Simply Math

A Comprehensive Guide
To Easy & Accurate
Chart Calculation

By Lauran Fowks & Lynn Sellon

Simply Math: A Comprehensive Guide to Easy
& Accurate Chart Calculation, 2nd Edition

ISBN: 0-9774332-1-8

Printed in the U.S.A.

Published by Twelfth House Press
16 Guilford Circle
Goldens Bridge, NY 10526

*We dedicate this book
with heartfelt thanks to Marie Mariani,
who has generously shared her love
and knowledge of astrology
with countless students over the years.*

Acknowledgements

Thanks go to the Nereids, Dolphins and Octopi of Kepler College, for your help in testing and providing feedback on the preliminary copy of this book, and to Lee Lehman, for supporting the trial run of *Simply Math* at Kepler College. To my children Amelie, Ben, and Doug, for patiently tolerating me for the three years it took to write this book. To Lynn, for your willingness to juggle a thousand meetings and phone calls, your uncanny ability to spot mistakes, and for your friendship through all the trials and triumphs of the book writing process.

Lauran Fowks

Thank you- To my husband Chris, for years of encouragement and support. To my sons Jonathan and Daniel, for your willingness to conduct spur of the moment math testing in several sections of this book, and to my daughter Lea, for giving me all those "I just have one more page to write" moments. To Lauran, your tireless dedication to seeing our "dream" through to reality along with your attention to detail and extensive knowledge of astrology made it all possible.

Lynn Sellon

Credits

Table of Contents

Introduction

Why We Wrote This Book

We met in the summer of 1994 at an astrology class and quickly realized we shared a passion for astrology. Serious about our studies, we challenged each other to become nationally certified, and worked together to master the math components needed for the certification exams. Between the two of us we had each taken a variety of correspondence courses and learned several chart calculation methods, but it seemed that none of the methods produced the level of accuracy we wanted. Call us perfectionists, but we refused to be satisfied unless we consistently hit the mark. After thoroughly investigating the logic behind each step of these methods we came up with our own formula combining the best of each, finding that it worked with perfect accuracy every time! We went on to pass the AFA student and professional exams and all levels of the NCGR exams the first time with excellent remarks. There are lots of different methods for constructing a chart out there - some are simpler but not as precise, others produce the same precision but are more difficult to understand or impossible to memorize. We believe that the system we teach encompasses the best of both worlds - straightforward and understandable procedures that consistently produce charts to within a minute of exactitude.

It is our hope that this book will help demystify the math requirements for certification. There are many sad tales of excellent astrologers who were unable to pass exams and be rightfully recognized because they could not get a handle on the math. It is unnecessary for math texts to enshroud the chart calculation process in an aura of mystery and confusion, or to get so bogged down with technical astronomical data that students give up. We believe that anyone can master the math if it is explained clearly and fully so that the reason behind each step is understood. Understanding is the key to remembering. If you know why you are doing what you are doing, you are far more apt to remember the steps required in an exam setting. If we can help even a handful of students move from math-phobic to Math Master, then we will have accomplished our purpose.

Why Learning the Math Will Make You a Better Astrologer

Why do we really need the math? If your interest in astrology is casual and you do not intend to practice professionally, you do not need the math. Computers can calculate everything you ever wanted to know and then some. But if you want to become certified as a professional you must know how to do all the calculations presented in this book. If you are serious about astrology, the benefits of understanding the math go well beyond just passing certification exams. You will gain the ability to quickly assess a chart. You will appreciate the ramifications of Standard Time versus Daylight Savings Time on house cusps. When you have a dubious birth time, you will be able to make adjustments in your head, recognizing how a variance of several minutes will affect a chart. You will see aspects immediately, and instantly be able to differentiate those that are generational from those that are not. You will know how long the effects of transits and progressions will last, and quickly estimate when aspects will perfect. Having a solid foundation of understanding in all areas of this subject, including the math, defines a professional. Most importantly, as professional astrologers we have a responsibility to our clients to provide a thorough interpretation of an accurate chart, as well as a responsibility to our astrological colleagues to uphold professional educational standards.

How to Use This Book

This book is organized into sections, with each section covering an aspect of chart calculation. Within each section you will find several lessons with exercises. Answers to all exercises and exams can be found in the Answer Key in the back of the book. We suggest you work through all lessons in order, as each lesson builds on the skills learned in previous lessons. Try your hand at the exercises provided at the end of each lesson, and when you are confident that you understand that lesson's material, move on to the next lesson. The amount of math may seem daunting at first glance, but we are confident that if you tackle it one step/lesson at a time, you will be able to master the math in no time.

In our experience the most common mistakes made by students are simple math errors. Although you may be tempted to skip over the first Math Basics lessons, we highly recommend that you take the time to master this section as all subsequent lessons require a thorough understanding of these concepts.

The following lesson plans are provided for astrologers studying for a particular certification exam. To the best of our knowledge these lessons cover the math requirements for each certification level indicated. However students should contact NCGR or AFA or other certification organization for complete information on current requirements.

> **NCGR Level 1:** Complete Lessons 1-14 (Natal Chart Calculation, Aspects)
>
> **NCGR Level 2:** Review Lessons 1-14
> Complete Lessons 15-26 (Other Points & Measurements, Secondary Progressions & Solar Arcs)
>
> **NCGR Level 3:** Review Lessons 1-26
> Complete Lessons 27, 29 & 30 (Solar Returns, Composites, Relocation)
> (Math requirements related to the use of the 90° and 360° dials are beyond the scope of this book.)
>
> **AFA Student Exam:** Complete Lessons 1-26 (Natal, Aspects & Other Measurements, Secondary Progressions, Solar Arcs)
>
> **AFA Professional Exam:** Review Lessons 1-26
> Complete Lessons 27, 29 & 30 (Solar Returns, Composites, Relocation)

For more information on NCGR and AFA certification, please contact the appropriate office at the following addresses:

National Council for Geocosmic Research
(Check website for name and address of current Education Director)
edu@geocosmic.org
http://www.geocosmic.org

American Federation of Astrologers
6535 S. Rural Road, Tempe, AZ 85283
Tele. (480) 838-1751
Email: AFA@msn.com
http://www.astrologers.com

Reference Materials Needed

You will need to have access to the following reference books in order to complete the lessons. All of these books are standard references that should be in the library of any astrologer:

The American Atlas, Expanded Fifth Edition, US Longitudes & Latitudes Time Changes and Time Zones, Compiled and Programmed by Thomas G. Shanks

The International Atlas, Expanded Fifth Edition, World Longitudes & Latitudes Time Changes and Time Zones, Compiled and Programmed by Thomas G. Shanks

The American Ephemeris for the 20th Century—Midnight, Revised Fifth Edition, By Neil F. Michelsen

The American Ephemeris for the 21st Century—Midnight, Expanded Second Edition, Programmed by Neil F. Michelsen Revisions by Rique Pottenger

The Michelsen Book of Tables, Compiled and Programmed by Neil F. Michelsen

All reference books are available from:

Astro Communications Services, Inc.
5521 Ruffin Road, San Diego, CA 92123
Tele. (800) 888-9983
http://www.astrocom.com

Section 1:

Math Basics

Lesson 1: Adding & Subtracting in a 60-Base System

Lesson 2: Converting 60-Base to Decimal

The lessons in this section are provided to help refresh the basic math skills needed to calculate a birth chart. Students who feel confident in their mathematical abilities can safely skip this section - you will not miss any chart calculation information. But those whose basic math skills may be a bit "rusty" will benefit greatly from working through this section, as all subsequent lessons require these basic skills.

Lesson 1: Math Basics I
Adding & Subtracting in a 60-Base System

Unlike common decimal-based mathematics which utilize units of 10, Time, Geographic Longitude & Latitude, and Zodiacal Longitude are all **sexagesimal**, meaning they have a base unit of 60. Adding and subtracting in a sexagesimal system can be a little tricky. This lesson focuses on how to add and subtract time and longitude. In Lesson 2, converting time and longitude to decimal and back again will be covered.

Before proceeding, take a minute to notice the similarities between notations of Time, Latitude/Longitude, and Zodiacal Longitude:

Time	Geographic Latitude & Longitude	Zodiacal Longitude
60 seconds = 1 minute	60 seconds = 1 minute	60 seconds = 1 minute
60 minutes = 1 hour	60 minutes = 1 degree	60 minutes = 1 degree
24 hours = 1 day	360 degrees = 1 full circle	30 degrees = 1 sign
Notated 00:00:00	Notated 00° W 00' 00"	12 signs = 1 full circle
(hours:mins:secs)	*(degrees, direction, mins, secs)*	Notated 00° ♈ 00' 00"
		(degrees, sign, mins, secs.)

Adding Hours, Minutes, and Seconds

Let's start with some simple addition. When adding time, it is important to keep the hours, minutes, and seconds columns in line. The columns are then added straight down. Seconds are added to seconds, minutes are added to minutes, and hours are added to hours. "Carrying over" is not done yet.

Example 1.

$$
\begin{array}{rl}
& 1{:}15{:}32 \quad \text{(1 hour, 15 minutes, 32 seconds)} \\
+ & 3{:}12{:}52 \quad \text{(3 hours, 12 minutes, 52 seconds)} \\
\hline
= & 4{:}27{:}84 \quad \text{(4 hours, 27 minutes, 84 seconds)}
\end{array}
$$

If, after adding, the minutes or seconds are greater than 60, then 60 is subtracted from that column and 1 is carried over to the next column. In the above example, the seconds column needs to be adjusted because 84 is greater than 60.

$$
\begin{array}{rl}
& 4{:}27{:}84 \\
- & \quad\quad\ 60 \\
+ & \quad\ 1{:}00 \\
\hline
= & 4{:}28{:}24
\end{array}
$$
} *Subtract 60 seconds, add 1 minute*

The adjusted time is 4 hours, 28 minutes, 24 seconds.

**Whenever the Seconds are Greater than 60,
Subtract 60 Seconds and Add 1 Minute.**

Example 2.

$$11:42:36$$
$$+ \ \underline{10:21:32}$$
$$= \ 21:63:68$$

In this example the seconds and the minutes columns both need to be adjusted, as follows:

$$21:63:68$$
$$- \quad\quad 60$$
$$+ \quad\quad \underline{1:00} \quad \Big\} \ \textit{Subtract 60 seconds, Add 1 minute}$$
$$= \ 21:64:08$$
$$- \quad\quad 60:00 \quad \Big\} \ \textit{Subtract 60 minutes, Add 1 hour}$$
$$+ \quad\quad \underline{1:00:00}$$
$$= \ 22:04:08 \quad \text{The adjusted time is 22 hours, 4 minutes, 8 seconds}$$

**Whenever the Minutes are Greater than 60,
Subtract 60 Minutes and Add 1 Hour.**

Example 3.

$$11:42:36$$
$$+ \ \underline{15:11:22}$$
$$= \ 26:53:58$$

In this case, the hours are now over 24, or one full day. 24 is then subtracted from the hours column, and the date is moved up by one day.

$$26:53:58$$
$$- \ \underline{24:00:00}$$
$$= \quad 2:53:58 \quad \textbf{on the following day}$$

It is very important to remember that when you subtract 24 hours, you need to add one day. If, say, we were calculating someone's birth time on May 5, 1984 above, this 24 hour change would now take us to 2:53:58 on May 6th, 1984.

**Whenever the Hours are Greater than 24,
Subtract 24 Hours and Add 1 Day.**

8

Subtracting Hours, Minutes, and Seconds

Subtracting time can be tricky when "borrowing" is required.

Example 4.

$$
\begin{array}{r}
\overset{4}{} \quad \overset{76}{} \quad \text{(subtract 1 hour, add 60 minutes)} \\
\cancel{5}:\cancel{16}:46 \\
- \quad 2:45:18 \\
\hline
= \quad 2:31:28
\end{array}
$$

In the example above 18 seconds can easily be subtracted from 46 seconds, but we can't subtract 45 minutes from 16 minutes. We must "borrow" one hour or 60 minutes from the hours column. When one hour is taken away from the hours column, 60 minutes must be added to the minutes column, resulting in 76 minutes. Now 45 can be subtracted from 76.

If you need to "borrow" more minutes,
Add 60 Minutes and Subtract 1 Hour

When subtracting hours there may be situations where more hours need to be subtracted than the number of hours listed, and there seems to be no place to "borrow" from. Remember that time is a continual process—you can "borrow" the previous day. If more hours are needed, add 24 hours and adjust the date back by one day to compensate for the day you "borrowed".

Example 5.

$$
\begin{array}{rl}
\overset{28}{} \qquad \overset{9}{} & \text{(subtract 1 day, add 24 hours)} \\
\cancel{4}:12:53 \quad \text{April } \cancel{10}, 2001 & \\
- \quad 16:06:10 & \\
\hline
= \quad 12:06:43 \quad \text{April 9, 2001} &
\end{array}
$$

Example 6.

$$
\begin{array}{rl}
\overset{21}{} \quad \overset{65}{} & \text{(subtract 1 hour, add 60 minutes)} \\
\cancel{22}:\cancel{05}:17 & \\
- \quad 11:48:09 & \\
\hline
= \quad 10:17:08 &
\end{array}
$$

Example 7.

$$
\begin{array}{rl}
\overset{32}{} \qquad \overset{4}{} & \text{(subtract 1 day, add 24 hours)} \\
\cancel{8}:48:30 \quad \text{January } \cancel{5}, 2003 & \\
- \quad 19:07:25 & \\
\hline
= \quad 13:41:05 \quad \text{January 4, 2003} &
\end{array}
$$

If you need to "borrow" more Hours,
Add 24 Hours and Subtract 1 Day

Adding & Subtracting Geographic Longitude & Latitude

All the techniques used for adding and subtracting time also apply to longitude and latitude.

Example 8.

Adding Longitude:

```
        45° 52' 38"
  +     26° 11' 08"
  =     71° 63' 46"
  -          60
  +          1°        } Subtract 60 minutes, add 1 degree
  =     72° 03' 46"
```

**Whenever the Minutes are Greater than 60,
Subtract 60 Minutes and Add 1 Degree.**

Example 9.

Subtracting Longitude:

```
        20  69     (subtract 1 minute, add 60 seconds)
      38° 21' 09"
  -   19° 16' 43"
  =   19° 04' 26"
```

**If you need to "borrow" more Seconds,
Add 60 Seconds and Subtract 1 Minute.**

**If you need to "borrow" more Minutes,
Add 60 Minutes and Subtract 1 Degree.**

Example 10.

360 degrees (one full circle around the globe) can be added if a greater number of degrees is needed to subtract:

```
      389°        (add 360 degrees)
       29° 52'
  -    85° 08'
  =   304° 44'
```

**If you need to "borrow" more Degrees,
Add 360 Degrees.**

Adding and Subtracting Zodiacal Longitude

Zodiacal Longitude is treated exactly the same as geographic longitude with the addition of one more "place" beyond degrees, that of signs. Although it is customary to notate zodiacal longitude with the sign following the degrees, as in *23° ♉ 37'*, when performing mathematical calculations it is easier to notate zodiacal longitude with the sign first, as in *♉ 23° 37'*, so that all values are in descending order (signs → degrees → minutes). Usually, seconds are rounded up to the nearest minute, unless extremely precise measurements are required, which is necesssary when calculating a solar return. Then, zodiacal positions are calculated to the nearest second. But for most calculations, zodiacal position only needs to be calculated to the nearest minute.

Example 11.

To add Zodiacal Longitude, first convert the sign to its numerical equivalent, as shown in the box to the right. Then proceed with the addition. Because each sign contains 30 degrees, if your answer produces a result with greater than 30°, subtract 30° and add one sign.

	♋ (4)	26°	15'
+		16°	32'
=	(4)	42°	47'
-		30	
+	(1)		
=	(5)	12°	47'

} *Subtract 30 degrees, add 1 sign*

Signs of the Zodiac Numbered
♈ = 1
♉ = 2
♊ = 3
♋ = 4
♌ = 5
♍ = 6
♎ = 7
♏ = 8
♐ = 9
♑ = 10
♒ = 11
♓ = 12

The answer is 12° 47' of the 5th sign, or 12° ♌ 47'.

**Whenever the Degrees are Greater than 30,
Subtract 30 Degrees and Add 1 Sign.**

Example 12.

	♑ (10)	18°	52'
+		75°	27'
=	(10)	93°	79'
-			60'
+		1°	
=	(10)	94°	19'
-		90°	
+	(3)		
=	(13)	04°	19'
-	(12)		
=	(1)	04°	19'

} *Subtract 60 minutes, add 1 degree*

} *Subtract 90 degrees, add 3 signs (90 degrees = 3 signs)*

12 signs = 1 full circle around the zodiac

The answer is 4° 19' of the 1st sign, or 4° ♈ 19'.

**Whenever the Signs are Greater than 12,
Subtract 12 Signs.**

Example 13.

Subtracting Zodiacal Longitude:

```
          5   56      (subtract 1 sign, add 30 degrees)
      ♍ (6) 26° 49'
    -          29° 13'
    =      (5) 27° 36'   = 27° ♌ 36'
```

**If you need to "borrow" more Degrees,
Add 30 Degrees and Subtract 1 Sign.**

Example 14.

```
          8   44      (subtract 1 sign, add 30 degrees)
      ♐ (9) 14° 37'
    -  ♊ (3) 23° 18'
    =      (5) 21° 19'   = 21° ♌ 19'
```

Example 15.

12 signs (one full circle around the zodiac) can be added if a greater number is needed in the signs column:

```
    +      (12)       (add 12 signs)
           0   73     (subtract 2 signs, add 60 degrees (2 x 30° = 60°))
       ♉ (2) 13° 49'
    -          65° 28'
    =  ♓ (12) 08° 21'   = 8° ♓ 21'
```

**If you need to "borrow" more Signs,
Add 12 Signs.**

Don't cross the wall without converting first!

Because we are all used to working in a decimal system and "carrying over" units of 10, it is easy to make careless mistakes when dealing with 60-base numbers. It helps to imagine a "wall" between units (hours- minutes-seconds or sign-degrees-minutes) that cannot be crossed without converting one unit into the other:

♐ (9)	18°	52'
+ ♉ (2)	23°	16'
= (11)	41°	68'
	+1°	-60'
+1	-30°	
= ♓ (12)	12°	08'

Convert Minutes to Degrees
Convert Degrees to Signs

Adding & Subtracting in Absolute Longitude

Each point on the zodiac can be described in two ways: in terms of its zodiacal sign and degree, and in terms of its degree of the 360° whole. **Absolute Longitude** is the name given to zodiacal longitude when it is expressed in degrees from 0 to 360 without the use of signs. For example, 20° ♉ can also be expressed as 50° in absolute longitude, because it is the 50th degree from 0° ♈, the starting point of the zodiac. Similarly, 15° ♐ is the same point as 255° in absolute longitude, and 29° ♓ is the same point as 359°. Often, addition and subtraction problems become easier if zodiacal degrees are converted to absolute longitude first. A table is provided on page 310 of the Appendix to help in converting zodiacal degrees into absolute longitude. Refer to this table now as you follow along below.

$$18° ♎ = 198°$$

$$27° ♑ = 297°$$

Notice that the absolute longitude equivalent takes the place of degree and sign only - any minutes or seconds must still be included:

$$14° ♏ 42' = 224° 42'$$

$$21° ♊ 32' 45'' = 81° 32' 45''$$

Example 16.

18° ♊ 45'	78° 45'	*Degrees can be converted to absolute longitude first, then added together*
+ 27° ♏ 12'	+ 237° 12'	
	= 315° 57', or 15° ♒ 57'	*The result is then converted back into zodiacal sign and degree*

Example 17.

Using absolute longitude in place of zodiacal signs is especially helpful when performing subtraction problems requiring sign changes:

	294° 87'	
25° ♑ 27'	~~295° 27'~~	*Degrees are converted to absolute longitude first, then subtracted*
- 9° ♋ 38'	- 99° 38'	
	= 195° 49', or 15° ♎ 49'	*The result is then converted back into zodiacal sign and degree*

Example 18.

Occasionally you may wish to leave an answer expressed in absolute longitude, for instance when calculating daily motion or solar arc in subsequent lessons:

	401°	*360° can be added if more degrees are needed*
11° ♉ 39'	~~41°~~ 39'	
- 14° ♓ 25'	- 344° 25'	
	= 57° 14'	

13

Converting to Absolute Longitude without a Table

Although the Table of Absolute Longitude makes converting to absolute longitude easier, you do not need to use a table to convert. Notice in the table below that each sign of the zodiac represents an additional 30°, starting with 0°♈. In an exam setting where the use of a table is not allowed, you can create your own conversion guide by simply listing the zodiacal signs in order. Starting with Aries as 0°, add 30° for each sign. This list can be used to convert to absolute longitude as follows:

23°♋ 48' is the same as 23 degrees + 90 degrees (because ♋ = 90°) + 48 minutes
or 113° 48' in absolute longitude

11°♍ 20' is the same as 11°+ 150° (♍ = 150°) + 20'
or 161° 20' in absolute longitude

27°♓ 53' is the same as 27°+ 330° (♓ = 330°) + 53'
or 357° 53' in absolute longitude

Degree Equivalents to Signs of the Zodiac
♈ = 0°
♉ = 30°
♊ = 60°
♋ = 90°
♌ = 120°
♍ = 150°
♎ = 180°
♏ = 210°
♐ = 240°
♑ = 270°
♒ = 300°
♓ = 330°

Lesson 1 Exercises

Complete the following problems on this and the following page. Answers can be found in the Answer Key in the Appendix.

Add the following time units.

1.   10:16:05 (Jan 3, 1985)
     +   3:02:20

2.   15:33:12 (Aug 8, 2002)
     +   4:45:08

3.   20:16:52 (May 5, 1973)
     +   7:38:15

4.   17:42:55 (June 10, 1953)
        9:30:00
     +   0:02:46

5.   3:08:40 (Feb 21, 1994)
        2:45:10
     +   0:03:18

6.   12:33:21 (Nov. 8, 1975)
        5:00:00
     +   0:01:12

Subtract the following time units:

7.   13:52:10 (Feb 10, 1997)
     -    6:43:52

8.   9:08:45 (Jun 20, 1962)
     -    4:36:15

9.   6:32:56 (Apr 13, 2003)
     -    12:45:15

Add the following zodiacal measurements:

10.   22° ♏ 49'
    + 14°   22'

11.   14° ♊ 53'
    + 28°   18'

12.   9° ♈ 30'
    + 26°   48'

Find the difference in degrees and minutes between the following zodiacal positions by converting the sign to its numerical equivalent:

13.   8° ♌ 26'
    - 23° ♋ 52'

14.   27° ♈ 09'
    - 19° ♓ 23'

15.   18° ♒ 42'
    - 7° ♎ 30'

Find the difference in degrees and minutes between the following zodiacal positions by converting the sign and degree to absolute longitude:

16.   26° ♑ 08'
    - 10° ♎ 29'

17.   19° ♊ 47'
    - 21° ♍ 12'

18.   4° ♐ 19'
    - 22° ♉ 37'

Lesson 2: Math Basics II
Converting 60-Base to Decimal

Several steps in the chart calculation process require expressing time, latitude, longitude, or zodiacal longitude in decimal form, because it is much easier to apply mathematical formulas to values expressed in the decimal system than it is to work with sexagesimal numbers. Then, after the formula has been applied, decimals are converted back into traditional sexagesimal notation - hours/minutes/seconds, or degrees/minutes/seconds. In this lesson, the process of converting sexagesimal to decimal, and back again, will be explained.

Converting Time Notation Into Decimals

We will start with some easy examples of converting time to decimal.

Example 1.

Let's express 3:42 (3 hours and 42 minutes) in decimal format. Minutes are 60ths of hours, so 3:42 is actually 3 hours and 42/60ths of an hour. 42 divided by 60 = .7. So 3:42 expressed as a decimal is 3.7 hours:

$$3:42 = 3 \text{ hours} + \frac{42}{60} = 3 \text{ hours} + .7 \text{ (because } 42 \div 60 = .7) = 3.7 \text{ hours}$$

Example 2.

$$12:53 = 12 \text{ hours} + \frac{53}{60} = 12 + .88 \text{ } (53 \div 60 = .88) = 12.88 \text{ hours}$$

Example 3.

$$4:13 = 4 + \frac{13}{60} = 4 + .22 \text{ } (13 \div 60 = .2166, \text{ rounded up to } .22) = 4.22 \text{ hrs}$$

Rounding up, Rounding down

Do you remember how to round off? The rules are:

If the value is less than half, round down. If the value is half or more, round up.

This is pretty straightforward in the decimal system:

    140.6 rounds up to 141   152.3 rounds down to 152   42.865 rounds up to 42.87

In the sexagesimal system, 60 is the base number, half of which is 30:

12:36:22 rounded to the nearest minute is 12:36
(22 seconds is less than half a minute - round down)

45° 16' 48" rounded to the nearest minute is 45°17'
(48" is more than half a minute - round up)

If seconds are less than 30, round down. If 30 or more, round up.

17

Converting to decimal gets more complicated when time is expressed to the second.

Example 4.

Let's convert a time of 5:18:52 to a decimal. First, 52 seconds is converted to a decimal of a minute, as follows:

$$5:18:52 = 5 \text{ hours, } 18 \text{ minutes} + \frac{52}{60} \text{ of a minute}$$

$$= 5 \text{ hours, } 18.87 \text{ min (because } 52 \div 60 = .87)$$

Then, using the new minutes value expressed as a decimal, convert the minutes to a decimal of an hour:

$$= 5 \text{ hours} + \frac{18.87}{60} \text{ of an hour}$$

$$= 5.31 \text{ hours (because } 18.87 \div 60 = .31)$$

The time of 5:18:52, expressed in decimal form, is 5.31 hours. Think about this logically. 18+ minutes is almost one third of an hour, and .31 is also almost one third. Whenever you do an involved mathematical computation like this, think about it logically afterward. Does the answer make sense? This will be your best safeguard against careless mistakes.

Now here are two more "short-form" conversions:

Example 5. 8:49:23

$\frac{23}{60}$ = .38 minutes ➡ $\frac{49.38}{60}$ = .82 hours ➡ Final time: 8.82 hours

(convert secs to mins)　　　(convert mins to hrs)　　　(expressed as decimal of hrs)

Example 6. 16:08:52

$\frac{52}{60}$ = .87 minutes ➡ $\frac{8.87}{60}$ = .15 hours ➡ Final time: 16.15 hours

(convert secs to mins)　　　(convert mins to hrs)　　　(expressed as decimal of hrs)

Suppose these two time values need to be expressed as a portion of an entire day. The process is exactly the same, but this time, instead of dividing by 60 (because there are 60 seconds in a minute, 60 minutes in an hour), we divide by 24 (because there are 24 hours in a day).

Example 7. 8:49:23 = 8.82 hours (as calculated above)　　$\frac{8.82}{24}$ = .37 of a day

Example 8. 16:08:52 = 16.15 hours (as calculated above)　　$\frac{16.15}{24}$ = .67 of a day

18

Converting Decimals Into Time Notation

Let us now convert decimals back into standard (sexagesmimal) time notation.

Example 9. .7 minutes (This value is less than a minute, so it will be expressed in seconds)
.7 x 60 (number of seconds in 1 minute) = 42
Answer: 42 seconds, or 0:00:42

Example 10. .4 hours (This value is less than an hour so it will be expressed in minutes)
.4 x 60 (number of minutes in 1 hour) = 24
Answer: 24 minutes, or 0:24:00

Example 11. .5 days (This value is less than a day, so it will be expressed in hours)
.5 x 24 (number of hours in 1 day) = 12
Answer: 12 hours, or 12:00:00

The above examples all resulted in a whole number of seconds, minutes, or hours, with no decimal remainders. Now let's try some more complicated examples:

Example 12. 392.65 minutes

This value represents 392 whole minutes, plus .65 of a minute which will be converted to seconds below.

First, divide whole minutes by 60 to determine the number of whole hours, then record whole hours as follows: 392 ÷ 60 = 6.53   6:_ _:_ _

Second, multiply the decimal remainder from the above computation by 60 to determine the number of whole minutes remaining after the hours are deducted. Round up or down if necessary, then record whole minutes. .53 x 60 = 31.8 minutes, rounded to 32 minutes.   6: 32:_ _

Last, refer back to the original decimal remainder and multiply by 60 to determine the seconds: .65 x 60 = 39 seconds   6: 32: 39

Example 13. 8.37 hours

First, record the whole hours as follows: 8:_ _:_ _

Second, multiply the remaining decimal portion by 60, to determine the number of minutes: .37 x 60 = 22.2 minutes

Then record the whole minutes as follows: 8: 22:_ _

Last, multiply .2, the remaining decimal, by 60 to determine the seconds: .2 x 60 = 12 seconds   8: 22: 12

Example 14. .37 days

.37 x 24 = 8.88 hours. Record the whole hours   8:_ _:_ _
= 8 hours, 52.8 minutes (.88 x 60 = 52.8). Record the whole minutes   8: 52:_ _
= 8 hours, 52 minutes, 48 seconds (.8 x 60 = 48) Record the whole seconds   8: 52: 48

Converting Geographic or Zodiacal Longitude & Latitude to Decimal

All the techniques used for converting time also apply to longitude and latitude.

Example 15. Converting Longitude into decimal notation:

$$72° \; 39'$$

$$= 72 + \frac{39}{60} \text{ degrees}$$

$$= 72.65° \quad (39 \div 60 = .65)$$

Example 16. Converting decimal back into standard Longitude notation:

33.63°	
Record whole degrees	33° _ _'
.63 x 60 = 37.8. Round off to whole minutes	33° 38'

Or, to convert to the nearest second:

Record whole degrees	33° _ _' _ _"
.63 x 60 = 37.8. Record whole minutes	33° 37' _ _"
.8 x 60 = 48. Record whole seconds	33° 37' 48'

Converting Absolute Longitude to Decimal

The previous lesson explained how to express zodiacal longitude in terms of absolute longitude, which is the numerical position of a zodiacal degree within the 360° whole. Many computational problems are simplified by expressing absolute longitude in decimal format, rather than expressing degrees and minutes separately.

Example 17. Converting zodiacal longitude to absolute longitude in decimal notation:

$$18° \triangleq 46' = 198° \; 46' \text{ (because } 18° \triangleq \text{ equals } 198° \text{ in absolute longitude)}$$

$$198° \; 46' = 198 + \frac{46}{60} = 198.77°$$

20

Converting Degrees to Minutes

Occasionally it is helpful to express a value in all minutes, rather than converting minutes into a decimal of a degree. In order to do this, the given degrees must be converted into the equivalent number of minutes. This is done by multiplying the degrees by 60.

Example 18.

18° expressed as minutes = 18 x 60 minutes = 1080 minutes

This is fairly straightforward when dealing with whole degrees, but can become a little trickier when dealing with values representing a combination of degrees and minutes:

Example 19.

22° 35' expressed as minutes = 22 x 60 minutes, plus the additional 35 minutes

= 1320 + 35 = 1355 minutes

Understand that it is just as correct to express this value in terms of degrees and decimals of degrees, which in this case would equal 22.58°. This represents the same value as 1355 minutes, it is simply a different way of expressing the same thing. One uses degrees as the unit of measurement, while the other uses minutes as units.

Example 20.

The chart calculation process often requires finding a proportion of degrees and minutes. This can easily be accomplished if the value is first converted into all minutes.

Let's find .75 (or 75%) of 13° 52'. First, the value is converted into all minutes:

13° 52' = 13 x 60 minutes + 52 minutes = 780 + 52 minutes = 832 minutes

Finding .75 (75%) of this value now becomes straightforward:

832 minutes x .75 = 624 minutes

Once the answer is determined, it can be converted back into degree/minute format by dividing by 60, as follows:

624 ÷ 60 = 10.4, or 10 whole degrees with a remainder of 24 minutes (.4 x 60 = 24')
This becomes 10° 24'

Do NOT confuse any decimal "remainder" to be minutes! In this example, 624 ÷ 60 = 10.4. This is NOT the equivalent of 10 degrees and 4 minutes. This result means 10 whole degrees, plus a remainder of 4/10ths of a degree, which is 24 minutes (60 minutes x .4 = 24).

Lesson 2 Exercises

Convert the following times into decimal notation. Answers can be found in the Answer Key in the Appendix.

1. 12:48

2. 3:52:15

3. 18:08:30

Convert the following decimals into standard time notation:

4. 12.63 hours

5. 4.14 hours

6. .69 days

Convert the following longitudes into decimal, or vice versa:

7. 45° W 36'

8. 23° 58'

9. 18.682°

Convert the following degree and minute values into all minutes, or vice versa:

10. 3° 52'

11. 12° 13'

12. 758'

Section 2:

Time

Lesson 3: Time & GMT

There are many different ways to denote time. This lesson begins by defining several terms used for time, then explains how to use an atlas to determine in which time zone any given birth place is located, how to decide whether or not Daylight Savings Time was in effect, and how to express a given time of birth in Greenwich Mean Time (GMT).

In the beginning, there was **Local Mean Time (LMT)**. Based on the Sun, Local Mean Time is easily measured using a sundial. When the Sun is directly overhead and a sundial's gnomon makes its shortest shadow, it is 12:00 noon. From noon to the following noon, the day is divided into 24 hours. Not that long ago each locality kept its own time according to LMT. When it was noon in one town, it was not quite noon in another town several miles to the west. This worked fine for centuries, because there was no need to precisely coordinate time between neighboring towns.

With the advent of the locomotive in the 1880's and the resulting train schedules, a more standardized method of timekeeping was needed. **Standard Time**, based on **Standard Time Zones**, was then adopted. In the United States, the railroads instituted standard time on November 18, 1883. Then, at the International Meridian Conference held in 1884, the International Date Line was drawn up and the world was divided into 24 standard time zones. Beginning with the Prime Meridian (0° Longitude) at Greenwich, England, 24 standard meridians of longitude, each 15° apart, were denoted as the theoretical "centers" of each time zone. (360°, or one complete circle around the globe, divided by 24 hours = 15°.) To either side of these standard time meridians, time zone boundaries were established. These boundaries have been moved around dramatically since their original introduction, and are still frequently adjusted for political or convenience reasons. Some countries have chosen not to base their standard time on these meridians at all. The time zone map below will give you a general idea of how the world's time zones are currently formatted, however a good reference such as *The ACS American Atlas* or *The ACS International Atlas* is needed to accurately determine the correct time zone for a locality.

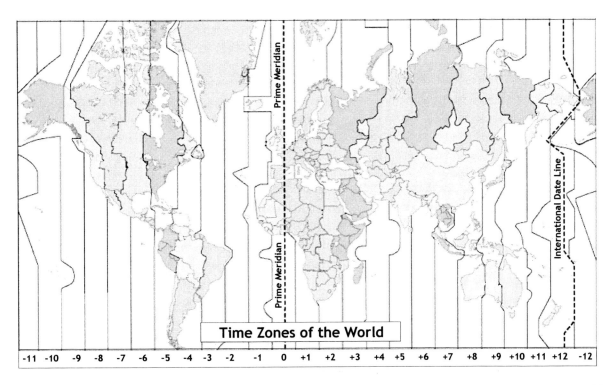

Time Zones of the World

| -11 | -10 | -9 | -8 | -7 | -6 | -5 | -4 | -3 | -2 | -1 | 0 | +1 | +2 | +3 | +4 | +5 | +6 | +7 | +8 | +9 | +10 | +11 | +12 | -12 |

The map to the right shows how the four time zones of the continental United States are divided. Notice that the standard time meridians on which the time for each zone is based is not necessarily located in the center of that zone. This is because boundaries are established for commercial or geographic convenience. For example, notice that the locality in western Texas marked by the star is located practically on the standard time meridian for Mountain Time (105°), yet it keeps its clocks according to Central Time, based on the 90° time meridian. This means that "clock noon" in this place will occur a full hour earlier than "true noon". It is not necessary to memorize these time zone boundaries, be-

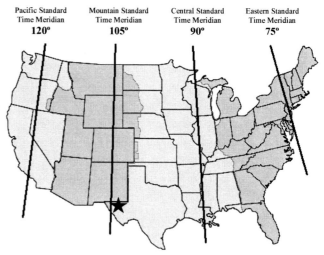

| Pacific Standard Time Meridian 120° | Mountain Standard Time Meridian 105° | Central Standard Time Meridian 90° | Eastern Standard Time Meridian 75° |

cause atlases contain all the information needed. For now, simply understand that standard time does not reflect the true solar time (local mean time) for a given location, and may differ by up to an hour or more.

Daylight Savings Time (DST or DT) is a method used to extend the evening daylight hours. In the Spring, clocks are adjusted an hour ahead to take advantage of longer daylight. Then in the Fall, when days become shorter and there is no extra daylight to spare, clocks are turned back an hour and "real" standard time is resumed. In the United States, Daylight Savings Time was first used in 1918, but its use was optional. Each locality could decide for itself whether or not to observe DST, and on which day it would begin and end. It was not until the Uniform Time Act of 1966 that the dates for the beginning and ending of DST were standardized, but to this day it is still not mandatory that all localities observe DST. For example, the State of Arizona does not use DST, but the Native American Reservations within Arizona do observe DST. Indiana is another state that varies from county to county. Therefore, in order to calculate a horoscope for a person born in either of these two states, it is necessary to check the actual town of birth to determine if DST was in effect. Additional exceptions have also been made to the Uniform Time Act over the years. For example, during the "energy crisis" years of 1974 and 1975, the start of DST was moved to January and February respectively. In 1986, a law was passed that permanently established the start of DST to be 2:00 am on the first Sunday in April, and the end of DST as 2:00 am on the last Sunday in October.

War Time (WT) and **Double War Time** are like Daylight Savings Time, but they do not necessarily begin in the Spring and end in the Fall. During World War II in the U.S., War Time was continuously in effect from February 9, 1942 to September 20, 1945. Some areas in Europe observed Double War Time, during which the clocks were moved ahead two hours instead of one.

Greenwich Mean Time (GMT) is simply the Local Mean Time for Greenwich, England. Because most **ephemerides** (tables of planetary positions) are kept according to GMT, it is necessary to convert the local time of birth to GMT in order to accurately determine the position of the planets at birth. We will cover how to convert local birth time to GMT in detail later in this lesson. **Universal Time (UT)** is just another name for Greenwich Mean Time (GMT).

Local Sidereal Time (LST) is local time based on the relative position of the stars, the word "sidereal" meaning "of the stars". LST is used to determine the Midheaven and other house cusps and is fully explained in Lesson 5. All other types of time covered in this lesson are "solar time" because they are based on the Sun's movement.

26

How to Use *The ACS American Atlas*

The ACS American Atlas contains listings for every city, town, and village in the United States, with references to time zones and time changes from 1883 to present. Take some time now to become familiar with this book. You will notice that each state section begins with a list of numbered time change tables, then a list of counties, then an alphabetical listing of cities and towns with various reference numbers following each listing.

Below is an excerpt from the New York section of *The American Atlas*. The first number following the name of the city or town refers to the county in which the town is located. Use this number to ensure that you have the correct town. For example, in the sample below there are two listings for Bellevue, NY, one in county 15, and one in county 47, as well as a Belleview with a different spelling. If you refer to the county listing at the beginning of the New York section, you will see that one Bellevue is in Erie County, and the other is in Schenectady County, which is quite a distance away. If you were to erect a birth chart using the coordinates for the wrong Bellevue, the chart you produced would not be accurate. If you are in doubt about which is the correct county to use, check with your client.

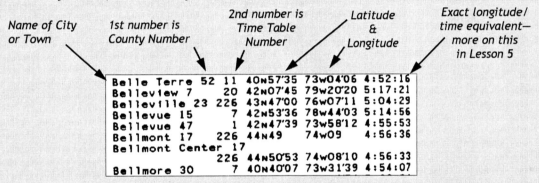

Let us check the time zone and time changes for a birth at 10:00 pm on November 8, 1944 in Belleview, NY, the second town listed in this *American Atlas* excerpt. This Belleview is located in county #7. Referring to the County list at the beginning of the New York State section, we find that this is Chautauqua county. The second number (20) refers to New York Time Table #20 located at the beginning of the New York State section. A copy of New York Time Table #20 is reproduced below.

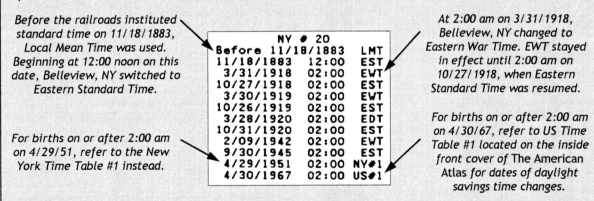

This 11/8/44 example birth falls between the listing for 2/09/1942, when Belleview began Eastern War Time (EWT), and 9/30/1945, when Eastern Standard Time (EST) was resumed. Therefore, we know that this birth time is given in Eastern War Time.

Now turn to the table located on the inside back cover of *The American Atlas*, reprinted below. You will see that Eastern War Time differs from Greenwich Mean Time by 4:00 hours.

The first letter of a time zone abbreviation denotes the zone. "E" stands for Eastern, "C" for Central, etc. The second letter denotes whether standard (S), daylight (D), or war (W) time was in effect.

EST = Eastern Standard Time
EDT = Eastern Daylight Time
EWT = Eastern War Time

and so on for each of the U.S. time zones.

Time Zones and Abbreviations

Abbr.	Name	Standard Meridian	Hours from Greenwich Mean Time Standard	Daylight (War)
A	Atlantic	60°	4:00	3:00
E	Eastern	75°	5:00	4:00
C	Central	90°	6:00	5:00
M	Mountain	105°	7:00	6:00
P	Pacific	120°	8:00	7:00
Y	Yukon	135°	9:00	8:00
AH	Alaska-Hawaii	150°	10:00	9:00
H	Hawaiian	157°30'	10:30	9:30
B	Bering	165°	11:00	10:00

Abbr.	Time Type
S	Standard
D	Daylight
W	War

Eastern War Time = 4:00

How to Use *The ACS International Atlas*

The ACS International Atlas is formatted similarly to *The ACS American Atlas*, with a few minor differences. Each town or village listing within a country is followed by first a province or division number if applicable, and second a Time Table number which refers to a Time Table located at the beginning of that country's section. Each Time Table lists the actual time difference from Greenwich Mean Time, instead of an abbreviated Time Zone name. Time zones located to the east of Greenwich are preceded by a minus (-) sign. Time zones to the west do not have a sign, but should be regarded as a positive (+) number.

Notice that a country's standard time may not necessarily be based on a standard time meridian which is a multiple of 15° from Greenwich, and so may not differ from GMT by a whole number of hours. Often a country will choose to base its time on the longitude of its capital city instead. For example, below is an excerpt from the Time Table listings for Iran. Notice that Standard Time was not adopted until January 1, 1916, at which time it was based on the longitude meridian of 51° 26' East, which is the longitude of its capital city Tehran. This resulted in a time difference of 3 hours and 26 minutes east of GMT (-3:26). In 1946, the longitude meridian was changed to 52° 30' East, resulting in a time difference of 3 hours 30 minutes east of GMT (-3:30).

ĪRĀN   PERSIA

Time Table	21 Mar 1979	0:00 -4:30
Before 1 Jan 1916 LMT	19 Sep 1979	0:00 -3:30
Begin Standard 51E26	21 Mar 1980	0:00 -4:30
1 Jan 1916 0:00 -3:26	23 Sep 1980	0:00 -3:30
Begin Standard 52E30	3 May 1991	0:00 -4:30
1 Jan 1946 0:00 -3:30	20 Sep 1991	0:00 -3:30
Begin Standard 60E00	21 Mar 1992	0:00 -4:30
1 Nov 1977 0:00 -4:00	23 Sep 1992	0:00 -3:30
21 Mar 1978 0:00 -5:00	21 Mar 1993	0:00 -4:30
21 Oct 1978 0:00 -4:00	23 Sep 1993	0:00 -3:30
Begin Standard 52E30	21 Mar 1994	0:00 -4:30
1 Jan 1979 0:00 -3:30	23 Sep 1994	0:00 -3:30

Determining Time Zones for U.S. Births

In order to calculate a birth chart, the time zone of birth must first be determined, then the birth time must be converted to Greenwich Mean Time (GMT). The next examples will demonstrate how to determine time zone differences to GMT. Then the last section of this lesson will demonstrate how to use this time zone information to express a birth time in GMT.

There are three steps to follow when identifying the standard time zone for a U.S. birth.

Step 1. Look up the city and state in *The American Atlas* to determine which time table applies to the birth date.

Step 2. Locate that time table in *The American Atlas* to find time zone and whether Daylight Savings, Standard Time or War Time was observed on the birth date.

Step 3. Use the "Time Zones and Abbreviations" table on the inside back cover of *The American Atlas* to identify how many "standard hours" away from Greenwich Mean Time the time zone identified in Step 2 represents.

Take out your copy of *The ACS American Atlas* and follow along in the next example.

Example 1.

Let's find out what time standard was in effect for a birth on September 15, 1952 at 10:15 am in Norfolk, Virginia.

Step 1. Look up the city and state in *The American Atlas* to determine which time table applies to the birth date. The time table is the second number given after the city name. In this case it is Virginia Table #6.

```
Nomini Grove 92
                 19 38N02'06 76w44'55 5:07:00
Nora 26          15 37N04'15 82w20'51 5:29:23
Norcross 35       4 37N21'01 80w42'01 5:22:48
Norcum Park 125 7 36N49'53 76w20'03 5:05:20
Nordick 91       15 36N42   82w18    5:29:12
Norfolk 121       6 36N50'48 76w17'08 5:05:09
Norfolk Highlands 101
                  6 36N48'56 76w13'56 5:04:56
```

Step 2. Locate that time table in *The American Atlas* to find time zone and whether Daylight Savings, Standard Time or War Time was observed on the birth date.

Table #6 can be found at the beginning of the "Virginia" pages. Under table VA #6, the birth date 9/15/52 falls between 4/27/52 and 9/28/52 during which time Eastern Daylight Time ("EDT") was observed.

VA # 6		
Before 11/18/1883		LMT
11/18/1883	12:00	EST
3/31/1918	02:00	EWT
10/27/1918	02:00	EST
3/30/1919	02:00	EWT
10/26/1919	02:00	EST
2/09/1942	02:00	EWT
9/30/1945	02:00	EST
4/28/1946	02:00	EDT
9/30/1946	00:00	EST
4/25/1948	02:00	EDT
9/26/1948	02:00	EST
4/27/1952	02:00	EDT
9/28/1952	02:00	EST
5/31/1962	00:00	EDT
9/04/1962	00:00	EST

Step 3. Use the "Time Zones and Abbreviations" table on the inside back cover of *The American Atlas* to identify how many "standard hours" away from Greenwich Mean Time the time zone identified in Step 2 represents.

Abbr.	Name	Standard Meridian	Hours from Greenwich Mean Time Standard	Daylight (War)
A	Atlantic	60°	4:00	3:00
E	Eastern	75°	5:00	4:00
C	Central	90°	6:00	5:00
M	Mountain	105°	7:00	6:00
P	Pacific	120°	8:00	7:00
Y	Yukon	135°	9:00	8:00
AH	Alaska-Hawaii	150°	10:00	9:00
H	Hawaiian	157°30'	10:30	9:30
B	Bering	165°	11:00	10:00

The Time Zones table indicates that EDT is four (4:00) hours away from GMT. Four hours would need to be added to the time in Norfolk, Virginia to know what time it was in Greenwich, England in GMT.

Example 2.

For this example, we will use a birth on May 2, 1969 at 8:00 am in Montgomery, Alabama. Looking up Montgomery, Alabama in *The American Atlas*, we find we are directed to Alabama Time Table #4.

Time Table #4 indicates that on April 30, 1967, Montgomery began following national Standard-to-Daylight Savings Time changes as per U.S. Time Table #1. However, before turning to that table it is important to understand that the U.S. Time Tables will only designate whether Standard Time or Daylight Savings Time was in effect; they will NOT give the time zone of any particular city or town. Therefore, before turning to U.S. #1, make note of the standard time zone shown in the state time table. This will give the first "letter" of the time zone abbreviation. In this example, the last time zone shown in Alabama Table #4, before the U.S. Table reference, is C̲ST, or Central Standard Time.

AL # 4		
Before 11/18/1883		LMT
11/18/1883	12:00	CST
3/31/1918	02:00	CWT
10/27/1918	02:00	CST
3/30/1919	02:00	CWT
10/26/1919	02:00	CST
5/18/1935	00:01	CDT
9/02/1935	00:01	CST
4/28/1940	02:00	CDT
9/29/1940	02:00	CST
7/21/1941	00:01	CDT
10/01/1941	00:01	CST
2/09/1942	02:00	CWT
9/30/1945	02:00	CST
4/30/1967	02:00	US#1

With this information in hand we can now turn to U.S. Table #1 on the inside front cover of *The American Atlas* to check for Daylight Savings Time. In this table, on April 27, 1969 clocks were changed to Daylight Savings Time. Combining this information with the time zone information from Alabama Table #4, we know that this birth is recorded in C̲D̲T, or Central Daylight Time. The "Time Zones and Abbreviations" table on the inside back indicates that this is 5:00 away from GMT.

U.S. #1		
10/27/1968	02:00	ST
4/27/1969	02:00	DT
10/26/1969	02:00	ST
4/26/1970	02:00	DT
10/25/1970	02:00	ST
4/25/1971	02:00	DT
10/31/1971	02:00	ST

When directed to a U.S. Time Table,
Use the last entry in the State Time Table to determine Time Zone (E, C, M or P).
Use the U.S. Time Table to determine Standard or Daylight Time (S̲T or D̲T)

Example 3.

Let's determine the time zone for a birth recorded as 4:00 pm on August 5, 1995 in San Francisco, California.

First, look up San Francisco, CA in *The American Atlas* and notice that only a county number is given. No Time Table number is designated.

```
San Fernando 19   34N16'55  118w26'17  7:53:45
Sanford 19                  34N04    118w18    7:53:12
San Francisco 38  37N46'30  122w25'06  8:09:40
San Francisco Int'l Airport 41
                  37N37    122w23    8:09:32
San Francisco Recreation Cam 55
                  38N33    121w17    8:05:08
```

Turn to the beginning of the California section and notice that a single Time Table is given for the entire state of California. This indicates that the entire state is in the Pacific Standard Time Zone and follows the same Time Table. Beginning on 4/30/67, California followed the U.S. Time Table #1.

```
CALIFORNIA TIME TABLE

4/25/1965    02:00    PDT
10/31/1965   02:00    PST
4/24/1966    02:00    PDT
10/30/1966   02:00    PST
4/30/1967    02:00    US#1
```

Locate the US #1 Table inside the front cover of *The American Atlas*. According to this table, Daylight Savings Time was in effect from April 2 to October 29 in 1995. We now know that this birth occurred in the Pacific Standard Time Zone, which is 8 hours from GMT, and that Daylight Savings Time was in effect.

```
          US # 1
10/30/1994   02:00    ST
4/02/1995    02:00    DT
10/29/1995   02:00    ST
4/07/1996    02:00    DT
10/27/1996   02:00    ST
```

The "Time Zones and Abbreviations" table on the inside back cover of *The American Atlas* indicates that PDT (Pacific Daylight Time) differs from GMT by 7 hours.

Abbr.	Name	Standard Meridian	Hours from Greenwich Mean Time	
			Standard	Daylight (War)
A	Atlantic	60°	4:00	3:00
E	Eastern	75°	5:00	4:00
C	Central	90°	6:00	5:00
M	Mountain	105°	7:00	6:00
P	Pacific	120°	8:00	7:00
Y	Yukon	135°	9:00	8:00
AH	Alaska-Hawaii	150°	10:00	9:00
H	Hawaiian	157°30'	10:30	9:30
B	Bering	165°	11:00	10:00

Finding Time Zone Differences for Non-U.S. Births

Because *The ACS International Atlas* lists time zones by their number of hours' difference to GMT rather than by the time zone name, identifying the standard time zone for a non-U.S. birth requires only two steps instead of three:

Step 1. **Look up the country and city in *The International Atlas* to determine which time table applies to the birth date.**

Step 2. **Locate the time table in *The International Atlas* to determine how many "standard hours" away from Greenwich Mean Time the time zone represents.**

Take out your copy of *The ACS International Atlas* and follow the steps in the example below.

Example 4.

Let us find the standard time zone observed for someone born in Paris, France on July 16, 1985.

Step 1. Locate Paris, France in *The ACS International Atlas*. The time table referenced is table #61, found at the beginning of the "France" section.

Parentis en Born	24	44N21	1W05	0:04:20
Pargny sur Saulx	88	48N46	4E50	-0:19:20
Parigné l'Evêque	47	47N56	0E22	-0:01:28
Paris	61	48N52	2E20	-0:09:20
Parmain	80	49N07	2E12	-0:08:48
Parthenay	24	46N39	0W15	0:01:00
Pas en Artois	122	50N09	2E30	-0:10:00

Step 2. Table #61 shows that after August 25, 1944, France's Time Table #1 is used. In table #1 this birth falls between 3/31/85 and 9/29/85 when the time observed in Paris was -2:00 standard hours away from (two hours earlier than) GMT. Two hours would need to be subtracted from the time in Paris, France to know what time it was in GMT.

Time Table # 61 Before 15 Mar 1891 LMT Begin Standard 2E20		
15 Mar 1891	0:01	TT#1
14 Jun 1940	0:00	-2:00
1 Nov 1942	3:00	-1:00
29 Mar 1943	2:00	-2:00
4 Oct 1943	3:00	-1:00
3 Apr 1944	2:00	-2:00
25 Aug 1944	0:00	TT#1

France TT #1		
27 Mar 1983	2:00	-2:00
25 Sep 1983	3:00	-1:00
25 Mar 1984	2:00	-2:00
30 Sep 1984	3:00	-1:00
31 Mar 1985	2:00	-2:00
29 Sep 1985	3:00	-1:00
30 Mar 1986	2:00	-2:00
28 Sep 1986	3:00	-1:00
29 Mar 1987	2:00	-2:00

Notice that *The ACS International Atlas* lists time zones by their number of hours' difference to GMT only and not by name. If you are curious to know the name of an international time zone, you can find this in *The Michelsen Book of Tables* "Table 1: Time Zones of the World", but this information is not really necessary. It is only the number of hours away from GMT, as it is listed in *The International Atlas*, that we need to know.

Expressing Time of Birth in GMT

The first step in chart calculation is to express a given time of birth in Greenwich Mean Time (GMT). **Ephemerides** (tables listing the zodiacal positions of the planets) are usually kept in GMT, so all birth times need to be converted to GMT in order to calculate the position of the planets at birth. The GMT of birth is also the basis for calculating the Sidereal Time of birth (covered in a later lesson), which is needed for determining house cusps. The remainder of this lesson will focus on how to express a given time of birth in GMT.

How to Convert a Birth Time into GMT

Three factors need to be taken into account when converting a given birth time to GMT:

- **Whether birth time is a.m. or p.m.**
- **Time Zone**
- **Time Zone adjustments (Daylight Time, War Time, Double War Time)**

The following three steps are taken to adjust for these factors:

Step 1. Record the Time of Birth exactly as given on the Birth Certificate, stating whether time is a.m. or p.m.

Step 2. Convert Birth Time to 24-Hour Format. Time should always be expressed in 24 Hour ("Military") Time to prevent any a.m./p.m. mistakes. This is done by adding 12 hours to any p.m. birth time to convert to 24-Hour time. The one exception is any time during the noon hour, such as 12:43 pm, which in effect already has 12 hours added. If the birth time is a.m., nothing needs to be done, unless the birth falls within the midnight hour, such as 12:43 am. Then 12 hours must be subtracted to express this time in 24-hour format, i.e. 00:43.

> **P.M. Births between 1:00 pm and 11:59 pm - Add 12 Hours**
> **A.M. Births between 12:00 am and 12:59 am - Subtract 12 Hours**

Step 3. Adjust for Time Zone. Determine the time zone of birth by looking up the birthplace in the relevant atlas. Time zones west of Greenwich are expressed as a positive number and are added to the given time of birth. Time zones east of Greenwich are expressed as a negative number and are subtracted from the given time of birth.

> **Western Births - Add Time Zone To Birth time**
> **Eastern Births - Subtract Time Zone From Birth time**

Ensure that the time zone adjustment includes any Daylight Savings Time changes in effect. If necessary, adjust for Daylight Savings Time manually. This step usually just applies to U.S. births, because *The ACS International Atlas* is formatted differently and any adjustments like DST are already included in the time zone adjustment value given. Use *The ACS American Atlas* to determine if Daylight Savings Time was in effect. If it was, one hour is subtracted from the standard time zone.

> **U.S. Daylight Savings Time - Subtract One Hour from Standard Time Zone**

Example 5.

Let's determine the GMT of birth for the same birth used in Example 3:

4:00 pm , August 5, 1995, San Francisco, California.

Steps 1 & 2. First record the time of birth exactly as given. Then convert the time to 24-hour format by adding 12 hours.

Given Time of Birth:	4:00 pm
PM adjustment	+ 12:00
Given Time expressed in 24-hour time:	16:00

Step 3. Check *The American Atlas* for time zone and time adjustments. In Example 3, we determined that this birth occurred in the Pacific Standard Time Zone, which is 8 hours from GMT, and that Daylight Savings Time was in effect. This information is now used to determine the GMT of birth, as follows:

1. Given Time of Birth:		4:00 pm
2. + PM Adjustment		+12:00
= Given Time expressed in 24-hour time:		16:00
3. Standard Time Zone (PST)	+8:00	
- DST Adjustment	-1:00	
= Time Zone Adjustment	+7:00 ———▶	+ 7:00
4. Sum of Steps 1-3 = GMT of birth		23:00

U.S. Daylight Savings Time - Subtract One Hour from Standard Time Zone

Example 6.

Let's determine the GMT of birth for a person born at 5:30 pm on the same day (August 5, 1995) in San Francisco.

1. Given Time of Birth:		5:30 pm
2. + PM Adjustment		+12:00
3. Standard Time Zone (PST)	+ 8:00	
- DST Adjustment	- 1:00	
= Time Zone Adjustment	+ 7:00 ———▶	+ 7:00
4. = GMT of birth		24:30

The result is greater than 24:00, yet there are only 24 hours in a day. At the time of this birth, it was actually 30 minutes past midnight on the following day in Greenwich, England in GMT. In order to express this birth time in GMT, the date must be changed. The GMT of this birth is 00:30 on August 6, 1995.

GMT of birth	24:30
- 24 hours (date change)	-24:00
GMT of birth	0:30 August 6, 1995

From this point on in our calculations, this birth must be treated as occurring on August 6, 1995.

**Whenever the GMT of birth is greater than 24:00,
subtract 24:00 hours and move the date <u>ahead</u> by one day.**

34

Example 7.

Let's determine the GMT for a birth occurring east of Greenwich:

10:50 am, June 10, 1969, Bombay, India

This is an a.m. birth, so 12 hours do not need to be added to express this in 24-hour time. Look up Bombay, India in *The International Atlas* and notice that Bombay follows India's Time Table #2. Turn to Time Table #2 at the beginning of the India section and there you will find that starting on October 15, 1945, Bombay's time differed from GMT by -5:30. Because there are no time changes listed after this date, we can safely assume that India does not make annual Daylight Savings Time adjustments. This is how the GMT of this birth is determined:

Given Time of Birth:	10:50 am
Time Zone Adjustment:	-5:30
GMT of Birth	5:20

Notice that, because this birth occurred east of Greenwich, the time difference to GMT is expressed in *The International Atlas* as a negative number, and is subtracted from the given time of birth.

**Time Zone Adjustments for Eastern Time Zones
are always <u>subtracted</u> from the Time of Birth**

Example 8.

Let's try another eastern birth, at 1:30 am on July 30, 1989, in Vienna, Austria. This is another morning birth, so no adjustment is needed to convert to 24-hour time. *The International Atlas* indicates that from March 26 to September 24, 1989, Austria's time differed from GMT by -2:00. We can safely assume that Austria uses Daylight Savings Time, because each Spring to each Fall Austria's time difference to GMT varies by an hour. However, *The International Atlas* has already taken these Daylight Savings Time adjustments into account when calculating Austria's time difference to GMT, so unlike dealing with U.S. births, no additional adjustment is needed.

Given Time of Birth:	1:30 am
Time Zone Adjustment	-2:00
	?

Here is another anomaly - the time zone adjustment is greater than the given time of birth. This indicates that when the birth took place in the early morning of July 30th in Vienna, it was not yet midnight of the day before in Greenwich, England. Therefore, 24 hours must be added and the date changed to a day <u>earlier</u> as follows:

Given Time of Birth:	1:30 am
Date Change	+24:00
Time Zone Adjustment	-2:00
GMT of Birth	23:30 July 29, 1989

From this point on in our calculations, this birth must be treated as occurring on July 29, 1989.

**Whenever the GMT of birth is less than 0:00,
add 24:00 hours and move the date <u>back</u> by one day.**

Lesson 3 Exercises

Try the following exercises to make sure you understand how to use the atlases. Use either The American Atlas *or* The International Atlas *to determine the correct time zone for each of the following birth dates. Express each time zone as the number of hours and minutes difference to GMT. State whether Daylight Savings Time (DT), War Time (WT), or Double War Time was in effect, if applicable. Then proceed to the exercises on the following four pages on calculating the GMT of Birth. Answers can be found in the Answer Key in the Appendix.*

1. 3:14 am, Dec. 10, 1944
   San Elizario, TX

2. 7:30 pm, June 14, 1968
   Bowling Green, IN

3. 4:40 pm, April 18, 1938
   Brooklyn, Kings Co., NY

4. 11:30 pm, Sept. 25, 1948
   Chattanooga, TN

5. 5:18 am, June 15, 1978
   Eugene, Oregon

6. 3:45 pm, February 8, 1946
   Honolulu, Hawaii

7. 9:35 pm, August 5, 1915
   Tokyo, Japan

8. 9:30 pm, Sept. 30, 1970
   Dingo, Australia

9. 7:00 am, May 10, 1942
   London, England

10. 1:15 pm, July 10, 1983
    Istanbul, Turkey

Convert the following birth times to GMT. Answers can be found in the Answer Key in the Appendix.

(Note: In order to make the first few exercises a little easier, we have reproduced the GMT portion of our Chart Calculation Form found in the Appendix. This form is provided to help you become acquainted with the steps needed for calculation. However, most certification exams do not allow the use of forms containing printed instruction, so the form should only be used until you feel comfortable with the process, then try practicing without it.)

11. 7:35 pm, September 10, 1985, Boise, Idaho

Part A: GMT of Birth

1. Given Time of Birth ____:____ am / pm

2. + PM Adjustment *(+12:00 if pm)* + ____:____

3. +/-Time Zone

    a. Standard Time Zone *(+W, -E)* ____:____

    b. DST Adjustment *(- 1:00 if DST)* - ____:____
    (Include only if not already factored into (a) above)

    c. = Time Zone Adjustment *(Enter on Line 3, right)* = ____:____ ⟶ +W,-E ____:____

                                      Subtotal = ____:____

4. +/- 24 hours if date change required +/- ____:____

5. = GMT of Birth   Date _____   Time = ____:____

---

12. 3:15 am, March 20, 1945, Brooklyn, Kings County, New York

Part A: GMT of Birth

1. Given Time of Birth ____:____ am / pm

2. + PM Adjustment *(+12:00 if pm)* + ____:____

3. +/-Time Zone

    a. Standard Time Zone *(+W, -E)* ____:____

    b. DST Adjustment *(- 1:00 if DST)* - ____:____
    (Include only if not already factored into (a) above)

    c. = Time Zone Adjustment *(Enter on Line 3, right)* = ____:____ ⟶ +W,-E ____:____

                                        Subtotal = ____:____

4. +/- 24 hours if date change required +/- ____:____

5. = GMT of Birth   Date _____   Time = ____:____

13. 12:40 pm, December 5, 1943, London, England

Part A: GMT of Birth

1. Given Time of Birth   ____:____ am / pm

2. + PM Adjustment *(+12:00 if pm)*   + ____:____

3. +/-Time Zone

    a. Standard Time Zone *(+W, -E)*   ____:____

    b. DST Adjustment *(- 1:00 if DST)*   - ____:____
    (Include only if not already factored into (a) above)

    c. = Time Zone Adjustment *(Enter on Line 3, right)* = ____:____ ⟶ +W,-E ____:____

                                              Subtotal = ____:____

4. +/- 24 hours if date change required   +/- ____:____

5. = GMT of Birth   Date _____   Time = ____:____

---

14. 3:30 am, April 12, 1986, Leningrad, Russia

Part A: GMT of Birth

1. Given Time of Birth   ____:____ am / pm

2. + PM Adjustment *(+12:00 if pm)*   + ____:____

3. +/-Time Zone

    a. Standard Time Zone *(+W, -E)*   ____:____

    b. DST Adjustment *(- 1:00 if DST)*   - ____:____
    (Include only if not already factored into (a) above)

    c. = Time Zone Adjustment *(Enter on Line 3, right)* = ____:____ ⟶ +W,-E ____:____

                                              Subtotal = ____:____

4. +/- 24 hours if date change required   +/- ____:____

5. = GMT of Birth   Date _____   Time = ____:____

15.   8:30 pm, August 5, 1972, Honolulu, Hawaii

Part A: GMT of Birth

1. Given Time of Birth   ___:___ am / pm

2. + PM Adjustment *(+12:00 if pm)*   +   ___:___

3. +/-Time Zone

    a. Standard Time Zone *(+W, -E)*   ___:___

    b. DST Adjustment *(- 1:00 if DST)*   - ___:___
    (Include only if not already factored into (a) above)

    c. = Time Zone Adjustment *(Enter on Line 3, right)* = ___:___ ⟶ +W,-E ___:___

                                            Subtotal = ___:___

4. +/- 24 hours if date change required   +/- ___:___

5. = GMT of Birth   Date _____   Time = ___:___

---

16.   11:45 am, February 11, 1957, Melbourne, Australia

Part A: GMT of Birth

1. Given Time of Birth   ___:___ am / pm

2. + PM Adjustment *(+12:00 if pm)*   +   ___:___

3. +/-Time Zone

    a. Standard Time Zone *(+W, -E)*   ___:___

    b. DST Adjustment *(- 1:00 if DST)*   - ___:___
    (Include only if not already factored into (a) above)

    c. = Time Zone Adjustment *(Enter on Line 3, right)* = ___:___ ⟶ +W,-E ___:___

                                            Subtotal = ___:___

4. +/- 24 hours if date change required   +/- ___:___

5. = GMT of Birth   Date _____   Time = ___:___

Now try one without the form:

17.   4:12 pm, March 19, 1959, Santa Fe, New Mexico

Lesson 4: Latitude, Longitude & Longitude/Time Equivalent

In order to pinpoint a location on the Earth, a coordinate system of **latitude** and **longitude** lines was developed. The intersection of these imaginary geographical lines identifies any location on earth in degrees, minutes, and seconds. As astrologers, we need to know the exact location of a birthplace, using latitude and longitude, in order to calculate an accurate birth chart. This lesson will briefly explain how latitude and longitude are measured, the relationship between time and longitude, and how to convert longitude to time.

Latitude

Lines of latitude are called **Parallels** because they are parallel to the Equator. Latitude parallels form the horizontal lines of the grid. The **Equator** (an imaginary circle around the middle of the Earth that is equidistant from both poles) is designated as 0 degrees latitude. Latitude indicates distance north or south of the Equator. Locations north of the Equator run from 0° - 90° north; locations south of the Equator run from 0° - 90° south. Lines of latitude never measure more than 90 degrees. In the example on the right New York, NY is located at Latitude 40° N 42' 51". (40 degrees, 42 minutes, 51 seconds North of the Equator.)

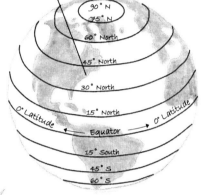

New York, NY is located at 40°N 42' 51"

Longitude

Lines of longitude are called **Meridians** and run from the North Pole to the South Pole, forming the vertical (or "long") lines of measurement. Longitude measures the distance east or west of the Prime Meridian, which is designated as 0 degrees longitude and runs through Greenwich, England. There are 360° around the earth's circumference resulting in longitude lines which run from 0° to 180° EAST of the Prime Meridian and 0° to 180° WEST of the Prime Meridian. (180° West of and 180° East of the Prime Meridian are actually the same line.) In the example on the right New York, NY is located at Longitude 74° W 00' 23" (74 degrees, 0 minutes, 23 seconds West of the Prime Meridian).

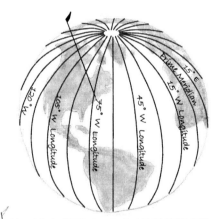

New York, NY is located at 74°W 00' 23"

Latitude + Longitude = Location

Any location can be pinpointed using both its longitude and latitude. In this example New York, NY is located at Longitude 74° W 00' 23" and Latitude 40° N 42' 51".

The Longitude-Time Connection

Longitude is used to calculate Local Mean Time, because longitude determines time - any location along the same longitudinal meridian will be experiencing the same time of day. Converting longitude to time is necessary because it identifies actual local mean time, and is part of the process used to calculate the house cusps for a place of birth. Local mean time, as you will remember from Lesson 3, is true local time based on the actual position of the Sun. The difference between a location's local mean time and GMT is called the **Longitude/Time Equivalent**, or the **Time Equivalent to Greenwich**.

Determining the Longitude/Time Equivalent

The ACS American Atlas and *ACS International Atlas* give an exact latitude and longitude for every location, as well as its longitude-time equivalent (see page 27). Some reference guides also have tables that help calculate the conversion of longitude to time, such as "Table III" provided in the back of *The Michelsen Book of Tables*. However some certification exams require students to demonstrate an understanding of the conversion of longitude to time without the use of Atlases and conversion tables. In order to pass these exams, you will need to understand the longitude-time conversion process explained in this lesson.

Converting Longitude to Time

Longitude and time are related because both measure the circumference of the Earth. One measures it in terms of degrees, and the other measures it in terms of hours.

One full rotation of the Earth = 360°
One full rotation of the Earth = 24 Hours

Or to phrase this another way, distance can be measured by time because it takes 24 hours or one day for the Earth to complete one full rotation of 360°. From this information we can derive the following:

If 360° = 24 hours
and 360 ÷ 24 = 15
then 15° = 1 hour

This tells us that the Earth rotates 15° each hour. It also tells us that for each 15° we are away from Greenwich, England, time will differ from GMT by one hour. Now let's reduce this further:

If 1 hour, or 60 minutes = 15°
and 60 ÷ 15 = 4
then 4 minutes of time = 1° of Longitude

The Earth rotates 1° every 4 minutes. Because of the Earth's rotational direction, local mean time in areas to the east will be later than local mean time in areas to the west.

For each degree of longitude away from the Prime Meridian, Local Mean Time will be
4 minutes ahead of GMT if the location is East of Greenwich,
or 4 minutes behind GMT if the location is West of Greenwich.

Example 1.

Boston, Massachusetts is located at longitude 71° W 03' 37", which can be rounded to 71° W 04'. (Longitude and latitude need only be expressed to the nearest whole minute for adequate accuracy.) Below are the steps needed to determine Boston's Longitude/Time Equivalent:

Step 1. Express Longitude in decimal form. (This process is covered in detail in lesson 2.)

$$71° \text{ W } 04'$$

$$= 71° + \frac{4}{60} \text{ degrees}$$

$$= 71.0666, \text{ rounded up to } 71.07°$$

Step 2. Multiply Longitude (in decimal form) by 4 minutes.

$$71.07° \times 4 \text{ (minutes per degree)} = 284.28 \text{ minutes}$$

Step 3. Convert this answer to Hours, Minutes and Seconds.

a) Convert whole minutes to hours. Record whole hours:

284 minutes ÷ 60 = 4.73 hours   4: _ _:_ _

b) Convert decimal remainder from "a" above to minutes.
Record whole minutes:

.73 (hours) x 60 = 43.8 minutes, rounded to 44 minutes   4: 44:_ _

c) Convert original decimal remainder from Step 2 to seconds.
Record whole seconds:

.28 (minutes) x 60 = 16.8 seconds, rounded to 17 seconds   4: 44: 17

Step 4. Determine sign (+/-) of result.

Longitude/time equivalents for western longitudes are expressed as a negative number, because western longitudes are earlier than GMT. Eastern longitude-time equivalents are expressed as a positive number, because eastern longitudes are later than GMT.

Boston's Longitude/Time Equivalent is -4: 44: 17.   - 4: 44: 17

This Longitude/Time Equivalent tells us that Local Mean Time in Boston is 4 hours, 44 minutes, and 17 seconds earlier than Local Mean Time in Greenwich, England (GMT).

You may notice that the sign of a location's longitude/time equivalent is **opposite** to that given in *The ACS Atlases*. This is because the atlases are starting with a location's local mean time and stating the time difference between LMT and GMT, while here we are starting with GMT and in effect traveling in the opposite direction to determine Local Mean Time. Manual calculations of Longitude-Time Equivalents may also differ from the values listed in an atlas or the Table by up to 2 seconds. This is due to rounding up/down and will not affect the accuracy of the birth chart.

Example 2.

Santa Cruz, California is located at longitude 122° W 01' 47", rounded to 122° W 02'.

Step 1. Express Longitude in decimal form.

$$122° 02' = 122 + \frac{02}{60} \text{ degrees}$$

$$= 122.0333°, \text{ rounded to } 122.03°$$

Step 2. Multiply Longitude by 4 minutes.

$$122.03 \times 4 \text{ minutes} = 488.12 \text{ minutes}$$

Step 3. Convert answer to Hours, Minutes, Seconds.

488 ÷ 60 = 8.13 hours	8:_ _:_ _
.13 hours x 60 = 7.8 minutes, rounded to 8	8: 08:_ _
.12 minutes (from original decimal remainder in Step 2) x 60 = 7.2 seconds, rounded to 7	8: 08: 07

Step 4. Determine sign (+/-) of result.

Western Longitude =   - 8: 08: 07

Santa Cruz's Longitude/Time Equivalent is –8:08:07.

Example 3.

Heidelberg, Germany is located at longitude 8° E 43'. (Notice that international longitudes are listed in *The International Atlas* already rounded to the nearest minute.)

Step 1.

$$8° 43' = 8° + \frac{43}{60} = 8.72 \text{ degrees}$$

Step 2.

$$8.72 \times 4 \text{ minutes} = 34.88 \text{ minutes}$$

Step 3. In this case, the longitude/time equivalent is less than an hour, so we can move right into converting the decimal into seconds:

.88 minutes x 60 = 52.8 seconds, rounded up to 53	0: 34:_ _
	0: 34: 53

Step 4.

Eastern Longitude =   + 0: 34: 53

Heidelberg's Longitude/Time Equivalent is + 0:34:53.

44

Example 4.

Lima, Peru is located at longitude 77° W 03'.

Step 1.

$$77° \ 03' = 77° + \frac{03}{60} = 77.05 \text{ degrees}$$

Step 2.

77.05 x 4 minutes = 308.2 minutes

Step 3.

308 ÷ 60 = 5.13 hours	5:_ _:_ _
.13 hours x 60 = 7.8 minutes, rounded to 8	5: 08:_ _
.2 minutes x 60 = 12 seconds	5: 08: 12

Step 4.

Western Longitude =	- 5: 08: 12

Lima's Longitude/Time Equivalent is -5:08:12.

Did you know you can approximate your latitude just by looking at the stars?

In the Northern Hemisphere, if one were to walk outside and point with one arm toward the North Star *Polaris*, the star located closest to the North Celestial Pole, and point with the other arm toward the northern horizon where the sky appears to meet the land, the angle created between the two arms would approximate the degree of latitude. At the North Pole, the North Star would be directly overhead and the angle between arms would be approximately 90°. At the Equator, the North Star would appear to be resting on the northern horizon, forming an angle of 0°. (In the Southern Hemisphere, there is not an obvious celestial marker for the South Celestial Pole, making this more difficult.)

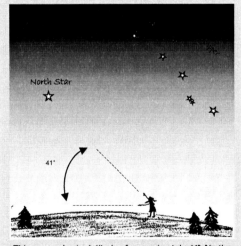

This person is at a latitude of approximately 41° North, which is shared by New York, Rome, and Madrid.

Lesson 4 Exercises

Determine the Longitude-Time Equivalent for the following locations. Answers can be found in the Answer Key in the Appendix.

1. Charlotte, North Carolina
   80° W 51'

2. Laramie, Wyoming
   105° W 35'

3. Miami, Florida
   80° W 12'

4. Rome, Italy
   12° E 29'

5. Hornby, New Zealand
   172° E 32'

6. Beijing, China
   116° E 25'

Lesson 5: Local Sidereal Time

"Sidereal" means "relative to the stars", and Local Sidereal Time (LST) tells us exactly what point of the starry zodiac is culminating at the Midheaven position in a given location at any given time. This lesson will explain what Local Sidereal Time is and how to convert the GMT of birth into Local Sidereal Time.

What is Sidereal Time?

Picture the celestial sphere—the starry background upon which the Sun, Moon, and planets move. While the planets appear to wander among the zodiacal constellations, the stars stay in fixed patterns and relationships to each other. From our perspective, the stars appear to be painted on a great inverted bowl suspended over the Earth, and the bowl as a whole moves and rotates according to the time of day and year. Imagine that we could reach up and mark a particular star on the celestial sphere with a highlighting pen. When that same star returned to its exact position in the sky, it would represent one sidereal day, or 24 sidereal hours.

What is Sidereal Time actually measuring?

The **Equinoctial Point** is that point on the celestial sphere where the Sun's apparent path, called the **Ecliptic** intersects with the **Celestial Equator**, which is simply the Earth's Equator projected out into space. There are two of these equinoctial points, designated as 0° Aries and 0° Libra. The Spring Equinoctial Point, or 0° Aries, is the actual point that is "highlighted" in sidereal time. When this precise point reaches the midheaven in a given location, it is **0:00** local sidereal time.

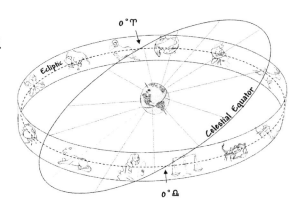

Sidereal vs. Solar Time

If the Earth simply rotated on its axis but did not simultaneously revolve around the Sun, Solar Time and Sidereal Time would be exactly the same. As the Earth made one full rotation in 24 solar hours, 0° Aries would return to its midheaven position in the sky at the same time each day, denoting the passing of 24 sidereal hours. But because the Earth also revolves around the Sun, by the time a full 24 solar-hour rotation has occurred, the Earth has moved a little bit in its orbit, and the stars are not in quite the same position anymore. From our perspective 0° Aries returns to midheaven position a little earlier, approximately 3 minutes and 56 seconds earlier each day. What this means is that a 24-hour sidereal "day" is actually just over 3 minutes and 56 seconds shorter than a 24-hour solar day. Reducing this further, one hour of sidereal time is 9.86 seconds shorter than one hour of solar time. Or phrased another way, one hour of Solar Time equals one hour and 9.86 seconds of Sidereal Time. In order to convert solar time to sidereal time, we need to add 9.86 seconds to each hour of solar time. This is called the **Solar/Sidereal time correction**.

"0 Hour" vs. Midnight

Let's take a little tangent here to clarify an important definition. In common language, when we use the term "midnight", we usually mean the end of a particular day. For instance, when we say "I'll meet you Friday at midnight", we mean that moment when Friday night ends and Saturday begins. This is very different than 0:00 or "0 Hour", which is the moment a day begins. If we were to say, "I'll meet you Friday at 0 hour", we would mean the moment Thursday became Friday –a full 24 hours earlier than the "midnight" just mentioned. Because of this difference in the common usage of the word "midnight", the title "Midnight Ephemeris" is a bit misleading. A midnight ephemeris is actually recording planetary positions at "0 hour" on any particular day (i.e. planetary positions for Thursday, November 6, 2003 at 0:00, meaning the moment Thursday 11/6/03 first begins). To avoid any misunderstanding, you will notice that in this workbook we use the designation "0 hour" instead of "midnight", and encourage students to do the same.

Converting GMT to LST (Local Sidereal Time)

There are four steps to convert a GMT of birth into Local Sidereal Time (abbreviated "LST"):

Step 1. Look up the Sidereal Time for 0 hr on the birth date in an ephemeris. Remember that if the birth date changed as a result of converting the given time of birth to GMT, you must use the new birth date for this step. (Refer to Lesson 3 if you don't understand this.)

Step 2. Add the GMT of birth to the Sidereal Time (above).

Step 3. Determine the Solar/Sidereal time correction on the GMT (explained below), **and add this to the Sidereal Time above.** *The Michelsen Book of Tables* includes a table to make this conversion process easier. In this lesson, we will show you how to use this table as well as how to calculate the solar-sidereal time correction manually.

Step 4. Add (if East longitude) or Subtract (if West longitude) the Longitude/Time Equivalent for the place of birth (explained in Lesson 4).

Example 1.

Let us convert a birth of 11:45 GMT on February 2, 1978 at Boston, Massachusetts into Local Sidereal Time.

Step 1. First, look up February 2, 1978 in *The ACS Midnight Ephemeris*. The second column titled "Sid. Time" gives the Sidereal Time at 0 hr GMT in hours:minutes:seconds. In the example below, notice that the Sidereal Time for 0 hr on February 2 is 8:47:20.

					LONGITUDE							**FEBRUARY 1978**	
Day	Sid.Time	☉	0 hr ☽	Noon ☽	True ☊	☿	♀	♂	♃	♄	♅	♆	♇
1 W	8 43 23	11♒46 4	11♏50 50	18♏45 12	7♎29.1	24♑26.0	14♒ 6.4	27♋46.8	26♌40.8	28♌20.1	16♏14.8	17♐41.8	16♎38.8
2 Th	8 47 20	12 46 58	25 44 51	2♐49 47	7R28.3	25 56.1	15 21.7	27R25.7	26R37.1	28R15.5	16 15.8	17 43.3	16R38.3
3 F	8 51 16	13 47 51	9♐59 53	17 14 50	7 25.4	27 27.1	16 37.0	27 5.2	26 33.6	28 10.9	16 16.8	17 44.8	16 37.8
4 Sa	8 55 13	14 48 43	24 34 13	1♑57 21	7 20.3	28 58.8	17 52.3	26 45.1	26 30.3	28 6.3	16 17.7	17 46.2	16 37.3

Step 2. Next, add the GMT of birth to this Sidereal Time. Express the GMT hours: minutes: seconds to lessen the chance of making an addition error.

$$
\begin{array}{lr}
\text{Sidereal Time at 0:00} & 8\!:\!47\!:\!20 \\
\text{GMT of Birth} & \underline{11\!:\!45\!:\!00} \\
& 19\!:\!92\!:\!20
\end{array}
$$

Step 3. Determine the Solar/Sidereal Time correction needed to convert the GMT of birth into Sidereal Time, and add this amount to the Sidereal Time above. In order to calculate this the GMT must be expressed as a decimal. (Refer to Lesson 2 if you need additional help on this step.)

$$11:45 \ = \ 11 \ \frac{45}{60} \ = \ 11.75 \text{ hours}$$

(45 divided by 60 = .75)

Now multiply the GMT hours by the conversion factor of 9.86 seconds. The result will always be <u>seconds</u>, not minutes.

The solar/sidereal time correction can never be more than 236 seconds (24 hours x 9.86), or just under 4 minutes.

11.75 x 9.86 seconds = 115.85 seconds
Round up to 116 seconds
116 seconds = 1 minute, 56 seconds

Then add these first three steps together:

Sidereal Time at 0 hr	8:47:20
+ GMT of Birth	11:45:00
+ Solar/Sidereal correction	1:56
=	19:93:76

(Notice that in this example the minutes and seconds are each greater than 60. Do not reduce these values until finished with the last step of this process, below.)

Step 4. The figure above (19:93:76) indicates the Sidereal Time of Birth in Greenwich, England. The longitude/time equivalent for the place of birth (discussed in lesson 4) is used to determine the Sidereal Time of Birth at the birth place - the <u>Local</u> Sidereal Time (LST). This figure will either be added to the Sidereal Time above if the birth place has an eastern longitude, or subtracted if the birth place has a western longitude. The example birth occurred in Boston, Massachusetts. We either look up Boston in *The American Atlas* and see that it has a longitude/time equivalent of 4:44:14, or calculate this value manually (as discussed in lesson 4). Boston has a western longitude and is therefore earlier than GMT, so this value is subtracted from the Sidereal Time above:

$$19:93:76$$
$$- 4:44:14$$
$$15:49:62$$

Or   15:50:02 = Local Sidereal Time of Birth

Occasionally, when adding or subtracting Sidereal Time, you may end up with a figure greater than 24 hours or less than 0 hours. If this happens, add or subtract a full 24 hours (24:00:00) as needed. There are no "days" in Sidereal Time, only the repetition of the 24-hour cycle as the "highlighted" point on the celestial sphere returns to its original position, so 24 hours can be added or subtracted without requiring any date change.

**24 hours of Sidereal Time can be added or subtracted as needed.
No date change is necessary.**

Example 2.

Let's determine the Sidereal Time of a birth occurring on May 5, 1945 in Sacramento, California, at a GMT of 8:15.

Sidereal Time at 0 hr on May 5, 1945:	14:50:00
+ GMT of Birth	8:15:00
+ Solar/Sidereal Time correction on GMT	1:21
(8.25 hrs x 9.86 secs = 81 secs = 1 min 21 secs)	
	22:66:21
- Longitude/Time Equivalent for Sacramento, CA	- 8:05:58
	14:60:23
= LST of Birth	= 15:00:23

} *Remember that you Can "borrow" minutes*

Example 3.

November 3, 1961, Mexico City, Mexico, 2:52 GMT.

Sidereal Time at 0 hr on November 3, 1961	2:48:03
+ GMT of Birth	2:52:00
+ Solar/Sidereal Time correction on GMT	:28
(2.87 hrs x 9.86 secs = 28 secs)	
	4:100:31
Add 24 hours in order to subtract L/TE below	+24: 00:00
	28:100:31
- Longitude/Time Equivalent for Mexico City	- 6: 36:36
	22:63:55
= LST of Birth	= 23:03:55

Example 4.

July 29, 1977, Heidelberg, Germany, 12:35 GMT. Notice that the longitude/time equivalent is **added to** the sidereal time, not subtracted, because Heidelberg's longitude is **east** of Greenwich.

Sidereal Time at 0 hr on July 29, 1977:	20:26:08
+ GMT of Birth	12:35:00
+ Solar/Sidereal Time correction on GMT	2:04
(12.58 hrs x 9.86 secs = 124 secs = 2 min 4 secs)	
	32:63:12
+ Longitude/Time Equivalent for Heidelberg	+ 0:34:52
=	32:97:64
	= 33:38:04
result is greater than 24 hours	- 24:00:00
= LST of Birth	= 9:38:04

Longitude/Time Equivalents for western births are subtracted from Sidereal Time
Longitude/Time Equivalents for eastern births are added to Sidereal Time

How to Use the Michelsen
Solar-Sidereal Time Correction Table

You will find many helpful tables in the back of the *Michelsen Book of Tables*. There are several different ways to calculate a birthchart, and most of these tables are used for these alternate methods but are not needed for the method taught in this book. Most certification exams require you to demonstrate your ability to erect a birthchart without reliance on tables, and this is why we teach the "why" and "how" behind each step of the calculation process. But occasionally exams do allow tables, so for students who don't get a kick out of math calculations, we provide handy alternatives where applicable.

Table II Solar-Sidereal Time Correction, found in the back of *The Book of Tables*, shortcuts calculating the solar-sidereal time correction used in Step 3 of this lesson. This is how the table is used:

First, using the GMT of birth,
find the number of hours of
GMT across the top

Next, find the number
of minutes of GMT down
either side

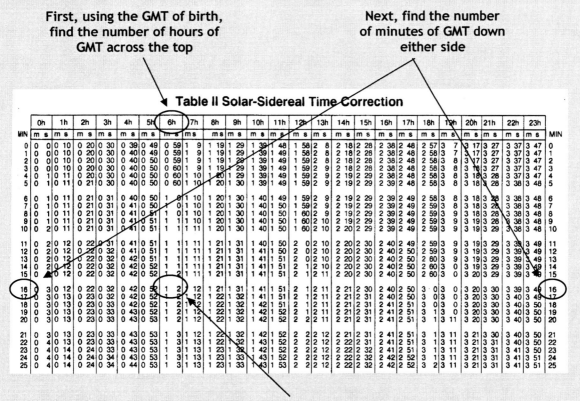

◄ **Table II Solar-Sidereal Time Correction**

Last, find where the hours column
and the minutes row meet. The value
located there gives you the minutes
and seconds of solar-sidereal
correction on the GMT of birth.

In the example above, the GMT of birth is 6:16. Locate 6 hours across the top, and 16 minutes down the side. Then follow the hours column down and the minutes row over until they intersect. There you will find "1 2". The solar-sidereal correction for this GMT of birth is 1 minute and 2 seconds, or 00:01:02.

Lesson 5 Exercises

Determine the LST of birth for the following births. Answers can be found in the Answer Key in the Appendix.

1. 6:29 GMT, February 16, 1985, Atlanta, Georgia

Sidereal Time at 0 hr on birth date   ____:____:____

+ GMT of birth   ____:____: 00

+ Solar/Sidereal Time Correction on GMT *(from Table or calculate below:)*   ____:____

(GMT *(as decimal)*_____ hrs x 9.86 secs = _____)   Subtotal = ____:____:____

+/- Longitude/Time Equivalent *(from Atlas or calculate below; -W, +E)*   +/- ____:____:____

(Longitude *(as decimal)* _____ x 4 min = _____)   Subtotal = ____:____:____

+/- 24:00:00 if required   +/- ____:____:____

= **LST of Birth**   **LST** = ____:____:____

---

2. 14:05 GMT, August 30, 1965, Athens, Greece

Sidereal Time at 0 hr on birth date   ____:____:____

+ GMT of birth   ____:____: 00

+ Solar/Sidereal Time Correction on GMT *(from Table or calculate below:)*   ____:____

(GMT *(as decimal)*_____ hrs x 9.86 secs = _____)   Subtotal = ____:____:____

+/- Longitude/Time Equivalent *(from Atlas or calculate below; -W, +E)*   +/- ____:____:____

(Longitude *(as decimal)* _____ x 4 min = _____)   Subtotal = ____:____:____

+/- 24:00:00 if required   +/- ____:____:____

= **LST of Birth**   **LST** = ____:____:____

Now try two without the form:

3. 8:45 GMT, March 4, 1942, Newark, New Jersey

4. 1:52 GMT, July 10, 1979, Vienna, Austria

Lesson 6: Section Review

In this lesson the steps from the preceding three lessons are combined and reviewed. This may seem like unnecessary repetition, but we have found that determining the correct GMT and LST of birth are areas where students frequently make mistakes. The best way to ensure against error is to practice over and over until the procedure becomes second nature. In the examples that follow, each step is cross-referenced to the lesson in which it was introduced, allowing you to easily refer back at any point in the process. So far we have covered how to find:

GMT of birth - used to calculate the positions of planets
LST of birth - used to calculate house cusps

Altogether there are 11 steps to determine the GMT and LST of birth, as shown on the reprinted sections of the Chart Calculation Form below:

Part A: GMT of Birth

1. Given Time of Birth   ____:____ am / pm

2. + PM Adjustment *(+12:00 if pm)*   +   ____:____

3. +/-Time Zone

     a. Standard Time Zone *(+W, -E)*   ____:____

     b. DST Adjustment *(- 1:00 if DST)*   - ____:____
      (Include only if not already factored into (a) above)

     c. = Time Zone Adjustment *(Enter on Line 3, right)* = ____:____ ⟶ +W,-E ____:____

                                                      Subtotal =   ____:____

4. +/- 24 hours if date change required   +/- ____:____

5. = GMT of Birth   Date _____   Time = ____:____

Part B: LST of Birth

6. Sidereal Time at 0 hr on birth date *(from ephemeris; use birth date from Step 5)*   ____:____:____

7. + GMT of birth *(from Step 5)*   ____:____: 00

8. + Solar/Sidereal Time Correction on GMT *(from Table or calculate below:)*   ____:____

     (GMT *(as decimal)*_____ hrs x 9.86 secs = _____)   Subtotal = ____:____:____

9. +/- Longitude/Time Equivalent *(from Atlas or calculate below; -W, +E)*   +/- ____:____:____

     (Longitude *(as decimal)* _____ x 4 min = _____)   Subtotal = ____:____:____

10. +/- 24:00:00 if required   +/- ____:____:____

11. = LST of Birth   LST = ____:____:____

Example 1

In this example we will calculate the GMT and LST of birth for an individual born:

March 3, 1962, 2:18 am CST
Chicago, Illinois   **Longitude: 87° W 39'**   **Latitude: 41° N 51'**

Part A: GMT of Birth

1. Given Time of Birth		2:18 am	*(Lesson 3)*
2. + PM Adjustment *(+ 12:00 if pm)*		----	*(Lesson 3)*
3. +/- Time Zone			
a. Standard Time Zone *(+W,-E)*	+ 6:00		*(Lesson 3)*
b. DST Adjustment *(-1:00 if DST)*	----		*(Lesson 3)*
c. = Time Zone Adjustment	6:00 ⟶	+ 6:00	
4. +/- 24 hours if date change is required		----	*(Lesson 3)*

5. = GMT of Birth   **Date = March 3, 1962**   **Time = 8:18**

Part B: LST of Birth

6. Sidereal Time at 0 hr on birth date *(from Ephemeris)*		10:41:09	*(Lesson 5)*
7. + GMT of birth *(from Step 5)*		+ 08:18:00	
8. + Solar/Sidereal Time correction on GMT *(from Table or calculate below:)*		+ 1:22	*(Lesson 5)*
(8.3 hrs x 9.86 secs = 82 seconds)			
	Subtotal =	18:60:31	
9. +/- Longitude/Time Equivalent *(from Atlas or calculate below; -W,+E)*		- 05:50:36	*(Lesson 4)*
(87.65° x 4 min = 350.6 min = 5:50:36)			
	Subtotal =	13:09:55	
10. +/- 24:00:00 if required		----	*(Lesson 5)*

11. = LST of Birth   **LST = 13:09:55**

A little trick to help remember whether to add or subtract:

In Part A we are calculating the time zone difference from the birth location to GMT. In Part B we are calculating the difference from GMT back to the birth location. One is the **inverse** of the other. If you **add** the Time Zone Adjustment in Step 3, then you will **subtract** the Longitude/Time Equivalent in Step 9. If you **subtract** the Time Zone Adjustment in Step 3, then you will **add** the Longitude/Time Equivalent in Step 9. You will never be adding or subtracting both.

+ Time Zone, - Long/Time Equivalent   or   **- Time Zone, + Long/Time Equivalent**

Example 2

In this example we will calculate the GMT and LST of birth for an individual born:

June 12, 1995, 9:15 pm PDT
Los Angeles, California   Longitude: 118° W 15'   Latitude: 34° N 03'

Part A: GMT of Birth

1. Given Time of Birth   9:15 pm   *(Lesson 3)*

2. + PM Adjustment *(+ 12:00 if pm)*   + 12:00   *(Lesson 3)*

3. +/- Time Zone

       a. Standard Time Zone *(+W,-E)*   + 8:00   *(Lesson 3)*

       b. DST Adjustment *(-1:00 if DST)*   - 1:00   *(Lesson 3)*

       c. = Time Zone Adjustment   + 7:00   ⟶   + 7:00

                                 Subtotal =   28:15

4. +/- 24 hours if date change is required   - 24:00   *(Lesson 3)*

5. = GMT of Birth   Date = June 13, 1995   Time =   4:15

Part B: LST of Birth

6. Sidereal Time at 0 hr on birth date *(from Ephemeris)*   17:23:21   *(Lesson 5)*

7. + GMT of birth *(from line 5)*   + 04:15:00

8. + Solar/Sidereal Time correction on GMT *(from Table or calculate below:)*   +   0:42   *(Lesson 5)*

     (4.25 hrs x 9.86 secs = 42 seconds)

                                 Subtotal =   21:38:63

9. +/- Longitude/Time Equivalent *(from Atlas or calculate below; -W,+E)*   -   07:53:00   *(Lesson 4)*

     (118.25° x 4 min = 473 min = 7:53:00)

                                 Subtotal =   13:45:63
                                              =   13:46:03

10. +/- 24:00:00 if required   ----   *(Lesson 5)*

11. = LST of Birth   LST =   13:46:03

In this example, one hour was deducted from the time zone for daylight savings time in Step 3. Notice also that the birth date changed to the following day once the birth time was converted to GMT - when 24 hours is subtracted in Step 4, one day must be added to the date of birth in Step 5 to compensate. Finally, if you used *The American Atlas* to find the Longitude/Time Equivalent in Step 9, you will have noticed that the atlas figure differs by two seconds. This is due to rounding off longitude to the nearest minute, while *The American Atlas* is calculated to the nearest second.

Example 3

In this example we will calculate the GMT and LST of birth for an individual born:

September 18, 1954, 9:12 pm
Stockholm, Sweden   Longitude: 18° E 03'   Latitude: 59° N 20'

Part A: GMT of Birth

1. Given Time of Birth		9:12 pm	*(Lesson 3)*
2. + PM Adjustment *(+ 12:00 if pm)*		+ 12:00	*(Lesson 3)*
3. +/- Time Zone			
a. Standard Time Zone *(+W,-E)*	- 1:00		*(Lesson 3)*
b. DST Adjustment *(-1:00 if DST)*	_____		*(Lesson 3)*
c. = Time Zone Adjustment	- 1:00 ⟶ - 1:00		
	Subtotal = 20:12		
4. +/- 24 hours *if date change is required*			*(Lesson 3)*

5. = GMT of Birth   Date = Sept. 18, 1954   Time =   20:12

Part B: LST of Birth

6. Sidereal Time at 0 hr on birth date *(from Ephemeris)*		23:45:31	*(Lesson 5)*
7. + GMT of birth *(from line 5)*		+ 20:12:00	
8. + Solar/Sidereal Time correction on GMT *(from Table or calculate below:)*		+ 3:19	*(Lesson 5)*
(20.2 hrs x 9.86 secs = 199 seconds)			
	Subtotal = 43:60:50		
9. +/- Longitude/Time Equivalent *(from Atlas or calculate below; -W,+E)*		+ 01:12:12	*(Lesson 4)*
(18.05° x 4 min = 72.2 min = 01:12:12)			
	Subtotal = 44:72:62		
	= 45:13:02		
10. +/- 24:00:00 if required		- 24:00:00	*(Lesson 5)*

11. = LST of Birth   LST =   21:13:02

Notice that because this is an eastern hemisphere birth, the time zone adjustment in Step 3 is subtracted, and the Longitude/Time Equivalent in Step 9 is added. Daylight Savings Time is not a consideration when using *The International Atlas* because any time adjustments like DST are already factored into the Time Table figures given. No date change was necessary when calculating the GMT. However, in the final step we ended up with a Sidereal Time greater than 24 hours. Remember that in sidereal time 24 hours can be added or subtracted without affecting the date because there are no "days" in sidereal time, only the repetition of the 24-hour cycle.

Lesson 6 Exercises

Determine the GMT and LST for the following births. Use the form following each exercise to do your calculations. Answers can be found in the Answer Key in the Appendix.

1.

July 11, 1975
8:45pm
Des Moines, Iowa
Latitude: 41° N 36', Longitude: 93° W 37'

Part A: GMT of Birth

1. Given Time of Birth _____:_____ am / pm

2. + PM Adjustment *(+12:00 if pm)* + _____:_____

3. +/- Time Zone

    a. Standard Time Zone *(+W, -E)* _____:_____

    b. DST Adjustment *(- 1:00 if DST)* - _____:_____
    (Include only if not already factored into (a) above)

    c. = Time Zone Adjustment *(Enter on Line 3, right)* = _____:_____ ⟶ +W,-E _____:_____

    Subtotal = _____:_____

4. +/- 24 hours if date change required +/- _____:_____

5. = GMT of Birth   Date _____   Time = _____:_____

Part B: LST of Birth

6. Sidereal Time at 0 hr on birth date *(from ephemeris; use birth date from Step 5)* _____:_____:_____

7. + GMT of birth *(from Step 5)* _____:_____: 00

8. + Solar/Sidereal Time Correction on GMT *(from Table or calculate below:)* _____:_____

    (GMT *(as decimal)*_____ hrs x 9.86 secs = _____)   Subtotal = _____:_____:_____

9. +/- Longitude/Time Equivalent *(from Atlas or calculate below; -W, +E)* +/- _____:_____:_____

    (Longitude *(as decimal)* _____ x 4 min = _____)   Subtotal = _____:_____:_____

10. +/- 24:00:00 if required +/- _____:_____:_____

11. = LST of Birth   LST = _____:_____:_____

2.

December 8, 1987
5:52 am
Tokyo, Japan
Latitude: 35° N 42', Longitude: 139° E 46'

Part A: GMT of Birth

1. Given Time of Birth   ____:____ am / pm

2. + PM Adjustment *(+12:00 if pm)*   +   ____:____

3. +/-Time Zone

    a. Standard Time Zone *(+W, -E)*   ____:___

    b. DST Adjustment *(- 1:00 if DST)*   - ____:____
      (Include only if not already factored into (a) above)

    c. = Time Zone Adjustment *(Enter on Line 3, right)*   = ____:____   ⟶   +W,-E ____:____

                              Subtotal =   ____:____

4. +/- 24 hours if date change required   +/- ____:____

5. = GMT of Birth   Date _____   Time = ____:____

Part B: LST of Birth

6. Sidereal Time at 0 hr on birth date *(from ephemeris; use birth date from Step 5)*   ____:____:____

7. + GMT of birth *(from Step 5)*   ____:____: 00

8. + Solar/Sidereal Time Correction on GMT *(from Table or calculate below:)*   ____:____

    (GMT *(as decimal)*_____ hrs x 9.86 secs = _____)   Subtotal = ____:____:____

9. +/- Longitude/Time Equivalent *(from Atlas or calculate below; -W, +E)*   +/- ____:____:____

    (Longitude *(as decimal)* _____ x 4 min = _____)   Subtotal = ____:____:____

10. +/- 24:00:00 if required   +/- ____:____:____

11. = LST of Birth   LST = ____:____:____

60

Now try one without the form:

3.

August 25, 1962
6:58 pm
Portland, Maine
Latitude: 43° N 40', Longitude: 70° W 15'

Section 3:

The Planets

Lesson 7: Daily Motion

Lesson 8: Finding Planets Using a Constant Multiplier

Lesson 9: Chiron & the Asteroids

Lesson 7: Daily Motion

The daily motion of a planet is the distance it seems to travel in twenty-four hours, expressed in degrees and minutes of arc. Determining daily motion is the first step in calculating the exact positions of the planets at birth. This lesson will cover how to calculate daily motion. The next lesson will focus on how to calculate the exact positions of the planets at birth based on their daily motion.

Finding Planetary Positions in the Ephemeris

Usually ephemerides list planet positions at either midnight (0 hour) or Noon GMT (Greenwich Mean Time). Calculating daily motion is a much simpler process if midnight positions are used, so in this book we will be using *The American Ephemeris for the 20th Century - Midnight Edition.*

Below is an example of an *ACS Ephemeris—Midnight Edition* page showing the planet positions for the first half of March, 1963:

MARCH 1963   **LONGITUDE**

Day	Sid.Time	☉	0 hr ☽	Noon ☽	True ☊	☿	♀	♂	♃	♄	♅	♆	♇
1 F	10 32 19	9♓40 57	17♉10 27	24♊19 5	28♋52.3	17♒26.9	25♑58.6	6♌54.8	21♓45.7	16♒49.9	2♍58.5	15♏37.2	10♍54.3
2 Sa	10 36 15	10 41 11	1♊22 54	8♊21 44	28D 50.2	18 54.3	27 7.7	6R 43.0	22 0.1	16 56.7	2R 55.9	15R 36.7	10R 52.8
3 Su	10 40 12	11 41 23	15 15 35	22 4 33	28 49.9	20 22.9	28 16.9	6 32.0	22 14.5	17 3.5	2 53.3	15 36.3	10 51.2
4 M	10 44 9	12 41 32	28 48 47	5♋28 31	28 50.8	21 52.6	29 26.2	6 21.8	22 29.0	17 10.2	2 50.7	15 35.7	10 49.6
5 Tu	10 48 5	13 41 40	12♋4 0	18 35 33	28 52.2	23 23.4	0♒35.6	6 12.4	22 43.4	17 16.9	2 48.1	15 35.2	10 48.1
6 W	10 52 2	14 41 46	25 3 25	1♌27 54	28R53.1	24 55.4	1 45.1	6 3.7	22 57.9	17 23.6	2 45.6	15 34.6	10 46.5
7 Th	10 55 58	15 41 49	7♌49 15	14 7 43	28 52.8	26 28.6	2 54.7	5 55.9	23 12.4	17 30.3	2 43.0	15 34.0	10 44.9
8 F	10 59 55	16 41 51	20 23 32	26 36 52	28 50.4	28 2.8	4 4.4	5 48.8	23 26.9	17 36.9	2 40.5	15 33.4	10 43.4
9 Sa	11 3 51	17 41 50	2♍47 53	8♍56 45	28 45.8	29 38.2	5 14.2	5 42.6	23 41.4	17 43.5	2 38.0	15 32.8	10 41.8
10 Su	11 7 48	18 41 47	15 3 35	21 8 32	28 38.7	1♓14.8	6 24.1	5 37.1	23 55.9	17 50.0	2 35.5	15 32.1	10 40.3
11 M	11 11 44	19 41 43	27 11 41	3♎13 13	28 29.8	2 52.4	7 34.0	5 32.4	24 10.4	17 56.5	2 33.0	15 31.4	10 38.7
12 Tu	11 15 41	20 41 36	9♎13 14	15 11 57	28 19.6	4 31.3	8 44.1	5 28.4	24 24.9	18 2.9	2 30.5	15 30.6	10 37.2
13 W	11 19 37	21 41 28	21 9 31	27 6 13	28 9.1	6 11.2	9 54.2	5 25.3	24 39.4	18 9.3	2 28.0	15 29.8	10 35.6
14 Th	11 23 34	22 41 18	3♏2 18	8♏58 5	27 59.2	7 52.4	11 4.4	5 22.9	24 54.0	18 15.7	2 25.6	15 29.0	10 34.1
15 F	11 27 31	23 41 6	14 53 56	20 50 16	27 50.8	9 34.7	12 14.7	5 21.2	25 8.5	18 22.0	2 23.2	15 28.2	10 32.6
16 Sa	11 31 27	24 40 52	26 47 32	2♐46 14	27 44.5	11 18.2	13 25.1	5D20.3	25 23.0	18 28.3	2 20.8	15 27.3	10 31.0

Each line represents a day of the month and gives positions for all planets. Be careful! Copying the wrong date starts the entire planetary calculation process with inaccurate data. It is helpful to use a ruler or long straight edge to underline the day of the month that you are working with to avoid mistakes.

The midnight (0 hour) GMT position of longitude is listed for the Sun, Moon, True ☊ (North Node of the Moon) and each planet. Because the Moon moves so rapidly, its position is given at both 0 hour and noon. We will be using the 0 hour Moon position only to calculate daily motion. Notice in *The ACS Ephemeris* page shown above, that at 0 hour GMT on March 3, 1963, the Sun (☉) is listed at 11° ♓ 41' 23" and the Moon (☽) is shown at 15° ♊ 15' 35".

The sign in which a planet is located is shown once on the first day of the month, unless it **ingresses**, or moves into a new sign. When a planet changes sign the new sign will then be shown. The planet will remain in that sign until another new sign is printed in the column. Look at the "0 hr" column for the Moon in the example above; the Moon moved into Virgo (♍) sometime before 0 hour on March 9th and remained in Virgo until some time on the 11th. Because planetary positions are only listed once a day at 0 hour (or twice a day in the case of the Moon), we know that if a planet is listed at a low degree of a new sign at 0 hour on a particular day, it changed sign some time during the previous day. Finding the exact time a planet changes sign in the ephemeris will be discussed on the following page.

Finding Planetary Ingress Information in the Ephemeris

At the bottom of each page in *The ACS Ephemeris* you will find a box containing additional information on the planets. Below we have reprinted the box provided for March and April 1963. Because data for two months is given on each page, the information in this box applies to both months, with the first month's data listed first.

The time that a planet actually changes signs is listed in the ***Ingress*** *column. The top half of the column applies to planetary ingresses occurring during the first month shown on the page, and the bottom half applies to the second month shown.*

The Moon is given its own column because it changes sign so frequently. The column on the left applies to lunar occurrences during the first month on a page, and the second column applies to the second month. These sections give data on the exact time and date of the Moon's last aspect before leaving a sign (on the left side of the column), and its ingress or entry into a new sign (on the right). Between its last aspect and its ingress into a new sign, the Moon is said to be ***Void of Course.***

Astro Data	Planet Ingress	Last Aspect	☽ Ingress	Last Aspect	☽ Ingress	☽ Phases & Eclipses		Astro Data
Dy Hr Mn	Dy Hr Mn	Dy Hr Mn	Dy Hr Mn	Dy Hr Mn	Dy Hr Mn	Dy Hr Mn		1 MARCH 1963
☽0S 12 4:13	♀ ♒ 4 11:41	1 16:07 ♀ △	♊ 1 21:39	2 14:04 ♃ △	♌ 2 14:45	2 17:17	☽ 11♊25	Julian Day # 23070
♂ D 16 17:21	☿ ♓ 9 5:26	3 12:31 ♃ □	♋ 4 2:08	4 5:30 ♄ ☍	♍ 5 0:20	10 7:49	○ 19♍01	Delta T 34.6 sec
☽0N 25 23:26	☉ ♈ 21 8:20	5 20:02 ♃ △	♌ 6 9:15	6 6:01 ♆ ⚹	♎ 7 11:49	18 12:08	☽ 27♐10	SVP 05♓46'42"
☿0N 27 22:00	☿ ♈ 26 3:52	8 16:57 ☿ ☍	♍ 8 18:34	9 5:32 ♄ △	♏ 10 0:14	25 12:10	● 4♈08	Obliquity 23°26'35"
	♀ ♓ 30 1:00	10 17:53 ♃ ☍	♎ 11 5:35	11 18:33 ♄ □	♐ 12 12:48			⚷ Chiron 10♓25.8
♃⚼♆ 4 12:28		12 17:54 ♄ △	♏ 13 17:51	14 12:21 ☉ △	♑ 15 0:27	1 3:15	☽ 10♋41	☽ Mean ☊ 27♋33.6
☽0S 8 10:23	♃ ♈ 4 3:19	15 21:06 ♃ △	♐ 16 6:27	17 2:52 ☉ □	♒ 17 9:34	9 0:57	○ 18♎28	
♃⚻♅ 10 12:14	☿ ♉ 9 22:03	18 12:08 ☉ □	♑ 18 17:35	19 12:44 ☉ ⚹	♓ 19 14:53	17 2:52	☽ 26♑23	1 APRIL 1963
♃0N 14 16:03	☉ ♉ 20 19:36	21 0:48 ☉ ⚹	♒ 21 1:21	21 11:19 ♀ ☌	♈ 21 16:30	23 20:29	● 2♉58	Julian Day # 23101
☽0N 22 10:34	♀ ♈ 24 3:39	22 14:16 ♀ ☌	♓ 23 5:04	23 2:56 ♄ ⚹	♉ 23 15:51	30 15:08	☽ 9♌33	Delta T 34.6 sec
♀0N 27 5:01		25 2:22 ☿ ☌	♈ 25 5:38	25 6:24 ☿ ☌	♊ 25 15:06			SVP 05♓46'39"
		26 23:11 ♀ ⚹	♉ 27 4:57	27 2:58 ♄ △	♋ 27 16:27			Obliquity 23°26'35"
		29 3:28 ♀ □	♊ 29 5:13	29 18:22 ☿ ⚹	♌ 29 21:25			⚷ Chiron 12♓21.3
		31 6:36 ♃ □	♋ 31 8:13					☽ Mean ☊ 25♋55.1

This first column gives information on miscellaneous planetary information, including the precise moment a planet turns retrograde or direct, the precise time a planet reaches 0° declination, and the precise time aspects between the outer planets perfect. Aspects and Declinations will be covered in other lessons.

This section gives the exact time and day of the Moon's Phases and Eclipses. Lunar Phases will be covered in detail in another lesson.

This last section contains additional astronomical data for each month. In this book we will only be utilizing the monthly listing for the zodiacal position of Chiron, which will be covered in Lesson 9. For detailed information explaining the rest of the data given in this column, please refer to the first few pages in your ACS Ephemeris.

To find when the Moon actually entered a new sign, take a look at the "☽ Ingress" columns above. There you will find the day, hour and minute in GMT that the Moon changed signs. In the excerpt above, the Moon changed from ♍ to ♎ on the 11th of March at 5:35 GMT. (Remember that because March is the first month listed on this page in *The ACS Ephemeris*, March's data is listed in the first column on the left.) Take a look at Venus in *The ACS Ephemeris* excerpt on the previous page and see that Venus changed from ♑ to ♒ sometime on March 4th. To find out exactly when it changed signs, look at the "Planet Ingress" column. Venus changed signs or "ingressed" into Aquarius on March 4th at 11:41 GMT.

Retrograde (℞) Motion

You will notice that in some instances the columns in the ephemeris are shaded. For example in the March 1963 excerpt on the first page of this lesson the "Mars" column is shaded during part of the month and there is an "R" shown at the top of that column. This indicates **retrograde motion**. Retrograde motion is the apparent backwards travel of a planet through the zodiac. The planets do not actually travel in reverse, but at certain places along their orbit they appear to be moving backwards from our perspective. Further down the "Mars" column on March 16th there is a "D" indicating that Mars began traveling forward or **Direct** on that date.

**Gray shaded columns in the Ephemeris
denote Retrograde (℞) Motion**

Unshaded columns denote Forward or Direct Motion

There are two different reasons why a planet may appear to move backwards, depending on whether the planet is an **inner** or **outer planet**. The inner planets are those that are closer to the Sun than the Earth, and so are "inside" the Earth's orbit. These are Mercury and Venus. Inner planets are also called **inferior planets**. The outer planets are "outside" the Earth's orbit, and include Mars, Jupiter, Saturn, Uranus, Neptune and Pluto. Outer planets are also called **superior planets**. The Sun and Moon are never retrograde.

Retrograde Motion of the Inner Planets

The inner planets (Mercury and Venus) appear to move backwards when they are on the same side of the Sun as we are and are "passing" us. Notice in the diagram to the right that Venus appears to be in Taurus when in position 'A', but as she passes the Earth in her swifter orbit and moves to position 'B', to us it looks as though she has moved backwards through Aries and into Pisces. In contrast, notice that Mercury, on the opposite side of the Sun from the Earth, is moving forward through Aries and towards Taurus, in **direct motion**.

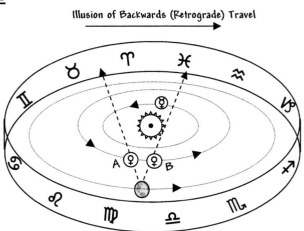

Illusion of Backwards (Retrograde) Travel

Mercury's orbit is much faster than the Earth's, completing one orbit around the Sun in only 88 days as compared to the 365 days it takes the Earth to complete one orbit. This means that there will be three or four occasions every year when Mercury will be passing the Earth, and creating the illusion of retrograde motion. Each time Mercury passes the Earth, it will appear retrograde for approximately 18 days, until it gets far enough ahead of us for its motion to appear direct again.

Venus orbits the Sun in 225 days. Once every year and a half or so, Venus will overtake the Earth and appear retrograde. Venus's retrograde period lasts for an average of six weeks.

Retrograde Motion of the Outer Planets

Outer planets also appear retrograde when they are on the same side of the Sun as the Earth, but for a different reason. In this case the Earth has the faster orbit, and as it passes a slower-moving outer planet, it creates the illusion that the outer planet is traveling backwards. Notice in the diagram to the right that Jupiter appears to be in Libra when the Earth is at position 'A', but seems to move backwards into Virgo as Earth moves ahead into position 'B'.

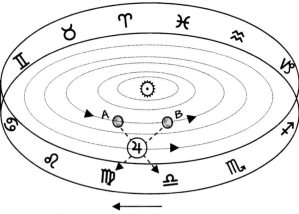

Illusion of Backwards (Retrograde) Travel

The outer planets from Jupiter to Pluto will retrograde once a year, when the Earth swings around in its orbit to overtake them again, with each retrograde period lasting from 4 to 6 months in length. But because Mars is closer to the Earth than the other outer planets and also moving along in its orbit quite rapidly, it takes the Earth longer than a year to catch up to Mars and "lap" it again. This means that there is a longer span from retrograde period to retrograde period with Mars. On average Mars will retrograde once every two years, with each retrograde period lasting approximately 3 months.

The Nodes of the Moon

Unlike the planets which are actual physical bodies, the Nodes of the Moon are mathematically determined points. They represent the two points where the Ecliptic, or path of the Sun, intersects with the path of the Moon. The Nodes are constantly moving in space from direct to retrograde, but on average they travel backwards through the zodiac. Therefore retrograde Nodes are the norm and not the exception. Notice that the South Node is always directly opposite the North Node.

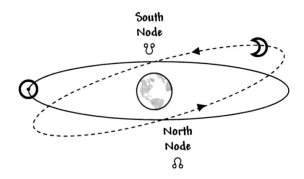

Rounding Off Planetary Positions

Zodiacal positions for the Sun and Moon are given to the nearest second of accuracy in *The ACS Ephemeris*, while the remaining planets are given to the nearest tenth of a minute, with minutes expressed in decimal format. All positions can be safely rounded to the nearest whole minute while still ensuring sufficient accuracy. For example, at 0 hour on March 1, 1963:

Sun, at 9° ♓ 40' 57", can be rounded up to 9° ♓ 41'

Mercury, at 17° ♒ 26.9', can be rounded up to 17° ♒ 27'

Determining the positions of the Sun and Moon to the nearest second is necessary when calculating Solar and Lunar Returns, which will be covered in Section 8 of this book. But for natal chart calculation, this level of precision is unnecessary.

Determining Daily Motion

Rarely does an astrologer erect a chart for someone born at exactly midnight GMT, so we need to manually calculate where the planets were at the time of birth based on the 0 hour information given in the ephemeris. The first step in this process is to calculate each planet's daily motion, or the distance it traveled in a twenty-four hour period. This is done by taking the planet's position listed at 0 hour on the day of birth and subtracting it from the 0 hour position on the following day.

Example 1.

Let's take the Sun on March 3, 1963 and determine its daily motion on that day. (Notice that the positions below have been rounded off to the nearest minute.)

0 hour position on March 4, 1963	♓ 12° 42'
- 0 hour position on March 3, 1963	♓ 11° 41'
= Daily Motion	1° 01'

The daily motion of the Sun on March 3, 1963 was 1° 01', or 61'.

Example 2.

Now let's take the Moon on the same date, as shown in the diagram above.

0 hour position on March 4, 1963	♊ 28° 49'
- 0 hour position on March 3, 1963	♊ 15° 16'
= Daily Motion	13° 33'

The daily motion of the Moon on March 3, 1963 was 13° 33'. The Moon's daily motion can range from 12 to 15 degrees or more because it moves so quickly.

**To determine a Planet's Daily Motion
Subtract the 0 hr position on the Birth Date
from its 0 hr position on the following day.**

Example 3.

When a planet is retrograde, as Mars was on March 3, 1963, its zodiacal position will be at a lesser degree the day after the birthday than on the birthday. In this case we need to subtract the larger degree from the lesser degree which means "subtracting up" to find the difference between the two 0 hour positions. It is very important to label a retrograde planet with a ℞ sign or minus sign. By doing this, you will know whether to add or subtract later in the calculation process.

Mars at 0 hour on March 4th: 6° ♌ 22' ℞ ↑ *"Subtract up" to find difference*
Mars at 0 hour on March 3rd: 6° ♌ 32' ℞

= Daily Motion   - 10' ℞

The daily motion of Mars on March 3rd was 10 minutes, retrograde.

**When a planet is retrograde
always subtract the lesser degree from the greater degree ("subtract up")
& mark your result with an "℞" to designate retrograde motion.**

Example 4.

Saturn, Uranus, Neptune and Pluto move so slowly that the daily travel distance may only be minutes. This is a tedious process, and once you get the hang of it you may want to do the necessary calculations in your head, but for the purpose of accuracy we advise taking the extra few minutes to calculate each position manually. Let's calculate the movement of Pluto on March 3, 1963.

Pluto at 0 hour on March 4th: 10° ♍ 50' ℞ ↑ *"Subtract up" to find difference*
Pluto at 0 hour on March 3rd: 10° ♍ 51' ℞

= Daily Motion   -1' ℞

Pluto traveled "backwards" one minute in this twenty four-hour time period.

Lesson 7 Exercises

Determine the daily motion for the Sun, Moon, Node, and all planets on the following two dates. A form is provided for the first exercise, but try the calculations without the form on the second exercise, on the following page. Answers can be found in the Answer Key in the Appendix.

1. May 10th, 1987

	☉	☽	☿	♀	♂	♃
1. Position at 0 hr on day After birth date _____						
2. Position at 0 hr on Birth date _____						
3. Line 1 - Line 2 = Total Daily Travel						

	♄	♅	♆	♇	☊
6. Position at 0 hr on day After birth date _____					
7. Position at 0 hr on Birth date _____					
8. Line 6 - Line 7 = Total Daily Travel					

2. April 15, 1985

Lesson 8: Finding Planets
Using a Constant Multiplier

The ACS Midnight Ephemeris lists planetary positions at midnight (0 hour) only, so calculating the exact longitude of a planet at any time other than midnight requires **interpolating** between two midnight positions. **Interpolation** is the calculation of an exact value between two known values based on it's proportion of the whole. This proportion is called the **constant multiplier**. In this lesson we explain how to calculate the constant multiplier, and how to apply it to a planet's daily motion to determine that planet's exact position at birth.

Finding the Constant Multiplier

The constant multiplier is a fraction representing the portion of time that has elapsed from midnight (0 hour) GMT to the time of birth. This portion of time can be multiplied against the daily motion of every planet, thus it is a "constant" value. The constant multiplier allows us to determine how much movement each planet made between midnight on the date of birth and the actual time of birth, enabling us to arrive at the exact planetary position at the time of birth.

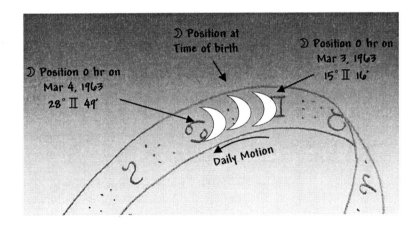

There are two steps to finding the constant multiplier:

Step 1. Convert the GMT of birth to decimal notation. The GMT of birth tells how much time has elapsed since 0 hour on the birth date.

Step 2. Divide the converted GMT of birth by 24 (hours) to determine what portion of the twenty-four hour period has elapsed since 0 hour on the birth date. **In order to maintain accuracy on the faster moving planets, always carry the constant multiplier out three decimal places.**

Because this same concept is also used for determining house cusps farther along in the chart calculation process, we refer to the constant multiplier used for finding planets (as covered in this lesson) as "**CM-1**" to differentiate it from those used for house cusps later.

Example 1.

Let's find the constant multiplier for a birth time of 8:18 GMT.

Step 1. Convert the GMT of Birth to decimal: $8:18 = 8 + \dfrac{18}{60}$ = 8.3 (because 18 ÷ 60 = .3)

Step 2. Divide by 24: 8.3 ÷ 24 = .345833 (of a day), rounded to .346

CM-1 = .346. This represents the fraction of the 24 hour period that has passed from midnight to the time of birth expressed as a decimal.

The constant multiplier must be carried out three decimal places to ensure accuracy. In addition, we suggest double-checking your math with the "eyeball" method. In this example, 8:18 GMT indicates that a little more than one third of the day has passed (24 ÷ 3 = 8). So the constant multiplier should be around one-third, or about .3. If the GMT had been 16:18, then the CM should be approximately two-thirds of the day or about .6.

Example 2.

Let's calculate the CM-1 for a GMT of birth of 4:15. We've reproduced below the "CM-1" section of the Chart Calculation Form found in the Appendix for this example.

CM-1
(Constant Multiplier for Part C: Planetary Position)

Convert GMT of Birth to decimal: _____4.25_____ ÷ 24 = **CM-1** ____.177____

The CM-1 for this GMT is .177, which is the portion of the 24 hour period that has passed since midnight on the date of birth.

Now let's "eyeball" double-check: In this case we know that a very small portion of the day has elapsed between 0 hour and a birth at four a.m. - less than a quarter. We would expect that the constant multiplier would also be less than a quarter of the day, or less than .25.

Understanding the logic behind the constant multiplier is very important, because the same concept is applied in several different stages of the chart calculation process as well as later on when calculating progressions. Make sure you really understand it before moving on.

Using the Constant Multiplier to Determine Exact Planetary Positions

Calculating planetary positions is a four part process:

Step 1. Determine the constant multiplier (as explained on the previous two pages).

Step 2. Determine the daily motion (as explained in the previous lesson). If more than a degree, convert motion into minutes.

Step 3. Multiply the daily motion of each planet by the constant multiplier from Step 1.

Step 4. Add (or subtract if retrograde) the result of step 3 to/from the planet position listed for 0 hour on the date of birth.

Information needed for planet calculations:

GMT of Birth

&

An Ephemeris for the year of birth

Notice that the location of birth does not matter when calculating the positions of the planets. The latitude and longitude of birth will be considered later when calculating house cusps to determine where in a chart the planets fall. The sign and degree of the planets will be exactly the same for everyone born on the same day and at the same GMT of birth, no matter where on earth the birth occurred.

In the next few examples we will explain how to calculate the exact position for several planets both direct and retrograde during the month of March, 1929. The relevant *ACS Ephemeris* page is reprinted below so that you can easily follow along.

MARCH 1929 **LONGITUDE**

Day	Sid.Time	☉	0 hr ☽	Noon ☽	True ☊	☿	♀	♂	♃	♄	♅	♆	♇
1 F	10 33 14	9♓55 29	12♏55 4	18♏59 11	24♉11.3	13♒ 4.7	24♈41.6	26♊36.1	6♉55.0	29♐14.6	5♈48.8	29♌44.1	16♋22.5
2 Sa	10 37 11	10 55 40	24 59 58	0♐58 3	24D 10.8	13 54.4	25 28.3	26 54.9	7 5.8	29 18.4	5 52.0	29R 42.4	16R 21.6
3 Su	10 41 8	11 55 50	6♐54 7	12 48 52	24R 11.1	14 47.4	26 14.1	27 14.1	7 16.7	29 22.0	5 55.2	29 40.8	16 21.2
4 M	10 45 4	12 55 58	18 42 59	24 37 10	24 11.0	15 43.4	26 58.9	27 33.7	7 27.7	29 25.5	5 58.4	29 39.2	16 20.5
5 Tu	10 49 1	13 56 5	0♑32 5	6♑28 22	24 9.6	16 42.3	27 42.7	27 53.7	7 38.7	29 29.0	6 1.6	29 37.6	16 19.9
6 W	10 52 57	14 56 10	12 26 40	18 27 31	24 6.0	17 43.8	28 25.4	28 14.0	7 49.9	29 32.3	6 4.8	29 35.9	16 19.3
7 Th	10 56 54	15 56 13	24 31 26	0♒38 53	23 59.9	18 47.9	29 7.1	28 34.6	8 1.2	29 35.6	6 8.1	29 34.3	16 18.8
8 F	11 0 50	16 56 15	6♒50 13	13 5 44	23 51.3	19 54.3	29 47.6	28 55.6	8 12.6	29 38.8	6 11.4	29 32.8	16 18.2
9 Sa	11 4 47	17 56 15	19 25 38	25 50 2	23 40.8	21 2.8	0♉26.9	29 17.0	8 24.1	29 41.9	6 14.7	29 31.2	16 17.7
10 Su	11 8 43	18 56 13	2♓18 56	8♓52 17	23 29.2	22 13.5	1 5.0	29 38.7	8 35.6	29 44.9	6 18.0	29 29.6	16 17.2
11 M	11 12 40	19 56 9	15 29 54	22 11 34	23 17.6	23 26.2	1 41.9	0♋ 0.6	8 47.3	29 47.8	6 21.3	29 28.0	16 16.7
12 Tu	11 16 37	20 56 3	28 56 57	5♈45 43	23 7.3	24 40.7	2 17.4	0 22.9	8 59.0	29 50.6	6 24.6	29 26.5	16 16.3
13 W	11 20 33	21 55 55	12♈37 29	19 31 50	22 59.1	25 57.1	2 51.5	0 45.5	9 10.8	29 53.4	6 27.9	29 25.0	16 15.8
14 Th	11 24 30	22 55 46	26 28 23	3♉26 45	22 53.6	27 15.1	3 24.2	1 8.5	9 22.7	29 56.0	6 31.3	29 23.4	16 15.4
15 F	11 28 26	23 55 34	10♉26 35	17 27 36	22D 50.8	28 34.8	3 55.4	1 31.7	9 34.7	29 58.6	6 34.6	29 21.9	16 15.0
16 Sa	11 32 23	24 55 20	24 29 31	1♊32 8	22 50.2	29 56.2	4 25.1	1 55.1	9 46.8	0♑ 1.0	6 38.0	29 20.4	16 14.7
17 Su	11 36 19	25 55 3	8♊35 14	15 38 42	22 50.8	1♓19.1	4 53.1	2 18.9	9 58.9	0 3.4	6 41.4	29 19.0	16 14.3
18 M	11 40 16	26 54 45	22 42 22	29 46 6	22R 51.5	2 43.4	5 19.5	2 42.9	10 11.1	0 5.7	6 44.8	29 17.5	16 14.0
19 Tu	11 44 12	27 54 24	6♋49 47	13♋53 15	22 51.2	4 9.3	5 44.1	3 7.2	10 23.4	0 7.8	6 48.2	29 16.1	16 13.7
20 W	11 48 9	28 54 1	20 56 16	27 58 39	22 49.0	5 36.6	6 7.0	3 31.8	10 35.8	0 9.9	6 51.6	29 14.7	16 13.5
21 Th	11 52 6	29 53 36	5♌ 0 4	12♌ 0 15	22 44.7	7 5.3	6 27.9	3 56.6	10 48.2	0 11.9	6 55.0	29 13.3	16 13.2
22 F	11 56 2	0♈53 8	18 58 47	25 55 19	22 38.2	8 35.5	6 47.0	4 21.6	11 0.7	0 13.8	6 58.4	29 11.9	16 13.0
23 Sa	11 59 59	1 52 38	2♍49 25	9♍40 41	22 30.2	10 7.0	7 4.0	4 46.9	11 13.3	0 15.6	7 1.8	29 10.5	16 12.8
24 Su	12 3 55	2 52 6	16 28 43	23 13 9	22 21.5	11 39.9	7 19.0	5 12.4	11 25.9	0 17.3	7 5.2	29 9.2	16 12.6
25 M	12 7 52	3 51 31	29 53 39	6♎30 0	22 13.2	13 14.1	7 31.9	5 38.1	11 38.7	0 18.9	7 8.7	29 7.8	16 12.5
26 Tu	12 11 48	4 50 55	13♎ 2 0	19 29 32	22 6.2	14 49.7	7 42.6	6 4.0	11 51.4	0 20.4	7 12.1	29 6.5	16 12.4
27 W	12 15 45	5 50 16	25 52 36	2♏11 16	22 1.0	16 26.7	7 51.0	6 30.2	12 4.2	0 21.8	7 15.5	29 5.2	16 12.3
28 Th	12 19 41	6 49 36	8♏25 42	14 36 9	21 58.0	18 5.0	7 57.2	6 56.6	12 17.1	0 23.1	7 18.9	29 4.0	16 12.2
29 F	12 23 38	7 48 54	20 42 54	26 46 23	21D 56.9	19 44.7	8 1.1	7 23.1	12 30.1	0 24.3	7 22.4	29 2.7	16 12.2
30 Sa	12 27 35	8 48 10	2♐47 1	8♐45 18	21 57.5	21 25.8	8R 2.6	7 49.9	12 43.1	0 25.4	7 25.8	29 1.5	16D 12.1
31 Su	12 31 31	9 47 24	14 41 49	20 37 7	21 58.9	23 8.2	8 1.7	8 16.9	12 56.1	0 26.4	7 29.2	29 0.3	16 12.1

Example 3.

Let's find the exact degree of the Sun for a birth on March 15, 1929, at 8:37 GMT.

Step 1. Determine the constant multiplier:

<table>
<tr><td colspan="2" align="center">CM-1
(Constant Multiplier for Part C: Planetary Position)</td></tr>
<tr><td>Convert GMT of Birth to decimal: ____8.62____ ÷ 24 = CM-1 ___.359___</td></tr>
</table>

Step 2. Determine the daily motion: If a degree or more convert to minutes.

Sun 0 hr position on March 16, 1929	♓ 24° 55'
- Sun 0 hr position on March 15, 1929	♓ 23° 56'
= Daily Motion	59'

The daily motion of the Sun from 0 hour March 15, 1929 to 0 hour March 16, 1929 was 59 minutes.

Step 3. Multiply the daily motion of each planet by the constant multiplier from Step 1:

Daily motion:	59'
x CM—1:	x .359
	= 21.18' , rounded down to 21'

The Sun moved 21.18 minutes between the 0 hour position on the 15th and the time of birth. This can be rounded to the nearest whole minute, or 21'.

Step 4. Add the result of step three to the 0 hour planet position listed for the date of birth:

0 hr Position on March 15, 1929	♓ 23° 56'
+ Movement from step 3	+ 21'
= Position at Birth	= ♓ 23° 77'
	= ♓ 24° 17' (- 60 minutes, + 1 degree)

The position of the Sun on March 15, 1929 at the time of birth is 24° ♓ 17'.

Calculating the Position of the Moon

The process gets a little trickier when calculating the Moon's position. The Moon moves very quickly, so we are dealing with a greater number of degrees and minutes of motion. The next example demonstrates how to determine the exact position of the Moon for the same birth: March 15, 1929, 8:37 GMT.

Example 4.

Step 1. Determine the constant multiplier:
We already know that this is **.359** from the previous example. Remember that the same CM is applied to all the planets for a specific birth time.

Step 2. Determine the daily motion:

Moon (0hr) on 3/16/29	♉ 24° 30'
Moon (0hr) on 3/15/29 -	♉ 10° 27'
= Daily Motion	14° 03'

Since the total daily motion is over a degree it must be converted to minutes:

$$14° \times 60 = 840' + 03' = \textbf{843'}$$

Step 3. Multiply the daily motion of each planet by the constant multiplier:

Daily Motion	843'
X CM-1	x .359
	= 302.637', rounded up to 303'

Since the result is over 60', it must be converted back to degrees and minutes:

$$303' \div 60 = 5.05°, \text{ or 5 degrees with a remainder of 3 minutes}$$
$$\text{Therefore, } 303' = 5° \ 03'$$

The movement of the Moon between 0 hour on the day of birth and the actual time of birth was: **5° 03'**.

Step 4. Add the result of step three to the 0 hour planet position listed for the date of birth.

Moon (0hr) on 3/15/29:	♉ 10° 27'
+ Movement from Step 3	+ 5° 03'
= Moon position at birth:	= ♉ 15° 30'

Keep in mind that the Moon's daily speed is not constant but varies from day to day, and within the course of a single day as well. While a computer can take these daily fluctuations into account, we cannot be that precise with manual calculation. This is because, by interpolating between midnight positions, we are in effect using the Moon's average during any particular day to determine its position at birth. Therefore, a manually-calculated position for the Moon may differ from a computer-calculated one by up to 3 minutes.

The Chart Calculation Form provided in the Appendix of this book has a handy calculation box for finding the planet positions. We will use the calculation form in the next examples. Extra dotted lines have been provided on the form in those steps where conversion of degrees to minutes and vice versa might be required, allowing more room for calculations.

Example 5.

Let's try one more calculation for the Moon showing a change of signs. We know that on March 17, 1929 the Moon changed signs from Taurus to Gemini sometime between March 16th and 17th. Lets calculate the position of the Moon for a birth on March 16, 1929 with a GMT of 22:49.

CM-1
(Constant Multiplier for Part C: Planetary Position)

Convert GMT of Birth to decimal: _____22.82_____ ÷ 24 = **CM-1** _____.951_____

	☽	
1. Position at 0 hr on day After birth date **(3/17/29)**	(02) 38° Ⅱ(03) 08° 35'	} *Subtract 1 sign, Add 30 degrees*
2. Position at 0 hr on Birth date **(3/16/29)**	♉(02) 24° 30'	
3. Line 1 - Line 2 = Total Daily Travel	14° 05' Or 845'	} *To convert to all minutes, Multiply degrees x 60, add minutes*
4. Line 3 X CM-1 _.951_ = Travel to birth time	804' Or 13° 24'	} *To convert back to degrees & minutes, Divide by 60, add remainder as minutes*
5. Add lines 2 + 4 = Position at Birth	♉(02) 37° 54' = Ⅱ (03) 7° 54'	} *Add 1 sign, Subtract 30 degrees*

The Moon in this case did change signs late in the day on the 16th. We also know this makes sense because the 0 hour position listed for the Moon on the 17th is at 8° Ⅱ, and the birth occurred a little more than an hour before 0 hour on the 17th.

Calculating Retrograde Planets

Example 6.

Let's calculate the position of Mercury for a birth on May 29, 1929 at 8:37 GMT. Take a look in your own *ACS Ephemeris* and find the page for May 1929. Notice that Mercury was retrograde on May 29th. The constant multiplier for this GMT was already calculated in Example 3, so CM-1 remains .359.

	☿	
1. Position at 0 hr on day After birth date **(5/30/29)**	♊ 22° 21' ℞	↑ *"Subtract up" to find difference*
2. Position at 0 hr on Birth date **(5/29/29)**	♊ 22° 26' ℞	
3. Line 1 - Line 2 = Total Daily Travel	- 05' ℞	
4. Line 3 X CM-1 **(.359)** = Travel to birth time	- 02' ℞	*"Adding" a negative number is the same as subtracting it*
5. Add lines 2 + 4 = Position at Birth	♊ 22° 24' ℞	

In this situation remember that we "subtract up" to find the daily motion on line 3. Then **subtract** the travel to birth time (line 4) from the 0 hour position on the day of birth (line 2) instead of adding because the planet is "moving backwards". When calculating retrograde planets, always mark your results on lines 3 and 4 with minus signs so that you will remember to subtract when determining the final position for line 5.

Remember to mark retrograde calculations with a ℞ symbol and a minus sign.

Always mark your final result with a ℞ symbol.

Example 7.

Now let's go back to our previous birth date of March 15, 1929 at 8:37 GMT used in Example 3. In that example we determined the CM-1 was .359. Below we have calculated all of the planet positions for this birth using the Chart Calculation Form found in the Appendix. When doing these calculations we find it easiest to copy down all of the planet positions from an ephemeris onto lines 1 and 2 of the form before beginning the math. Then, you can close your ephemeris and just concentrate on doing the calculations on the form.

	☉	☽	☿	♀	♂	♃
1. Position at 0 hr on day After birth date (3/16/29)	23° 115' ♓ 24° 55'	♉ 24° 30'	♒ 29° 56'	3° 85' ♉ 4° 25'	♋ 1° 55'	♉ 9° 47'
2. Position at 0 hr on Birth date (3/15/29)	♓ 23° 56'	♉ 10° 27'	♒ 28° 35'	♉ 3° 55'	♋ 1° 32'	♉ 9° 35'
3. Line 1 - Line 2 = Total Daily Travel	59'	14° 03' = 843'	1° 21' = 81'	30'	23'	12'
4. Line 3 X CM-1 (.359) = Travel to birth time	21'	303' = 5° 03'	29'	11'	8'	4'
5. Add lines 2 + 4 = Position at Birth	♓ 23° 77' =♓ 24° 17'	♉ 15° 30'	♒ 28° 64' =♒ 29° 04'	♉ 3° 66' = ♉ 4° 06'	♋ 1° 40'	♉ 9° 39'

	♄	♅	♆	♇	☊	
6. Position at 0 hr on day After birth date (3/16/29)	♐ 29° 61' ♐ 30° ♑ 0° 01'	♈ 6° 38'	♌ 29°20'Rx	♌ 16°15'Rx	♉ 22°50'Rx	
7. Position at 0 hr on Birth date (3/15/29)	♐ 29° 59'	♈ 6° 35'	♌ 29°22'Rx	♌ 16°15'Rx	♉ 22°51'Rx	
8. Line 6 - Line 7 = Total Daily Travel	2'	3'	- 2' Rx	0	- 1'	
9. Line 8 X CM-1 (.359) = Travel to birth time	1'	1'	- 1' Rx	0	0	
10. Add lines 7 + 9 = Position at Birth	♑ 0° 00'	♈ 6° 36'	♌ 29°21'Rx	♌ 16°15'Rx	♉ 22° 51'	

Lesson 8 Exercises

Calculate the Constant Multiplier and the planet positions for someone born on October 12, 1987, 16:44 GMT. Answers can be found in the Answer Key in the Appendix.

CM-1
(Constant Multiplier for Part C: Planetary Position)

Convert GMT of Birth to decimal: _____ ÷ 24 = CM-1 _____

	☉	☽	☿	♀	♂	♃
1. Position at 0 hr on day After birth date _____						
2. Position at 0 hr on Birth date _____						
3. Line 1 - Line 2 = Total Daily Travel						
4. Line 3 X CM-1 _____ = Travel to birth time						
5. Add lines 2 + 4 = Position at Birth						

	♄	♅	♆	♇	☊	
6. Position at 0 hr on day After birth date _____						
7. Position at 0 hr on Birth date _____						
8. Line 6 - Line 7 = Total Daily Travel						
9. Line 8 X CM-1 _____ = Travel to birth time						
10. Add lines 7 + 9 = Position at Birth						

Lesson 9: Chiron & Asteroids

Occasionally you may need to calculate positions of celestial bodies by interpolating between data given at intervals other than daily, such as weekly or monthly. It is common for ephemeredes to list less commonly used bodies such as Chiron and asteroids at these intervals. Locating exact positions for these bodies has not been required in the past on certification exams, but we felt it would be helpful to know how to handle these calculations nonetheless. In this lesson we will explain how to interpolate between monthly intervals for Chiron, and 10-day intervals for asteroids. Once you understand this concept, it can be applied to any value given at any interval.

Chiron & Monthly Interpolation

The ACS Ephemeris lists Chiron's position at 0 hour on the first of each month only. You can find this information in the box entitled "Astro Data" at the bottom right of each page. You will remember from Lesson 7 on Daily Motion that this box covers information for both months listed on each page. The example to the right covers the months of March and April 1963.

Chiron's position at 0 hour on March 1, 1963 →

Chiron's position at 0 hour on April 1, 1963 →

Astro Data
1 MARCH 1963
Julian Day # 23070
Delta T   34.6 sec
SVP 05♓46'42"
Obliquity 23°26'35"
⚷ Chiron 10♓25.8
☽ Mean ☊ 27♋33.6

1 APRIL 1963
Julian Day # 23101
Delta T   34.6 sec
SVP 05♓46'39"
Obliquity 23°26'35"
⚷ Chiron 12♓21.3
☽ Mean ☊ 25♋55.1

The procedure for calculating Chiron's position is similar to the process used to locate planets, but with a slight difference. Where before we were determining the portion of the **day** that had elapsed from midnight GMT to the time of birth, now we are determining the portion of the **month** that has elapsed from the first of the month to the time **and day** of birth.

Six steps are needed to calculate a celestial position when only monthly information is given:

Step 1. Determine the constant multiplier CM-1. This is the same constant multiplier used for planets. You will remember that CM-1 tells us what portion of the day has elapsed since 0 hour on the birth date to the time of birth.

Step 2. Add the "day number of the birth date minus 1" to CM-1. For instance, if the birth occurred on May 9th, you will add 8 to CM-1. This tells us the total number of full days (8) and partial days (CM-1) that have elapsed from the beginning of the month to the day and time of birth.

Step 3. Divide the result from Step 2 by the total number of days in the month of birth. The result is your "Monthly Constant Multiplier". For example, if the birth month is May, divide Step 2 by 31 days, because there are 31 days in May. If the birth month is February, divide Step 2 by 28 days, unless a leap year was in effect, in which case divide by 29. If you are unsure how many days were in the month in question, check an ephemeris. This step gives you the portion of the month that has elapsed to the exact time and day of birth.

Step 4. Determine the monthly motion of the celestial body. If more than a degree, convert to minutes. This is done by subtracting the position on the 1st of the birth month from the position on the 1st of the following month.

Step 5. Multiply the monthly motion (Step 4) by the "Monthly Constant Multiplier" (Step 3). The result will be the celestial body's movement from the 1st of the month to the time of birth.

Step 6. Add the result of Step 5 to the position given on the first of the birth month.

Example 1.

Let's calculate Chiron's position for a birth date on March 10, 1963, 20:29 GMT.

Step 1. Determine the constant multiplier CM-1. This is the same CM-1 used for planets.

CM-1
(Constant Multiplier for Part C: Planetary Position)

Convert GMT of Birth to decimal: ___20.48___ ÷ 24 = **CM-1** ___.853___

Step 2. Add the "day number of the birth date minus 1" to CM-1.

This birth occurred on the 10th of March	9.
+ CM-1 as calculated in Step 1	+ .853
	= 9.853

This tells us that 9.853 days have passed since the start of the month to the time of birth.

Step 3. Divide the result from Step 2 by the total number of days in the month of birth. The result is the "Monthly Constant Multiplier". In this case, March contains 31 days:

$$9.853 ÷ 31 = .318$$

This tells us that this birth occurred exactly .318 of the way through the month, making .318 the monthly constant multiplier.

Step 4. Determine the monthly motion of the celestial body. If more than a degree, convert to minutes. This is determined by subtracting Chiron's position on March 1st from Chiron's position on April 1st.

	11 81
0 hour, April 1, 1963	✕ ̶1̶2̶° ̶2̶1̶'
- 0 hour, March 1, 1963	- ✕ 10° 26'
= monthly motion	= 1° 55', or 115'.

Step 5. Multiply the monthly motion (Step 4) by the "Monthly Constant Multiplier" (Step 3).

$$115' \times .318 = 36.57', \text{ rounded to } 37'$$

Step 6. Add the result of Step 5 to the position given on the first of the birth month.

Now simply add 37 minutes to Chiron's position on March 1st to arrive at Chiron's placement at the time of birth.

0 hour, March 1, 1963	✕ 10° 26'
+	37'
	= ✕ 10° 63', or 11° ✕ 03'

Chiron's position on March 10, 1963 20:29 GMT is 11° ✕ 03'.

10-Day Interpolation

From time to time you may run across ephemeredes that list celestial information at intervals other than daily or monthly. Demetra George's work on asteroids, *Asteroid Goddesses*, contains an ephemeris listing the positions of the sixteen most popular asteroids at 10-day intervals. In order to pinpoint an asteroid's position using this type of ephemeris, you will need to understand how to interpolate between 10-day periods. This is a little trickier than monthly interpolation, but if you think about each step logically, you will be able to make these calculations without difficulty.

Below is an excerpt from the *Asteroid Goddesses* ephemeris for the beginning of 1963:

1963	Ceres	Pallas	Juno	Vesta	Psyche	Eros	Sappho	Amor	Lilith	Toro	Pandora	Icarus	Diana	Hidalgo	Urania	Chiron
Jan 8	17♍26	12♋59R	26♍53	28♍51	12♏46	28♏00	14♈36	02♈05	19♏34	05♒30	27♐10	13♑00	24♒11	28♈00	16♐31	07♓25
18	17 41R	09 54	27 15R	00♎08	15 13	05♐12	18 59	04 35	22 18	15 25	01♑12	17 55	27 38	00♉49	20 42	07 54
28	17 11	07 36	26 52	00 43	17 22	12 07	23 35	07 22	24 48	26 06	05 11	22 38	01♓12	04 32	24 49	08 27
Feb 7	15 59	06 24	25 47	00 31R	19 13	18 44	28 21	10 24	26 59	07♓33	09 06	27 08	05 38	09 02	28 50	09 03
17	14 11	06 21D	24 03	29♍31	20 40	25 01	03♉15	13 38	28 49	19 43	12 57	01♒28	08 34	14 11	02♑44	09 40
27	11 59	07 20	21 49	27 47	21 42	01♑00	08 14	17 04	00♐15	02♈31	16 43	05 38	12 20	19 54	06 30	10 18
Mar 9	09 40	09 11	19 21	25 28	22 15	06 37	13 17	20 38	01 13	15 43	20 21	09 40	16 08	26 04	10 04	10 57
19	07 33	11 43	16 54	22 54	22 17R	11 52	18 22	24 19	01 40	29 04	23 50	13 32	19 58	02♊35	13 26	11 34
29	05 52	14 48	14 44	20 24	21 47	16 42	23 29	28 08	01 35R	12♉20	27 09	17 15	23 47	09 21	16 34	12 11
Apr 8	04 50	18 17	13 04	18 21	20 45	21 03	28 36	02♉01	00 55	25 15	00♒14	20 48	27 37	16 16	19 22	12 45
18	04 30D	22 04	12 00	16 58	19 15	24 54	03♊43	06 00	29♏42	07♊37	03 04	24 11	01♈25	23 14	21 50	13 16
28	04 52	26 05	11 34	16 23	17 24	28 07	08 49	10 02	28 01	19 19	05 35	27 21	05 11	00♋11	23 52	13 44

These are the steps needed to calculate celestial positions using a 10-day ephemeris:

Step 1. Determine the constant multiplier CM-1, as before.

Step 2. Determine how many full days have elapsed from the next earliest listing in the ephemeris to the birth date. Add this number of days to CM-1. For example, if a birth occurred on April 16, 1963, notice in the ephemeris (above) that the next earliest date given is April 8. Eight full days have elapsed from 0 hour April 8th to 0 hour April 16th (16 - 8 = 8). We would then add 8 to the CM-1.

Step 3. Divide the result from Step 2 by 10. This will give you the portion of the 10-day period that has elapsed to the day and time of birth.

Step 4. Determine the 10-day motion of the celestial body. If more than a degree, convert to minutes. This is done by subtracting the celestial body's position on the next earliest listed date from its position on the next latest listed date in the ephemeris.

Step 5. Multiply the 10-day motion (Step 4) by the "10-Day Constant Multiplier" (Step 3). The result will be the celestial body's movement from the next earliest listed position to the time of birth.

Step 6. Add the result of Step 5 to the position given on the next earliest date. The result will be the exact position at birth.

Example 2.

Let's calculate the position of the asteroid Pallas for the same date: March 10, 1963, 20:29 GMT.

Step 1. Determine the constant multiplier CM-1. This is the same constant multiplier used for the planets, which was calculated in Example 1 to be .853.

Step 2. Determine how many full days have elapsed from the next earliest listing in the ephemeris to the birth date. Add this number of days to CM-1. Look at the ephemeris excerpt on the previous page and notice that our target birth date of March 10th falls between the listings for March 9th and March 19th. March 9th is the next earliest listing, which is one day earlier than the birth date:

$$
\begin{array}{lr}
\text{Number of days elapsed from next earliest listing} & 1 \\
\text{+ CM-1 as calculated in Step 1} & +\quad .8533 \\
\hline
& =\quad 1.8533
\end{array}
$$

This tells us that 1.853 days have passed since the earlier listed time and the time of birth.

Step 3. Divide the result from Step 2 by 10.

$$1.8533 \div 10 = .185$$

This tells us that this birth occurred exactly .185 of the way through this ten day period.

Step 4. Determine the 10-day motion of the celestial body. If more than a degree, convert to minutes. This is determined by subtracting the March 9th position from the March 19th position.

$$
\begin{array}{lllll}
\text{0 hour, March 19, 1963} & & \circledcirc & 11° & 43' \\
\text{- 0 hour, March 9, 1963} & - & \circledcirc & 9° & 11' \\
\hline
\text{= monthly motion} & = & & 2° & 32', \text{ or } 152'.
\end{array}
$$

Step 5. Multiply the 10-day motion (Step 4) by the "10-Day Constant Multiplier" (Step 3).

$$152' \times .185 = 28.12', \text{ rounded to } 28'$$

Step 6. Add the result of Step 5 to the position given on the next earliest date.

$$
\begin{array}{llll}
\text{0 hour, March 9, 1963} & \circledcirc & 9° & 11' \\
+ & & & 28' \\
\hline
= \circledcirc & & 9° & 39'
\end{array}
$$

Pallas's position on March 10, 1963 20:29 GMT is 9° ⊚ 39'.

One final note on retrogrades: Remember that retrograde asteroids should be handled exactly the same as retrograde planets. In Step 4, subtract the lesser degree from the greater degree to determine overall motion, then mark your result with a ℞ symbol and a minus sign so you will remember to subtract the travel from the next earliest listing in the ephemeris in Step 6. Always mark your final result with a ℞ symbol.

Lesson 9 Exercises

Use the ACS Ephemeris to locate Chiron's position in Exercise 1, and the reprinted excerpt from Asteroid Goddesses in this lesson to locate Ceres' position in Exercise 2. Answers can be found in the Answer Key in the Appendix.

1. Determine Chiron's position on February 11, 1963 13:39 GMT.

2. Determine the position of the asteroid Ceres for the same birth date.

Section 4:

The Houses

Lesson 10: House Cusps Part 1
Finding the Midheaven & Imum Coeli

The astrological houses form the structure of the birth chart and fix the zodiac in time and space. This lesson will explain houses and house divisional systems in general, then demonstrate how to calculate the Midheaven and Imum Coeli for northern latitude births using the Placidus house system. Calculations for the Ascendant and remaining houses will be covered in the next lesson. Southern latitude births require special handling and are covered separately in lesson 12.

What Are Houses?

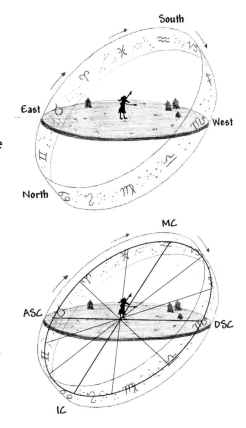

The astrological houses are based on the **diurnal motion** of the Earth, which is its daily rotation on its axis (*diurnal* means "daily"). The daily turning of the Earth creates the impression that the zodiac belt itself is rotating. Just like the Sun and the planets, the stars of the zodiac will rise in the east, culminate overhead, set in the west, continue on to their lower culmination or "midnight" position, then rise again. The astrological houses are derived from this daily cycle and divide the zodiac into twelve segments, much like placing a 12-slice pie transparency over the circle of the zodiac. These pie segments or houses anchor the signs and planets on a mundane level, allowing us to apply their symbolism to the various areas of our lives.

Remember from Lesson 5 on Local Sidereal Time that the zodiac makes one full rotation every 24 sidereal hours, or one sidereal day. At this speed, it takes only 4 minutes for each degree of the zodiac to rise. This means that rising and culminating degrees are quickly changing as the minutes tick by. While everyone born within a several-hour time frame will have planets located at roughly the same zodiacal degree, it is the swift changes due to the Earth's diurnal motion, frozen in time at the moment of birth by the houses, that makes each birth chart truly unique.

Many House Systems

Dividing the heavens into twelve houses is a very simple concept, but working out the details of exactly where and how to divide has been a major debate among astrologers for centuries. As a result, there are over twenty different house systems, each based on varying theories. Some of the simplest use one particular point in the zodiac to be the basis point and divide the rest into twelve equal segments from there. Others use complicated formulas to divide up the pie, based either on time, space, or other astronomical measurements. Basically, what all house systems are doing is assigning a particular zodiacal degree to be the **cusp**, or boundary, between each of the twelve astrological houses. In this book, we use the **Placidus** system, which is one of the more commonly used systems of house division in the United States. If Placidus is not your house system of choice, we hope you will put preferences aside as you learn house cusp calculation using a Table of Houses. Then once you have mastered the math, you can substitute the Table of Houses for your preferred system.

The Chart Angles

Most house systems agree that four astronomically defined points create the four **angles** of the birth chart: the **Ascendant**, **Midheaven**, **Descendant**, and **Imum Coeli**. These four points form the horizontal and vertical axes of the birth chart and divide it into four **quadrants** of three houses each.

The **Midheaven**, or *Medium Coeli*, meaning "middle of the sky" in Latin and abbreviated "**MC**", is the most elevated degree of the zodiac at any given time. In many house systems including the Placidus system, the Midheaven denotes the 10th house cusp. The Midheaven is not the same as the **Zenith**, which is the point on the celestial sphere directly overhead. The Midheaven is always a point along the ecliptic, which you will remember is the Sun's apparent path through the sky. In equatorial regions, the Zenith and the Midheaven may at certain times coincide, but in the Northern Hemisphere, the Midheaven will usually be found to the south of the Zenith.

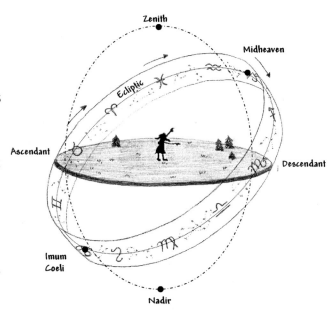

The *Imum Coeli*, meaning "bottom of the sky" in Latin and abbreviated "**IC**", is always the opposite point of the zodiac from the Midheaven. Once you have found the Midheaven, just a sign change will give you the IC. The IC is often referred to as the **Nadir**, but this terminology is incorrect. Technically, the Nadir is the point on the celestial sphere directly opposite the Zenith, as illustrated in the diagram to the right. The Imum Coeli denotes the 4th house cusp in most house systems, and together with the Midheaven forms the vertical axis of the birth chart.

The **Ascendant**, abbreviated "**ASC**", is that point of the zodiac where the **celestial horizon** intersects with the Ecliptic in the east. The celestial horizon is not the same as the visible horizon. Where the visible horizon is marred with hills and valleys, trees and other obstructions, the celestial horizon is a great circle parallel to the visible horizon but passing through the center of the Earth, dividing the Earth into two equal halves. Picture a great imaginary circular plane, like the rings of Saturn but extending indefinitely into space. Where this plane intersects with the ecliptic in the east is the Ascendant. In most house systems the Ascendant forms the cusp of the 1st house.

The **Descendant**, abbreviated "**DSC**", is the point of the zodiac directly opposite the Ascendant, where the celestial horizon intersects with the ecliptic in the west. In most house systems, the descendant forms the cusp of the 7th house, and together with the Ascendant forms the horizontal axis of the birth chart. The DSC is always the same degree and minute as the ASC but in the opposite sign.

How to Use *The Michelsen Book of Tables*

Tables of Houses contain sets of tables giving exact zodiacal degrees for each angle and house cusp at various sidereal times and latitudes. In this book we will be using *The Michelsen Book of Tables* which contains two separate sets of tables, one for the Koch house system and one for Placidus. We will only be using the Placidus tables, found on pages 78-122.

Leaf through *The Book of Tables* now and notice that there are individual tables for every four minutes of sidereal time, arranged in sidereal time order. The Midheaven degree and minute for each time given is found at the top center of each table. The Midheaven is the same for all latitudes, but the remaining house cusps will vary according to latitude. Notice that the table gives house cusps for every five degrees of latitude from 0°-20°, then for every degree of latitude from 20°- 60°. How to use these values and degrees will be thoroughly explained in this and the next two lessons.

Sidereal Time in hrs/ mins/secs is shown in the upper left of each table. Tables give data in 4 minute increments

The Midheaven is shown at the top of each table, calculated to the nearest minute of zodiacal longitude

This figure gives the right ascension of the Midheaven, used in some calculation methods but not needed for the method taught in this book.

The 11th, 12th, ASC (1st), 2nd, & 3rd house cusps are then listed for each degree of latitude

Although the MC is not affected by latitude, other house cusps are. Different values are given for the 11th, 12th, ASC (1st), 2nd, & 3rd house cusps for each 5° of latitude from 0-20° North, then for each degree from 20-60° North.

Here are the house cusps by degree and minute for a birth at latitude 40°N, 4:24:00 LST. Follow each column up to find the sign for each cusp. In this example, the 11th house cusp is 11°♋ 53', the 12th cusp is 13°♌ 20', and so on.

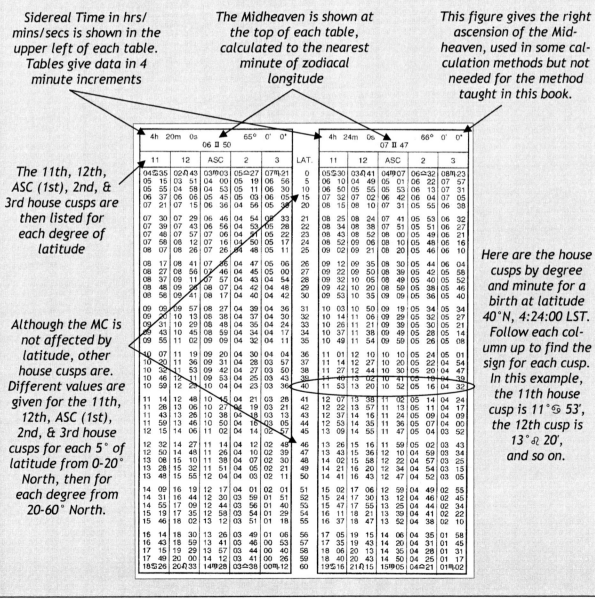

93

Signs of Long & Short Ascension

You have probably noticed that chart angles are rarely ever a neat 90° apart, dividing the birth chart into four equal quadrants. This is another phenomenon we can attribute to the tilt of the Earth. Because the Earth's axis is at a 23½° angle to the zodiac belt, some signs appear to take longer to rise over the horizon, while others appear to rise more quickly. Those that take longer to rise are the signs from Cancer to Sagittarius in the northern hemisphere. These are called **Signs of Long Ascension**. Those that rise more quickly are called **Signs of Short Ascension**, and include Capricorn through Gemini. This phenomenon is what causes **interceptions**; when an entire sign of the zodiac becomes contained within a single house without "owning" the cusp of that house, it is said to be **intercepted**. Notice in the lower chart to the right that the entire sign of Gemini is contained within the 11th house, yet does not "own" any cusp. Distorted houses and resultant interceptions become more pronounced the farther away from the Equator you are. Because the angles of the chart are formed by opposite points, opposite quadrants will also become equally distorted. If you have a larger 1st quadrant and a smaller 2nd quadrant, you will also have a larger 3rd quadrant and a smaller 4th quadrant, and vice versa. Notice in the same chart to the right how opposite quadrants are equally expanded or contracted. Also notice that the sign Sagittarius in the 5th house is intercepted. Whenever a sign is intercepted, its opposite sign will also be intercepted.

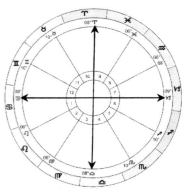

Chart for Accra, Ghana, near the Equator at 5°N

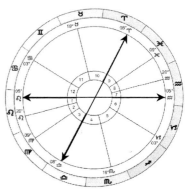

Chart for same time & longitude as above, but for Edinburgh, Scotland at 56°N

Calculating the MC & IC

To calculate a Midheaven for a birth chart, we need the LST (local sidereal time) of birth and *The Book of Tables* introduced on the previous page. As previously mentioned, these tables give the Midheaven and other house cusps for sidereal times in 4 minute increments. If we are lucky enough to have an LST which is given in a table of houses, all we need do is copy the Midheaven right out of the table. Usually however the LST of birth will fall somewhere between two times shown in the tables. This requires **interpolation** between the Midheavens listed in those two tables in order to arrive at an exact Midheaven for a particular LST.

Interpolation is the process of calculating an exact value between two known values based on its proportion of the whole. Interpolation was done earlier when we calculated the planets at a particular time using the earlier and later ephemeris positions. Now this same procedure is used to calculate the Midheaven using the earlier and later positions given in the tables of houses.

In order to interpolate, we need to determine where between two given sidereal times the LST of birth falls, and what portion of the difference between these two given sidereal times it represents. This is done by finding a **Constant Multiplier** based on elapsed sidereal time, which we will call "CM-2" to differentiate it from the constant multiplier "CM-1" used for planetary motion, which is a separate calculation altogether.

Calculating the MC and IC is a two-part process:
First determine a constant multiplier,
Then use the constant multiplier to find the MC & IC.

Example 1.

Let's find the constant multiplier for an LST of 4:22:56. Look in *The Book of Tables* to find a listing for 4:20:00 (4h 20m 0s) and another for 4:24:00, four minutes later.

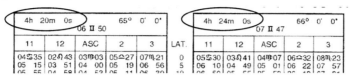

The first step is to determine how much time has elapsed from the earlier listed time in *The Book of Tables* to the target LST. This is done by subtracting the earlier listed time from the LST:

	4:22:56	*Given LST*
-	4:20:00	*Next earlier Sidereal Time in Table*
=	2:56	*Difference*

Next convert this difference into decimal notation:

$$2:56 = 2 + \frac{56}{60} = 2.93 \text{ minutes}$$

This tells us that 2.93 out of a possible 4 minutes have elapsed from the earlier listed Sidereal Time to the target LST. All that remains is to express this as a fraction, and do the math:

$$\frac{2.93}{4} = 2.93 \div 4 = .7325, \text{ rounded down to } .73$$

The constant multiplier (CM-2) for this LST of birth is .73.

**Notice that CM-2 needs only to be calculated
to two decimal places for sufficient accuracy.**

Example 2.

The Chart Calculation Form provided in the Appendix of this book has a handy calculation box for CM-2 on the second page. Let's do another example using this section of the form. For this example, we will calculate the constant multiplier for an LST of 15:51:08.

CM-2	
(Constant Multiplier for LST Interpolation)	
LST of Birth	15 : 51 : 08
- Next lowest Sid Time from Table	- 15 : 48 : 00
=	3 : 08
Convert result to decimal	3.13
÷ 4 = CM-2	.78

First, subtract the next lowest Sidereal Time found in the tables from the birth LST, leaving a difference of 3 minutes, 8 seconds.

Convert 3:08 to decimal notation, which is 3.13.

Then divide 3.13 by 4, which results in .78.

The CM-2 for this LST is .78.

Using the Constant Multiplier to find the MC & IC

Now that the constant multiplier has been determined, it can be used to interpolate between the earlier and later Midheavens shown in *The Book of Tables* to arrive at the exact MC for the LST of birth. Because the CM-2 represents the portion of time that has elapsed since the earlier listed Sidereal Time, it also represents the portion of zodiacal longitude that has elapsed since the earlier listed Midheaven. Once we have found the Midheaven, we just need to change the sign to its opposite for the IC. Let's go through this process in a few examples.

Example 3.

For this example we will go back to Example 1 and use the already calculated CM-2 to locate the Midheaven for this birth. We know that the LST of birth is 4:22:56, which resulted in a CM-2 of .73. Look at the reproduced tables on the previous page, and notice that the MC for the earlier sidereal time (4:20:00) is 06° Gemini 50', while the MC for the later sidereal time (4:24:00) is 07° Gemini 47'. Let's find the difference in degrees and minutes between these two Midheavens:

$$
\begin{array}{rll}
 & 06 \quad 107 \\
\text{II} & \cancel{07} \; \cancel{47}' & \textit{later given MC} \\
-\quad \text{II} & 06° \; 50' & \textit{earlier given MC} \\
\hline
= & \qquad 57' & \textit{difference}
\end{array}
$$

This tells us that there is a 57 minute difference between the two given Midheavens. Now we can apply the CM-2 to this figure to determine what portion has elapsed to the LST of birth:

$$57' \times .73 = 41.61, \text{ rounded up to } 42'$$

42 minutes of zodiacal longitude have elapsed between the earlier listed Midheaven, and the Midheaven for the LST of birth. Now add this figure to the earlier Midheaven value, and the result is the Midheaven of birth:

$$
\begin{array}{rll}
\text{II} & 06° \; 50' & \textit{earlier given MC} \\
+ \qquad\quad & 42' & \textit{+ value determined by CM-2} \\
\hline
= \quad \text{II} & 06° \; 92' & \\
= \quad \text{II} & 07° \; 32' & \textit{= Midheaven for LST of birth}
\end{array}
$$

The Midheaven for this LST of birth (4:22:56) is 7° II 32'. The IC will therefore be 7° ♐ 32', because Sagittarius is the opposite sign to Gemini.

Sign Polarities:
♈ - ♎
♉ - ♏
♊ - ♐
♋ - ♑
♌ - ♒
♍ - ♓

Example 4.

Let's calculate the Midheaven for the LST from Example 2. This LST (15:51:08) resulted in a constant multiplier (CM-2) of .78.

Step 1. List MC for later Sid. Time in Table, which in this case is 15:52:00   ♐ (09) 00° 11'

Step 2. List MC for earlier Sid. Time in Table, which in this case is 15:48:00   - ♏ (08) 29° 13'

Step 3. Subtract to find the difference   58'

Step 4. Multiply this difference by CM-2, which in this case in .78   58' x .78 = 45'

Step 5. Add the amount found in Step 4 to the earlier MC listed in Step 2   ♏ (08) 29° 13'
                                                      +   45'

The Midheaven for this LST of birth is 29° ♏ 58'   ♏ (08) 29° 58'

Therefore, the IC for this LST will be 29° ♉ 58', because Taurus is the opposite polarity to Scorpio.

Example 5.

Let's do one more example, this time going through the complete process starting with finding the constant multiplier, then applying it to determine the Midheaven. For this example, let's use an LST of 10:11:15.

```
                            CM-2
              (Constant Multiplier for LST Interpolation)

LST of Birth                         10 : 11 : 15

- Next lowest Sid Time from Table  - 10 : 08 : 00

                                 =     3 : 15

Convert result to decimal              3.25

                      ÷ 4 = CM-2        .81
```

                                            (05) 30°

1. MC at Later Sid Time (10:12:00)   ♍ (06) 00° 57'

2. MC at Earlier Sid Time (10:08:00)   ♌ (05) 29° 54'

3. Line 1 - Line 2 =   01° 03'   or 63'

4. Line 3 X CM-2 (.81) =   +   51'

5. Add lines 2 + 4 =   ♌ (05) 29° 105'

                          = ♍ (06) 00° 45'

The Midheaven for this LST is 00° ♍ 45'. The IC is 00° ♓ 45'.

Lesson 10 Exercises

Calculate the Constant Multiplier, MC and IC for the following two LSTs. The relevant portions of the Chart Calculation Form are reproduced for your use in completing the first exercise, but try the second exercise without these aids. Answers can be found in the Answer Key in the Appendix.

1. 8:51:42 LST

<table>
<tr><td colspan="2" align="center">CM-2
(Constant Multiplier for LST Interpolation)</td></tr>
<tr><td>LST of Birth</td><td>___:___:___</td></tr>
<tr><td>- Next lowest Sid Time from Table</td><td>- ___:___:___</td></tr>
<tr><td></td><td>= ___:___</td></tr>
<tr><td>Convert result to decimal</td><td>_____</td></tr>
<tr><td align="right">÷ 4 = CM-2</td><td>_____</td></tr>
</table>

1. MC at Later LST	
2. MC at Earlier LST	
3. Line 1 - Line 2 =	
4. Line 3 X CM-2 _____ =	
5. Add lines 2 + 4 =	

2. 14:10:45 LST

Lesson 11: House Cusps Part 2
Finding the Ascendant & Intermediate House Cusps

While locating the Midheaven requires only the local sidereal time of birth, locating the Ascendant and other house cusps takes into account the birth latitude as well. This results in a calculation process that requires three different interpolation procedures - much more involved than the Midheaven calculations covered in the previous lesson. Although complex, this computation is not beyond anyone's mathematical abilities provided they understand the reason behind each step of the process. This lesson explains how to calculate house cusps while working through several examples. This is a big lesson - be prepared to spend a little more time on it than on previous lessons.

As with the previous lesson, we will just be dealing with northern hemisphere births. Southern latitude births require special handling and are covered in Lesson 12.

Three Interpolation Procedures Required

Because the Ascendant and other house cusps take into account latitude as well as birth time, three different calculations must be made before each house cusp can be located:

Step 1. First, calculate the house cusp for the exact LST of birth for the next highest latitude by interpolating between next lowest and next highest sidereal times. This is the same procedure used in the last lesson when we calculated the Midheaven.

Step 2. Next, calculate the house cusp for the exact LST of birth for the next lowest latitude by interpolating between next lowest and next highest sidereal times. Again, this is the same procedure used to calculate the Midheaven in the last lesson, except that we are using values from *The Book of Tables* for a different latitude than in Step 1 above.

Step 3. Finally interpolate between these two results for the exact latitude of birth.

Notice that Steps 1 & 2 are interpolating between time, while Step 3 interpolates between latitudes. Because this third step is based on a proportion of a different value (latitude as opposed to time), the constant multiplier used in Step 3 will be different than the one used in the first two steps. This procedure will become clear as we work through an example.

Example 1.

In this example we will calculate an Ascendant for a person born in Albany, New York (42°N 39' 09", 73°W 45' 24"). Let's say we have already calculated an LST of birth at 19:54:49. For house cusp calculation the only information needed is the LST and **latitude** of birth - 42°N 39' 09", which can be rounded to 42°N 39'. (Longitude was already taken into account when the LST was calculated and so is no longer needed.)

Information needed for house cusp calculation:

LST of Birth: 19:54:49
Latitude of Birth: 42°N 39'

Finding the Constant Multipliers

Let's look in *The Book of Tables* and find the nearest Sidereal Time and Latitude listings:

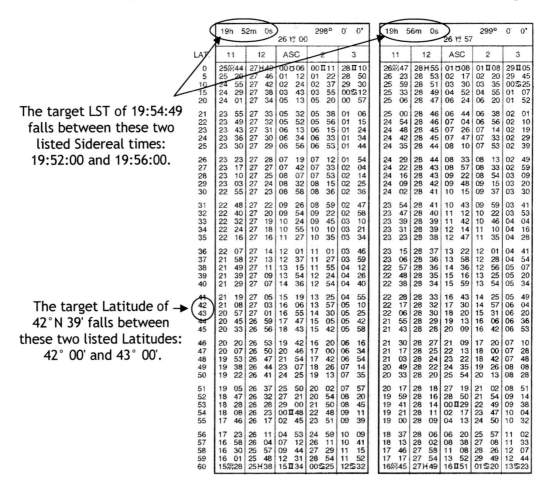

The target LST of 19:54:49 falls between these two listed Sidereal times: 19:52:00 and 19:56:00.

The target Latitude of → 42°N 39' falls between these two listed Latitudes: 42° 00' and 43° 00'.

	19h 52m 0s — 298° 0' 0' — 26 ♑ 00					19h 56m 0s — 299° 0' 0' — 26 ♑ 57				
LAT.	11	12	ASC	2	3	11	12	ASC	2	3
0	25♒44	27♓48	00♉06	00♊11	28♊10	26♒47	28♓55	01♉08	01♊08	29♊05
5	25 20	27 46	01 12	01 22	28 50	26 23	28 53	02 17	02 20	29 45
10	24 55	27 42	02 24	02 37	29 30	25 59	28 51	03 30	03 35	00♋25
15	24 29	27 38	03 43	03 55	00♋12	25 33	28 49	04 52	04 55	01 07
20	24 01	27 34	05 13	05 20	00 57	25 06	28 47	06 24	06 20	01 52
21	23 55	27 33	05 32	05 38	01 06	25 00	28 46	06 44	06 38	02 01
22	23 49	27 32	05 52	05 56	01 15	24 54	28 46	07 04	06 56	02 10
23	23 43	27 31	06 13	06 15	01 24	24 48	28 45	07 26	07 14	02 19
24	23 36	27 30	06 34	06 33	01 34	24 42	28 45	07 47	07 33	02 29
25	23 30	27 29	06 56	06 53	01 44	24 35	28 44	08 10	07 53	02 39
26	23 23	27 28	07 19	07 12	01 54	24 29	28 44	08 33	08 13	02 49
27	23 17	27 27	07 42	07 33	02 04	24 22	28 43	08 57	08 33	02 59
28	23 10	27 25	08 07	07 53	02 14	24 16	28 43	09 22	08 54	03 09
29	23 03	27 24	08 32	08 15	02 25	24 09	28 42	09 48	09 15	03 20
30	22 55	27 23	08 58	08 36	02 36	24 02	28 41	10 15	09 37	03 30
31	22 48	27 22	09 26	08 59	02 47	23 54	28 41	10 43	09 59	03 41
32	22 40	27 20	09 54	09 22	02 58	23 47	28 40	11 12	10 22	03 53
33	22 32	27 19	10 24	09 45	03 10	23 39	28 39	11 42	10 46	04 04
34	22 24	27 18	10 55	10 10	03 21	23 31	28 39	12 14	11 10	04 16
35	22 16	27 16	11 27	10 35	03 34	23 23	28 38	12 47	11 35	04 28
36	22 07	27 14	12 01	11 01	03 46	23 15	28 37	13 22	12 01	04 41
37	21 58	27 13	12 37	11 27	03 59	23 06	28 36	13 58	12 28	04 54
38	21 49	27 11	13 15	11 55	04 12	22 57	28 36	14 36	12 56	05 07
39	21 39	27 09	13 54	12 24	04 26	22 48	28 35	15 16	13 25	05 20
40	21 29	27 07	14 36	12 54	04 40	22 38	28 34	15 59	13 54	05 34
41	21 19	27 05	15 19	13 25	04 55	22 28	28 33	16 43	14 25	05 49
42	21 08	27 03	16 06	13 57	05 10	22 17	28 32	17 30	14 57	06 04
43	20 57	27 01	16 55	14 30	05 25	22 06	28 30	18 20	15 31	06 20
44	20 45	26 59	17 47	15 05	05 42	21 55	28 29	19 13	16 06	06 36
45	20 33	26 56	18 43	15 42	05 58	21 43	28 28	20 09	16 42	06 53
46	20 20	26 53	19 42	16 20	06 16	21 30	28 27	21 09	17 20	07 10
47	20 07	26 50	20 46	17 00	06 34	21 17	28 25	22 13	18 00	07 28
48	19 53	26 47	21 54	17 42	06 54	21 03	28 24	23 22	18 42	07 48
49	19 38	26 44	23 07	18 26	07 14	20 49	28 22	24 35	19 26	08 08
50	19 22	26 41	24 25	19 13	07 35	20 33	28 20	25 54	20 13	08 28
51	19 05	26 37	25 50	20 02	07 57	20 17	28 18	27 19	21 02	08 51
52	18 47	26 32	27 21	20 54	08 20	19 59	28 16	28 50	21 54	09 14
53	18 28	26 28	29 00	21 50	08 45	19 41	28 14	00♊29	22 49	09 38
54	18 08	26 23	00♊48	22 48	09 11	19 21	28 11	02 17	23 47	10 04
55	17 46	26 17	02 45	23 51	09 39	19 00	28 09	04 13	24 50	10 32
56	17 23	26 11	04 53	24 59	10 09	18 37	28 06	06 20	25 57	11 02
57	16 58	26 04	07 12	26 11	10 41	18 13	28 02	08 38	27 08	11 33
58	16 30	25 57	09 44	27 29	11 15	17 46	27 58	11 08	28 26	12 07
59	16 01	25 48	12 31	28 54	11 52	17 17	27 54	13 52	29 49	12 44
60	15♒28	25♓38	15♊34	00♋25	12♋32	16♒45	27♓49	16♊51	01♋20	13♋23

To find each house cusp, there are three separate calculations to make:

First calculate each house cusp for the exact LST of birth **as if** the birth latitude was exactly 43° N 00'. In order to do this we will have to interpolate between the two Sidereal Times of 19:52:00 and 19:56:00 given in the Table, just as we did when calculating the Midheaven in the previous lesson.

Next calculate each house cusp for the exact LST of birth **as if** the birth latitude was exactly 42° N 00', interpolating between Sidereal Times again as above.

Finally, using the two house cusps found in Steps 1 and 2, interpolate between them according to latitude to arrive at a final house cusp for the exact birth latitude of 42°N 39'.

Notice that the first two steps involve interpolating between **time.** These steps will use the same constant multiplier used for finding the Midheaven (CM-2). The third step, however, involves interpolating between **latitudes**, and requires a completely different constant multiplier, which we will call "CM-3".

First CM-2 is calculated as explained in the previous lesson.

```
┌─────────────────────────────────────────────────────────────┐
│                           CM-2                                │
│              (Constant Multiplier for LST Interpolation)      │
│                                                               │
│   LST of Birth                              19 : 54 : 49      │
│                                                               │
│   - Next lowest Side Time from Table      -  19 : 52  00      │
│                                                               │
│                                         =       2 : 49        │
│                                                               │
│   Convert result to decimal                     2.82          │
│                                                               │
│                              ÷ 4 = CM-2          .71           │
│                                                               │
└─────────────────────────────────────────────────────────────┘
```

Now let's calculate CM-3, for use in latitude interpolation. Notice that the procedure is exactly the same as for the CM-2 calculation above, except that where we used **LST** of Birth and Next Lowest **LST** from the Tables, here we are substituting **Latitude** of Birth and Next Lowest **Latitude** from the Tables.

After filling in the Latitude of Birth and Next Lowest Latitude from the Tables, subtract the next lowest latitude from the birth latitude. In this example this leaves a difference of 39 minutes. Then divide 39 by 60 to convert this difference to a decimal of a whole degree. Dividing by 60 gives us the proportion of a whole degree of latitude represented by the birth latitude.

```
┌─────────────────────────────────────────────────────────────┐
│                           CM-3                                │
│            (Constant Multiplier for  Latitude Interpolation)  │
│                                                               │
│   Latitude of Birth                         42 ° 39 '         │
│                                                               │
│   - Next lowest Latitude from Table         42 ° 00 '         │
│                                                               │
│                                         =      ° 39 '         │
│                                                               │
│   Convert result to decimal      CM-3 =        .65            │
│                                                               │
│   Exception: If Birth Latitude is                             │
│   less than 20°, divide result by 5    ÷ 5 = CM-3 _____    │
│                                                               │
└─────────────────────────────────────────────────────────────┘
```

Notice that there is an additional line in the calculation box for Birth Latitudes under 20°. This is because *The Book of Tables* lists house cusps in 5 degree increments instead of 1 degree increments for latitudes under 20°. For these births, we must divide the decimal result by 5 in order to arrive at the proportion of 5 degrees represented by the target birth latitude.

Now with these two constant multipliers in hand (CM-2 and CM-3), we are ready to calculate the house cusps.

Understanding Constant Multipliers

Trying to memorize formulas for calculating the various constant multipliers needed in chart calculation can be overwhelming and is not necessary if you understand the logic behind the process. Each constant multiplier is determining a **proportion**, expressed as a **decimal**, of a particular **whole**. Notice below how all three constant multipliers used to erect a chart follow the same basic "formula":

When we calculate CM-1, we are determining what portion of a day has elapsed to the time of birth in GMT. We use CM-1 when we are interpolating between 0-hours, to pinpoint each planet's location. Because all days contain a total of 24 hours, the denominator is always 24.

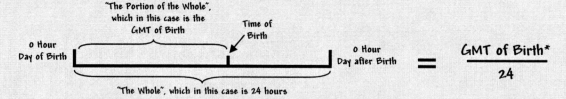

CM-2 tells us the portion of time that has elapsed from the earlier listed sidereal time to the LST of birth. CM-2 is used when interpolating between listed sidereal times, to pinpoint house cusps at a single latitude. If you are using *The Michelsen Book of Tables*, the denominator will always be 4, because it arranges its tables in 4-minute increments. If you are using another set of tables, you must adjust the denominator to reflect the increment between earlier and later listed sidereal times in your tables.

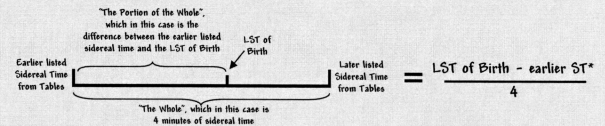

We use CM-3 to interpolate between Latitudes. It tells us what portion the birth latitude represents between next lowest and next highest latitudes listed in the Tables. If the birth latitude is 20° or higher, the denominator will be 1, because the Tables list latitudes in 1° increments. If the birth latitude is less than 20°, the denominator will be 5, because the Tables list these lower latitudes in 5° increments. Remember that dividing a number by 1 will always result in the number itself, so it is not necessary to actually divide if your denominator is 1.

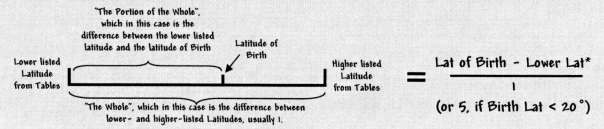

* Remember that each numerator (marked with an asterisk*) must be expressed in the same type of unit as its denominator before you can divide:

GMT of birth must be expressed in hours and decimals of hours for CM-1
The difference between LSTs must be expressed in minutes and decimals of minutes for CM-2
The difference between Latitudes must be expressed in degrees and decimals of degrees for CM-3

Using the Two Constant Multipliers to Interpolate

First, let's determine the Ascendant for the target LST of 19:54:49 at **43° N 00'**. This process is exactly the same as the process used to find the Midheaven in the previous lesson:

Step 1. List the ASC for later Sid Time in Table, which in this case is 19:56:00	♉ 18° 20'
Step 2. List the ASC for earlier Sid Time in Table, which in this case is 19:52:00	- ♉ 16° 55'
Step 3. Subtract to find the difference	1° 25'
	or 85'
Step 4. Multiply this difference by CM-2, which in this case in .71	85' x .71 = 60'
Step 5. Add the amount found in Step 4 to the earlier ASC listed in Step 2	♉ 16° 55'
	+ 60'
The Ascendant for 19:54:49 LST at 43° N 00' is 17° ♉ 55'.	= ♉ 16°115'
	or ♉ 17° 55'

Now repeat the entire process, but for a latitude of **42° N 00'**:

1. ASC at Later Sid Time (19:56:00)	♉ 17° 30'
2. ASC at Earlier Sid Time (19:52:00)	♉ 16° 06'
3. Line 1 - Line 2 =	1° 24' or 84'
4. Line 3 X CM-2 (.71) =	60'
5. Add lines 2 + 4 =	♉ 16° 66' or ♉ 17° 06'

We have determined the Ascendant at 43° latitude, and at 42° latitude. Now we must interpolate between these two values to arrive at the exact Ascendant for the birth location of 42° N 39'. **For this final step, CM-3 is used instead of CM-2:**

1. ASC at Higher Latitude (43°)	♉ 17° 55'
2. ASC at Lower Latitude (42°)	♉ 17° 06'
3. Line 1 - Line 2 =	49'
4. Line 3 X CM-3 (.65) =	32'
5. Add lines 2 + 4 =	♉ 17° 38'

The Ascendant for this birth is 17° ♉ 38'. The Descendant will be the same degree and minute of the opposite sign, or 17° ♏ 38'.

Example 2.

Let's go through this whole process again, this time more briefly, for the 11th house cusp. First, calculate the 11th house cusp at 43° N:

At 43°: 1. 11th cusp at Later Sid Time (19:56:00)   ♒ 22° 06'

2. 11th cusp at Earlier Sid Time (19:52:00)   ♒ 20° 57'

3. Line 1 - Line 2 =   1° 09' or 69'

4. Line 3 X CM-2 (.71) =   49'

5. Add lines 2 + 4 =   ♒ 20° 106' Or ♒ 21° 46'

Then, calculate the 11th house cusp at 42° N:

At 42°: 1. 11th cusp at Later Sid Time (19:56:00)   ♒ 22° 17'

2. 11th cusp at Earlier Sid Time (19:52:00)   ♒ 21° 08'

3. Line 1 - Line 2 =   1° 09' or 69'

4. Line 3 X CM-2 (.71) =   49'

5. Add lines 2 + 4 =   ♒ 21° 57'

Finally, interpolate between these two results for latitude:

1. 11th cusp at Higher Latitude (43°)   ♒ 21° 46'

2. 11th cusp at Lower Latitude (42°)   ♒ 21° 57'

3. Line 1 - Line 2 =   -11'

Notice here that the house cusp is moving backward from the lower to the higher latitude instead of forward. You will find that this is a very common occurrence. In cases like this, you must "subtract up", as you did when calculating the daily motion for retrograde planets, in order to find the difference on line 3. Then, the difference should be recorded as a negative number, so that after the constant multiplier is applied on line 4, the result is **subtracted** from line 2 instead of added, as follows. This produces an 11th house cusp of 21° ♒ 50' for an LST of 19:54:49.

4. Line 3 X CM-3 (.65) =   -7'

5. Add lines 2 + 4 =   ♒ 21° 50'

(Remember that adding a negative number is the same as subtracting it.)

**Whenever you find house cusps moving backwards instead of forwards,
Record the difference as a negative number.**

104

Example 3.

Let's calculate all house cusps for a birth with an LST of 15:51:08 in San Jose, California, latitude 37° N 20'. For this example we will use the Chart Calculation Form from the Appendix. First, we need to calculate the two constant multipliers, using the boxes for CM-2 and CM-3:

CM-2
(Constant Multiplier for LST Interpolation)

LST of Birth	15 : 51 : 08
- Next lowest Sid Time from Table	- 15: 48 00
=	3: 08
Convert result to decimal	3.13
÷ 4 = CM-2	.78

CM-3
(Constant Multiplier for Latitude Interpolation)

Latitude of Birth	37 ° 20 '
- Next lowest Latitude from Table	37 ° 00 '
=	° 20 '
Convert result to decimal = CM-3 =	.33

Exception: If Birth Latitude is less than 20°, divide result by 5   ÷ 5 = CM-3 _____

Next, transcribe the house cusps shown in the Tables onto lines 1 and 2 of the form for latitude 37°, and onto lines 6 and 7 for latitude 38°. We find it easiest to do all the transcribing at once; then we can close *The Book of Tables* and concentrate on doing the calculations.

Notice that boxes are provided for the Midheaven calculation in the "Higher latitude" section on the top of the form. You will remember from the previous lesson that the Midheaven is not affected by latitude - it is included here just for the sake of convenience.

Notice also that in this example, latitude interpolation (Steps 11-15 on the following page) produced negative house cusp movement on all but one of the cusp calculations. As previously mentioned, this is a common occurrence that one needs to be wary of. Whenever you find you need to "subtract up" to find the difference between house cusps on line 13 of the form, always mark your result with a minus sign so that it will be subtracted instead of added on line 15.

Finally, remember that house cusps opposite to those calculated contain the same degrees and minutes, but in the opposite sign. Therefore, the house cusps in this example are as follows:

MC = 29° ♏ 58' ↔ IC = 29° ♉ 58'   ASC = 11° ♒ 34' ↔ DSC = 11° ♌ 34'
11th = 22° ♐ 07' ↔ 5th = 22° ♊ 07'   2nd = 26° ♓ 54' ↔ 8th = 26° ♍ 34'
12th = 14° ♑ 10' ↔ 6th = 14° ♋ 10'   3rd = 3° ♉ 17' ↔ 9th = 3° ♏ 17'

House Cusp Calculation for Higher Latitude

Latitude __38__ °	MC	11th	12th	ASC	2nd	3rd
1. House Cusps at Later Sid Time **(15:52:00)**	♐ 00° 11'	♐ 22° 10'	♑ 14° 04'	♒ 11° 24'	♓ 27° 11'	♉ 03° 37'
2. House Cusps at Earlier Sid Time **(15:48:00)**	♏ 29° 13'	♐ 21° 16'	♑ 13° 05'	♒ 10° 06'	♓ 25° 47'	♉ 02° 28'
3. Line 1 - Line 2 =	58'	54'	59'	1° 18' = 78'	1° 24' = 84'	1° 09' = 69'
4. Line 3 X CM-2 **(.78)** =	45'	42'	46'	61'	66'	54'
5. Add lines 2 + 4 =	♏ 29° 58'	♐ 21° 58'	♑ 13° 51'	♒ 10° 67' = ♒ 11° 07'	♓ 25° 113' = ♓ 26° 53'	♉ 02° 82' = ♉ 03° 22'

House Cusp Calculation for Lower Latitude

Latitude __37__ °		11th	12th	ASC	2nd	3rd
6. House Cusps at Later Sid Time **(15:52:00)**		♐ 22° 23'	♑ 14° 32'	♒ 12° 04'	♓ 27° 13'	♉ 03° 29'
7. House Cusps at Earlier Sid Time **(15:48:00)**		♐ 21° 29'	♑ 13° 33'	♒ 10° 46'	♓ 25° 49'	♉ 02° 20'
8. Line 6 - Line 7 =		54'	59'	1° 18' = 78'	1° 24' = 84'	1° 09' = 69'
9. Line 8 X CM-2 **(.78)** =		42'	46'	61'	66'	54'
10. Add lines 7 + 9 =		♐ 21° 71' = ♐ 22° 11'	♑ 13° 79' = ♑ 14° 19'	♒ 10° 107' = ♒ 11° 47'	♓ 25° 115' = ♓ 26° 55'	♉ 02° 74' = ♉ 03° 14'

Latitude Interpolation

		11th	12th	ASC	2nd	3rd
11. House Cusps at Higher Latitude (from line 5)		♐ 21° 58'	♑ 13° 51'	♒ 11° 07'	♓ 26° 53'	♉ 03° 22'
12. House Cusps at Lower Latitude (from line 10)		♐ 22° 11'	♑ 14° 19'	♒ 11° 47'	♓ 26° 55'	♉ 03° 14'
13. Line 11 - Line 12 =		- 13'	- 28'	- 40'	- 02'	08'
14. Line 13 X CM-3 **(.33)** =		- 4'	- 9'	- 13'	- 01'	03'
15. Add lines 12 + 14 = **House Cusps at Birth**		♐ 22° 07'	♑ 14° 10'	♒ 11° 34'	♓ 26° 54'	♉ 03° 17'

Lesson 11 Exercises

Calculate both Constant Multipliers and all house cusps for the following birth, using the forms below and on the following page. Then fill in the zodiacal degree and minute for each house cusp below. Answers can be found in the Answer Key in the Appendix.

17:24:49 LST
Houston, Texas 29° N 46'

CM-2
(Constant Multiplier for LST Interpolation)

LST of Birth   ___:___:___

- Next lowest Sid Time from Table   - ___:___:___

                                        =   ___:___

Convert result to decimal   _____

                       ÷ 4 = **CM-2** _____

CM-3
(Constant Multiplier for Latitude Interpolation)

Latitude of Birth   ____° ____'

- Next lowest Latitude from Table   - ____° ____'

                                   =   ____° ____'

Convert result to decimal   = **CM-3** = _____

Exception: If Birth Latitude is less than 20°, divide result by 5   ÷ 5 = **CM-3** _____

1st Cusp _____		7th Cusp _____
2nd Cusp _____		8th Cusp _____
3rd Cusp _____		9th Cusp _____
4th Cusp _____		10th Cusp _____
5th Cusp _____		11th Cusp _____
6th Cusp _____		12th Cusp _____

House Cusp Calculation for Higher Latitude

Latitude _____ °	MC	11th	12th	ASC	2nd	3rd
1. House Cusps at Later Sid Time						
2. House Cusps at Earlier Sid Time						
3. Line 1 - Line 2 =						
4. Line 3 X CM-2 _____ =						
5. Add lines 2 + 4 =						

House Cusp Calculation for Lower Latitude

Latitude _____ °		11th	12th	ASC	2nd	3rd
6. House Cusps at Later Sid Time						
7. House Cusps at Earlier Sid Time						
8. Line 6 - Line 7 =						
9. Line 3 X CM-2 _____ =						
10. Add lines 7 + 9 =						

Latitude Interpolation

		11th	12th	ASC	2nd	3rd
11. House Cusps at Higher Latitude (from line 5)						
12. House Cusps at Lower Latitude (from line 10)						
13. Line 11 - Line 12 =						
14. Line 13 X CM-3 _____ =						
15. Add lines 12 + 14 = **House Cusps at Birth**						

Lesson 12: Southern Latitude Births

Southern latitude births require special handling because the Southern Hemisphere has a different orientation to the Ecliptic. In this lesson, we will explain why southern latitude births are different and demonstrate the entire process of calculating a southern latitude birth chart.

Southern Signs of Long & Short Ascension

For calculation purposes, the most crucial difference between the northern and southern hemispheres lies in the signs of long and short ascension. You will remember from Lesson 10 that due to the tilt of the Earth, some signs rise slower and some faster than others. In the southern hemisphere, these signs are swapped around - signs of short ascension in the north rise slowly in the south and vice versa.

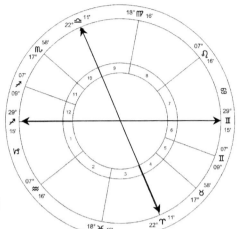

Northern Latitude Chart
40°N 00', 40°W 00'

To illustrate this phenomenon, look at the two charts to the right. Both are calculated for the same date and GMT, same latitude and longitude, except one is in the north and the other in the south. Notice that both have a Midheaven of 22°♎ 11'. This is because the Midheaven is not affected by latitude and will be the same for all locations sharing the same longitude, as you will remember from Lesson 10. But notice that all other house cusps are off by varying amounts. In the northern chart, the 1st house is very large, while in the southern chart the 1st house is very small. Notice also that the house containing Sagittarius in the northern chart is small, while the Sagittarius house in the southern chart is very large. This is all due to the difference in signs of long and short ascension.

None of this would matter if we were using a Table of Houses calculated for southern latitudes, but most Tables readily available are calculated for northern latitudes only. This means that the signs of long and short ascension as they apply to northern latitudes have been factored in. Because the signs of long and short ascension are opposite in the south, we need to make adjustments manually. This is done by adding 12 hours of sidereal time and then swapping each sign for its opposite. By making these changes we are "tricking" the northern latitude Table of Houses into trading long ascension for short ascension, and vice versa.

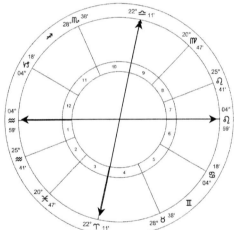

Southern Latitude Chart
40°S 00', 40°W 00'

The Southern View of the Ecliptic

Another difference between the two hemispheres is that where northerners face south to view the ecliptic, southerners must face north. This means that the Midheaven in a southern latitude birth chart is actually the northernmost point on the ecliptic, not the southernmost point as it is in the north. While this does not affect chart calculation at all, it is good to keep in mind that the Midheaven is not always in the south. (Note: The Earth rotates from west to east for us all, so the Ascendant is still in the east and the Descendant still in the west in southern charts.)

Southern Latitude Chart Calculations

This all boils down to two extra steps that must be done to calculate a chart for a southern latitude birth:

1) Add or Subtract 12 hours (12:00:00) to the LST
2) Reverse signs on all house cusps

All other calculations are handled exactly the same as they are for northern latitude births.

Do NOT reverse the signs for planetary positions -
The planets are in the same signs for all locations regardless of hemisphere.

Let us demonstrate this by working through two examples. In the first example below, the LST adjustment is demonstrated. Then in Example 2, we will go through the entire process for a southern latitude birth.

Example 1.

Let's calculate the LST for a birth on January 6, 1979, Melbourne, Australia, 3:54 GMT.

Sidereal Time at 0 hr on January 6, 1979	6:59:55
+ GMT of Birth	+ 3:54:00
+ Solar/Sidereal Time correction on GMT	+ :38
(3.9 hrs x 9.86 secs = 38 secs)	
	9:113:93
+ Longitude/Time equivalent for Melbourne	+ 9:39:52 (Eastern Longitude = +)
	= 18:152:145
= LST of Birth	or 20:34:25
Southern Latitude Adjustment	- 12:00:00
= "LST +12"	= 8:34:25

Although 20:34:25 is the actual local sidereal time for this birth, we must subtract 12 hours and use the resultant "LST +12" in place of the actual LST in order to calculate house cusps using a table of houses for northern latitudes. Notice that the 12-hour Southern Latitude Adjustment can be either added or subtracted, depending on which is easier. In this case it was easier to subtract 12 hours because the LST was greater than 12, but we could have just as correctly added 12 hours and arrived at the same answer, as shown below:

= LST of Birth	= 20:34:25
Southern Latitude Adjustment	+ 12:00:00
= "LST +12"	= 32:34:25
+/- 24:00:00 if required	- 24:00:00
= "LST +12"	= 8:34:25

For Southern Latitude Births,
If the LST is greater than 12:00:00, Subtract 12 Hours
If the LST is less than 12:00:00, Add 12 Hours

Example 2.

Let's calculate the houses for someone born in a southern latitude location. We will skip the planets here, because calculating the planets for southern latitude births is done exactly the same as for northern latitude births. The following birth data will be used:

April 29, 1924   **9:19 pm NZT**
Fairlie, New Zealand   **44°S 06' 170°E 50'**

First, calculate the GMT of birth. This is done just as it is for northern births:

Given Time of Birth:	9:19 pm
+ PM Adjustment	+ 12:00
Time Zone Adjustment:	-11:30
= GMT of Birth	9:49

Next, use the GMT above to calculate the LST of birth. As in the previous example, notice the extra step at the end of this calculation where 12 hours of sidereal time is added:

Sidereal Time at 0 hr on April 29, 1924	14:26:41
+ GMT of Birth	+ 9:49:00
+ Solar/Sidereal Time correction on GMT	+ 1:37
(9.8 hrs x 9.86 secs = 97 secs)	
	= 23:76:78
+ Longitude/Time equivalent for Fairlie	+ 11:23:20 (Eastern Longitude = +)
	= 34:99:98
	or 35:40:38
- 24 hours, if result is greater than 24:00:00	- 24:00:00
= LST of Birth	= 11:40:38
+ Southern Latitude Adjustment	**+ 12:00:00**
= "LST +12"	**= 23:40:38**

In this case it was easier to add 12 hours to the LST of Birth to adjust for southern latitude, rather than subtracting it. From now on in our house cusp calculations, we will proceed as if the "LST +12", or 23:40:38, was the actual sidereal time of birth, substituting it whenever the LST is called for. Follow along as we calculate the house cusps for this birth on the next few pages.

When calculating Southern Latitude Births,
Treat the "LST +12" as if it were the actual LST of Birth

Next, calculate the two constant multipliers needed for house cusp calculation, CM-2 and CM-3. These are calculated the same as for northern births, except that the "LST +12" is substituted for the LST of Birth in the CM-2 calculation:

CM-2
(Constant Multiplier for LST Interpolation)

LST of Birth	23 : 40 : 38
- Next lowest Sid Time from Table	- 23 : 40 : 00
=	0 : 38
Convert result to decimal	.63
÷ 4 = CM-2	.16

CM-3
(Constant Multiplier for Latitude Interpolation)

Latitude of Birth	44 ° 06 '
- Next lowest Latitude from Table	- 44 ° 00 '
=	° 06 '
Convert result to decimal = CM-3 =	.1

Exception: If Birth Latitude is less than 20°, divide result by 5   ÷ 5 = CM-3 _____

Finally, we can calculate the house cusps using the calculation form on the next page. Notice that this is done exactly as it is when calculating house cusps for northern births, but we are substituting the "LST +12" for the LST of birth. Once all cusps are calculated we will reverse all the signs. The final house cusps for this birth are listed below.

1st Cusp	17° ♑ 11'		7th Cusp	17° ♋ 11'
2nd Cusp	5° ♒ 40'		8th Cusp	5° ♌ 40'
3rd Cusp	27° ♒ 05'		9th Cusp	27° ♌ 05'
4th Cusp	24° ♓ 43'		10th Cusp	24° ♍ 43'
5th Cusp	1° ♉ 14'		11th Cusp	1° ♏ 14'
6th Cusp	12° ♊ 14'		12th Cusp	12° ♐ 14'

**After calculating House Cusps,
Reverse all Signs for Southern Latitude Births**

House Cusp Calculation for Higher Latitude

Latitude __45__ °	MC	11th	12th	ASC	2nd	3rd
1. House Cusps at Later Sid Time (23:44:00)	♓ 25° 38'	♉ 2° 23'	♊ 13° 39'	♋ 18° 30'	♌ 6° 43'	♌ 27° 59'
2. House Cusps at Earlier Sid Time (23:40:00)	♓ 24° 33'	♉ 1° 12'	♊ 12° 37'	♋ 17° 42'	♌ 5° 54'	♌ 27° 03'
3. Line 1 - Line 2 =	1° 5' = 65'	1° 11' = 71'	1° 02' = 62'	48'	49'	56'
4. Line 3 X CM-2 (.16) =	10'	11'	10'	8'	8'	9'
5. Add lines 2 + 4 =	♓ 24° 43' ♍	♉ 1° 23'	♊ 12° 47'	♋ 17° 50'	♌ 5° 62' = ♌ 6° 02'	♌ 27° 12'

House Cusp Calculation for Lower Latitude

Latitude __44__ °		11th	12th	ASC	2nd	3rd
6. House Cusps at Later Sid Time (23:44:00)		♉ 2° 13'	♊ 13° 02'	♋ 17° 48'	♌ 6° 20'	♌ 27° 51'
7. House Cusps at Earlier Sid Time (23:40:00)		♉ 1° 02'	♊ 12° 00'	♋ 16° 59'	♌ 5° 30'	♌ 26° 55'
8. Line 6 - Line 7 =		1° 11' = 71'	1° 02' = 62'	49'	50'	56'
9. Line 8 X CM-2 (.16) =		11'	10'	8'	8'	9'
10. Add lines 7 + 9 =		♉ 1° 13'	♊ 12° 10'	♋ 16° 67' = ♋ 17° 07'	♌ 5° 38'	♌ 26° 64' = ♌ 27° 04'

Latitude Interpolation

		11th	12th	ASC	2nd	3rd
11. House Cusps at Higher Latitude (from line 5)		♉ 1° 23'	♊ 12° 47'	♋ 17° 50'	♌ 6° 02'	♌ 27° 12'
12. House Cusps at Lower Latitude (from line 10)		♉ 1° 13'	♊ 12° 10'	♋ 17° 07'	♌ 5° 38'	♌ 27° 04'
13. Line 11 - Line 12 =		10'	37'	43'	24'	8'
14. Line 13 X CM-3 (.1) =		1'	4'	4'	2'	1'
15. Add lines 12 + 14 = **House Cusps at Birth**		♉ 1° 14' ♏	♊ 12° 14' ♐	♋ 17° 11' ♑	♌ 5° 40' ♒	♌ 27° 05' ♒

Lesson 12 Exercises

Calculate the GMT and LST of birth and all house cusps for the following birth, using the forms below and on the following two pages. Then fill in the zodiacal degree and minute for each house cusp where requested on the next page. Answers can be found in the Answer Key in the Appendix.

January 9, 1974
3:25 am
Sydney, Australia 33°S 52' 151°E 13'

Part A: GMT of Birth

1. Given Time of Birth _____:_____ am / pm

2. + PM Adjustment *(+12:00 if pm)* + _____:_____

3. +/-Time Zone

    a. Standard Time Zone *(+W, -E)* _____:_____

    b. DST Adjustment *(- 1:00 if DST)* - _____:_____
    (Include only if not already factored into (a) above)

    c. = Time Zone Adjustment *(Enter on Line 3, right)* = _____:_____ ⟶ +W,-E _____:_____

                                   Subtotal = _____:_____

4. +/- 24 hours if date change required +/- _____:_____

5. = GMT of Birth   Date _____   Time = _____:_____

Part B: LST of Birth

6. Sidereal Time at 0 hr on birth date *(from ephemeris; use birth date from Step 5)* _____:_____:_____

7. + GMT of birth *(from Step 5)* _____:_____: 00

8. + Solar/Sidereal Time Correction on GMT *(from Table or calculate below:)* _____:_____

    (GMT *(as decimal)*_____ hrs x 9.86 secs = _____)   Subtotal = _____:_____:_____

9. +/- Longitude/Time Equivalent *(from Atlas or calculate below; -W, +E)* +/- _____:_____:_____

    (Longitude *(as decimal)* _____ x 4 min = _____)   Subtotal = _____:_____:_____

10. +/- 24:00:00 if required +/- _____:_____:_____

11. = LST of Birth   LST = _____:_____:_____

12. Southern Latitude Adjustment *(+/- 12:00:00 if Southern Latitude)* +/- _____:_____:_____

13. **"LST + 12"** *(use in place of LST for Southern Latitude births)* LST+12 = _____:_____:_____

CM-2
(Constant Multiplier for LST Interpolation)

LST of Birth   ___:___:___

- Next lowest Sid Time from Table   - ___:___:___

                                     =   ___:___

Convert result to decimal   _____

                      $\div$ 4 = CM-2   _____

CM-3
(Constant Multiplier for Latitude Interpolation)

Latitude of Birth   ___° ___'

- Next lowest Latitude from Table   - ___° ___'

                              =   ___° ___'

Convert result to decimal   = CM-3 =   _____

*Exception: If Birth Latitude is
less than 20°, divide result by 5* $\div$ 5 = CM-3 _____

1st Cusp	_____	7th Cusp	_____
2nd Cusp	_____	8th Cusp	_____
3rd Cusp	_____	9th Cusp	_____
4th Cusp	_____	10th Cusp	_____
5th Cusp	_____	11th Cusp	_____
6th Cusp	_____	12th Cusp	_____

House Cusp Calculation for Higher Latitude						
Latitude _____°	MC	11th	12th	ASC	2nd	3rd
1. House Cusps at Later Sid Time						
2. House Cusps at Earlier Sid Time						
3. Line 1 - Line 2 =						
4. Line 3 X CM-2 _____ =						
5. Add lines 2 + 4 =						

House Cusp Calculation for Lower Latitude						
Latitude _____°		11th	12th	ASC	2nd	3rd
6. House Cusps at Later Sid Time						
7. House Cusps at Earlier Sid Time						
8. Line 6 - Line 7 =						
9. Line 3 X CM-2 _____ =						
10. Add lines 7 + 9 =						

Latitude Interpolation						
		11th	12th	ASC	2nd	3rd
11. House Cusps at Higher Latitude (from line 5)						
12. House Cusps at Lower Latitude (from line 10)						
13. Line 11 - Line 12 =						
14. Line 13 X CM-3 _____ =						
15. Add lines 12 + 14 = **House Cusps at Birth**						

Section 5:

Natal Chart Calculation Review

Lesson 13: Natal Chart Calculation Review
& Filling in the Chart Wheel

Natal Chart Exams

Lesson 13: Natal Chart Calculation Review
& Filling in the Chart Wheel

If you have worked through all the previous lessons, you have now learned everything you need to know to calculate a birth chart! In this lesson we will put together everything covered thus far, reviewing the entire process from start to finish. As we do, we will list the most common errors students tend to make which can result in failure on certification exams. Use these lists to check yourself to ensure you are not making the same mistakes. After reviewing natal chart calculations, we will discuss how to use the information gathered to fill in a chart wheel. Finally, try testing yourself by taking the three Natal Chart Exams at the end of this lesson, one with the aid of the Chart Calculation Form and one without.

Natal Chart Review

Let's review how to calculate a natal chart in "short form" using the following birth data:

April 9, 1968
12:13 pm CST
Des Moines, Iowa
41°N 36', 93°W 37'

Part A: GMT of Birth

1. Given Time of Birth			12:13 pm
2. + PM Adjustment (+ 12:00 if pm)			---
3. +/- Time Zone			
a. Standard Time Zone (+W,-E)	+ 6:00		
b. DST Adjustment (-1:00 if DST)	----		
c. = Time Zone Adjustment	6:00		+ 6:00
4. +/- 24 hours if date change is required			----
5. = GMT of Birth Date = April 9, 1968		Time =	18:13

Common Errors: Calculating the GMT of Birth

1. Not converting the given time of birth to 24-hour format correctly. Remember that 12:00-12:59 am and pm are anomalies.

2. Not taking Daylight Savings Time into account, or subtracting an additional hour for DST when it is already included in the time zone figure on line 3a.

3. Adding or subtracting east or west time zones incorrectly.

4. Not changing the GMT **date** of birth if a 24-hour adjustment was required.

   Remember that if the GMT is incorrect, the entire chart will be incorrect!

Part B: LST of Birth

6. Sidereal Time at 0 hr on birth date *(from Ephemeris)*		13:09:12	*(Lesson 5)*
7. + GMT of birth *(from Step 5)*		+ 18:13:00	
8. + Solar/Sidereal Time correction on GMT *(from Table or calculate below:)*		+ 3:00	*(Lesson 5)*
(18.22 hrs x 9.86 secs = 180 seconds)			
	Subtotal =	31:25:12	
9. +/- Longitude/Time Equivalent *(from Atlas or calculate below; -W,+E)*		- 06:14:29	*(Lesson 4)*
(93.62° x 4 min = 374.48 min = 6:14:29)			
	Subtotal =	25:10:43	
10. +/- 24:00:00 if required		- 24:00:00	*(Lesson 5)*
11. = LST of Birth	LST =	1:10:43	

Common Errors: Calculating the LST of Birth

1. Copying the wrong Sidereal Time from the ephemeris.

2. Writing the GMT of birth as minutes:seconds instead of hours:minutes.

3. Calculating the Solar-Sidereal time correction for a time other than the GMT of birth.

4. Adding the wrong Solar-Sidereal time correction to the GMT, especially adding hours: minutes instead of minutes:seconds.

5. Adding or subtracting east or west longitude time equivalents incorrectly. Remember this will always be the **opposite** function to that performed on line 3, GMT calculation.

6. Forgetting to add 12 hours to a southern latitude birth LST.

Remember that if the LST is incorrect, all house cusps will subsequently be incorrect!

CM-1
(Constant Multiplier for Part C: Planetary Position)

Convert GMT of Birth to decimal: __18.22__ ÷ 24 = **CM-1** __.759__

Part C: Planetary Position

	☉	☽	☿	♀	♂	♃
1. Position at 0 hr on day After birth date **(4/10/68)**	19° 71' ♈ ~~20° 11'~~	♌ 36° 51' ~~♍ 6° 51'~~	4° 73' ~~♈ 5° 13'~~	♈ 1° 21'	8° 92' ~~♉ 9° 32'~~	♌ 26° 03' Rx
2. Position at 0 hr on Birth date **(4/9/68)**	♈ 19° 12'	♌ 23° 11'	♈ 3° 25'	♈ 0° 07'	♉ 8° 48'	♌ 26° 05' Rx
3. Line 1 - Line 2 = Total Daily Travel	59'	13° 40' = 820'	1° 48' = 108'	1° 14' = 74'	44'	-2' Rx
4. Line 3 X CM-1 **(.759)** = Travel to birth time	45'	622' = 10° 22'	82' = 1° 22'	56'	33'	-2' Rx
5. Add lines 2 + 4 = Position at Birth	♈ 19° 57'	♌ 33° 33' = ♍ 3° 33'	♈ 4° 47'	♈ 0° 63' = ♈ 1° 03'	♉ 8° 81' = ♉ 9° 21'	♌ 26° 03' Rx

	♄	♅	♆	♇	☊	
6. Position at 0 hr on day After birth date **(4/10/68)**	♈ 15° 59'	♍ 26° 12' Rx	♏ 26° 04' Rx	♍ 20° 48' Rx	♈ 18° 43'	
7. Position at 0 hr on Birth date **(4/9/68)**	♈ 15° 51'	♍ 26° 15' Rx	♏ 26° 05' Rx	♍ 20° 50' Rx	♈ 18° 43'	
8. Line 6 - Line 7 = Total Daily Travel	8'	- 3' Rx	- 1' Rx	- 2' Rx	0	
9. Line 8 X CM-1 **(.759)** = Travel to birth time	6'	- 2' Rx	- 1' Rx	- 2' Rx	0	
10. Add lines 7 + 9 = Position at Birth	♈ 15° 57'	♍ 26° 13' Rx	♏ 26° 04' Rx	♍ 20° 48' Rx	♈ 18° 43'	

Common Errors: Calculating Planetary Positions

1. Copying planet positions for the wrong day, either by accident or by using the date of the local birth and not the revised date according to GMT.

2. Adding the results of a retrograde planet to the planet position on the date of birth instead of subtracting.

3. Forgetting to mark the final results for retrograde planets with an Rx symbol.

<table>
<tr><th colspan="2">CM-2
(Constant Multiplier for LST Interpolation)</th><th colspan="2">CM-3
(Constant Multiplier for Latitude Interpolation)</th></tr>
</table>

CM-2 (Constant Multiplier for LST Interpolation)	CM-3 (Constant Multiplier for Latitude Interpolation)
LST of Birth 1 : 10 : 43	Latitude of Birth 41 ° 36 '
- Next lowest LST from Table of Houses - 1 : 08 : 00	- Next lowest Lat from Table of Houses - 41 ° 00 '
= 2 : 43	= ___° 36 '
Convert result to decimal 2.72	Convert result to decimal = CM-3 = .6
÷ 4 = CM-2 .68	Exception: If Birth Latitude is less than 20°, divide result by 5 ÷ 5 = CM-3 _____

Part D: House Cusps

House Cusp Calculation for Higher Latitude

Latitude __42__°	MC	11th	12th	ASC	2nd	3rd
1. House Cusps at Later LST (1:12:00)	♈ 19° 30'	♉ 26° 28'	♋ 3° 02'	♌ 4° 01'	♌ 24° 01'	♍ 18° 27'
2. House Cusps at Earlier LST (1:08:00)	♈ 18° 26'	♉ 25° 24'	♋ 2° 07'	♌ 3° 14'	♌ 23° 11'	♍ 17° 29'
3. Line 1 - Line 2 =	1° 04' = 64'	1° 04' = 64'	55'	47'	50'	58'
4. Line 3 X CM-2 (.68) =	44'	44'	37'	32'	34'	39'
5. Add lines 2 + 4 =	♈ 18° 70' = ♈ 19° 10'	♉ 25° 68' = ♉ 26° 08'	♋ 2° 44'	♌ 3° 46'	♌ 23° 45'	♍ 17° 68' = ♍ 18° 08'

House Cusp Calculation for Lower Latitude

Latitude __41__°		11th	12th	ASC	2nd	3rd
6. House Cusps at Later LST (1:12:00)		♉ 26° 14'	♋ 2° 31'	♌ 3° 30'	♌ 23° 46'	♍ 18° 24'
7. House Cusps at Earlier LST (1:08:00)		♉ 25° 10'	♋ 1° 37'	♌ 2° 42'	♌ 22° 55'	♍ 17° 26'
8. Line 6 - Line 7 =		1° 04' = 64'	54'	48'	51'	58'
9. Line 8 X CM-2 (.68) =		44'	37'	33'	35'	39'
10. Add lines 7 + 9 =		♉ 25° 54'	♋ 1° 74' = ♋ 2° 14'	♌ 2° 75' = ♌ 3° 15'	♌ 22° 90' = ♌ 23° 30'	♍ 17° 65' = ♍ 18° 05'

122

Latitude Interpolation			11th	12th	ASC	2nd	3rd
11. House Cusps at Higher Latitude (from line 5)			♉ 26° 08'	♋ 2° 44'	♌ 3° 46'	♌ 23° 45'	♍ 18° 08'
12. House Cusps at Lower Latitude (from line 10)			♉ 25°54'	♋ 2° 14'	♌ 3° 15'	♌ 23° 30'	♍ 18° 05'
13. Line 11 - Line 12 =			14'	30'	31'	15'	03'
14. Line 13 X CM-3 (.6) =			8'	18'	19'	9'	2'
15. Add lines 12 + 14 = **House Cusps at Birth**			♉ 25°62' = ♉ 26° 02'	♋ 2° 32'	♌ 3° 34'	♌ 23° 39'	♍ 18° 07'

Common Errors: Calculating the House Cusps

1. Using longitude instead of latitude to calculate CM-3.

2. Copying the wrong line of data from a table of houses. (We like to use the edge of a Post-it Note® to underline the line of data we are working with because it stays put and won't shift.)

3. Not noticing sign changes when copying data from a table of houses.

3. Adding the results of a cusp that is "moving backwards" instead of subtracting.

4. Forgetting to flip cusp signs for a southern latitude chart.

Filling in the Chart Wheel

Now that all calculations are finished, all that remains is completing the chart wheel. In general, all notations should be made in the standard format, as follows:

26° ♉ 48' ℞
(Degree - Sign - Minute, Retrograde where applicable)

Be sure to include the degree sign (°) and the minute sign ('). This is very important, because as you begin to insert information in some of the more awkward quadrants of the chart, it becomes less clear which figure represents degrees and which minutes unless each is marked.

First, enter the six calculated house cusps around the wheel perimeter. These should be entered as you would normally read - either left to right, or top down. All figures should be "right side up" so that the chart wheel does not have to be turned to be read. Then enter the remaining six house cusps using the degree and minute of its opposite house but with the opposite sign.

Calculated House Cusps		Derived House Cusps	
MC (10th Cusp)	19° ♈ 10'	IC (4th Cusp)	19° ♎ 10'
11th Cusp	26° ♉ 02'	5th Cusp	26° ♏ 02'
12th Cusp	2° ♋ 32'	6th Cusp	2° ♑ 32'
ASC (1st Cusp)	3° ♌ 34'	DSC (7th Cusp)	3° ♒ 34'
2nd Cusp	23° ♌ 39'	8th Cusp	23° ♒ 39'
3rd Cusp	18° ♍ 07'	9th Cusp	18° ♓ 07'

Next, look around the chart and check for interceptions. If you find that a sign has been "skipped", you will know that an interception exists. Notice in the example that the sign Taurus is on the 11th house cusp, and Cancer is on the 12th cusp. This means that the sign Gemini is intercepted in the 11th house. Remember that whenever a sign is intercepted, its opposite sign will also be intercepted. Make note of the interception on the chart wheel by writing in the intercepted sign between the two relevant house cusps, as was done with Gemini and Sagittarius in the 11th and 5th houses on the chart wheel opposite.

Finally, enter the planets and nodes. Remember that the South Node (☋) is always the same degree and minute of the opposite sign to the North Node (☊). All planet symbols should be written to the outer edge of the house, followed by its degree-sign-minute written in a single line from the outside in, like a spoke of a wheel. Retrograde symbols are entered last after the minutes. **Be sure to enter the planets in the correct zodiacal order.** Sometimes it helps to list the planets and nodes in zodiacal order on a scrap paper first. This is especially helpful if there are several planets located in the same sign or house, as is the case for the sign Aries and the 9th house in this example. When determining where to enter a planet, keep in mind that the degrees of the zodiac increase **counter-clockwise** around the wheel. In the example, the Sun at 19° ♈ 57' falls to the 10th house side of the MC at 19° ♈ 10', because 19° 57' comes after 19° 10'. Similarly, notice that Neptune at 26° ♏ 04' falls to the 5th house side of the 5th cusp at 26° ♏ 02', because 26° 04' comes after 26° 02'. Once all planets have been entered, double check the order of your entries by starting at 0° Aries and moving around the wheel counter-clockwise, ensuring that all planets and house cusps are ordered correctly.

Planetary Positions	
♀	1° ♈ 03'
☿	4° ♈ 47'
♄	15° ♈ 57'
☊	18° ♈ 43'
☉	19° ♈ 57'
♂	9° ♉ 21'
♃	26° ♌ 03' ℞
☽	3° ♍ 33'
♇	20° ♍ 48' ℞
♅	26° ♍ 13' ℞
☋	18° ♎ 43'
♆	26° ♏ 04' ℞

124

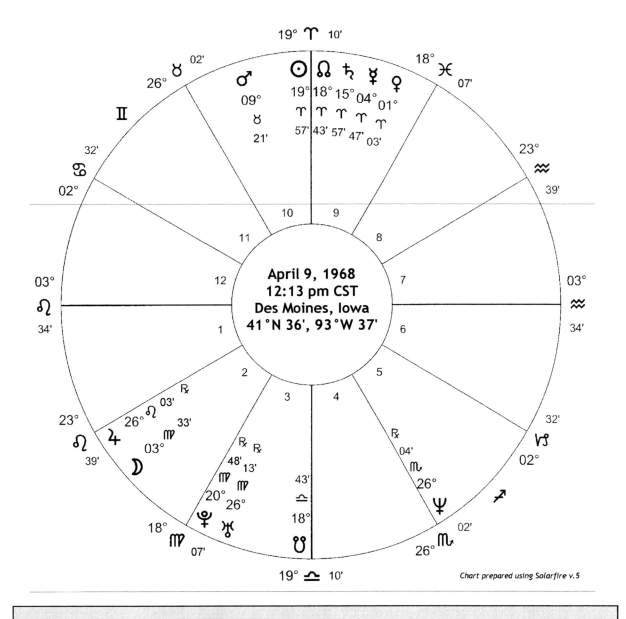

19° ♈ 10'

Chart prepared using Solarfire v.5

April 9, 1968
12:13 pm CST
Des Moines, Iowa
41°N 36', 93°W 37'

19° ♎ 10'

Common Errors: Filling in the Chart Wheel

1. Planets written to the wrong side of a house cusp, or not in proper order.

2. Retrograde symbols not entered where applicable.

3. Degrees and minutes not properly labeled.

4. Omitting a planet or node by mistake. (If you have entered all 10 planets and both nodes, you should have 12 items entered on the chart wheel.)

4. Messy illegible handwriting.

5. Intercepted signs not noted.

Natal Chart Exams

Three tests are provided here for your use. The first test allows the use of the chart calculation form, but the next two tests ask you to try the calculations from memory. Remember that most certification exams do not allow students to use preprinted calculation forms, so these tests are more along the lines of what you can expect in a certification exam setting.

Exam No. 1. *Calculate all planetary positions and house cusps for the following birth, using the forms below and on the next two pages. Then fill in the chart wheel on page 129. Answers can be found in the Answer Key in the Appendix.*

August 15, 1983   5:52 am
Cairo, Egypt 30°N 03' 31°E 15'

Part A: GMT of Birth

1. Given Time of Birth   ____:____ am / pm

2. + PM Adjustment *(+12:00 if pm)*   +   ____:____

3. +/-Time Zone

    a. Standard Time Zone *(+W, -E)*   ____:____

    b. DST Adjustment *(- 1:00 if DST)*   - ____:____
    (Include only if not already factored into (a) above)

    c. = Time Zone Adjustment *(Enter on Line 3, right)* = ____:____ ⟶ +W,-E ____:____

                                        Subtotal = ____:____

4. +/- 24 hours if date change required   +/- ____:____

5. = GMT of Birth   Date _____   Time = ____:____

Part B: LST of Birth

6. Sidereal Time at 0 hr on birth date *(from ephemeris; use birth date from Step 5)*   ____:____:____

7. + GMT of birth *(from Step 5)*   ____:____: 00

8. + Solar/Sidereal Time Correction on GMT *(from Table or calculate below:)*   ____:____

    (GMT *(as decimal)*_____ hrs x 9.86 secs = _____)   Subtotal = ____:____:____

9. +/- Longitude/Time Equivalent *(from Atlas or calculate below; -W, +E)*   +/- ____:____:____

    (Longitude *(as decimal)* _____ x 4 min = _____)   Subtotal = ____:____:____

10. +/- 24:00:00 if required   +/- ____:____:____

11. = LST of Birth   LST = ____:____:____

12. Southern Latitude Adjustment *(+/- 12:00:00 if Southern Latitude)*   +/- ____:____:____

13. "LST + 12" *(use in place of LST for Southern Latitude births)*   LST+12 = ____:____:____

CM-1

(Constant Multiplier for Part C: Planetary Position)

Convert GMT of Birth to decimal: _____ ÷ 24 = **CM-1** _____

	☉	☽	☿	♀	♂	♃
1. Position at 0 hr on day After birth date _____						
2. Position at 0 hr on Birth date _____						
3. Line 1 - Line 2 = Total Daily Travel						
4. Line 3 X CM-1 _____ = Travel to birth time						
5. Add lines 2 + 4 = Position at Birth						

	♄	♅	♆	♇	☊	
6. Position at 0 hr on day After birth date _____						
7. Position at 0 hr on Birth date _____						
8. Line 6 - Line 7 = Total Daily Travel						
9. Line 8 X CM-1 _____ = Travel to birth time						
10. Add lines 7 + 9 = Position at Birth						

CM-2

(Constant Multiplier for LST Interpolation)

LST of Birth ___:___:___

- Next lowest LST from Table of Houses - ___:___:___
_____

= ___:___

Convert result to decimal _____

÷ 4 = **CM-2** _____

CM-3

(Constant Multiplier for Latitude Interpolation)

Latitude of Birth ____° ____'

- Next lowest Lat from Table of Houses - ____° ____'
_____

= ____° ____'

Convert result to decimal = **CM-3** = _____

Exception: If Birth Latitude is less than 20°, divide result by 5 ÷ 5 = **CM-3** _____

House Cusp Calculation for Higher Latitude

Latitude _____°	MC	11th	12th	ASC	2nd	3rd
1. House Cusps at Later LST						
2. House Cusps at Earlier LST						
3. Line 1 - Line 2 =						
4. Line 3 X CM-2 _____ =						
5. Add lines 2 + 4 =						

House Cusp Calculation for Lower Latitude

Latitude _____°		11th	12th	ASC	2nd	3rd
6. House Cusps at Later LST						
7. House Cusps at Earlier LST						
8. Line 6 - Line 7 =						
9. Line 3 X CM-2 _____ =						
10. Add lines 7 + 9 =						

Latitude Interpolation

		11th	12th	ASC	2nd	3rd
11. House Cusps at Higher Latitude (from line 5)						
12. House Cusps at Lower Latitude (from line 10)						
13. Line 11 - Line 12 =						
14. Line 13 X CM-3 _____ =						
15. Add lines 12 + 14 = **House Cusps at Birth**						

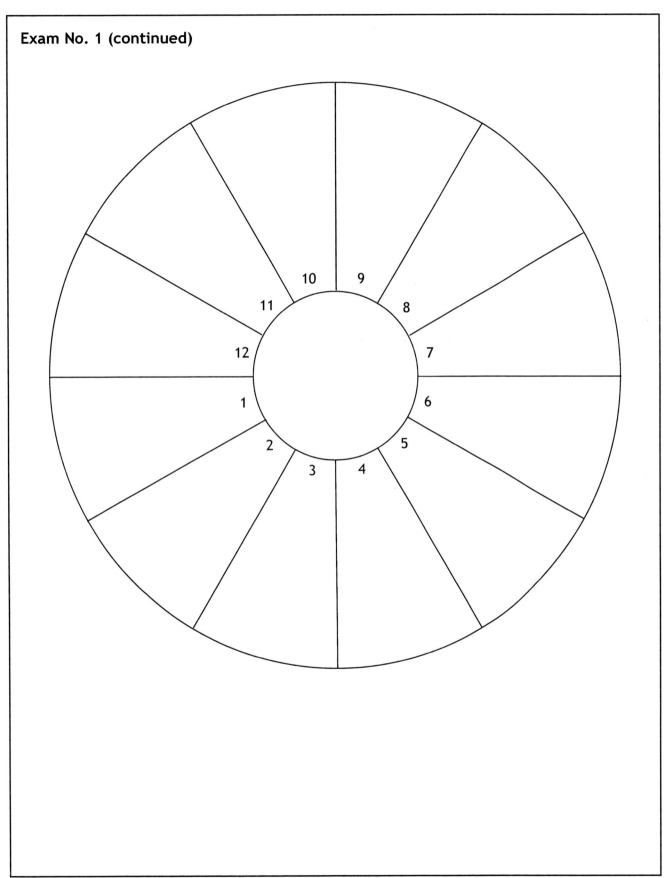

Exam No. 2. *Calculate the GMT, LST, and all planetary positions and house cusps for the following birth, without the use of forms. Blank pages have been provided following this page for your work. Then fill in the chart wheel below. Answers can be found in the Answer Key.*

April 10, 1995
10:50 pm
Seattle, WA
47° N 36' 122° W 20'

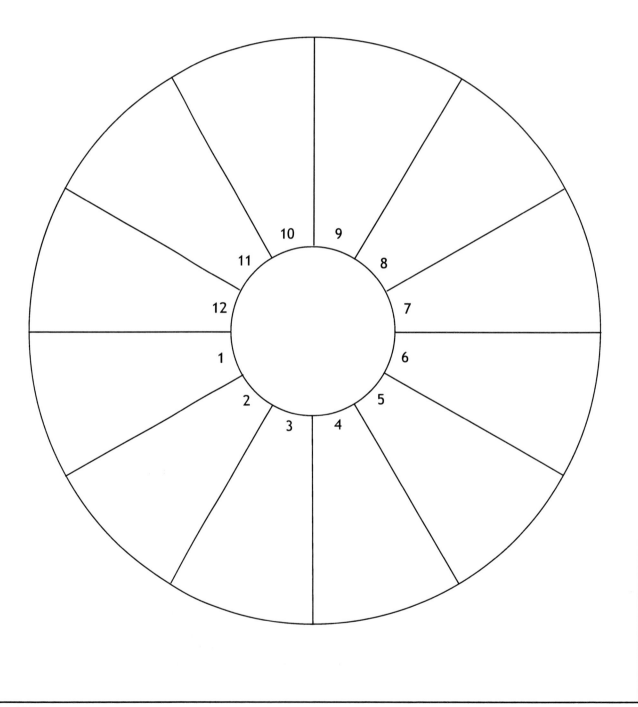

Exam No. 3. *Calculate the GMT, LST, and all planetary positions and house cusps for the following birth, without the use of forms. Blank pages have been provided following this page for your work. Then fill in the chart wheel below. Answers can be found in the Answer Key.*

January 5, 1961
4:45 am
Perth, Australia
31° S 57' 115° E 51'

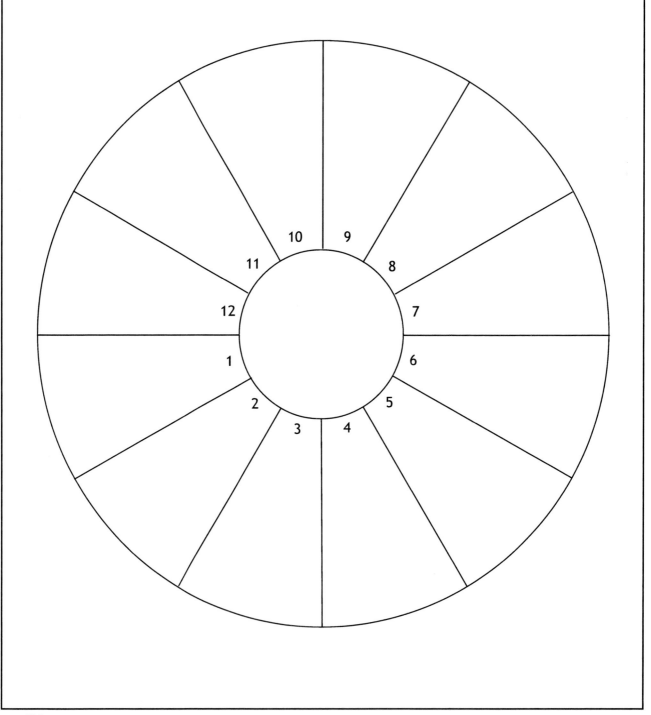

Section 6:

Aspects
&
Other Points and Measurements

Lesson 14: Aspects

Aspects are angular relationships between planets or points. This lesson will cover how to determine whether an aspect or angle exists between two planets or points; how to use **orbs**, or distances between points qualifying the existence of an aspect; and how to determine if an aspect is applying or separating. Finally how to fill out an **Aspectarian** will be demonstrated.

Major Aspects

Aspects are simply angles created by the distance or arc between two points, and are established by dividing the circle by various numbers. The **Major Aspects**, also called the **Ptolemaic Aspects** after the 2nd century astrologer Claudius Ptolemy, are based on a division of the circle by either 1, 2, 3, 4, or 6, as listed below. The word "aspect" stems from the Latin *aspecto*, meaning to look at or observe, and in fact Ptolemy described the "view" from one planet to another as an indicator of the type of relationship between the two.

> **Conjunction (☌)**, 360° divided by 1; points sharing the same degree are in conjunction.
>
> **Opposition (☍)**, 360° divided by 2; points 180° apart are in opposition.
>
> **Trine (△)**, 360° divided by 3; points 120° apart form a trine.
>
> **Square (□)**, 360° divided by 4; points 90° apart form a square.
>
> **Sextile (✶)**, 360° divided by 6; points 60° apart form a sextile.

Conjunction (☌):

Dividing the circle by 1 results in a conjunction (360 ÷ 1 = 360°). A conjunction occurs if two points or planets occupy the same place in the zodiac, and signifies a blending of energy.

Opposition (☍):

Dividing the circle by 2 produces two points directly opposite each other (360 ÷ 2 = 180°). Any two points that are separated by 180° form an opposition, signifying two opposite points of view.

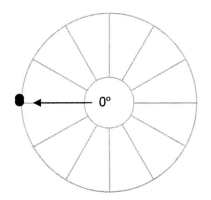

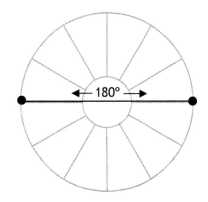

Trine (△): A Trine is produced when the chart is divided by 3 (360° ÷ 3 = 120°). Signs of the same **element** (Fire, Earth, Air and Water) form trines and are said to create an easy flow of energy. Any two points that are separated by 120 degrees form a Trine.

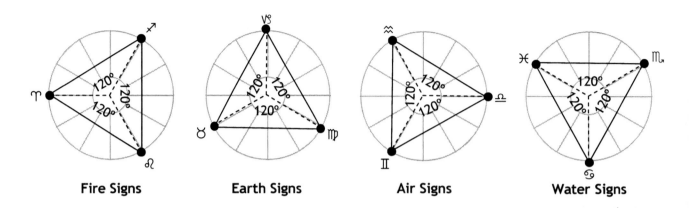

| **Fire Signs** | **Earth Signs** | **Air Signs** | **Water Signs** |

Square (□): A Square is produced when the chart is divided by 4 (360° ÷ 4 = 90°). Signs of the same **modality** (Cardinal, Fixed and Mutable) form squares and are believed to create stress resulting in increased energy. Any two points that are separated by 90 degrees form a square.

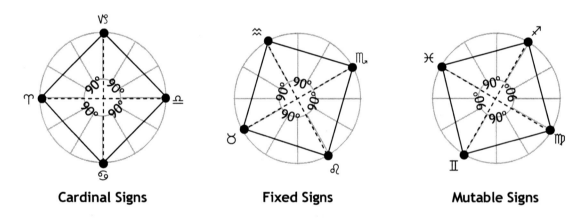

| **Cardinal Signs** | **Fixed Signs** | **Mutable Signs** |

Sextile (✶): A Sextile is formed when the chart is divided by 6 (360° ÷ 6 = 60°). Fire and Air signs form sextiles, as do Earth and Water signs. A sextile is believed to create opportunity. Any two points that are separated by 60 degrees form a sextile.

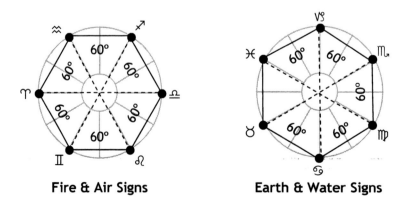

| **Fire & Air Signs** | **Earth & Water Signs** |

Minor Aspects

Minor aspects are formed by dividing the circle by larger numbers. These include:

Semisextile (⊻), 360° divided by 12, points that are 30° apart form a semisextile.

Semisquare (∠), 360° divided by 8 (Octile series), points that are 45° apart form a semi-square.

Sesquisquare (⬚), Points that are 135° apart form a sesquisquare, also called a **sesquiquadrate**. This aspect is based on a multiple of the division of 360° by 8 (Octile series).

Quincunx (⊼), Points that are 150° apart form a Quincunx, which is based on a multiple of the division of 360° by 12.

Further divisions of the circle in multiples of 5, (Quintile series) , 7 (Septile series), 9 (Nonile series), and 16 (Semioctile series) are sometimes referred to as **Harmonics**, aspects related by divisions of the chart by the same number.

Orbs

An **Orb** is a range of degrees surrounding exactitude which qualifies the existence of an aspect. An orb provides a guideline to gauge whether a planet within a few degrees of an exact aspect qualifies as being in aspect. The orbs used by various astrologers differ according to each astrologer's personal preferences, however most astrologers agree that the closer an aspect is to being exact, the stronger its influence. Most astrologers give the Sun and the Moon a wider orb than other planets. If the Sun is 100° away from another planet, although not an exact 90° angle, it would still be considered in orb of a square if a 10° orb was allowed. With a 10° orb, any planet between 80° and 100° away from the Sun would be considered in orb of a square to the Sun. In an exam, the allowable orbs are usually provided. In this lesson, the following orbs will be used for all planets when calculating aspects:

Glyph	Aspect	Orb	Range of Orb
☌	Conjunction	8°	352° - **0°** - 8°
☍	Opposition	8°	172° - **180°** - 188°
△	Trine	8°	112° - **120°** - 128°
□	Square	8°	82° - **90°** - 98°
✳	Sextile	6°	54° - **60°** - 66°
⊻	Semisextile	3°	27° - **30°** - 33°
∠	Semisquare	4°	41° - **45°** - 49°
⬚	Sesquisquare	2°	133° - **135°** - 137°
⊼	Quincunx	2°	148° - **150°** - 152°

Orbs qualify the existence of aspects between two planets or points.

Aspect Patterns

The Grand Square, Grand Trine, T-Square, Yod, and Mystic Rectangle are aspect patterns formed by multiple aspects within charts. They are most easily recognized by the shapes created:

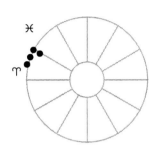

Stellium:
Three or more points
in conjunction

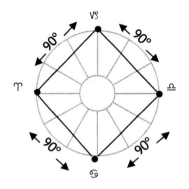

Grand Square or Grand Cross:
Four points 90° apart, usually in
the same modality (Cardinal,
Fixed or Mutable)

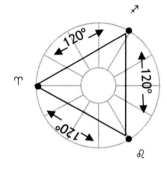

Grand Trine:
Three points 120° apart,
usually in the same Element
(Fire, Earth, Air or Water)

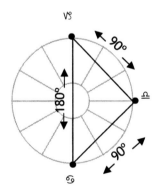

T-Square:
Two points in opposition and
both points forming a square
to a third point.

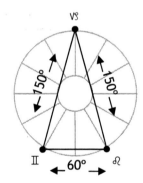

Yod:
Two points Sextile one another
while both form a Quincunx to
a third point.

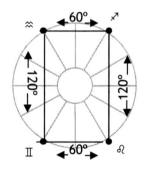

Mystic Rectangle:
Two Trines, two Sextiles
and two Oppositions.

Arc

Two arcs exist between any two points in a chart - a shorter arc and a longer arc. Notice in the diagram to the right that the distance between the Sun at 0°♈ and Mars at 0°♐ can be measured in two ways: via a longer arc measured counterclockwise from 0°♈ to 0°♐ equaling 240° or via a shorter arc measured clockwise from 0°♐ to 0°♈ equaling 120°.

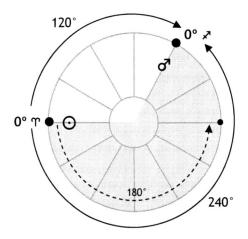

The closest distance or **shortest arc** between two points is used to determine the existence of an aspect. If that distance is equal to or within orb of an aspect, then an aspect exists. Notice that 180° is the largest "short arc" possible. Once the distance between the two points reaches 180° then the opposite arc begins to diminish and becomes the shorter arc. The sum of the shorter arc and the longer arc will always equal 360°.

Calculating the Arc Between Two Points

There are three steps involved when calculating the closest distance between points:

Step 1. Convert the zodiacal degrees and minutes of the planets or points to absolute longitude.

Step 2. Subtract the lesser degree from the greater degree.

Step 3. If the result is more than 180°, subtract 360° to find the shortest arc. Disregard the minus sign of the result - the minus sign simply indicates that the arc is being measured in the opposite direction.

Example 1.

Let's find the distance between 28° Capricorn and 13° Sagittarius, which when converted to absolute longitude become 298° and 253° respectively. The lesser degree is subtracted from the greater degree as follows:

Greater Degree		298°
- Lesser Degree	-	253°
= Arc	=	45°

The closest distance between these two points is 45 degrees. These two points are in semi-square aspect to each other.

Example 2.

Now let's find the distance between 26°♓ 14' and 2°♈ 06'. Converted to absolute longitude, 26°♓ 14' = 356.23° and 2°♈ 06' = 2.1°.

Greater Degree	356.23°
- Lesser Degree	- 2.10°
	= 354.13°
- 360° if greater than 180°	- 360.00°
= Arc	= 5.87°

Notice that in this example the initial result was greater than 180° and therefore represented the longer arc instead of the shorter arc. 360° needed to be subtracted from this arc to determine the shorter arc. The result of 5.87 or 5° 52' represents the closest distance between these two points. These two points are within orb of a conjunction.

Example 3.

Now let's find the distance between 6°♋ 41' and 10°♏ 05':

Greater Degree	220.08°
- Lesser Degree	- 96.68°
= Arc	= 123.40°

The closest distance between these two points is **123.4° or 123° 24'**. This distance would be within orb of a Trine.

Example 4.

Now let's find the distance between 10°♒ 05' and 1°♉ 29':

Greater Degree	310.08°
- Lesser Degree	- 31.48°
	= 278.60°
- 360° if greater than 180°	- 360.00°
= Arc	= 81.40°

The closest distance between these two points is **81.4° or 81° 24'**. Notice that this distance is slightly under 82° and is not within the given orb of 8° for a square.

Applying and Separating Aspects

Planetary movement creates a continuing cycle of varying relationships and aspects between planets and points. As a result aspects are either **applying** or **separating**. **Applying aspects** occur when a faster moving planet is within orb of a slower moving planet or point and is approaching exactitude. **Separating aspects** occur when a faster moving planet is moving away and exiting the orb of an aspect. A **partile aspect** is one that is exact to the degree. The closer an aspect is to exact, the stronger its influence will be. Applying aspects are considered stronger than separating aspects because they are building in strength as they approach exactitude.

The faster moving planet is the determining factor in whether an aspect is applying or separating. In order to determine which planet is faster it is helpful to know the **planetary cycles**, or the time it takes each planet to progress through the zodiac in its orbit around the Sun. The Moon, for instance, will always be the planet applying or separating in aspect to any other planet because it is the fastest planet. When two planets with similar speeds are in aspect, an ephemeris must be consulted to determine which of the two planets is moving more quickly in its orbit and is thus either applying or separating from the other. Further, a planet that is normally faster moving may become the slower planet if it is retrograde or about to become retrograde. Always consult an ephemeris when in doubt.

Planetary Cycles

☽ - 28 days	♃ - 12 years
☉ - 1 year	♄ - 29 years
☿ - 1 year (always within 28° of the Sun)	♅ - 84 years
♀ - 1 year (always within 48° of the Sun)	♆ - 165 years
♂ - 2 years	♇ - 245 years

In the chart to the right, notice that the Moon at 6°♋41' is applying toward a trine to the Sun at 10° ♏ 05'. Both the Moon and Sun are in water signs. As the Moon moves through the sign of Cancer, it will reach 10°♋ at which point it will form an exact trine to the Sun at 10°♏.

The Moon is separating from a square to Venus at 5° ♎ 02' by a little more than 1°. Both the Moon and Venus are in cardinal signs.

The Sun at 10° ♏ 05' is separating from an opposition to the North Node at 2°♉ 06'. The Sun is the faster moving point in this instance.

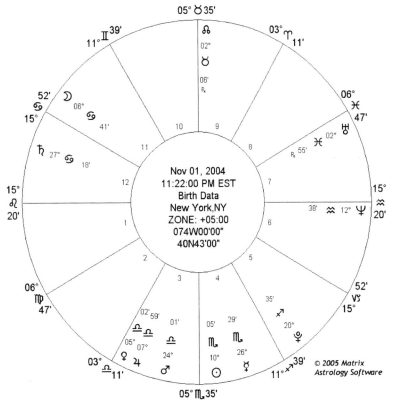

Nov 01, 2004
11:22:00 PM EST
Birth Data
New York,NY
ZONE: +05:00
074W00'00"
40N43'00"

© 2005 Matrix
Astrology Software

The Aspectarian

An **Aspectarian** is a grid showing the aspects between all planets and sensitive points in a chart. Although easily generated by a computer, most certification exams require students to calculate aspects and complete an aspectarian manually. Knowing how to calculate aspects and orbs manually fosters a greater understanding of a computer generated aspectarian and allows an astrologer to make more informed interpretations.

An aspectarian is read from top to bottom and across from left to right. If an aspect exists between two points in a chart, the symbol for the relevant aspect is placed in the grid where the column and the row corresponding to the two planets forming the aspect meet. The aspectarian below shows the aspects between planets and points in the chart on the previous page. Notice that in addition to the aspect symbol, the orb of the aspect and whether it is applying ("a") or separating ("s") is also indicated.

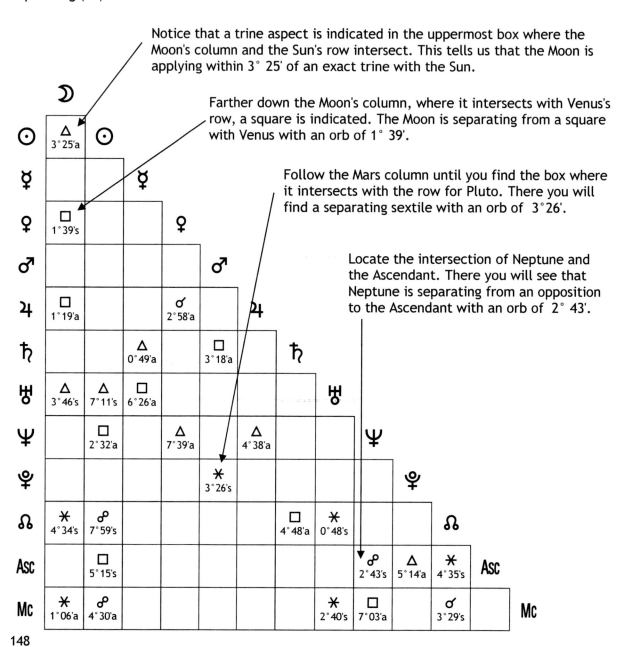

Notice that a trine aspect is indicated in the uppermost box where the Moon's column and the Sun's row intersect. This tells us that the Moon is applying within 3° 25' of an exact trine with the Sun.

Farther down the Moon's column, where it intersects with Venus's row, a square is indicated. The Moon is separating from a square with Venus with an orb of 1° 39'.

Follow the Mars column until you find the box where it intersects with the row for Pluto. There you will find a separating sextile with an orb of 3°26'.

Locate the intersection of Neptune and the Ascendant. There you will see that Neptune is separating from an opposition to the Ascendant with an orb of 2° 43'.

Calculating Aspects using the Aspect Calculation Form

Let's manually calculate the aspects for the natal chart shown on page 147 using the Aspect Calculation Form provided in the Appendix. Although this process is extremely tedious, we find it is the best way to calculate precise aspects and orbs. A blank Aspect Calculation Form has been included in the Appendix for this purpose.

There are five steps needed to calculate aspects using the Aspect Calculation Form:

Step 1. Record the zodiacal degree and minute of each planet and point across the top of the form and down the left side, then convert all positions to absolute longitude.

Step 2. List the allowable orbs being used at the bottom of the form and determine the degree range for each aspect.

Step 3. Starting with the Moon, find the distance between the Moon and each planet by subtracting the lesser longitude from the greater longitude. If any results are greater than 180°, subtract 360° and record that result. Repeat this process for all remaining planets and points.

Step 4. Determine if the difference in each case is within orb of an aspect. Circle those that are and note the aspect symbol.

Step 5. If required, transcribe the circled aspects to an aspectarian. If orbs are also required, find the difference between the result from Step 3 and the number of degrees represented by the aspect if exact.

Example 5.

Notice that in the partial aspect calculation form below, the zodiacal position of each planet and its equivalent absolute longitude has been recorded in the top row as well as down the left hand column. Calculations are then made to find the difference between the planet shown at the top of each column and the planet listed on the left side of each row.

	☽ 6° ♋ 41' 96.68	☉ 10° ♏ 05' 220.08	☿ 26° ♏ 29' 236.48	♀ 5° ♎ 02' 185.03	♂ 24° ♎ 01' 204.02
☽ 6° ♋ 41' 96.68		-96.68 =123.4 △	-96.68 =139.8	-96.68 =88.35 □	-96.68 =107.34
☉ 10° ♏ 05' 220.08			-220.08 =16.4	220.08 =35.05	220.08 =16.06
☿ 26° ♏ 29' 236.48				236.48 =51.45	236.48 =32.46 ⚹

Notice that the Sun's absolute longitude is 220.08°, and the Moon's absolute longitude is 96.68°. The difference between these is 123.4° and is recorded in the box where the Sun's column and Moon's row intersect. This falls within the allowable range of 112°-128° for a trine, if using an 8° orb. If the exact orb of this aspect was needed, we would simply find the difference between 123.4° and 120° which represents an exact trine.

On the following page a full Aspect Calculation Form has been used to calculate both major and minor aspects for this chart.

	☽ 6°♋41' 96.68	☉ 10°♏05 220.08	☿ 26°♏29 236.48	♀ 5°♎02 185.03	♂ 24°♎01 204.02	♃ 7°♎59 187.98	♄ 27°♋18 117.3	♅ 2°♓55' 332.92	♆ 12°♒38 312.63	♇ 20°♐35 260.58	☊ 2°♉06 32.1	ASC 15°♌20 135.33	MC 5°♉35 35.58
☽ 6°♋41' 96.68		96.68 =123.4 △	96.68 =139.8	96.68 =88.35 □	96.68 =107.3	96.68 =91.3 □	96.68 =20.62	96.68 =236.24 △-360 123.76	96.68 =215.95 -360 144.05	96.68 =163.9	96.68 =64.58 ✶	96.68 =38.65	96.68 =61.1 ✶
☉ 10°♏05 220.08			220.08 =16.4	220.08 =35.05	220.08 =16.06	220.08 32.1 ⊻	220.08 =102.78	220.08 =112.84 △	220.08 =92.55 □	220.08 =40.5	220.08 =188.7 ☍	220.08 =84.75 □	220.08 =184.5 ☍
☿ 26°♏29 236.48				236.48 51.48	236.48 32.46 ⊻	236.48 48.5 ∠	236.48 119.18 △	236.48 96.44 □	236.48 76.15	236.48 24.1	236.48 204.38 -360 155.62	236.48 101.15	236.48 200.09 -360 159.1
♀ 5°♎02' 185.03					185.03 18.99	185.03 2.95 ♂	185.03 67.73	185.03 147.89	185.03 127.6 △	185.03 75.55	185.03 152.93	185.03 49.7	185.03 149.45 ⊼
♂ 24°♎01' 204.02						204.02 16.04	204.02 86.72 □	204.02 128.9	204.02 108.61	204.02 56.56 ✶	204.02 171.92	204.02 68.69	204.02 168.44
♃ 7°♎59' 187.98							187.98 70.68	187.98 144.94	187.98 124.65 △	187.98 72.6	187.98 155.88	187.98 52.65	187.98 152.4
♄ 27°♋18' 117.3								117.3 215.62 -360 144.38	117.3 195.33 -360 164.67	117.3 143.28	117.3 85.2 □	117.3 18.03	117.3 81.72
♅ 2°♓55' 332.92									332.92 20.29	332.92 72.34	332.92 300.82 -360 ✶59.18	332.92 197.59 -360 162.41	332.92 297.34 -360 ✶62.66
♆ 12°♒38' 312.63										312.63 52.05	312.63 280.53 -360 79.47	312.63 177.3 ☍	312.63 277.06 □-360 82.95
♇ 20°♐35' 260.58											260.58 228.48 -360 131.52	260.58 125.25 △	260.58 225 -360 ⊡135
☊ 2°♉06' 32.1												32.1 103.23	32.1 3.48 ♂
ASC 15°♌20' 135.33													135.33 99.75
MC 5°♉35' 35.58													

Given Allowable Orbs

Aspect	Orb	Range
♂	8°	352° - 0° - 8°
⊻	3°	27° - 30° - 33°
∠	4°	41° - 45° - 49°
✶	6°	54° - 60° - 66°
□	8°	82° - 90° - 98°
△	8°	112° - 120° - 128°
⊡	2°	133° - 135° - 137°
⊼	2°	148° - 150° - 152°
☍	8°	172° - 180° - 188°

Calculating Orbs Mathematically

Often, certification exams require students to identify the closest aspect in a chart. In order to answer this question, orbs need to be calculated for each aspect found on the Aspect Calculation Form. The aspect with the smallest orb is the closest aspect in a chart.

To determine the actual orb, take the arc found in the aspect calculations and subtract the arc of the aspect if exact. This process will give the exact orb for the aspect between two points.

	☽ 6° ♋ 41' 96.68	☉ 10° ♏ 05 220.08	☿ 26° ♏ 29 236.48	♀ 5° ♎ 02 185.03	♂ 24° ♎ 01 204.02	♃ 7° ♎ 59 187.98	♄ 27° ♋ 18 117.3	♅ 2° ♓ 55' 332.92	♆ 12° ♒ 38 312.63	♇ 20° ♐ 35 260.58	☊ 2° ♉ 06 32.1
☽ 6° ♋ 41' 96.68		96.68 =123.4 △	96.68 =139.8	96.68 =88.35 □	96.68 =107.3	96.68 =91.3 □	96.68 =20.62	96.68 =236.24 △-360 123.76	96.68 =215.95 -360 144.05	96.68 =163.9	96.68 =64.58 ✶

Example 6.

Let's find the exact orb of the trine between the Sun and Moon in the aspectarian above and determine if it is applying or separating.

$$\begin{array}{ll} \text{Arc between Moon and Sun} & 123.4° \\ \text{- Arc of exact Trine} & -120° \\ \hline \text{= exact orb of aspect} & 3.4° \text{ orb} \end{array}$$

The Moon at 6° ♋ 41' is the faster moving planet and is applying by an orb of 3.4° to a Trine to the Sun at 10° ♏ 05'.

Always check the sign and degree of the faster moving planet to determine if it is applying or separating from the slower planet or point.

Example 7.

Now let's determine the exact orb between the Moon and Venus:

$$\begin{array}{ll} \text{Arc between Moon and Venus} & 88.35° \\ \text{- Arc of exact Square} & -90° \\ \hline \text{= exact orb of aspect} & -1.65° \text{ orb} \end{array}$$

The Moon at 6° ♋ 41' is separating by an orb of 1.65 from a square to Venus at 5° ♎ 02'. Even though the Moon is in Cancer and "moving towards" Libra, the square became exact when it was at 5° ♋ 02', the same degree and minute as Venus' position.

Lesson 14 Exercises

Determine the aspects using the given allowable orbs for all planets and personal points for the chart below, using the Aspect Calculation Form on the following page. Fill in the aspectarian, then answer the three questions below. Answers can be found in the Answer Key in the Appendix.

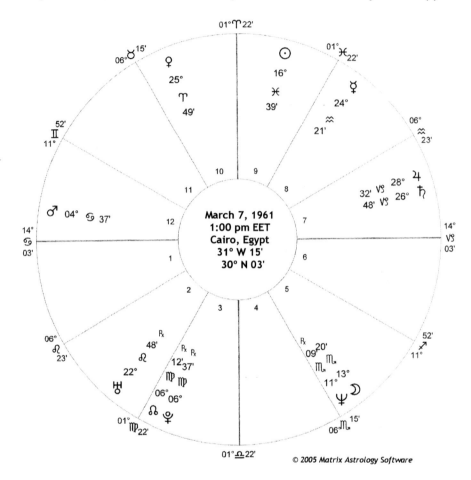

© 2005 Matrix Astrology Software

	Major Aspects			Minor Aspects	
Aspect	Orb	Range	Aspect	Orb	Range
☌	8°	352° - 0° - 8°	⚺	3°	27° - 30° - 33°
✶	6°	54° - 60° - 66°	∠	4°	41° - 45° - 49°
□	8°	82° - 90° - 98°	⚌	2°	133° - 135° - 137°
△	8°	112° - 120° - 128°	⚻	2°	148° - 150° - 152°
☍	8°	172° - 180° - 188°			

1. The closest aspect in the chart is:_____

2. What was the last aspect made by the Moon? _____

3. What is the next aspect made by the Moon? _____

152

Aspect Calculation Form

	☽	☉	☿	♀	♂	♃	♄	♅	♆	♇	☊	ASC	MC
☽													
☉													
☿													
♀													
♂													
♃													
♄													
♅													
♆													
♇													
☊													
ASC													
MC													

Lesson 15: Declinations

Declinations measure a planet or point's distance north or south of the Celestial Equator. Many astrologers believe that relationships between planets sharing similar or opposite declinations are significant and should be considered along with other aspects in a chart. This lesson provides an overview of declinations, how to calculate them, and how to determine if two points are in a **parallel** or **contraparallel** relationship to each other.

Different Coordinate Systems

Let's start by defining three different coordinate systems that exist for measuring the position of a planet or other point in space. All calculations covered in previous lessons have used measurements from the **Ecliptic System**. In this system, the Ecliptic forms the horizontal plane. A

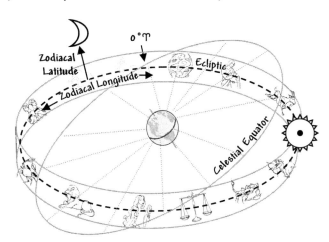

planet's position east of 0° Aries along the Ecliptic is called its **zodiacal longitude**. Its position north or south of the Ecliptic is called **zodiacal latitude**. Because the Sun is always on the Ecliptic, its zodiacal latitude will always be 0°. The Moon and other planets, with orbits close to the same plane as the Earth's, generally have zodiacal latitudes of less than 9° north or south of the Ecliptic. In fact, it is this 18° zone on either side of the Ecliptic that defines the zodiac belt. Pluto's orbit deviates more than the other planets resulting in zodiacal latitudes of up to 17° north or south.

The **Equatorial System** uses the Celestial Equator as its horizontal plane. You will recall from Lesson 5 that the Celestial Equator is simply the Earth's Equator projected out into space. A planet's distance east of 0° Aries measured along the Celestial Equator is called **right ascension**. Its distance north or south of the Celestial Equator is called **declination**. In the diagram to the

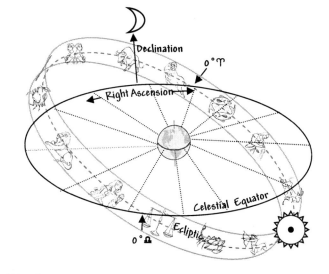

right notice that the Ecliptic is at a 23½° slant to the Celestial Equator. This angle is called the **obliquity of the Ecliptic**. When the Sun is located at the equinoctial points 0° Aries or 0° Libra its declination will be 0°, but at all other times the Sun will have either a northern declination, if located in the signs Aries through Virgo, or a southern declination, if located in Libra through Pisces. Its greatest declination occurs at the solstice points 0° Cancer or 0° Capricorn when it is 23½° North or South. The Moon and planets are on slightly different orbital planes and therefore have a greater possible range of declination.

A third system called the **Horizon System** uses the celestial horizon as its horizontal plane. Coordinates are given in **Azimuth**, which is an object's compass bearing, and **Altitude**, which is its distance in degrees above or below the celestial horizon. This is the system generally used in celestial navigation.

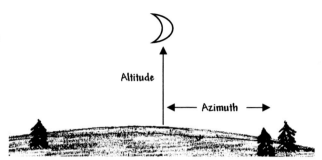

Parallels & Contraparallels of Declination

When two planets share the same degree of declination and are on the same side of the Celestial Equator they are considered **parallel** (‖), because they both share the same plane of parallel to the Celestial Equator. Generally a 1° orb is allowed for parallels. Notice in the diagram below that the Sun at 17° and Mercury at 18° are within a degree of each other and are both south of the Celestial Equator. Therefore, the Sun and Mercury are parallel. This is notated ☉‖☿. The Moon at 8°north and Uranus at 8°north are also parallel, because they share the same degree of declination and are both north of the Celestial Equator. In horoscope delineation a parallel is thought to function similarly to a weak conjunction. When two planets are both conjunct and parallel, the conjunction is strengthened.

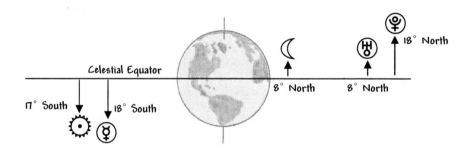

When two planets share the same degree of declination but one is north of the Celestial Equator and the other is south, they are considered **contraparallel** (⸗). In the diagram above, Mercury and Pluto are contraparallel because Mercury's declination is 18° south and Pluto's declination is 18° north. This is notated ☿⸗♇. The Sun at 17° south is also contraparallel Pluto, because it is within a 1° orb. Contraparallels are thought to function similarly to weak oppositions. When two planets are in opposition to each other and also contraparallel, the opposition is made stronger.

Planets within one degree of orb in the same polarity are Parallel (‖)

Planets within one degree of orb but in opposite polarities are Contraparallel (⸗)

Calculating Planetary Declinations

The steps required to calculate planetary declinations are very similar to those used to calculate the zodiacal positions of the planets in Lesson 8:

Step 1. Determine a constant multiplier using the GMT of Birth. This is the same constant multiplier "CM-1" used for determining planetary positions as explained in lesson 8.

Step 2. Determine the daily change in declination. This is done by taking the planet's declination at 0 hour on the day of birth and subtracting it from the 0 hour position on the following day. If the result is more than a degree, convert it to minutes.

Step 3. Multiply the daily change in declination for each planet (from Step 2) by the constant multiplier (from Step 1). The result represents the change in declination from 0 hour to the time of birth.

Step 4. Add (or subtract) the result of Step 3 to (from) the declination at 0 hour on the date of birth. The result is the planet's exact declination at the time of birth.

As with the zodiacal positions of the planets, location of birth does not affect planetary declinations. These will be exactly the same for everyone born on the same day at the same GMT.

The next two examples demonstrate how to calculate declinations for planets both north and south of the Celestial Equator, using the partial ephemeris listing for the month of September 1987 reprinted below. Notice that declinations are listed with a plus sign indicating a northern declination and a minus sign indicating a southern declination. When transcribing declinations from an ephemeris in preparation for calculation, it is important to transcribe these signs along with the degree and minute values, as positive (northern) values will be added and negative (southern) values will be subtracted during the calculation process. We suggest you also add an 'N' or 'S' to help alleviate possible confusion.

Northern Declinations are indicated by + or 'N'
Southern Declinations are indicated by - or 'S'

GMT +0:00 Tropical Geocentric Decl	Moon ☽	Sun ☉	Mercury ☿	Venus ♀	Mars ♂	Jupiter ♃	Saturn ♄	Uranus ♅	Neptune ♆	Pluto ♇	True Node ☊
Sep 8 1987	−05°53'	+05°59'	+00°04'	+05°36'	+08°43'	+09°45'	−21°14'	−23°24'	−22°19'	+00°57'	+00°57'
Sep 9 1987	+01°05'	+05°36'	−00°41'	+05°06'	+08°29'	+09°43'	−21°14'	−23°24'	−22°19'	+00°56'	+00°57'
Sep 10 1987	+07°50'	+05°14'	−01°26'	+04°37'	+08°14'	+09°41'	−21°15'	−23°24'	−22°19'	+00°55'	+00°57'
Sep 11 1987	+14°01'	+04°51'	−02°10'	+04°07'	+07°59'	+09°40'	−21°15'	−23°24'	−22°19'	+00°54'	+00°57'
Sep 12 1987	+19°22'	+04°28'	−02°54'	+03°37'	+07°45'	+09°38'	−21°15'	−23°24'	−22°19'	+00°53'	+00°58'
Sep 13 1987	+23°38'	+04°05'	−03°37'	+03°07'	+07°30'	+09°36'	−21°16'	−23°24'	−22°19'	+00°52'	+00°58'
Sep 14 1987	+26°40'	+03°42'	−04°20'	+02°36'	+07°15'	+09°34'	−21°16'	−23°24'	−22°19'	+00°51'	+00°58'
Sep 15 1987	+28°21'	+03°19'	−05°02'	+02°06'	+07°00'	+09°33'	−21°17'	−23°24'	−22°19'	+00°50'	+00°58'
Sep 16 1987	+28°39'	+02°56'	−05°44'	+01°36'	+06°45'	+09°31'	−21°17'	−23°24'	−22°20'	+00°49'	+00°58'
Sep 17 1987	+27°37'	+02°33'	−06°25'	+01°05'	+06°30'	+09°29'	−21°18'	−23°24'	−22°20'	+00°48'	+00°58'
Sep 18 1987	+25°19'	+02°10'	−07°06'	+00°35'	+06°15'	+09°26'	−21°18'	−23°24'	−22°20'	+00°48'	+00°58'

Declination ephemeris prepared using Solarfire v.5

You will find that not all ephemerides include planetary declinations. In order to calculate declinations, you will need an ephemeris that lists them such as *The Astrolabe World Ephemeris 2001-2050,* or a computer-generated declination ephemeris like the example above, generated using the *Solarfire* program. Notice that the Moon is often listed first, before the Sun, in most computer-generated declination ephemeredes.

Example 1.

Let's find the exact declination of the Sun for a birth on September 8, 1987 at 8:37 GMT.

Step 1. Determine a constant multiplier using the GMT of Birth. This is the same constant multiplier "CM-1" used for determining planetary positions as explained in Lesson 8.

CM-1
(Constant Multiplier for Part C: Planetary Position)

Convert GMT of Birth to decimal: __8.62__   ÷ 24 = **CM-1**   ___.359___

Step 2. Determine the daily change in declination. This is done by taking the planet's declination at 0 hour on the day of birth and subtracting it from the 0 hour position on the following day. If the result is more than a degree, convert it to minutes.

Sun 0 hr declination on September 9, 1987	+5° 36' N
- Sun 0 hr declination on September 8, 1987	- +5° 59' N
= Daily declination change	- 23'

The daily change in declination of the Sun from 0 hour September 8, 1987 to 0 hour September 9, 1987 was (minus) - 23 minutes. Remember that declinations can be either a positive (North) or negative (South) number, so be sure to include the sign in your calculations and mark the result accordingly.

Step 3. Multiply the daily change in declination for each planet by the constant multiplier. The result represents the change in declination from 0 hour to the time of birth.

Daily change:	- 23'
x CM—1:	x .359
=	- 8.25, rounded to 8'

The declination of the Sun changed –8 minutes between 0 hour on September 8th and 8:37 GMT, the time of birth. Remember that if the daily change has a minus sign, the result in this step will also have a minus sign.

Step 4. Add (or subtract) the result of Step 3 to (from) the declination at 0 hour on the date of birth. The result is the planet or point's exact declination at the time of birth.

0 hr Position on September 8, 1987	+ 5° 59' N
+/- declination change (step 3)	- 08'
= Declination at Birth	+ 5° 51' N

The declination of the Sun on September 8, 1987 at the time of birth was 5° 51' North.

Example 2.

In this example let's determine the exact declination of the Moon for the same birth.

Step 1. Determine a constant multiplier using the GMT of Birth. This is **.359** from the previous example. Remember that the same CM-1 is applied to all planetary declinations for a specific birth time.

Step 2. Determine the daily change in declination.

Moon (0hr) on 9/9/87	+1° 05' N
Moon (0hr) on 9/8/87	- - 5° 53' S
= Daily change in declination	6° 58'

Notice in this example that the Moon has changed from a northern declination to a southern declination during this 24 hour period. As a result, we are subtracting a negative number (the southern declination value) which is the same as adding a positive number. Therefore, the Moon's total change in declination from 5° 53' South to 1° 05' North was +6° 58', or 6° 58' traveling northward. Refer to the diagram at the bottom of this page for an illustration of the Moon's movement in this example.

Step 3. Multiply the daily change in declination for each planet by the constant multiplier. The result represents the change in declination from 0 hour to the time of birth.

Daily change in declination 6° 58', or 418'	
X CM-1	x .359
=	150', or 2° 30'

The Moon's change in declination from 0 hour on the day of birth to the GMT of birth was +2° 30'.

Step 4. Add (or subtract) the result of Step 3 to (from) the declination at 0 hour on the date of birth. The result is the planet or point's exact declination at the time of birth.

Moon (0hr) on 9/8/87:	- 5° 53' S
+ Declination change (Step 3)	+ 2° 30'
= Moon declination at birth:	= - 3° 23' S

In this step, the change in declination is being added to a negative number. The result is negative 3° 23' , or 3° 23' South.

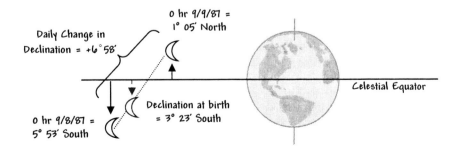

Calculating the Declination of the Ascendant and Midheaven

Just like the planets, each point along the Ecliptic will have a declination either north or south of the Celestial Equator. While planetary movement creates changing declinations however, the Ecliptic remains in a fixed relationship to the Celestial Equator. This gives each degree of the zodiac along the Ecliptic a fixed declination.

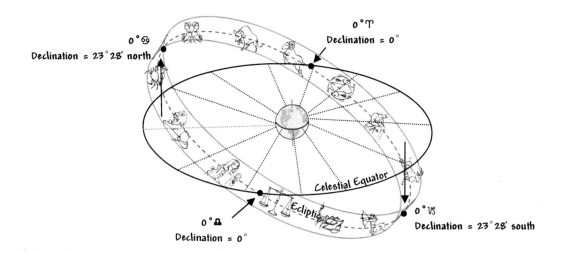

Calculating the declination of the Ascendant and Midheaven in a chart requires a few steps, but is easily done by using the **Table of Declination of Degrees on the Ecliptic** included on page 312 in the Appendix. This table lists the declination of each degree of the zodiac along the ecliptic. These values are then used to interpolate in order to arrive at an exact declination for the degree and minute of the Ascendant and Midheaven.

There are four steps to determine the declination of a point along the ecliptic:

Step 1. Determine a constant multiplier. This is done by converting the minutes of the point in question into a decimal of a degree. This decimal becomes the constant multiplier.

Step 2. Determine the change in declination between the next highest and next lowest zodiacal degree. This is done by subtracting the declination of the next lowest degree from that of the next highest degree. If the result is more than a degree, convert it to minutes.

Step 3. Multiply the change in declination by the constant multiplier. The result represents the change in declination from the next lowest degree to the point in question.

Step 4. Add (or subtract) the result of Step 3 to (from) the declination of the next lowest zodiacal degree. The result is the point's exact declination.

Example 3.

In this example we will use the relevant portions of the Declination Calculation Form provided in the Appendix of this book to demonstrate calculation of the declination of an Ascendant located at **23° ♎ 15'**.

Step 1. Determine a constant multiplier. This is done by converting the minutes of the point in question, in this case the Ascendant, into a decimal of a degree. Notice how we have converted 15 minutes to .25 in the upper portion of the form to the right. This will be the constant multiplier.

Step 2. Determine the change in declination between the next highest and next lowest zodiacal degree. This is done by subtracting the next lowest zodiacal listing from the next highest zodiacal listing found in the **Table of Declination of Degrees on the Ecliptic**, as shown in boxes 1, 2 and 3 of the form on the right. This results in a change of 22'.

Step 3. Multiply the change in declination by the constant multiplier. The result represents the change in declination from the next lowest degree to the point in question. See box 4 of the form on the right.

Step 4. Add the result of Step 3 to the declination of the next lowest zodiacal degree. The result is the point's exact declination. In this example, the Ascendant 23° ♎ 15' has a declination of 9° 03' South.

Example 4.

Now let's repeat the process for a Midheaven located at **0° ♌ 49'**. Notice the steps taken on the form to the right to arrive at a final declination for the Midheaven of 19° 59' North.

Ascendant Declination Calculation	
Zodiacal Position **23° ♎ 15'** Convert minutes to decimal (15'÷60) = CM **.25** *(use for Step 4 below)*	**Asc**
1. **Declination** of next highest listed zodiacal degree **24° ♎ 00'**	- 9° 19' S
2. **Declination** of next lowest listed zodiacal degree **23° ♎ 00'**	- 8° 57' S
3. Line 1 - Line 2 = Change in Declination	- 22'
4. Line 3 x CM **.25**	- 5.5' - or 6'
Add lines 2+4 = **ASC** Declination at Birth (N = +, S = -)	- 8° 63' S, Or - 9° 03' S

Midheaven Declination Calculation	
Zodiacal Position **0° ♌ 49'** Convert minutes to decimal (49'÷60) = CM **.82** *(use for Step 4 below)*	**MC**
1. **Declination** of next highest listed zodiacal degree **1° ♌ 00'**	+ 19° 57' N
2. **Declination** of next lowest listed zodiacal degree **0° ♌ 00'**	+ 20° 10' N
3. Line 1 - Line 2 = Change in Declination	-13'
4. Line 3 x CM **.82**	-11'
Add lines 2+4 = **MC** Declination at Birth (N = +, S = -)	**+ 19° 59' N**

Determining Parallel & Contraparallel Aspects

Determining if any two planets or points in a chart are in parallel or contraparallel aspect can be done simply by listing the declinations in ascending order, then scanning the list to see if any are within one degree of orb.

Example 5.

For this example we will use declinations which have already been calculated using the following birth data:

September 15, 1987, 8:37 GMT
Greenwich, England

The declinations of the planets, ASC and MC are listed in ascending order in the table to the right. The orb between any two declinations is then found by calculating the difference between them.

In this example, the orb between Venus and the North Node is found by determining the difference between their declinations:

$$\begin{array}{r} ♀ \ 1° \ 55' \ N \\ - \ ☊ \ 0° \ 59' \ N \\ \hline = \quad 56' \end{array}$$

The difference between Venus and the North Node is less than 1°. They both have northern declinations and are therefore considered parallel. This is notated ♀ ‖ ☊.

The difference between Pluto and the North Node is also less than 1°. They are also parallel, notated ♇ ‖ ☊.

The difference between Jupiter and the Ascendant is also less than 1°, however in this case Jupiter has a northern declination while the Ascendant has a southern declination. They are contraparallel, which is notated ♃ ⫲ Asc .

Parallel and contraparallel aspects are noted in an aspectarian the same way any other aspect is noted between two planets, using the ‖ and ⫲ symbols.

Declinations Listed in Ascending order
♇ 0° 50' N
☊ 0° 59' N
♀ 1° 55' N
☉ 3° 11' N
☿ 5° 17' S
♂ 6° 55' N
Asc 9° 13' S
♃ 9° 32' N
Mc 19° 59' N
♄ 21° 17' S
♆ 22° 20' S
♅ 23° 24' S
☽ 28° 28' N

1° orb is used for Parallels & Contraparallels

As with any other aspect, note Parallels & Contraparallels in an aspectarian using the ‖ and ⫲ symbols

162

Example 6.

Using the Declination Calculation Form from the Appendix and the declination ephemeris shown on page 157, let's calculate the declination of all planets, Ascendant and Midheaven for the following birth:

September 16, 1987 6:00 GMT
Asc: 28° ♋ 16'   MC: 12° ♈ 18'

Declinations of the outer planets and nodes change minimally in a 24-hour day, so interpolation is usually not necessary. Spaces are provided to fill in these declinations directly from the ephemeris.

(N = +, S = -)	☽	☉	☿	♀	♂	♃	♄
1. Declination 0 hr day after birth date **9/17/87**	+27° 37' N	+2° 33' N	-6° 25' S	+1° 05' N	+6° 30' N	+9° 29' N	-21° 18' S
2. Declination 0 hr on Birth date **9/16/87**	+28° 39' N	+2° 56' N	-5° 44' S	+1° 36' N	+6° 45' N	+9° 31' N	-21° 17' S
3. Line 1 - Line 2 = Total Daily Change in Declination	-62'	-23'	-41'	-31'	-15'	-2'	-1'
4. Line 3 X CM-1 **.250** = Declination change to Birth GMT	-16'	-6'	-10'	-8'	-4'	-1'	0'
5. Add lines 2 + 4 = Declination at Birth (N = +, S = -)	+28° 23' N	+2° 50' N	-5° 54' S	+1° 28' N	+6° 41' N	+9° 30' N	-21° 17' S

♅ 23° 24' S   Ψ 22° 20' S   ♇ +0° 49' N   ☊ +0° 58' N

Ascendant Declination Calculation		Midheaven Declination Calculation		Declinations Listed in Ascending order
Zodiacal Position **28° ♋ 16'** Convert minutes to decimal = CM **.27** *(use for Step 4 below)*	**Asc**	Zodiacal Position **12° ♈ 18'** Convert minutes to decimal = CM **.3** *(use for Step 4 below)*	**MC**	♇ 0° 49' N
1. **Declination** of next highest listed zodiacal degree **29° ♋ 00'**	+20° 23' N	1. **Declination** of next highest listed zodiacal degree **13° ♈ 00'**	+5° 08' N	☊ 0° 58' N
				♀ 1° 28' N
2. **Declination** of next lowest listed zodiacal degree **28° ♋ 00'**	+20° 35' N	2. **Declination** of next lowest listed zodiacal degree **12° ♈ 00'**	+4° 45' N	☉ 2° 50' N
				MC 4° 52' N
3. Line 1 - Line 2 = Change in Declination	-12'	3. Line 1 - Line 2 = Change in Declination	23'	☿ 5° 54' S
4. Line 3 x CM **.27**	-3'	4. Line 3 x CM **.3**	7'	♂ 6° 41' N
				♃ 9° 30' N
Add lines 2+4 = ASC Declination at Birth (N = +, S = -)	+20° 32' N	Add lines 2+4 = MC Declination at Birth (N = +, S = -)	+4° 52' N	Asc 20° 32' N
				♄ 21° 17' S
				Ψ 22° 20' S
				♅ 23° 24' S
				☽ 28° 23' N

Parallel and Contraparallel Aspects

♇ ∥ ☊   ♇ ∥ ♀   ♀ ∥ ☊   ☿ ♯ ♂   ASC ♯ ♄

Lesson 15 Exercises

Using the declination ephemeris provided below and the calculation form provided on the following page, calculate the declinations of the planets, Ascendant, and Midheaven for the following birth. The zodiacal degrees of the ASC and MC have been provided. Then determine if any parallel or contra-parallel aspects exist. Answers can be found in the Answer Key in the Appendix.

February 2, 1995 at 8:02 GMT
Ascendant: 21° ≈ 23'
Midheaven: 13° ♐ 55'

GMT +0:00 Tropical Geocentric Decl	Moon ☽	Sun ☉	Mercury ☿	Venus ♀	Mars ♂	Jupiter ♃	Saturn ♄	Uranus ♅	Neptune ♆	Pluto ♇	True Node ☊
Feb 1 1995	−08°31'	−17°17'	−12°29'	−20°32'	+16°38'	−21°14'	−09°03'	−21°11'	−20°49'	−07°01'	−14°47'
Feb 2 1995	−04°07'	−17°00'	−12°37'	−20°37'	+16°46'	−21°15'	−09°00'	−21°11'	−20°49'	−07°01'	−14°43'
Feb 3 1995	+00°21'	−16°43'	−12°49'	−20°42'	+16°55'	−21°17'	−08°57'	−21°10'	−20°48'	−07°01'	−14°40'
Feb 4 1995	+04°40'	−16°26'	−13°03'	−20°46'	+17°03'	−21°18'	−08°55'	−21°09'	−20°48'	−07°01'	−14°38'
Feb 5 1995	+08°41'	−16°08'	−13°19'	−20°50'	+17°12'	−21°19'	−08°52'	−21°09'	−20°48'	−07°00'	−14°37'
Feb 6 1995	+12°13'	−15°49'	−13°37'	−20°53'	+17°20'	−21°20'	−08°50'	−21°08'	−20°47'	−07°00'	−14°37'
Feb 7 1995	+15°12'	−15°31'	−13°57'	−20°55'	+17°29'	−21°22'	−08°47'	−21°08'	−20°47'	−07°00'	−14°37'
Feb 8 1995	+17°29'	−15°12'	−14°16'	−20°58'	+17°37'	−21°23'	−08°44'	−21°07'	−20°46'	−07°00'	−14°37'
Feb 9 1995	+19°02'	−14°53'	−14°36'	−20°59'	+17°45'	−21°24'	−08°41'	−21°06'	−20°46'	−07°00'	−14°36'
Feb 10 1995	+19°44'	−14°34'	−14°56'	−21°00'	+17°53'	−21°25'	−08°39'	−21°06'	−20°46'	−06°59'	−14°35'
Feb 11 1995	+19°34'	−14°15'	−15°14'	−21°01'	+18°02'	−21°26'	−08°36'	−21°05'	−20°45'	−06°59'	−14°34'
Feb 12 1995	+18°30'	−13°55'	−15°32'	−21°01'	+18°09'	−21°27'	−08°33'	−21°04'	−20°45'	−06°59'	−14°31'
Feb 13 1995	+16°32'	−13°35'	−15°49'	−21°00'	+18°17'	−21°28'	−08°31'	−21°04'	−20°45'	−06°59'	−14°28'
Feb 14 1995	+13°45'	−13°15'	−16°05'	−20°59'	+18°25'	−21°29'	−08°28'	−21°03'	−20°44'	−06°58'	−14°24'
Feb 15 1995	+10°15'	−12°55'	−16°19'	−20°58'	+18°32'	−21°30'	−08°25'	−21°02'	−20°44'	−06°58'	−14°19'
Feb 16 1995	+06°11'	−12°34'	−16°32'	−20°55'	+18°40'	−21°31'	−08°22'	−21°02'	−20°44'	−06°58'	−14°16'
Feb 17 1995	+01°44'	−12°13'	−16°44'	−20°53'	+18°47'	−21°32'	−08°20'	−21°01'	−20°43'	−06°58'	−14°12'
Feb 18 1995	−02°51'	−11°52'	−16°54'	−20°49'	+18°54'	−21°33'	−08°17'	−21°00'	−20°43'	−06°57'	−14°10'
Feb 19 1995	−07°21'	−11°31'	−17°03'	−20°45'	+19°00'	−21°34'	−08°14'	−21°00'	−20°43'	−06°57'	−14°08'
Feb 20 1995	−11°30'	−11°10'	−17°10'	−20°41'	+19°07'	−21°34'	−08°11'	−20°59'	−20°42'	−06°57'	−14°07'
Feb 21 1995	−15°01'	−10°48'	−17°15'	−20°36'	+19°13'	−21°35'	−08°09'	−20°59'	−20°42'	−06°56'	−14°07'
Feb 22 1995	−17°41'	−10°27'	−17°19'	−20°30'	+19°19'	−21°36'	−08°06'	−20°58'	−20°42'	−06°56'	−14°07'
Feb 23 1995	−19°15'	−10°05'	−17°22'	−20°24'	+19°25'	−21°37'	−08°03'	−20°57'	−20°41'	−06°56'	−14°07'
Feb 24 1995	−19°38'	−09°43'	−17°23'	−20°17'	+19°30'	−21°37'	−08°00'	−20°57'	−20°41'	−06°56'	−14°07'
Feb 25 1995	−18°47'	−09°21'	−17°22'	−20°10'	+19°35'	−21°38'	−07°57'	−20°56'	−20°41'	−06°55'	−14°06'
Feb 26 1995	−16°46'	−08°58'	−17°20'	−20°02'	+19°40'	−21°39'	−07°55'	−20°56'	−20°40'	−06°55'	−14°03'
Feb 27 1995	−13°47'	−08°36'	−17°17'	−19°54'	+19°45'	−21°40'	−07°52'	−20°55'	−20°40'	−06°54'	−14°01'

Declination ephemeris prepared using Solarfire v.5

(N = +, S = -)	☽	☉	☿	♀	♂	♃	♄
1. Declination 0 hr day after birth date _____							
2. Declination 0 hr on Birth date _____							
3. Line 1 - Line 2 = Total Daily Change in Declination	- - - - -	- - - - -	- - - - -				
4. Line 3 X CM-1 _____ = Declination change to Birth GMT	- - - - -	- - - - -	- - - - -				
5. Add lines 2 + 4 = Declination at Birth (N = +, S = -)	- - - - -	- - - - -	- - - - -	- - - - -	- - - - -	- - - - -	- - - - -

♅ _____   ♆ _____   ♇ _____   ☊ _____

Ascendant Declination Calculation		Midheaven Declination Calculation		Declinations Listed in Ascending order
Zodiacal Position _____ Convert minutes to decimal = CM _____ *(use for Step 4 below)*	**Asc**	Zodiacal Position _____ Convert minutes to decimal = CM _____ *(use for Step 4 below)*	**MC**	
1. **Declination** of next highest listed zodiacal degree		1. **Declination** of next highest listed zodiacal degree		
2. **Declination** of next lowest listed zodiacal degree		2. **Declination** of next lowest listed zodiacal degree		
3. Line 1 - Line 2 = Change in Declination		3. Line 1 - Line 2 = Change in Declination		
4. Line 3 x CM _____		4. Line 3 x CM _____		
Add lines 2+4 = ASC Declination at Birth (N = +, S = -)		Add lines 2+4 = MC Declination at Birth (N = +, S = -)		

Parallel and Contraparallel Aspects

Lesson 16: Midpoints & Antiscia

In addition to planets, nodes, and angles, charts contain other **sensitive points** that can produce effects when stimulated via aspect, transit, or progression. This lesson will focus on calculating two types of sensitive points in a chart: **Midpoints,** the center point between two points, and **Antiscia**, points equidistant to and on opposite sides of the 0° Cancer/0° Capricorn axis. Other types of sensitive points will be covered in the following two lessons.

Midpoints

A **Midpoint** is the center point of zodiacal arc between two given points. Midpoints can be calculated between planets, Ascendant, Midheaven, or any other two points in a chart. Many astrologers believe that midpoints are sensitive points in a chart, combining and acting as a collection point for the energy of the two points on either side.

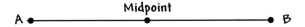

Because the zodiac is a circle, any two points will have two midpoints, a nearer midpoint and a farther midpoint. Notice in the chart below that there are two midpoints between 8° Leo and 22° Scorpio. The nearer midpoint bisects or divides equally the shortest distance between the two points and is the strongest midpoint. The second farther midpoint is 180° away, directly opposite the nearer midpoint, and bisects the longer arc between the two points. In this lesson all of the examples will demonstrate locating the nearer midpoint between two points in a chart.

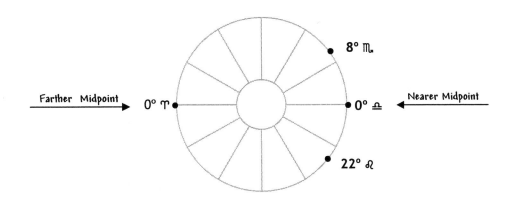

The farther midpoint is always 180° away from the nearer midpoint.

Midpoints are given primary importance in **Uranian Astrology** and **Cosmobiology.** Uranian Astrology and Cosmobiology techniques are beyond the scope of this book, however please refer to the bibliography in the Appendix for further reading recommendations on these subjects.

Calculating Midpoints

Calculating midpoints is most easily done if zodiacal longitude is first converted to absolute longitude. Please refer to Lesson 1 if you need to review this process.

There are three steps to calculating midpoints:

Step 1. Convert degrees of two planetary positions or points to absolute longitude. Convert minutes to a decimal.

Step 2. Add the absolute longitude of the two positions together.

Step 3. Divide the sum of Step 2 by two, then convert the answer back into zodiacal longitude. The result is the midpoint.

Example 1.

Let's find the midpoint between 3° Taurus and 12 ° Libra.

Step 1. Convert degrees of two planetary positions or points to absolute longitude.

3° ♉ = 33° in absolute longitude
12 ° ♎ = 192° in absolute longitude

Step 2. Add the absolute longitude of the two positions together.

$$33°$$
$$+ \quad 192°$$
$$= \quad 225°$$

Step 3. Divide the sum of Step 2 by two, then convert the answer back into zodiacal longitude. The result is the midpoint.

225° ÷ 2 = 112.5° = 22° ♋ 30'

The nearer midpoint is 22° ♋ 30'.

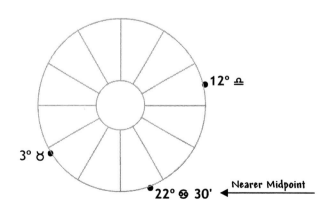

Example 2.

Now let's find the midpoint between 5° ♓ 12' and 5° ♍ 06'.

1. Convert to absolute longitude: 335.2
                                  +   155.1
2. Add the two together: 490.3

3. Divide the sum by two:

     490.3 ÷ 2 = 245.15 = 5° ♐ 09'

In this example the two original points 5° ♓ 12'
and 5° ♍ 06' are in opposition.   As a result there is
not a nearer and farther midpoint—both midpoints
(5° ♐ 09' as calculated above and its opposite 5° ♊ 09')
are equidistant from the original points and will be
equally strong.

Midpoint
5° ♐ 09'

5° ♓ 12'

5° ♍ 06'

Midpoint
5° ♊ 09'

**When two points are in opposition
both midpoints will be equally strong.**

Example 3.

In this example let's calculate the midpoint between 27° ♓ 15' and 7° ♈ 06'.

       357.25
   +   7.10
      364.35   364.35 ÷ 2 = 182.18 or 2° ♎ 11'

Notice that the calculation resulted in the farther midpoint 2° ♎ 11' instead of the nearer
midpoint 2° ♈ 11'. When calculating midpoints between points located from 0° Capricorn to 0°
Cancer it is possible to have the result be the farther midpoint. It is always helpful to check the
result against a chart wheel to confirm that the answer is actually the nearer midpoint. If you
find a calculation results in the farther midpoint, simply swap the sign for its opposite to designate the nearer midpoint.

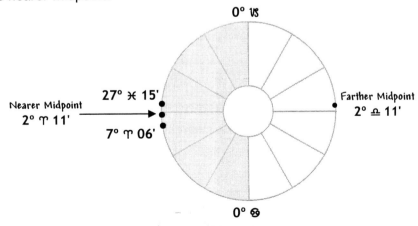

0° ♑

27° ♓ 15'

Nearer Midpoint
2° ♈ 11'

7° ♈ 06'

Farther Midpoint
2° ♎ 11'

0° ♋

**When calculating midpoints between points located from 0°♑ to 0°♋
the result may be the farther midpoint.**

169

Antiscia

Antiscia are points equidistant from the 0° Cancer/0° Capricorn axis. The **Solstice Points** 0° Cancer and 0° Capricorn serve as midpoints for antiscia, creating a symmetrical or "mirror image" relationship between a point and its **antiscion** (the singular form of "antiscia"). Some astrologers believe that planets in antiscia function similarly to a weak conjunction.

Degrees within the signs of the zodiac form pairs in antiscia. Each pair will have either 0° Cancer or 0° Capricorn as its nearest midpoint.

0° Cancer (Midpoint)
Gemini - Cancer
Taurus - Leo
Aries - Virgo

0° Capricorn (Midpoint)
Pisces - Libra
Aquarius - Scorpio
Capricorn - Sagittarius

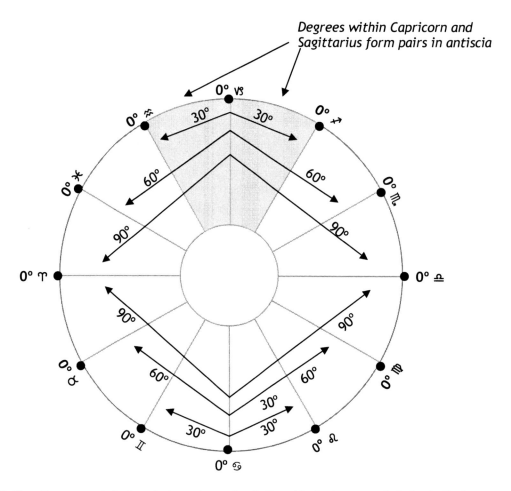

Degrees within Capricorn and Sagittarius form pairs in antiscia

Notice the symmetrical or "mirror image" relationship between points in Antiscia.

Calculating Antiscia

Antiscia are always calculated from the closest solstice point. There are two steps to calculating a planet or point's antiscion:

Step 1. Convert the planet or point's position to absolute longitude and minutes to a decimal.

Step 2. If the result of Step 1 is 179° 59' or less use the Cancer formula:

$$90° + (90° - degree) = Antiscion$$

If the result of Step 1 is 180° 00' or greater use the Capricorn formula:

$$270° + (270° - degree) = Antiscion$$

These formulas determine the distance from the closest solstice point to the planet or point in question and then add that distance to the solstice point to find the point's antiscion on the opposite side of the 0° Cancer/0° Capricorn axis.

Example 1.

Let's calculate the antiscion of **5° ♍ 20'**.

Step 1. Convert the planet or point's position to absolute longitude and minutes to a decimal.

$$5° ♍ 20' = 155.33°$$

Step 2. If the result of step one is 179° 59' or less use the Cancer formula:

$$90° + (90° - degree) = Antisicion$$

In this case 155° is less than 179° so the Cancer formula is used.

$$90° + (90° - 155.33°) = 90° + -65.33° = 24.67°$$
$$24.67° = 24° ♈ 40'$$

90° - 155.33° results in a negative number which is then subtracted from the solstice point. Remember that adding a negative number is the same as subtracting a positive number. The result is 24° ♈ 40', which is the antiscion of 5° ♍ 20'. These two points are "mirror images" of each other, with each point exactly 65° 20' to either side of 0° Cancer.

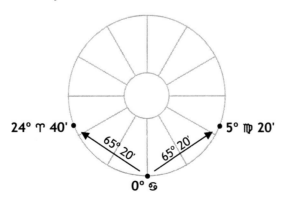

Example 2.

Now let's calculate the antiscion of **12° ♒ 17'**.

Step 1. $\qquad\qquad\qquad\qquad$ 12° ♒ 17' = 312.28°

Step 2. The result of Step 1 is greater than 180° 00' so we will use the Capricorn formula:

$$270° + (270° - \text{degree}) = \text{Antiscion}$$

$$270° + (270° - 312.28°) = 270° + -42.28° = 227.72°$$
$$227.72° = 17° ♏ 43'$$

17° ♏ 43' is the antiscion of 12° ♒ 17'. These two points are exactly 42° 17' to either side of 0° Capricorn.

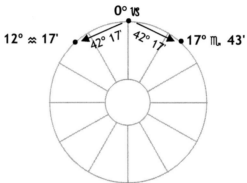

Example 3.

In this final example let's find the antiscion of **14° ♐ 52'**.

Step 1. $\qquad\qquad\qquad\qquad$ 14° ♐ 52' = 254.87°

Step 2. $\qquad\qquad$ 270° + (270° - 254.87°) = 270° + 15.13° = 285.13°
$$285.13° = 15° ♑ 08'$$

15° ♑ 08' is the antiscion of 14° ♐ 52'.

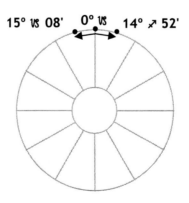

Lesson 16 Exercises

Calculate the following sensitive points in this chart. Answers can be found in the Answer Key in the Appendix.

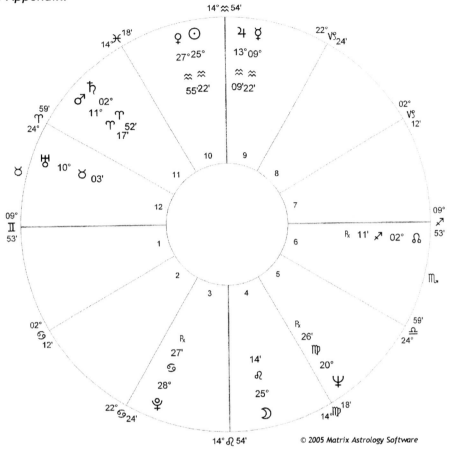

© 2005 Matrix Astrology Software

1. ♆/♇ Midpoint

2. ASC/MC Midpoint

3. ☉/☽ Midpoint

4. Antiscion of ♅

5. Antiscion of ☉

6. Antiscion of ASC

Lesson 17: Arabic Parts

Arabic Parts, also called **Lots**, are mathematically-derived points found by adding the zodiacal positions of two astrological points and then subtracting the zodiacal position of a third point. Their use in the judgment and interpretation of astrological charts has been in practice for centuries. This lesson gives an overview of Arabic Parts and explains how to calculate the three most popular Parts: **Part of Fortune, Part of Spirit, and Part of Marriage.**

Arabic Parts

Arabic Parts date back to at least the Hellenistic period, and may in fact be much older. The oldest surviving mention of Arabic Parts is found in the *Liber Hermetis*, an ancient text on Egyptian and Hermetic astrology which may date back as far as the 3rd century BCE. Although the parts are not Arabic in origin, the name "Arabic Parts" was acquired because Arabian astrologers during the Medieval period made extensive use of them and added many additional parts of their own. At that time over a hundred different Arabic Parts were in use, each with its own formula.

All Arabic Parts take the distance between two planets or points and then project that same distance from a third point, usually the Ascendant, to find the location of the Part. Written in "short form", all Arabic Parts use the following formula:

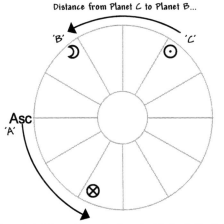

Distance from Planet C to Planet B...

Is projected forward from the Ascendant to locate the Part...

$$Part = A + (B - C)$$

$$Usually, \ Part = ASC + (Planet \ "B" - Planet \ "C")$$

Depending on the type of Arabic part, each is thought to reveal information regarding one's earthly expression and experience in different areas of life.

Sect

An important consideration in the calculation of most Arabic Parts is the **sect** of the chart involved. 'Sect' simply means 'division', and in this usage divides charts into two types: day births belonging to the **diurnal sect**, and night births belonging to the **nocturnal sect**. The sect of a chart was extremely important in traditional astrology and affected the interpretation of all other astrological factors. So important was the classification of sect that you will find most Arabic Parts have different formulas for day charts and night charts.

Determining whether a chart is diurnal or nocturnal is straightforward: If the Sun is above the Ascendant-Descendant axis, the chart is a day chart. If it is below this axis, the chart is a night chart. In most house systems, the Sun will be placed in houses 1 - 6 in a nocturnal chart, and in houses 7 - 12 in a diurnal chart.

Sun above Ascendant/Descendant Axis = Day Birth

Sun below Ascendant/Descendant Axis = Night Birth

The Part of Fortune

The Part of Fortune, or *Pars Fortuna* as it is called in Latin, is thought to indicate material success and show where one finds good fortune through no action of one's own but as if through sheer good luck. Its symbol is ⊗. There are two formulas for the Part of Fortune according to the sect of the chart. To calculate it, first determine if the birth occurred during the day or night, then follow the appropriate formula. Zodiacal positions can be converted to absolute longitude first in order to make addition and subtraction easier.

Formula for Day Births: Ascendant + Moon - Sun = Part of Fortune (⊗)

Formula for Night Births: Ascendant + Sun - Moon = Part of Fortune (⊗)

Example 1.

Let's calculate the Part of Fortune for a day birth with the following positions for the Sun, Moon and Ascendant:

Sun: 5° ♍ 10'   Moon: 18° ♏ 17'   Ascendant: 23° ♍ 13'

Part of Fortune: Day Birth			
Ascendant		173.22	(23° ♍ 13' in absolute longitude)
+ Moon	+	228.28	(18° ♏ 17' in absolute longitude)
- Sun	-	155.17	(5° ♍ 10' in absolute longitude)
	=	246.33	
= Part of Fortune	=	6° ♐ 20'	

Example 2.

Now let's calculate the Part of Fortune for a night birth with the following positions:

Sun: 20° ♈ 59'   Moon: 10° ♑ 04'   Ascendant: 8° ♐ 25'

Notice in this example the result is a negative number, so 360° was added to find the Part of Fortune. As explained in Lesson 1, 360° can be added or subtracted as required without affecting the accuracy of the answer.

Part of Fortune: Night Birth			
Ascendant		248.42	(8° ♐ 25' in absolute longitude)
+ Sun	+	20.98	(20° ♈ 59' in absolute longitude)
- Moon	-	280.07	(10° ♑ 04' in absolute longitude)
	=	- 10.67	
	+	360.00	+ or - 360°
	=	349.33	
= Part of Fortune	=	19° ♓ 20'	

The Part of Spirit

While the Part of Fortune is related to simple good fortune, the Part of Spirit, or *Pars Spiritus*, is related to conscious choices and actions, and is thought to describe one's future. In fact, medieval astrologer Guido Bonatti (13th century) referred to it as the "Part of Things to Come". The Ascendant, Sun and Moon are again the significant points used, but now in a different order. Here, the formula used for the Part of Fortune for night births becomes the Part of Spirit for day births, and the formula used for the Part of Fortune for day births becomes the formula for the Part of Spirit for night births:

Formula for Day Births: Ascendant + Sun - Moon = Part of Spirit

Formula for Night Births: Ascendant + Moon - Sun = Part of Spirit

Example 4.

Let's calculate the Part of Spirit for a day birth:

Sun: 5° ♍ 10'   Moon: 18° ♏ 17'   Ascendant: 23° ♍ 13'

Part of Spirit: Day Birth			
Ascendant		173.22	(23° ♍ 13' in absolute longitude)
+ Sun	+	155.17	(5° ♍ 10' in absolute longitude)
- Moon	-	228.28	(18° ♏ 17' in absolute longitude)
	=	100.11	
= Part of Spirit	=	**10° ♋ 07'**	

Example 5.

Now let's calculate the Part of Spirit for a night birth. Notice that in this example 360° needed to be subtracted from our result in order to arrive at the Part of Spirit:

Sun: 20° ♈ 59'   Moon: 10° ♑ 04'   Ascendant: 8° ♐ 25'

Part of Spirit: Night Birth			
Ascendant		248.42	(8° ♐ 25' in absolute longitude)
+ Moon	+	280.07	(10° ♑ 04' in absolute longitude)
- Sun	-	20.98	(20° ♈ 59' in absolute longitude)
	=	507.51	
	-	360.00	+ or - 360°
	=	147.51	
= Part of Spirit	=	**27° ♌ 31'**	

The Part of Marriage

There are several different formulas for calculating the Part of Marriage. Presented here is the Part of Marriage according to Bonatti. In this case, different formulas are not applied for day or night births but rather for males and females.

Males (Day or Night) = Ascendant + Venus - Saturn = Part of Marriage

Females (Day or Night) = Ascendant + Saturn - Venus = Part of Marriage

Example 6.

In the next two examples let's calculate the Part of Marriage for a married couple:

Male: Ascendant: 4° ♎ 35'   Venus: 4° ♓ 12'   Saturn: 25° ♐ 41'

Part of Marriage: Male			
Ascendant		184.58	(4° ♎ 35' in absolute longitude)
+ Venus	+	334.20	(4° ♓ 12' in absolute longitude)
- Saturn	-	265.68	(25° ♐ 41' in absolute longitude)
	=	253.10	
= Part of Marriage	=	13° ♐ 06'	

Example 7.

Female: Ascendant: 23° ♍ 13' Saturn: 12° ♐ 06' Venus: 23° ♍ 27'

Part of Marriage: Female			
Ascendant		173.22	(23° ♍ 13' in absolute longitude)
+ Saturn	+	252.10	(12° ♐ 06' inabsolute longitude)
- Venus	-	173.45	(23° ♍ 27' in absolute longitude)
	=	251.87	
= Part of Marriage	=	11° ♐ 52'	

Some Interesting Arabic Parts

There are hundreds of formulas for various parts, too many to include here, but we thought it would be fun to include the formulas for a few more. As with the three parts covered previously, not only is the house and sign position of each part considered, but the general condition of each part should be assessed to determine whether the significations of the part in question will be easily attained or not.

Part of Happiness

This part signifies the extent of a native's honor, wisdom, victory, and happiness.

Formula for Day Birth: ASC + Jupiter - Part of Spirit
Formula for Night Birth: ASC + Part of Spirit - Jupiter

Part of Life

This part signifies the overall condition and vitality of the body.

Formula for Day Birth: ASC + Saturn - Jupiter
Formula for Night Birth: ASC + Jupiter - Saturn

Part of Excellence

This part signifies whether a native will or will not achieve a reputation of excellence.

Formula for Day Birth: ASC + Part of Spirit - Part of Fortune
Formula for Night Birth: ASC + Part of Fortune - Part of Spirit

Part of Labor

This part signifies whether a native will or will not make money at his labors.

Formula for Day Birth: ASC + Part of Fortune - Part of Spirit
Formula for Night Birth: ASC + Part of Spirit - Part of Fortune

If your interest has been sparked and you would like to investigate additional Arabic Parts, we suggest you read Robert Zoller's *The Arabic Parts in Astrology: A Lost Key to Prediction* (see Bibliography for details).

Lesson 17 Exercises

Calculate the Part of Fortune, Part of Spirit, and the Part of Marriage for this individual. Answers can be found in the Answer Key located in the Appendix.

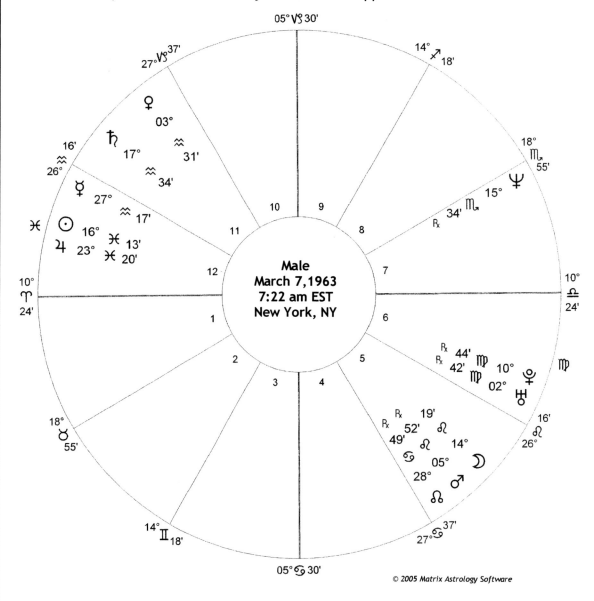

Male
March 7, 1963
7:22 am EST
New York, NY

© 2005 Matrix Astrology Software

Calculate the Part of Fortune, Part of Spirit, and the Part of Marriage for this individual.
Answers can be found in the Answer Key located in the Appendix.

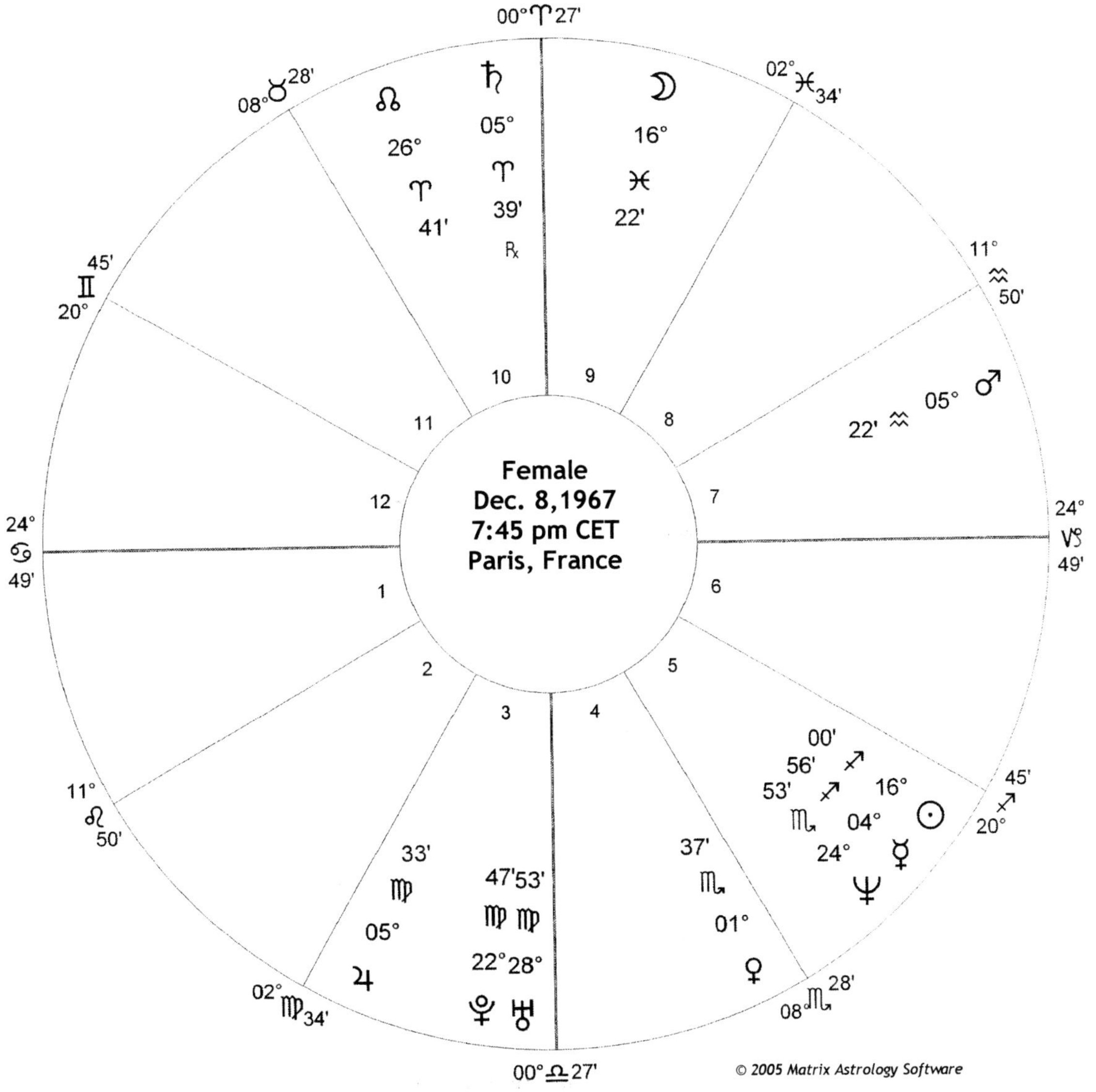

00° ♈ 27'

08° ♉ 28'

☊
26°
♈
41'

♄
05°
♈
39'
Rx

☽
16°
♓
22'

02° ♓ 34'

11°
♒
50'

♂
05°
22' ♒

24°
♑
49'

45'
♊
20°

24°
♋
49'

Female
Dec. 8,1967
7:45 pm CET
Paris, France

10   9

11   8

12   7

1   6

2   5

3   4

00'
56' ♐
53' ♐   16°
♏   04°   ☉
24°
☿
♄

45'
♐
20°

37'
♏
01°

♀

08° ♏ 28'

11°
♌
50'

33'
♍
05°
♃

47'53'
♍ ♍
22° 28°
♇ ♅

02° ♍ 34'

00° ♎ 27'

© 2005 Matrix Astrology Software

181

Lesson 18: Equatorial Ascendant & Vertex

The **Equatorial Ascendant** and **Vertex** are two personal points used by many Uranian astrologers. This lesson will begin with a very brief explanation of the five Great Circles which are factors in determining the location of many points in the horoscope including the Equatorial Ascendant and Vertex. This will be followed by an explanation of how to calculate these two points.

Great Circles

As explained in previous lessons, the Ascendant, Descendant, Midheaven, and Imum Coeli are all points along the Ecliptic rather than actual celestial bodies. Each one of these points is formed by the intersection of the Ecliptic with **Great Circles** - imaginary planes passing through the center of the Earth and projected out into the celestial sphere. The **Equatorial Ascendant** and **Vertex** are also points along the Ecliptic established by the intersection of great circles. You may find it helpful to understand which great circles are involved in determining the location of these points.

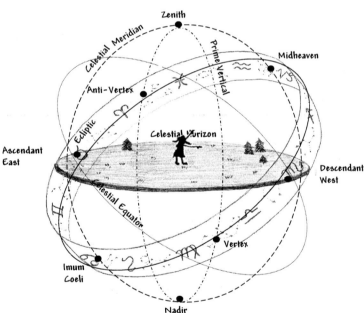

The Ecliptic is a great circle formed by the orbit of the Earth projected onto the celestial sphere. It is often referred to as the apparent path of the Sun.

The Celestial Horizon (not the same as the visible horizon) is a great circle parallel to the plane of the visible horizon which passes through the center of the Earth. The Ascendant, Descendant, and the Equatorial Ascendant are all determined by locating the points in the east and west where the Celestial Horizon intersects with the Ecliptic.

The Celestial Equator is the Earth's Equator projected into space. The Celestial Equator intersects with the Ecliptic at 0 degrees Aries and 0 degrees Libra.

The Celestial Meridian is a great circle that passes through due north and due south on the celestial horizon and through the Zenith directly above and the Nadir directly below. The Midheaven and the Imum Coeli are located at the points where the Celestial Meridian intersects with the highest point on the Ecliptic and the lowest point on the Ecliptic respectively.

The Prime Vertical is a great circle passing through the east and west points on the celestial horizon, overhead through the Zenith and down through the Nadir. The Prime Vertical and the Celestial Meridian intersect at right angles at the Zenith and Nadir.

The Vertex & Anti-Vertex - The point where the Prime Vertical intersects the Ecliptic in the west is called the **Vertex**, and the point directly opposite this in the east is called the **Anti-Vertex**. Some astrologers believe that the Vertex indicates a fated area of the chart bringing persons and circumstances beyond the individual's control.

The Equatorial Ascendant is formed by the intersection of the celestial horizon, Celestial Equator, and the Ecliptic in the east. It is the rising degree of the Ascendant if the location of birth were on the Equator. The significance of the Equatorial Ascendant is not widely agreed upon. Some astrologers feel that the Equatorial Ascendant represents how a native *believes* he presents himself to the world, in contrast to the natal Ascendant which represents how others perceive him.

Calculating the Equatorial Ascendant

The Equatorial Ascendant is the rising degree at the sidereal time of birth if the birth had occurred at 0° latitude on the Equator. You will recall that when calculating the natal Ascendant and other house cusps, the sidereal time of birth and latitude are used in three different interpolation procedures. When calculating the Equatorial Ascendant only one interpolation procedure is needed for sidereal time. Interpolation between latitudes is not necessary because values for 0° 00', the latitude of the Equator, can be taken directly out of a Table of Houses.

There are two steps to calculating the Equatorial Ascendant:

Step 1. Determine a constant multiplier based on the Local Sidereal Time (LST) of birth.
This will be the same "CM-2" used for house cusp calculation.

Step 2. Using a Table of Houses and the CM-2 found in Step 1, interpolate between listed sidereal times to calculate an Ascendant at 0° Latitude. The result is the Equatorial Ascendant.

The Equatorial Ascendant is the ascending degree at the Equator (0° Latitude) at the LST of Birth

184

Example 1.

In this example Let's calculate the Equatorial Ascendant for a birth in Albany, New York.

Birth information: Albany, New York
42°N 39', 73°W 45'
LST of birth: 19:54:49

To calculate the Equatorial Ascendant the only information needed is the **Local Sidereal Time** of birth. The **latitude of the Equator (0°)** is substituted for the birth latitude. (The longitude of birth was already taken into account when the LST was calculated.)

Step 1. Determine a constant multiplier based on the Local Sidereal Time (LST) of birth.
This will be the same "CM-2" used for house cusp calculation.

CM-2	
(Constant Multiplier for LST Interpolation)	
LST of Birth	19 :54 : 49
- Next lowest Sid Time from Table	- 19 : 52 : 00
=	2 : 49
Convert result to decimal	2.82
÷ 4 = CM-2	.71

Step 2. Using a Table of Houses and the CM-2 found in Step 1, interpolate between listed sidereal times to calculate an Ascendant at 0° Latitude. The result is the Equatorial Ascendant.

Latitude 0°	Equatorial ASC
1. Asc at Later Sid Time **19:56:00**	♉ 1° 08'
2. Asc at Earlier Sid Time **19:52:00**	- ♉ 0° 06'
3. Line 1 - Line 2 =	1° 02' or 62'
4. Line 3 X CM-2 = **.71**	44'
5. Add lines 2 + 4 = **Equatorial Ascendant**	♉ 0°50'

Example 2.

Now let's calculate one more Equatorial Ascendant for a birth in San Jose, California.

Birth information: San Jose, California
37°N 20', 121°W 54'
LST of birth: 15:51:08

Equatorial Ascendant Calculation			
CM-2 *(Constant Multiplier for LST Interpolation)*		**Latitude 0°**	**Equatorial ASC**
LST of Birth	15 : 51 : 08	1. Asc at Later Sid Time 15:52:00	≈ 25° 44'
- Next lowest Sid Time from Table	- 15 : 48 : 00	2. Asc at Earlier Sid Time 15:48:00	≈ 24° 42'
	= 3 : 08	3. Line 1 - Line 2 =	1° 02' 62'
Convert result to decimal	3.13	4. Line 3 X CM-2 = **.78**	48'
÷ 4 = CM-2	.78	5. Add lines 2 + 4 = **Equatorial Ascendant =**	≈ 24° 90' ≈ 25° 30'

The Equatorial Ascendant is the degree on the Ecliptic rising over the Celestial Horizon in the East, if birth had occurred at the same LST on the Equator.

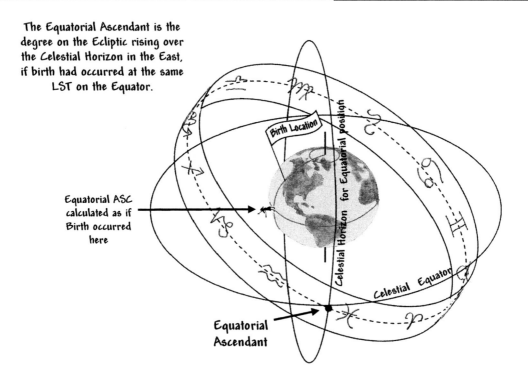

Equatorial ASC calculated as if Birth occurred here

Equatorial Ascendant

Calculating the Vertex

The procedure for calculating the Vertex follows the same basic steps used to calculate a natal Ascendant, but different factors are used. In brief, the natal IC is substituted for the MC and a new "Ascendant" is calculated by interpolating between Midheavens (instead of sidereal times) listed in a Table of Houses. Then, a "co-latitude" is substituted for the birth latitude and the final latitude interpolation is done.

There are six steps needed to calculate the Vertex:

Step 1. Determine the co-latitude of birth, which is done by subtracting the birth latitude from 90°. ("Co-latitude" is explained on the following page.)

Step 2. Calculate a Constant Multiplier for Vertex interpolation (CM-V). This is done by substituting the natal IC for the Midheaven; calculating the difference between it and the next lowest listed MC in the Table of Houses; and determining what proportion of the full increment between next lowest and next highest listed Midheavens this represents.

Step 3. Calculate a Constant Multiplier for Latitude interpolation (CM-3), using the co-latitude instead of the birth latitude.

Step 4. Interpolate between Ascendants shown in a Table of Houses for the higher Midheaven value, using CM-V calculated in Step 2.

Step 5. Interpolate between Ascendants shown in a Table of Houses for the lower Midheaven value, also using CM-V.

Step 6. Finally, Interpolate between Ascendants calculated in Steps 4 & 5 above, using the co-latitude constant multiplier CM-3 found in Step 3.

Since this is a different process than that previously used to calculate house cusps we will take it one step at a time. Let's start by working through a couple of examples to determine the co-latitude of birth and the necessary constant multipliers before moving into the complete Vertex calculation.

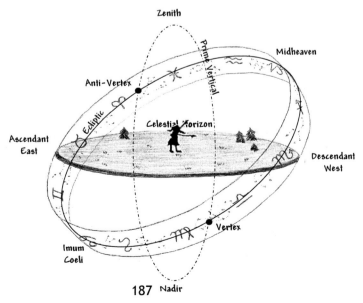

187

Finding the Co-Latitude

Co-Latitude is the angular measurement of a location's distance from one of the poles instead of from the Equator. The co-latitude of birth is easily calculated by subtracting the birth latitude from 90°.

Example 1.

Let's calculate the co-latitude of **35° N 00'**.

90°:	90° 00'
- Birth Latitude	- 35° 00' North
= Co-Latitude	= 55° 00'

The sum of the co-latitude and the birth latitude should equal 90°. Use this to double-check your result.

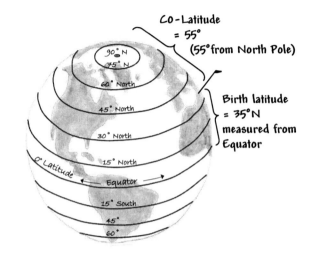

Example 2.

Now let's find the co-latitude for a birth latitude of **40° S 43'**. In this case we will need to convert minutes to a decimal before subtracting.

90°:	90.00°
- Birth Latitude:	- 40.72° South (latitude expressed as a decimal)
	= 49.28° = 49° 17' South

Co-Latitude = 49° S 17'.

Example 3.

Let's calculate one more co-latitude for a birth Latitude of **37° N 20'**.

90°:	90.00°
- Birth latitude:	- 37.33° North (latitude expressed as a decimal)
	= 52.67° = 52° 40' North

Co-Latitude = 52° N 40'.

90° - Birth Latitude = Co-Latitude

Check your Calculation: Co-Latitude + Birth Latitude should equal 90°

Determining a Constant Multiplier for Vertex Interpolation

The next step in Vertex calculation is to determine a constant multiplier for interpolation based on the degree and minute of the natal IC, which will be substituted for and used as if it were the Midheaven. This procedure is most easily explained by working through an example.

Example 4.

Let's calculate a constant multiplier for Vertex interpolation for the following birth information:

Birth Latitude: 37° N 20'   IC: 29 ♉ 58'

First, find an MC listed in *The Book of Tables* which is the next lowest and closest to the **IC** of the birth chart. In this case **29° ♉ 13'** is lower and closest. Then locate the next highest MC.

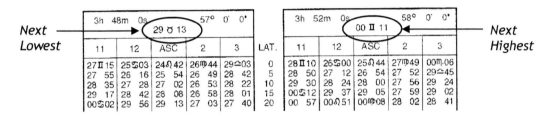

Next, find the difference between the natal IC and the next lowest listed MC, as in the example in "Part A" on the CM-V Form below. Then, subtract the lower listed MC **29° ♉ 13'** from the higher listed MC **00° ♊ 11'** to determine the interval between them, as in "Part B" shown below. This is similar to the procedure used for house cusp interpolation between listed sidereal times, however unlike sidereal time listings which are all 4 minutes apart, the interval between midheaven listings will almost always vary. Finally, divide the result from Part A by the interval found in Part B to find the constant multiplier:

CM-V
(Constant Multiplier for Vertex Interpolation)

A. IC of Birth   ♉   29°   58'

     - Next lowest MC from Table   - ♉   29°   13'

     = Difference   45'

                                  ♉   29°   71'

B. Higher listed MC   ~~♊   00°   11'~~

     - Lower listed MC   - ♉   29°   13'

     = Interval between MCs   58'

         (A) __45__ ÷ *(B)* __58__ = CM-V: __.78__

Divide the difference from part A by interval from B.

Example 5.

Let's continue calculating the Vertex using the same birth information:

Birth Latitude: 37° N 20'   IC: 29 ♉ 58'

First, calculate CM-3 using the co-latitude **52° N 40'** calculated in Example 3. Notice that the calculation process is exactly the same as that used to calculate the CM-3 for natal house cusp calculation, with the exception that the **co-latitude** is substituted for the **latitude** of birth.

CM-3		
(Constant Multiplier for Latitude Interpolation)		
Co-Latitude of Birth		52° 40'
- Next lowest Latitude from Table		52° 00'
	=	___° 40'
Convert result to decimal = **CM-3** =		___.67
Exception: If Co-Latitude is less than 20°, divide result by 5	÷ 5 = CM-3	_____

Next, the Ascendant is calculated by interpolating between the lower listed and higher listed Midheavens, using the **IC** of **29° ♉ 58'** as if it were the **MC** in *The Book of Tables*. The result is the Vertex.

First, the Vertex is calculated at the higher co-latitude 53°:

At 53°:
1. ASC at Higher listed MC (00° ♊ 11')   ♍ 7° 55'
2. ASC at Lower listed MC (29° ♉ 13')   ♍ 7° 14'
3. Line 1 - Line 2 =   41'
4. Line 3 X CM-Vertex (.78) =   32'
5. Add lines 2 + 4 =   ♍ 7° 46'

Then it is calculated at the lower co-latitude 52°:

At 52°:
1. ASC at Higher listed MC (00° ♊ 11')   ♍ 7° 38'
2. ASC at Lower listed MC (29° ♉ 13')   ♍ 6° 56'
3. Line 1 - Line 2 =   42'
4. Line 3 X CM-Vertex (.78) =   33'
5. Add lines 2 + 4 =   ♍ 6° 89'
                                                                    ♍ 7° 29'

Last, interpolate between the two results for latitude:

1. ASC at Higher Latitude (53°)   ♍ 7° 46'
2. ASC at Lower Latitude (52°)   ♍ 7° 29'
3. Line 1 - Line 2 =   17'
4. Line 3 X CM-3 (.67) =   11'
5. Add lines 2 + 4 =   **Vertex** =   ♍ 7° 40'

The Vertex for a birth at latitude 37° N 20' with an of IC of 29° ♉ 58 is **7° ♍ 40'** .

Example 6.

Let's use the form provided in the appendix and reproduced below to calculate a Vertex for a birth at a latitude of 40° N 43' with an IC of 22° ♐ 09':

<table>
<tr>
<td colspan="2">Vertex Calculation for:

Name: Example 6

Birth Latitude: 40° N 43'   Birth IC: 22° ♐ 09'

Co-Latitude:
　90°:   90.00°

　- Birth Latitude (as decimal):   - 40.72° N

　　　　　　　　　　　　　　 49.28°
= Co-Latitude: = <u> = 49° 17' N </u></td>
<td colspan="2" align="center">Vertex Interpolation
At Higher Latitude</td>
</tr>
<tr>
<td>Co-Latitude   <u> 50 </u> °</td>
<td>ASC</td>
</tr>
<tr>
<td>1. ASC at Higher MC <u> 22°♐ 39' </u></td>
<td>♓ 12° 14'</td>
</tr>
<tr>
<td>2. ASC at Lower MC <u> 21°♐ 44' </u></td>
<td>♓ 10° 06'</td>
</tr>
<tr>
<td>3. Line 1 - Line 2 =</td>
<td>2° 08'
= 128'</td>
</tr>
<tr>
<td>4. Line 3 X CM-V <u> .45 </u> =</td>
<td>58'</td>
</tr>
<tr>
<td>5. Add lines 2 + 4 =</td>
<td>♓ 10°64'
= ♓ 11° 04'</td>
</tr>
<tr>
<td colspan="2" align="center">CM-V
(Constant Multiplier for Vertex Interpolation)

A. IC of Birth   ♐ 22° 09'
　- Next lowest MC from Table   - ♐ 21° 44'
　= Difference   25'

B. Higher listed MC   ♐ 22° 39'
　- Lower listed MC   - ♉ 21° 44'
　= Interval between MCs   55'

(A) <u> 25 </u> ÷ (B) <u> 55 </u> = CM-V: <u> .45 </u>
Divide the difference from part A by interval from B.</td>
<td colspan="2" align="center">Vertex Interpolation
At Lower Latitude</td>
</tr>
<tr>
<td>Co-Latitude   <u> 49 </u> °</td>
<td>ASC</td>
</tr>
<tr>
<td>6. ASC at Higher MC <u> 22°♐ 39' </u></td>
<td>♓ 12° 51'</td>
</tr>
<tr>
<td>7. ASC at Lower MC <u> 21°♐ 44' </u></td>
<td>♓ 10° 46'</td>
</tr>
<tr>
<td>8. Line 6 - Line 7 =</td>
<td>2° 05'
= 125'</td>
</tr>
<tr>
<td>9. Line 8 X CM-V <u> .45 </u> =</td>
<td>56'</td>
</tr>
<tr>
<td>10. Add lines 7 + 9 =</td>
<td>♓ 10° 102'
= ♓ 11° 42'</td>
</tr>
<tr>
<td colspan="2" align="center">CM-3
(Constant Multiplier for Latitude Interpolation)

Co-Latitude of Birth   49° 17'
- Next lowest Latitude from Table   49° 00'
　　　　　　　　　　　 =   17'

Convert result to decimal   = CM-3 <u> .28 </u>

Exception: If Co-Latitude is
less than 20°, divide result by 5   ÷ 5 = CM-3 <u>   </u></td>
<td colspan="2" align="center">Vertex Latitude
Interpolation</td>
</tr>
<tr>
<td>11. Asc at Higher Latitude
(from line 5)</td>
<td>♓ 11° 04'</td>
</tr>
<tr>
<td>12. Asc. at Lower Latitude
(from line 10)</td>
<td>♓ 11° 42'</td>
</tr>
<tr>
<td>13. Line 11 - Line 12 =</td>
<td>- 38'</td>
</tr>
<tr>
<td>14. Line 13 X CM-3 <u> .28 </u> =</td>
<td>- 11'</td>
</tr>
<tr>
<td>15. Add lines 12 + 14 =
Vertex at Birth</td>
<td>♓ 11° 31'</td>
</tr>
</table>

Lesson 18 Exercises

Find the Equatorial Ascendant and the Vertex for this chart. Answers can be found in the Answer Key in the Appendix.

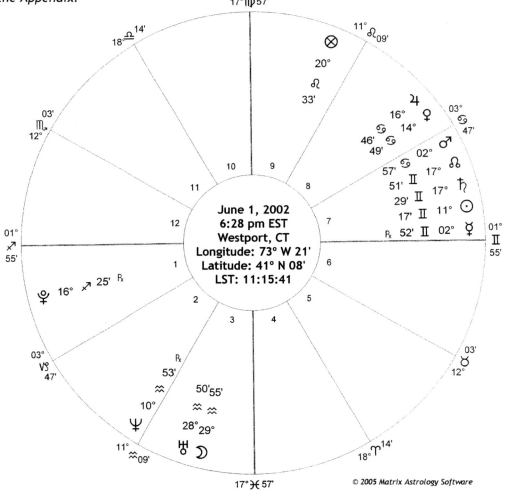

© 2005 Matrix Astrology Software

Equatorial Ascendant Calculation

CM-2	Latitude 0°	Equatorial ASC
(Constant Multiplier for LST Interpolation)		
	1. Asc at Later Sid Time	
LST of Birth _____		
- Next lowest Sid Time from Table - _____	2. Asc at Earlier Sid Time	
= _____		
	3. Line 1 - Line 2 =	
Convert result to decimal _____	4. Line 3 X CM-2 = _____	
÷ 4 = CM-2 _____	5. Add lines 2 + 4 = **Equatorial Ascendant**	

Vertex Calculation for:	Vertex Interpolation At Higher Latitude	
Name:_____	**Co-Latitude** _____°	**ASC**
Birth Latitude: _____ Birth IC: _____	1. ASC at Higher MC _____	
Co-Latitude:	2. ASC at Lower MC _____	
90°: **90.00°**	3. Line 1 - Line 2 =	
- Birth Latitude *(as decimal)*: - _____	4. Line 3 X CM-V _____ =	
= Co-Latitude: = _____	5. Add lines 2 + 4 =	

CM-V *(Constant Multiplier for Vertex Interpolation)*	Vertex Interpolation At Lower Latitude	
A. IC of Birth _____	**Co-Latitude** _____°	**ASC**
- Next lowest MC from Table - _____	6. ASC at Higher MC _____	
= Difference _____	7. ASC at Lower MC _____	
B. Higher listed MC _____	8. Line 6 - Line 7 =	
- Lower listed MC - _____	9. Line 8 X CM-V _____ =	
= Interval between MCs _____	10. Add lines 7 + 9 =	
*(A)*_____ ÷ *(B)*_____ = **CM-V:** _____ *Divide the difference from part A by interval from B.*		

CM-3 *(Constant Multiplier for Latitude Interpolation)*	Vertex Latitude Interpolation	
Co-Latitude of Birth _____	11. Asc at Higher Latitude (from line 5)	
- Next lowest Latitude from Table _____	12. Asc. at Lower Latitude (from line 10)	
= _____	13. Line 11 - Line 12 =	
Convert result to decimal = **CM-3** _____	14. Line 13 X CM-3 _____ =	
Exception: If Co-Latitude is less than 20°, divide result by 5 ÷ 5 = CM-3 _____	15. Add lines 12 + 14 = **Vertex at Birth**	

Lesson 19: Lunar Phases & Eclipses

The lunar phases in effect at the time of birth and by progression add additional insight to chart interpretation. This lesson will cover how to determine the phase of the Moon at the time of birth, the progressed lunar phase, and the phase relationship between any two planets in a chart. This is followed by a brief explanation of eclipses.

The Astronomy of Lunar Phases

Every 29½ days the Moon makes one complete revolution around the Earth. As a result, the light reflected by the Moon from the Sun changes, giving rise to the waxing and waning lunar cycle we observe from Earth. Once every 29½ days when the Moon is between the Earth and Sun in its orbit, a New Moon occurs and the Sun and the Moon appear to rise together in the same region of the sky. Over the course of a month, the combination of the Moon's orbit around the Earth and the Earth's own rotation causes the Moon to rise and set 50 minutes later each day. This phenomenon is called **daily retardation**. Two weeks after a New Moon, daily retardation has resulted in the Moon rising a full 12 hours after the Sun, at sunset. This is the Full Moon. Then two weeks later, the Moon's cycle once again brings it into alignment with the Sun, and another New Moon occurs. The period of time between a New Moon and the following New Moon 29½ days later is called a **lunation**.

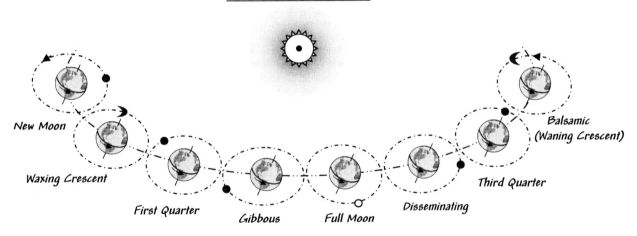

The Phases of the Moon

New Moon

Waxing Crescent

First Quarter

Gibbous

Full Moon

Disseminating

Third Quarter

Balsamic (Waning Crescent)

Waxing & Waning

An interesting way to identify the waxing crescent and the waning crescent is by the shape.

The **Waxing Crescent** is shaped like a "D", seemingly <u>d</u>etermined to forge ahead through a new cycle.

The **Waning Crescent** is shaped like a "C", <u>c</u>ompleting its cycle and heading back to the new phase.

Waxing Crescent

Waning Crescent

195

Lunar Phases in the Natal Chart

Each phase of the Moon, determined by the number of degrees from the Sun's zodiacal position to the zodiacal position of the Moon, has its own symbolic meaning. There are eight phases, each containing 45° (360° ÷ 8 = 45°), summarized below:

New Phase: 0° to 45°
The New Phase begins with a conjunction between the Sun and the Moon, then moves through a semisextile and culminates in a semisquare, symbolizing a beginning, fresh start or new energy.

Crescent Phase: 45° to 90°
The Crescent Phase begins with a semisquare between the Sun and the Moon, moves through a sextile indicating tremendous energy, and ends with a square indicating possible difficulty in letting go and moving forward.

First Quarter Phase: 90° to 135°
The First Quarter Phase begins with a square, moves through a trine, and finishes with a sesquisquare. A native in this phase is thought to be operating in crisis mode which facilitates change.

Gibbous Phase: 135° to 180°
The Gibbous Phase progresses from a sesquisquare through the quincunx and culminates in an opposition. This phase indicates a need for analysis and readjustment.

Full Phase: 180° to 225°
The Full Phase begins at the opposition and ends at the waning sesquisquare, initiating the second half of the lunar cycle and signifying completion and reflection.

Disseminating Phase: 225° to 270°
The Disseminating Phase moves through the waning trine and ends at the waning square, bringing a desire to share information gathered through the first five phases.

Third Quarter Phase: 270° to 315°
The Third Quarter Phase starts at the waning square, spans the waning sextile, and ends at the waning semisquare. In this phase, interactions with others brings about greater social consciousness, ultimately motivating change.

Balsamic Phase: 315° to 360°
The Balsamic Phase starts at the waning semisquare and ends at the next New Moon. This phase brings an internal commitment towards new beginnings and acceptance of another New Phase.

Calculating Lunar Phases

Lunar phases are calculated quite simply by finding the difference between the zodiacal position of the Sun (slower moving planet) and the Moon (faster moving planet). Here is the procedure expressed as a formula:

Moon - Sun = Lunar Phase

To calculate a lunar phase mathematically, it is helpful to first convert the zodiacal degree of the natal Sun and Moon to absolute longitude. This is the method used throughout this lesson. If the Sun is at a higher degree than the Moon, add 360° to make subtraction possible.

Lunar Phases can also be determined by using a Lunar Phase Dial. A Lunar Phase Dial has been provided on page 315 of the Appendix which can be cut out and assembled to help identify phase relationships without having to do any calculations.

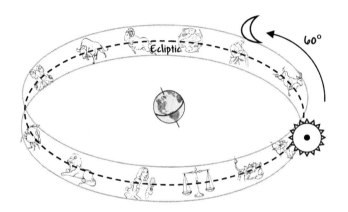

In the diagram to the right, the Moon at 1° ≈ 00' and the Sun at 1° ♐ 00' are 60° apart and are in a Crescent Phase. This is calculated:

Moon	301°	(1° ≈ 00')
- Sun	- 241°	(1° ♐ 00')
= Lunar Phase	60°	

Example 1.

Let's calculate the lunar phase between a natal **Moon** at **2° ♏ 04'** and natal **Sun** at **20° ♈ 59'**.

Moon	212.07°	←	*Zodiacal positions are*
- Sun	- 20.98°	←	*converted to absolute*
= Lunar Phase	= 191.09		*longitude.*

The natal lunar phase is within the Full Phase, which spans the degree range 180°-225°.

To determine the Lunar Phase: Moon - Sun = Lunar Phase

If required, add 360° to the Moon's position to facilitate subtraction.

Example 2.

Now let's calculate the lunar phase between a natal Moon at **13° ♐ 52'** and Natal Sun at **26° ♓ 06'**. In this case, the Moon is at a lower degree than the Sun. 360° must be added to the Moon's position to make it possible to subtract the Sun:

Moon		253.87°
	+	360.00 ◄——— *360° can be added to facilitate subtraction*
subtotal		613.87
- Sun	-	356.10°
= Lunar Phase	=	257.77

The lunar phase in this example is the Disseminating Phase, which spans 225°-270°.

It is very important in instances where the Sun is at a higher degree than the Moon that the subtraction order is NOT reversed. DO NOT subtract the Moon from the Sun as the result will not be the correct lunar phase.

Calculating Progressed Lunar Phases

Progressions are symbolic methods of advancing a chart through time and will be thoroughly covered in Section 7 of this book. Once you have completed Section 7 and understand progressions, you may wish to calculate the Progressed Lunar Phase. This is accomplished by subtracting the Progressed Sun from Progressed Moon as shown in the examples below. Again, if the Sun is at a greater degree than the Moon, simply add 360° to the Moon before subtracting.

Example 3.

Let's calculate the progressed Lunar phase between a progressed Moon at **25°♌ 32'** and a progressed Sun at **12° ♊ 15'**.

Prog. Moon		145.53°
- Prog. Sun	-	72.25°
= Prog. Lunar Phase	=	73.28

The progressed lunar phase is Crescent.

Example 4.

Now let's calculate the progressed Lunar phase between a progressed Moon at **29°♍ 47'** and a progressed Sun at **14° ♏ 35'**:

Moon		179.78°
	+	360.00
subtotal		539.78
- Sun	-	224.58°
= Lunar Phase	=	315.20

The progressed lunar phase is Balsamic.

To determine the Progressed Lunar Phase:

Progressed Moon - Progressed Sun = Progressed Lunar Phase

198

Calculating phases between other planets in a chart

Like the Sun and Moon, any two planets can be in a phase relationship. Many astrologers believe that the phase between two planets has meaning and may reveal information about the way in which those planets will express their energies.

Calculating the phase between two planets is done in the same manor as calculating lunar phases: The degree of absolute longitude of the slower moving planet is subtracted from the degree of absolute longitude of the faster moving planet. If the degree of the slower moving planet is greater than the degree of the faster moving planet, add 360° to the faster moving planet before subtracting.

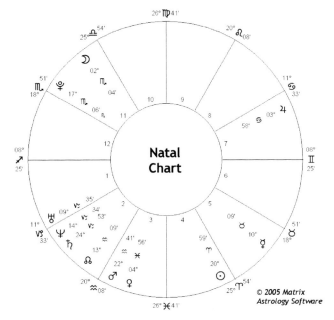

Example 6.

Let's calculate the phase between Saturn and Venus in the chart to the right. Venus is the faster moving planet of the two, so Saturn's position will be subtracted from Venus's position to determine the phase:

Venus (faster)	334.93°
- Saturn (slower)	- 294.88°
= Phase	= 40.05

These two planets are in a New Phase.

Example 7.

Now let's calculate the phase between Jupiter and Mercury in the same chart. In this case Mercury is the faster planet and Jupiter is the slower planet, so Jupiter will be subtracted from Mercury. Because Jupiter is at a higher degree than Mercury, 360° must be added to make subtraction possible:

Mercury (faster)		40.15°
	+	360.00
subtotal		400.15
- Jupiter (slower)	-	93.97°
= Phase	=	306.18

Mercury and Jupiter are in a Third Quarter relationship with each other.

Faster Planet - Slower Planet = Planetary Phase

Eclipses

Remember from Lesson 15 that the Sun and Moon do not always share the same declination. While the Sun will always be located on the Ecliptic, the Moon's declination varies to the north and south of this plane. This means that, during a New Moon or Full Moon, the Moon and Sun are not always in perfect alignment when seen from the Earth. When the Moon and Sun are in perfect alignment, however, an eclipse occurs.

A **Solar Eclipse** occurs at a New Moon when the Moon is directly between the Earth and the Sun, thus blocking the light of the Sun from reaching Earth.

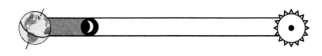

A **Lunar Eclipse** occurs at a Full Moon when the Earth is directly between the Sun and the Moon, blocking the light of the Sun from reaching the Moon.

A **Total Eclipse** is one in which the Sun, in a solar eclipse, or the Moon, in a lunar eclipse, is blocked completely. But due to the slight incline of the orbit of both the Earth and Moon, when eclipses occur they are not always total. **Partial Eclipses** occur when all three bodies are almost but not quite in perfect alignment so that the Moon or Sun is only partially blocked. Every six months, a solar and a lunar eclipse will occur, but most of these will be partial. Total eclipses only occur every few years and will then only be visible from specific locations on Earth.

Finding Eclipses in *The ACS Ephemeris*

Information on eclipses can be found in the "Phases & Eclipses" box at the bottom of each page in *The ACS Ephemeris*. The top half of the box shows lunar activity for the first month listed on the page, and the bottom section of the box lists activity for the second month. The date, hour and minute of each lunar event is given followed by the phase occurring and the zodiacal degree at which it occurred. Solar Eclipses are denoted with a black conjunction symbol (☌) and Lunar Eclipses are marked with a black opposition symbol(☍).

☽ Phases & Eclipses		
Dy Hr Mn		
7 6:36	☽	14♌52
13 21:34	●	21♏32
13 21:44:49	☀ P	0.928
21 2:03	☽	28♒47
29 6:31	○	7♊03
29 6:26	♐T	1.087
6 15:49	☽	14♍33
13 9:27	●	21♐23
20 22:26	☽	29♓04
28 23:05	○	7♋15

For November & December 1993

The Phases & Eclipses box to the right covers the months November and December 1993. Notice the black conjunction symbol immediately following the new moon glyph on the 13th of the top month November. A partial solar eclipse occurred at 21:44:49 GMT on that date. At the end of November, a total solar eclipse occurred on the 29th at 6:26 GMT.

The Prenatal Eclipse

The **prenatal eclipse** is the last eclipse (solar or lunar) to occur before a birth. Many astrologers believe that the zodiacal degree of the prenatal eclipse is a sensitive point in the birth chart. To locate the prenatal eclipse, simply find the birthdate in an ephemeris and scan backwards in time until locating the first eclipse. If the prenatal eclipse is a lunar eclipse, traditionally the degree of the Moon is used rather than the degree of the Sun.

Lesson 19 Exercises

Calculate the Phases between the planets listed below using the following chart. Answers can be found in the Answer Key in the Appendix.

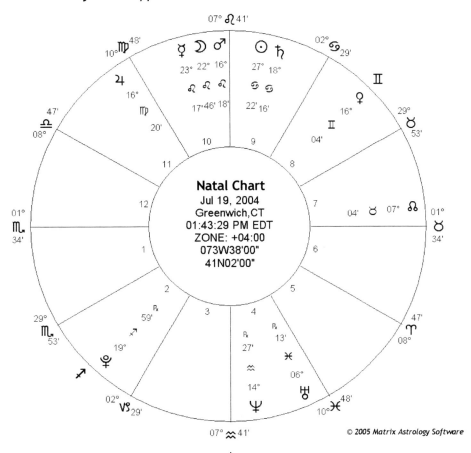

07° ♌ 41'

10°♍48'

23° 22° 16°
☿ ☽ ♂

27° 18°
☉ ♄

02° ♋ 29'

♃
16°

♌ ♌ ♌
♊

17'46' 18'

22' 16'

Ⅱ

♍
20'

10

9

04'

♀
16°

Ⅱ

47'
♎
08°

11

8

29°
♉
53'

12

Natal Chart
Jul 19, 2004
Greenwich, CT
01:43:29 PM EDT
ZONE: +04:00
073W38'00"
41N02'00"

7

04' ♉ 07° ☊

01°
♉
34'

01°
♏
34'

1

6

2

5

47'
♈
08°

29°
♏
53'

℞
59'

3

4

℞
13'

02° ♑ 29'

℞
27'
♓
14°
♇
♒
19°

06°
ℍ
♅
10° ♓ 48'

♆

07° ♒ 41'

© 2005 Matrix Astrology Software

---

1. Calculate the natal Lunar Phase.

2. Calculate the phase between Pluto and Mercury.

3. Calculate the phase between Mars and Venus.

4. At what degree and on what date did the prenatal eclipse occur?

Lesson 20: Section Exam

This lesson provides you with an opportunity to test yourself on all techniques covered in this section of the book. This exam is typical of a certification exam and does not include pre-printed calculation forms. Answers can be found in the Answer Key in the Appendix.

All of the questions relate to the following chart. Use the allowable orbs given below for any question relating to aspects.

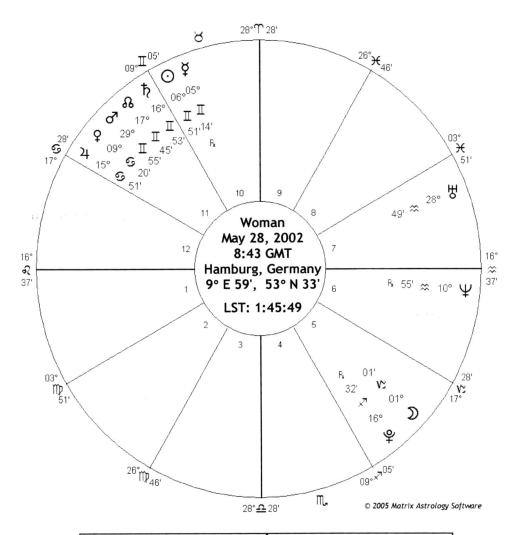

Woman
May 28, 2002
8:43 GMT
Hamburg, Germany
9° E 59', 53° N 33'

LST: 1:45:49

© 2005 Matrix Astrology Software

Aspect	Orb	Aspect	Orb
Conjunction	8°	Semi-sextile	3°
Opposition	8°	Semi-square	4°
Trine	8°	Sextile	6°
Square	8°	Sesquisquare	2°
Sextile	6°	Quincunx	2°

1. Calculate the aspects in the chart, then complete the aspectarian below.

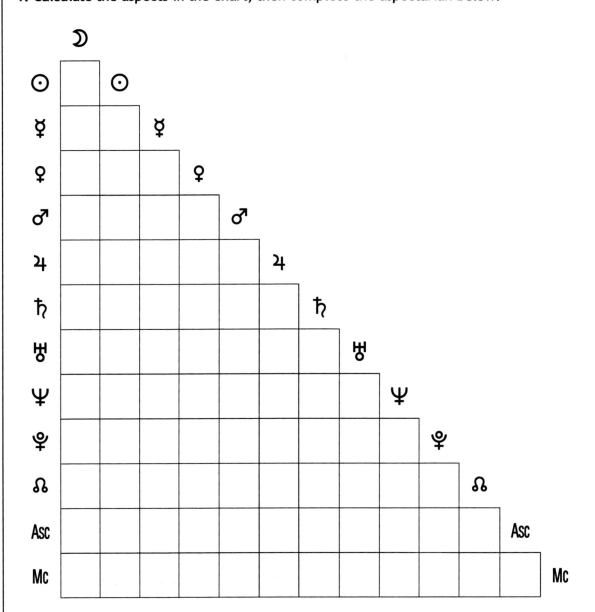

2. Calculate the Declinations of all planets, Ascendant and Midheaven in the chart, using the declination ephemeris provided on the facing page.

GMT +0:00 Tropical Geocentric Decl	Moon ☽	Sun ☉	Mercury ☿	Venus ♀	Mars ♂	Jupiter ♃	Saturn ♄	Uranus ♅	Neptune ♆	Pluto ♇	True Node ☊
May 1 2002	−24°37'	+14°57'	+22°52'	+22°08'	+23°00'	+23°12'	+21°04'	−12°43'	−17°24'	−12°44'	+22°56'
May 2 2002	−24°55'	+15°15'	+23°08'	+22°23'	+23°06'	+23°11'	+21°05'	−12°42'	−17°24'	−12°44'	+22°56'
May 3 2002	−23°52'	+15°33'	+23°23'	+22°37'	+23°12'	+23°11'	+21°06'	−12°42'	−17°24'	−12°44'	+22°56'
May 4 2002	−21°40'	+15°51'	+23°35'	+22°50'	+23°17'	+23°10'	+21°07'	−12°41'	−17°24'	−12°44'	+22°56'
May 5 2002	−18°33'	+16°08'	+23°44'	+23°03'	+23°22'	+23°09'	+21°08'	−12°41'	−17°24'	−12°43'	+22°56'
May 6 2002	−14°41'	+16°25'	+23°52'	+23°16'	+23°27'	+23°08'	+21°09'	−12°40'	−17°24'	−12°43'	+22°56'
May 7 2002	−10°18'	+16°42'	+23°57'	+23°27'	+23°32'	+23°07'	+21°10'	−12°40'	−17°24'	−12°43'	+22°56'
May 8 2002	−05°33'	+16°59'	+24°00'	+23°38'	+23°36'	+23°07'	+21°11'	−12°39'	−17°24'	−12°43'	+22°55'
May 9 2002	−00°36'	+17°15'	+24°01'	+23°49'	+23°41'	+23°06'	+21°12'	−12°39'	−17°24'	−12°43'	+22°55'
May 10 2002	+04°26'	+17°31'	+24°00'	+23°58'	+23°45'	+23°05'	+21°13'	−12°39'	−17°24'	−12°42'	+22°54'
May 11 2002	+09°21'	+17°47'	+23°57'	+24°07'	+23°49'	+23°04'	+21°14'	−12°38'	−17°24'	−12°42'	+22°54'
May 12 2002	+13°59'	+18°02'	+23°52'	+24°16'	+23°53'	+23°03'	+21°15'	−12°38'	−17°24'	−12°42'	+22°54'
May 13 2002	+18°06'	+18°17'	+23°45'	+24°23'	+23°56'	+23°02'	+21°16'	−12°38'	−17°24'	−12°42'	+22°53'
May 14 2002	+21°28'	+18°32'	+23°36'	+24°30'	+23°59'	+23°01'	+21°17'	−12°37'	−17°24'	−12°42'	+22°53'
May 15 2002	+23°50'	+18°46'	+23°26'	+24°36'	+24°03'	+23°00'	+21°18'	−12°37'	−17°24'	−12°42'	+22°53'
May 16 2002	+24°58'	+19°00'	+23°14'	+24°42'	+24°06'	+22°59'	+21°19'	−12°37'	−17°24'	−12°41'	+22°53'
May 17 2002	+24°43'	+19°14'	+23°00'	+24°47'	+24°08'	+22°58'	+21°20'	−12°36'	−17°24'	−12°41'	+22°53'
May 18 2002	+23°02'	+19°28'	+22°44'	+24°51'	+24°11'	+22°57'	+21°21'	−12°36'	−17°24'	−12°41'	+22°54'
May 19 2002	+19°59'	+19°41'	+22°27'	+24°54'	+24°13'	+22°56'	+21°21'	−12°36'	−17°24'	−12°41'	+22°54'
May 20 2002	+15°45'	+19°54'	+22°09'	+24°57'	+24°15'	+22°55'	+21°22'	−12°36'	−17°24'	−12°41'	+22°54'
May 21 2002	+10°36'	+20°06'	+21°50'	+24°59'	+24°17'	+22°53'	+21°23'	−12°36'	−17°24'	−12°41'	+22°54'
May 22 2002	+04°47'	+20°18'	+21°29'	+25°00'	+24°19'	+22°52'	+21°24'	−12°35'	−17°24'	−12°40'	+22°54'
May 23 2002	−01°20'	+20°30'	+21°08'	+25°01'	+24°20'	+22°51'	+21°25'	−12°35'	−17°24'	−12°40'	+22°53'
May 24 2002	−07°25'	+20°42'	+20°46'	+25°01'	+24°22'	+22°50'	+21°26'	−12°35'	−17°24'	−12°40'	+22°53'
May 25 2002	−13°05'	+20°53'	+20°23'	+25°00'	+24°23'	+22°49'	+21°27'	−12°35'	−17°24'	−12°40'	+22°53'
May 26 2002	−17°58'	+21°03'	+20°01'	+24°58'	+24°23'	+22°47'	+21°28'	−12°35'	−17°24'	−12°40'	+22°53'
May 27 2002	−21°45'	+21°14'	+19°38'	+24°56'	+24°24'	+22°46'	+21°28'	−12°35'	−17°25'	−12°40'	+22°53'
May 28 2002	−24°08'	+21°24'	+19°16'	+24°53'	+24°25'	+22°45'	+21°29'	−12°35'	−17°25'	−12°40'	+22°53'
May 29 2002	−25°03'	+21°33'	+18°54'	+24°49'	+24°25'	+22°44'	+21°30'	−12°35'	−17°25'	−12°40'	+22°53'
May 30 2002	−24°30'	+21°43'	+18°33'	+24°45'	+24°25'	+22°42'	+21°31'	−12°35'	−17°25'	−12°39'	+22°53'
May 31 2002	−22°41'	+21°51'	+18°13'	+24°40'	+24°25'	+22°41'	+21°32'	−12°35'	−17°25'	−12°39'	+22°53'

Declination ephemeris prepared using Solarfire v.5

3. What is the closest aspect in this Chart? _____.

4. Which was the last aspect made by the Moon? _____.

5. What will be the next Ptolemaic aspect made by the Moon? _____.

6. What aspect is made between Mars and the Ascendant? _____.

7. What is the midpoint between Saturn and Jupiter? _____.

8. Calculate the antiscion of the Sun _____ .

9. Calculate the antiscion of the Moon _____.

10. Calculate the Natal Lunar Phase _____.

11. Calculate the Part of Fortune _____.

12. Calculate the Equatorial Ascendant _____ & the Vertex _____.

Section 7:

Secondary Progressions

Lesson 21: Introduction to Progressions
& The Adjusted Calculation Date

The term **progression** encompasses several methods used in predictive astrology to "progress" or advance a birthchart through time. This lesson includes a brief description of the most common methods. We then focus on secondary progressions, and explain the Adjusted Calculation Date (ACD) which is used in the calculation process.

What are progressions?

An important part of an astrologer's job is to help clients with current issues by looking at the natal chart in relation to inner development and personal growth, and progressions are techniques that help to reveal this growth. While the effects of planetary transits on a birthchart are often associated with the external events in a life, progressions are believed to relate to the gradual unfoldment of life on an inner level.

All progressions are symbolic methods of advancing a chart. The most common progression methods described in this lesson are based on an analogy between the earth's daily rotation on its axis and its annual revolution around the Sun. This "day for a year" principle is common in biblical symbolism, where prophetic time periods given in days are believed to be metaphorical for years, and where certain scriptures imply that a year of life on earth is equivalent to a day for God. As you will see below, secondary progressions follow this metaphor exactly, while other methods draw on it a little more loosely. Although each is different, these progression methods have stood the test of time and have been shown to be effective for forecasting and gaining insight into inner emotional and spiritual change.

Secondary progressions advance the birth chart one day for each year of life. Secondary progressions are the most common progression method used by modern western astrologers, and the remainder of this lesson will explain them in detail.

Solar arc directions are based solely on the Sun's daily motion. To calculate solar arc directions, the Sun is moved forward a day for each year of life, then the difference in degrees and minutes between this progressed position and its natal position, called the **solar arc**, is added to every planet and house cusp in the natal chart, so that all planets and house cusps move at the same rate of speed. Solar arc directions are also commonly used and are covered in Lesson 26.

Primary directions were first described by Ptolemy in the 1st century CE. In this system, one year of life is equivalent to the time it takes for 1 degree to pass over the Midheaven, or about 4 minutes, measured in right ascension along the Celestial Equator rather than along the Ecliptic. Thus, a lifetime is the equivalent of just 5 or 6 hours. Primary directions are rarely used by astrologers today due to the complicated computations required.

Tertiary directions correlate each day to a lunar month, instead of a solar year. Because tertiary directions move much faster than day-for-a-year directions, they are generally used for timing specific events rather than gaining insight into long-term developments. Like primary directions, tertiary directions are not commonly used.

Converse directions are based on the same symbolic correlations as the techniques described above, but move the chart backwards through time instead of forwards. Converse secondary progressions move the chart backwards one day for each year of life, converse tertiary directions move the chart backwards one day for each month of life, and so on.

211

Secondary Progressions

Secondary progressions take the most literal interpretation of the "day for a year" principle in that each day after birth is thought to represent each successive year of life. In this system, to get a rough idea of where the progressed planets will be for someone born July 5, 1983 at age 25, we would count 25 days from July 5, 1983 and look at the planetary positions on that date, as shown below:

Birthday → (5 Tu)

Count 25 days

Progressed Planets at age 25 → (30 Sa)

JULY 1983 **LONGITUDE**

Day	Sid.Time	☉	0 hr ☽	Noon ☽	True ☊	☿	♀	♂	♃	♄	♅	♆	♇
1 F	18 33 55	8♋36 54	10♓29 13	16♓28 39	24♊59.8	28♊19.9	23♌ 3.7	1♋ 9.3	2♐15.5	27♎43.4	5♐50.6	27♐33.3	26♎43.3
2 Sa	18 37 52	9 34 6	22 30 20	28 34 47	24R 58.5	0♋24.6	23 52.3	1 49.7	2R 10.7	27D 43.4	5R 48.7	27R 31.8	26R 43.1
3 Su	18 41 49	10 31 18	4♈42 33	10♈54 10	24D 57.8	2 30.8	24 40.0	2 30.1	2 6.0	27 43.5	5 46.8	27 30.2	26 43.0
4 M	18 45 45	11 28 30	17 10 8	23 30 59	24 57.8	4 38.4	25 27.0	3 10.5	2 1.5	27 43.7	5 44.9	27 28.6	26 42.8
5 Tu	18 49 42	12 25 42	29 57 11	6♉29 10	24 58.4	6 47.1	26 13.2	3 50.8	1 57.2	27 44.0	5 43.1	27 27.1	26 42.7
6 W	18 53 38	13 22 55	13♉ 7 17	19 51 50	24 59.6	8 56.6	26 58.5	4 31.0	1 53.0	27 44.3	5 41.3	27 25.5	26 42.7
7 Th	18 57 35	14 20 8	26 42 58	3♊40 44	25 0.9	11 6.5	27 43.0	5 11.3	1 48.9	27 44.8	5 39.5	27 24.0	26D 42.6
8 F	19 1 31	15 17 21	10♊45 3	17 55 38	25 2.0	13 16.7	28 26.5	5 51.4	1 45.1	27 45.4	5 37.8	27 22.4	26 42.6
9 Sa	19 5 28	16 14 35	25 12 4	2♋33 45	25R 2.5	15 26.8	29 9.1	6 31.6	1 41.4	27 46.1	5 36.1	27 20.9	26 42.7
10 Su	19 9 24	17 11 49	9♋59 53	17 29 35	25 1.9	17 36.5	29 50.8	7 11.7	1 37.8	27 46.9	5 34.5	27 19.4	26 42.7
11 M	19 13 21	18 9 3	25 1 46	2♌35 18	25 0.3	19 45.6	0♍31.4	7 51.8	1 34.5	27 47.8	5 32.8	27 17.9	26 42.8
12 Tu	19 17 18	19 6 17	10♌ 8 59	17 41 38	24 57.7	21 54.0	1 10.9	8 31.8	1 31.3	27 48.8	5 31.3	27 16.5	26 43.0
13 W	19 21 14	20 3 32	25 12 7	2♍39 23	24 54.5	24 1.3	1 49.3	9 11.8	1 28.2	27 49.9	5 29.7	27 15.0	26 43.1
14 Th	19 25 11	21 0 46	10♍ 2 30	17 20 43	24 51.2	26 7.4	2 26.6	9 51.7	1 25.4	27 51.1	5 28.2	27 13.5	26 43.3
15 F	19 29 7	21 58 0	24 33 26	1♎40 14	24 48.3	28 12.2	3 2.7	10 31.6	1 22.7	27 52.4	5 26.8	27 12.1	26 43.6
16 Sa	19 33 4	22 55 14	8♎40 53	15 35 17	24 46.4	0♌15.6	3 37.5	11 11.5	1 20.2	27 53.7	5 25.4	27 10.7	26 43.9
17 Su	19 37 0	23 52 29	22 23 30	29 5 42	24D 45.7	2 17.5	4 11.0	11 51.3	1 17.9	27 55.2	5 24.0	27 9.3	26 44.2
18 M	19 40 57	24 49 43	5♏42 7	12♏13 8	24 46.1	4 17.7	4 43.2	12 31.1	1 15.7	27 56.8	5 22.6	27 7.9	26 44.5
19 Tu	19 44 53	25 46 57	18 39 5	25 0 26	24 47.3	6 16.3	5 14.0	13 10.9	1 13.8	27 58.5	5 21.4	27 6.5	26 44.9
20 W	19 48 50	26 44 12	1♐17 34	7♐30 57	24 49.0	8 13.2	5 43.3	13 50.6	1 12.0	28 0.2	5 20.1	27 5.1	26 45.3
21 Th	19 52 47	27 41 27	13 41 0	19 48 8	24R 50.3	10 8.3	6 11.1	14 30.2	1 10.4	28 2.1	5 18.9	27 3.8	26 45.7
22 F	19 56 43	28 38 43	25 52 43	1♑55 9	24 50.8	12 1.7	6 37.3	15 9.8	1 9.0	28 4.0	5 17.8	27 2.5	26 46.2
23 Sa	20 0 40	29 35 58	7♑55 44	13 54 47	24 50.0	13 53.3	7 1.9	15 49.4	1 7.8	28 6.1	5 16.6	27 1.2	26 46.7
24 Su	20 4 36	0♌33 15	19 52 36	25 49 27	24 47.4	15 43.2	7 24.9	16 29.0	1 6.7	28 8.2	5 15.6	26 59.9	26 47.3
25 M	20 8 33	1 30 31	1♒45 35	7♒41 13	24 43.2	17 31.3	7 46.1	17 8.5	1 5.8	28 10.5	5 14.6	26 58.6	26 47.9
26 Tu	20 12 29	2 27 49	13 36 36	19 31 58	24 37.5	19 17.7	8 5.4	17 48.0	1 5.1	28 12.8	5 13.6	26 57.4	26 48.5
27 W	20 16 26	3 25 7	25 27 31	1♓23 33	24 30.7	21 2.2	8 23.0	18 27.4	1 4.6	28 15.2	5 12.6	26 56.1	26 49.1
28 Th	20 20 22	4 22 26	7♓20 17	13 18 2	24 23.4	22 45.1	8 38.6	19 6.8	1 4.3	28 17.7	5 11.8	26 54.9	26 49.8
29 F	20 24 19	5 19 45	19 17 5	25 17 47	24 16.5	24 26.2	8 52.2	19 46.2	1D 4.2	28 20.3	5 10.9	26 53.7	26 50.5
30 Sa	20 28 16	6 17 6	1♈20 30	7♈25 37	24 10.6	26 5.5	9 3.8	20 25.5	1 4.2	28 23.0	5 10.1	26 52.6	26 51.2
31 Su	20 32 12	7 14 27	13 33 36	19 44 52	24 6.2	27 43.2	9 13.4	21 4.8	1 4.4	28 25.8	5 9.4	26 51.4	26 52.0

In secondary progressions, each planet moves at a rate according to its own daily speed. Each year the progressed Sun will move ahead by its daily motion of around 58-60 minutes, exactly as it does in solar arc directions, but every other planet will progress at its own individual rate. The fast-moving Moon may advance 14° or more each year, while slow movers like Saturn and the outer planets may move only 1-2 minutes. In fact, the outer planets and Nodes move so slowly via secondary progression that they are not usually considered in interpretation. In secondary progressions, planets can speed up, slow down, travel forwards or backwards and change direction, just as they do over the course of 2-3 months, the equivalent of a lifetime by progression.

Notice in the example above that on the birth date, Jupiter was at 1°♐ 57' and retrograde. By age 25, Jupiter had traveled backwards to 1°♐ 4' and changed to direct motion. Venus was slowly grinding to a halt, in preparation for turning retrograde on August 3rd, which by progression will correlate to this person's 29th year. In contrast, the Moon had made nearly an entire trip through the zodiac, starting in Taurus and progressing all the way around to Aries by age 25.

The table below gives the average daily speed of each planet, corresponding to its average yearly rate by progression. Keep in mind that these are averages; the actual rate of progression will depend on at what point in its cycle each planet is located, and whether it is direct or retrograde.

Average Daily Speed of the Planets = Average Annual Speed by Progression			
Sun	1 degree per day (year)	**Saturn**	2 minutes per day (year)
Moon	13 degrees per day (year)	**Uranus**	Less than ½ minute per day (year)
Mercury	1 degree per day (year)	**Neptune**	Less than ½ minute per day (year)
Venus	1 degree per day (year)	**Pluto**	Less than ½ minute per day (year)
Mars	30 minutes per day (year)	**Nodes**	5 minutes per day (year)
Jupiter	5 minutes per day (year)		

The "Personal Year"

In all progressions, when we talk about a year of life we are referring to a year from birthday to birthday, which we will call the "personal year". Naturally, when a birthday is not on January 1st the personal year will not coincide with the calendar year. Below, the personal year is illustrated for a birth on July 5, 1983. Notice also that what is labeled the "first personal year" refers to the first year of life from birth to age one. Similarly, when someone says "the 29th year", they are in fact referring to the year from age 28 to age 29, when the person is 28 years of age, not 29.

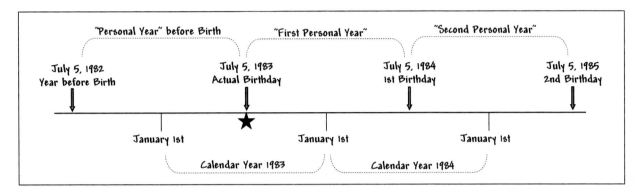

A Day = A Year

In "day for a year" symbolism, each personal year from birthday to birthday corresponds symbolically to each "personal day" - that is, each 24-hour period running from birth <u>time</u> to birth <u>time</u> each day after birth. The first year after birth corresponds to the first 24 hours after birth, the second year to the second 24 hours, and so on. In symbolic terms, each 24-hour "personal day" corresponds to one "progressed year".

Let us say a birth occurred at 8:00 am GMT on July 5, 1983. Each 24-hour period, running from 8:00 am to 8:00 am, will correspond to a "personal year" running from birthday to birthday, which in this case is July 5th to July 5th each year. By the first birthday, this person's planets will have "progressed" to their actual positions at 8:00 am on July 6, 1983, exactly 24 hours after birth. By the second birthday, the progressed planets will be located at their actual positions at 8:00 am on July 7, 1983, two complete days after birth, and so on.

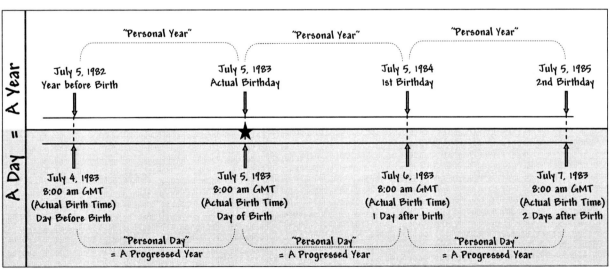

The Adjusted Calculation Date

As you can see, the time of birth plays a large part in determining the positions of progressed planets. If we wanted to pinpoint where the progressed planets would be on each birthday for this person, we would need to calculate a complete natal chart for each equivalent progressed date and time, such as a chart for 8:00 am GMT on July 6, 1983 to show progressions on the first birthday, a chart for 8:00 am GMT on July 7, 1983 to show progressions on the second birthday, and so on. Needless to say this is a lot of work, and luckily a much simpler method has been devised. This method involves the use of the **Adjusted Calculation Date**, abbreviated "**ACD**". The "ACD" is a date that represents the equivalent of 0 hour GMT for a particular individual.

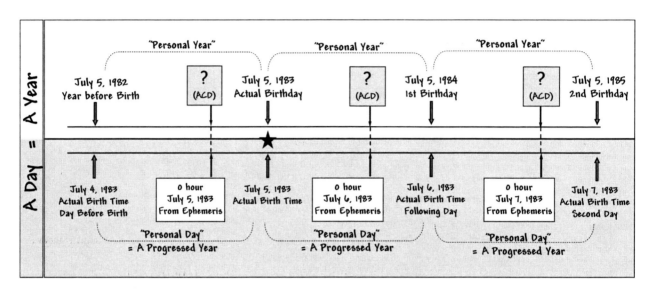

In "day for a year" symbolism, any given time during a day will correspond to a certain day during a year. Therefore, 0-hour on any day will correspond to a specific date during each personal year. That date is called the Adjusted Calculation Date, or ACD. In the diagram above we have indicated where 0-hour GMT falls within each "personal day". The specific day during this person's "personal year" corresponding to 0-hour will be this person's ACD. Notice that because this birth occurred at 8:00 am GMT, which is one-third of the way through a 24-hour day, the "actual birth time" arrows fall one-third of the way between the 0 hour GMT markings. This person's ACD will therefore fall one-third of a year before each actual birthday, or 122 days before each July 5th (because 1/3 of 365 days = 122). 122 days before July 5th falls on March 4, 1983 in this case. (We will go into more detail on how to calculate a precise ACD later in this lesson. For now just grasp that the ACD represents the exact date during one's personal year that is the symbolic equivalent to 0 hour GMT.)

Everyone's ACD will be different, because it is determined by taking the number of days equivalent to a person's GMT of birth, and projecting that number of days back from the birthday within the personal year. In other words, the portion of the day that elapsed from 0-hour until the time of birth in GMT is converted into a proportionate number of days of a year, which we will call the "ACD Interval". Then the ACD Interval is subtracted from the birthdate to arrive at the ACD. This is illustrated in the diagram at the top of the facing page.

(Note: "0 Hour" does NOT represent January 1st - remember that in progressions all symbolic equivalences relate to the personal year and not the calendar year.)

Remember from the natal chart calculation lessons that the GMT of Birth represents the portion of the day that elapsed from 0-hour on the birth date to the actual time of birth. This is illustrated in the lower half of the diagram below. We are now taking this same proportion and projecting it back from the birth date to arrive at the ACD, shown in the upper half of the diagram.

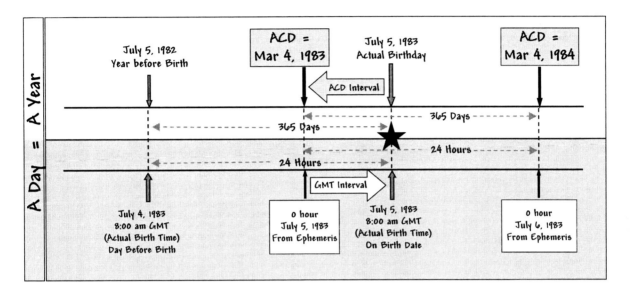

Why Have an ACD?

Before we get involved in the specifics of learning to calculate the ACD, let's clarify why we need to know this date and how it will be used. The ACD is like a progressions "shortcut" - it's a fast and accurate way to pinpoint the positions of all progressed planets once a year without needing to go through the bother of erecting a full chart. Each person's ACD is equivalent to their own personal "0-hour" each year - it tells when the progressed planetary positions listed in the ephemeris will be exact for that person.

Once a person's ACD has been determined, it never needs to be calculated again. Every year on the ACD, the positions of the progressed planets taken straight out of the ephemeris will be accurate without any extra calculations needed at all. Then, if progressed planets need to be pinpointed on any other day of the year, positions can be interpolated between ACDs. (This procedure will be covered in detail in the next lesson).

The ACD is also a great way to quickly estimate when a progressed planet will change sign or house, or when a progressed aspect will perfect (become exact), by simply looking in the ephemeris. This is especially helpful for estimating the position of the progressed Moon which moves 12 or more degrees each year, without needing to erect a chart or run to a computer. If an exact date is needed for any progressed event, then the ACD can be used to pinpoint it. (How to do this will be covered in lesson 24.)

The ACD concept should be mastered by all astrologers even if, once certified, you never intend to hand calculate a chart again. The ability you will gain to quickly assess and time progressions will be worth every minute spent.

Finding the Adjusted Calculation Date

Three steps are needed to determine the ACD:

Step 1. Use the GMT of Birth to calculate CM-1, which represents the portion of the day that has elapsed from 0 hour to the time of birth. This is the same CM-1 used when calculating a natal chart. (Refer to Lesson 8 if you need to review this procedure.)

Step 2. Multiply 365 days by CM-1. The result is the "ACD Interval" and represents the same proportion of days to a year as the time of birth's hours and minutes are to a day. Round off to the nearest whole number.

Step 3. Starting with the birthdate as '0', count <u>back</u> the number of days found in Step 2. This date is the ACD. Just as 0-hour on the birth date is always before the actual time of birth, the ACD will always be earlier in the year than the birth date, and may even extend back into the previous calendar year depending on the date and time of birth. (To simplify this step, we have provided a Table of Numbered Days in the Appendix of this book. Using the Table in place of counting days is demonstrated in Example 1, below.)

Example 1.

Let's determine the ACD for a birth at 10:30 GMT on March 17, 1962.

Step 1. Use the GMT of Birth to calculate CM-1. As was done when calculating CM-1 for a natal chart in lesson 8, convert the GMT of birth to a decimal, then divide by 24 hours, carrying the answer out to 3 decimal places.

CM-1

Convert GMT of Birth to decimal: ___10.5___ ÷ 24 = **CM-1** ___.438___

Step 2. Multiply 365 days by CM-1. The result is the "ACD Interval".

$$365 \times .438 = 159.87, \text{ rounded to 160 days}$$

160 days out of 365 represents the same proportion as 10:30, the GMT of birth, represents out of 24 hours. Another way to express this is:

$$\frac{10.5 \ (GMT)}{24} = \frac{160}{365}$$

Step 3. Starting with the birthdate as '0', count <u>back</u> the number of days found in Step 2. This date is the ACD. This step can be done manually or with the aid of our handy Table of Numbered Days found in the Appendix. Both methods will be demonstrated.

The Manual Method: The birth date is March 17, 1962. Starting with the birth date as '0', we can count back in the ephemeris 160 days, which will land us on October 8, 1961, or we can take a shortcut as follows: Not counting the birth date, 16 full days have elapsed in March. To this figure, we add as many full months of days as is necessary until arriving at the first subtotal <u>greater than</u> the number of days needed. (If you have forgotten how many days are in each month of a year, refer to your ephemeris.)

March	16	
February	28	Subtotal = 44
January	31	Subtotal = 75
December	31	Subtotal = 106
November	30	Subtotal = 136
October	31	Subtotal = 167

The subtotal is now 7 days over the target of 160 days. The ACD will be the first day <u>following</u> 7 whole days in the month of October, or October 8, 1961.

Using the Table of Numbered Days: An even shorter method for arriving at the ACD is to use the handy Table of Numbered Days found in the Appendix. Use the Table to find the numbered day of the year corresponding to the birth date, then subtract the ACD Interval from this. The result will be the number corresponding to the ACD. Two years are included in the Table to simplify calculations in cases where the ACD extends back into the previous calendar year.

In the example, the numbered day corresponding to March 17, the birth date, is 76. The ACD Interval of 160 cannot be subtracted from this number, so the numbered day corresponding to March 17th from the second year, which is 441, will be used instead:

Birthday	441
ACD Interval	- 160
= ACD	281

Look up "281" in the Table and find that this number corresponds to October 8th of the previous calendar year. Therefore, the ACD for this example is October 8, 1961.

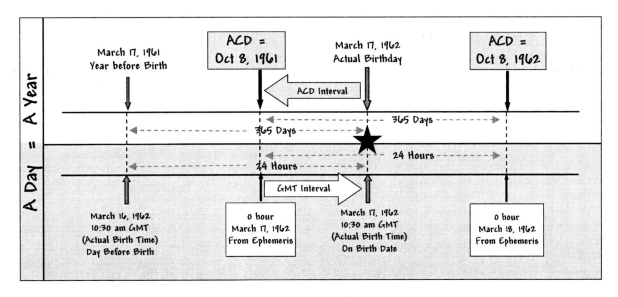

Example 2.

Let's calculate the ACD for a birth on April 10, 1997, at 2:15 GMT.

Step 1. Use the GMT of Birth to calculate CM-1.

> # CM-1
>
> Convert GMT of Birth to decimal: __2.25__ ÷ 24 = **CM-1** ___.094___

Step 2. Multiply 365 days by CM-1. The result is the "ACD Interval".

365 x .094 = 34.31, rounded to 34 days

Step 3. Starting with the birthdate as '0', count <u>back</u> the number of days found in Step 2. This date is the ACD.

April 10	Day # 100
- ACD Interval	- 34
= ACD	= Day # 66, or March 7, 1997

This informs us that, if we count in an ephemeris one day for each year, the positions found for 0 hour on that day will correspond to this person's progressed planets on the March 7th <u>before</u> that birthday. For instance, the planetary positions listed in an ephemeris for the day after his birth will correspond to his progressed planets on the ACD before his 1st birthday, or March 7, 1998, as shown in the diagram below. Similarly, ephemeris positions listed 10 days after his birth (April 20, 1997) will correspond to his exact progressed planets on the ACD before his 10th birthday, or March 7, 2007. If we were to run a computerized chart for this person, progressed to March 7, 2007, the planets would be in the exact same positions as those shown in an ephemeris for 0 hour on April 20, 1997, 10 days after his birth.

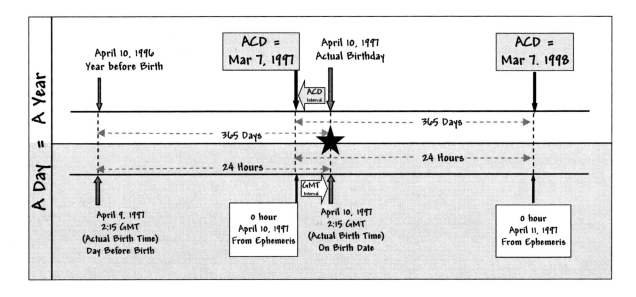

Example 3.

Let's calculate the ACD for a birth on April 10, 1997, at 23:06 GMT.

Step 1. Use the GMT of Birth to calculate CM-1.

CM-1

Convert GMT of Birth to decimal: ___23.1___ ÷ 24 = CM-1 ___.963___

Step 2. Multiply 365 days by CM-1. The result is the "ACD Interval".

365 x .963 = 351.495, rounded to 351 days

Step 3. Starting with the birthdate as '0', count <u>back</u> the number of days found in Step 2. This date is the ACD.

April 10   =   Day # 465
- ACD Interval   - 351

= ACD   = Day # 114, or April 24, 1996

Notice in this example that the day of birth was almost over by the birth time at 23:06 GMT. In the same way, this person's "ACD year" was almost over as well. For this person, the planets listed in an ephemeris for 0 hour on the day following his birth will correspond to the positions of his progressed planets on April 24, 1997, just 14 days after his birth date.

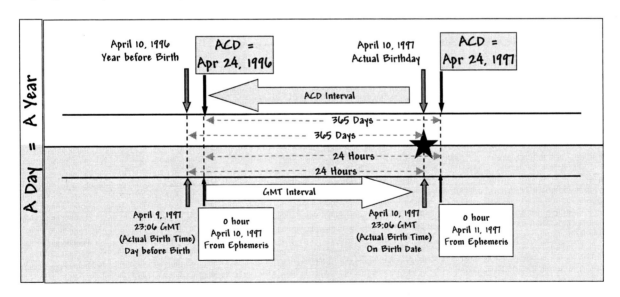

One final point to keep in mind when determining the ACD:

If the birth date changed when converting the time of birth to GMT, Always use the <u>GMT date</u> as the Birth date.

(If this is still confusing, review lesson 3 on finding the GMT of birth.)

Lesson 21 Exercises

Determine the ACD for each of the following births. Answers can be found in the Answer Key in the Appendix.

1. December 12, 1983, 3:55 GMT

2. July 16, 1995, 20:33 GMT

3. November 30, 1996, 13:45 GMT

Lesson 22: Using an ACD
To Locate Progressed Planets

The previous lesson covered how to find an ACD based on the time and date of birth. In this lesson, the ACD will be used to locate progressed planets on any given day by either progressing to the ACD itself, or by interpolating between ACDs to progress to any other date.

Progressing Planets to the ACD

Lesson 21 explained that using the ACD simplifies pinpointing the positions of progressed planets once a year. Each year the positions of the planets given in a midnight ephemeris on a specific day after the birthday will correlate with the positions of the progressed planets on the ACD before the same-numbered birthday, as follows:

Ephemeris positions 1 day after birth = Progressed positions on ACD before 1st birthday
Ephemeris positions 5 days after birth = Progressed positions on ACD before 5th birthday
Ephemeris positions 50 days after birth = Progressed positions on ACD before 50th birthday
and so on.

**The planetary positions given in an ephemeris for 0-hour "X" days after birth
will always correspond to the progressed planetary positions
on the ACD occurring <u>before</u> the same-numbered birthday.**

Progressing planets to an ACD requires two very simple steps:

Step 1. First, determine the correct day in the ephemeris to represent the target age.
This is accomplished by either counting days in the ephemeris, starting with the birth date as "0", or by using the Table of Numbered Days. When dealing with advanced ages, using the Table will save time and counting.

Step 2. Second, specify the year of the target ACD, according to the target age. The ACD month and day will always be the same; the ACD year is determined by adding the target age to the birth ACD as calculated in the previous lesson. As explained in that lesson, this ACD may fall in the calendar year of birth, or the previous calendar year, depending on the time and date of birth.

Remember, when counting days in the ephemeris,

**Always Count from the Birthday in the <u>Birth Year</u>,
NOT the Progressed Year.**

**The birth date itself is "0".
The first day <u>following</u> the birth date is Day 1.**

Example 1.

Let's progress the planets for a person born on April 10, 1997, at 23:06 GMT, to the ACD before the 23rd birthday. We have already determined this person's birth ACD to be April 24, 1996 in Example 3 of the previous lesson.

First, determine the correct day in the ephemeris to represent the target, which is the ACD before the 23rd birthday. This can be accomplished by either counting 23 days from the birthdate in the ephemeris, or by using the Table of Numbered Days as follows:

$$
\begin{aligned}
\text{April 10 (Birthday)} &= \text{Day \# 100} \\
\text{+ Progressed Age} &\quad \underline{+\ 23} \\
&= \text{Day \# 123, \ or May 3, 1997}
\end{aligned}
$$

This indicates that the planetary positions listed in the ephemeris 23 days after the birth date, or May 3, 1997, will correspond to the progressed planets on the ACD before the 23rd birthday. Now let's pinpoint exactly where the ACD before the 23rd birthday falls:

$$
\begin{aligned}
\text{Birth ACD} &\quad \text{April 24, 1996 (calculated in Lesson 21, Example 3)} \\
\text{+ Progressed age} &\quad \underline{+\qquad\ 23} \\
= \text{ACD before 23rd birthday} &\quad = \text{April 24, 2019}
\end{aligned}
$$

The planetary positions at 0 hour on May 3, 1997 correspond to April 24, 2019 by progression. If we were to progress this person's natal chart to April 24, 2019, the progressed positions of all planets would be exactly those listed for 0 hour on May 3, 1997, as shown in *The ACS Ephemeris* below:

LONGITUDE **MAY 1997**

Day	Sid.Time	☉	0 hr ☽	Noon ☽	True ☊	☿	♀	♂	♃	♄	♅	♆	♇
1 Th	14 35 51	10♉39 47	22♒23 23	29♒30 13	27♍56.0	1♉42.9	18♉ 1.5	16♍48.1	19♒30.1	14♈ 3.4	8♒36.7	29♑57.5	4♐52.5
2 F	14 39 47	11 38 1	6♓38 51	12♓49 0	27 57.1	1R11.9	19 15.5	16 50.8	19 37.0	14 10.4	8 37.2	29 57.5	4 51.0
3 Sa	14 43 44	12 36 13	21 0 20	28 12 28	27R58.2	0 44.4	20 29.4	16 54.2	19 43.8	14 17.3	8 37.8	29 57.5	4 49.5
4 Su	14 47 40	13 34 24	5♈24 56	12♈37 12	27 58.1	0 20.8	21 43.4	16 58.3	19 50.5	14 24.2	8 38.3	29 57.4	4 48.0
5 M	14 51 37	14 32 34	19 48 41	26 58 46	27 56.2	0 1.3	22 57.3	17 3.1	19 56.9	14 31.1	8 38.8	29 57.3	4 46.5

This can be checked against a computer. Below are two computer-generated charts - the chart on the left is the natal chart, and the chart on the right is the natal chart progressed to April 24, 2019. Notice that the planetary positions in the progressed chart agree with the ephemeris listings highlighted above:

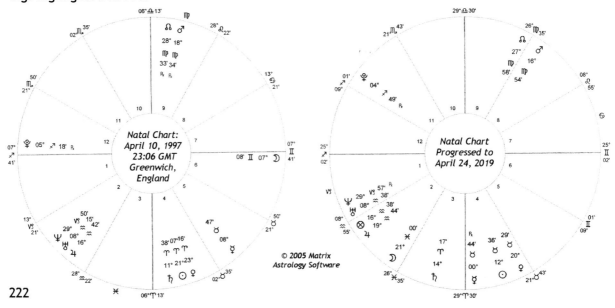

© 2005 Matrix
Astrology Software

Natal Chart:
April 10, 1997
23:06 GMT
Greenwich,
England

Natal Chart
Progressed to
April 24, 2019

222

Use your ACD to Estimate your Progressed Moon

Are you still not sure what the ACD is and why it is needed? If so, finding your own ACD and using it to estimate the position of your progressed Moon will help to demonstrate the ACD's value. Do you know where your progressed Moon is roughly located right now? Follow these steps to find out.

First, determine your ACD.

What is your GMT time and date of birth? (Remember that if your birthdate changed when determining your GMT of birth, you must use the GMT date here and not the given date.)

Birth Time: _____ GMT

Birth Date: _____

Convert your GMT of birth to a decimal, then divide by 24 to determine what portion of the day had already elapsed by the time you were born:

____.____ *hours* ÷ 24 = _____

Now multiply 365 by this portion to find the equivalent number of days, also called the "ACD Interval":

X 365 = _____

Finally, count back this number of days from your birthday. What date do you land on? This is your Birth ACD. *(You can use the Table of Numbered Days to help you with this step.)*

Birth ACD = _____

Then, use your ACD to estimate where your progressed Moon is located right now.

What is today's date? This will be your "target date".

Today's Date _____

Which ACD is nearest to this date - the current year's ACD, last year's ACD, or next year's ACD? Remember that the month and day of your ACD will always be the same, only the year will change.

Nearest ACD _____*

Subtract the year of your Birth ACD from the year of this nearest ACD. The answer tells you how many days to count ahead in the ephemeris. Then open your ephemeris to the **year** and **month** of your birth. Starting with your GMT birthdate as "0", count forward this number of days.

Nearest ACD Year _____

Birth ACD Year - _____

= _____

What date did you land on? This is the equivalent ephemeris date.

Equivalent Ephemeris Date _____

What was the Moon's position at 0 hour on this date? Your progressed Moon was at this exact position on the date of the nearest ACD you determined at * above.

Moon's 0-hr position _____

To estimate where your progressed Moon is located today, add 1° for each month that has passed since your nearest ACD. For example, if your ACD falls in February and it is now May, add 3°, because 3 months have passed. 1° per month is a rough estimate of the progressed Moon's speed, because the Moon travels roughly 12° per day which corresponds to 12° per year by progression. If the ACD you chose as the nearest has not yet occurred, then subtract 1° for each month left to go between now and then. (To determine your progressed Moon's exact position, follow the steps shown under "Progressing Planets to a Day other than the ACD" later in this lesson.)

Progressed Moon's estimated position

_____

Example 2.

For this example we will use the same birth data used in Example 1 of the previous lesson: March 17, 1962, 10:30 GMT. In that lesson the birth ACD was calculated as October 8, 1961. Now let's progress this person's planets to the ACD before the 40th birthday. First, determine which day falls 40 days after the date of birth:

$$\begin{array}{rl} \text{March 17 (Birthday)} = & \text{Day \# 76} \\ \text{+ Progressed Age} & \underline{+ \ 40} \\ = & \text{Day \#116} \ = \text{April 26, 1962} \end{array}$$

Day number 116 in the table corresponds to April 26th. Therefore, the planetary positions given in the ephemeris for April 26th after the birthday, or April 26, 1962, will correspond to the positions of this person's progressed planets on the ACD before the 40th birthday, or October 8, 2001:

$$\begin{array}{ll} \text{ACD} & \text{October 8, 1961} \\ \text{+ Progressed age} & \underline{+ \qquad\qquad 40} \\ = \text{ACD before 40th birthday} & = \text{October 8, 2001} \end{array}$$

If we were to run a computer-generated chart for this person and progress it to October 8, 2001, we would find that all of the planets had progressed to the exact positions listed at 0 hour on April 26, 1962 in the ephemeris.

Actual planetary positions 0 hour April 26, 1962 = October 8, 2001 by progression

Adjusting the Table of Numbered Days to Accommodate Leap Years

Progressing planets to an ACD is quite simple, but there is one caveat to be aware of, and that involves dealing with leap years. When a birth occurs <u>before February 29th</u> in a leap year, and the age to which you are progressing the planets corresponds to a date <u>after February 29th</u>, you must take the extra day into account. Naturally, if you are manually counting days in the ephemeris, February 29th will be there to be counted and you will arrive at the correct ephemeris day corresponding to the appropriate progressed year of age. But if you are using the Table of Numbered Days to arrive at your target ephemeris date, you must add one to every day following February 28th. This is because the Table does not take leap year into account. Let's demonstrate this with an example.

Example 3.

For this example, let's use someone born January 28, 1960 (a leap year), at 3:00 am, which produces an ACD of December 13, 1959. Now let's say we want to locate their progressed planets for the ACD before their 35th birthday. If we count 35 days from January 28, 1960 in the ephemeris, we land on March 3, 1960. But if we use the "Numbered Days in a Year" Table, we land on March 4th:

$$\begin{array}{rl} \text{January 28 (Birthday)} = & \text{Day \# 28} \\ \text{+ Progressed Age} & \underline{+ \ 35} \\ = & \text{Day \# 63, or March 4 (Incorrect!)} \end{array}$$

March 3, 1960 is the correct day corresponding to this person's 35th ACD. If the Table is used, then add one every day occurring after February 28th to account for February 29th. If one day is added, March 3rd becomes day #63 instead of #62.

**When Using the Table of Numbered Days
and working with a leap year,
add 1 to all days after February 28.**

Progressing Planets to a Day Other Than the ACD

As you can see, progressing planets to the ACD is quite straightforward. Once the appropriate day is determined, all that needs to be done is to read the planetary positions straight out of the ephemeris. But what happens if we want to pinpoint progressed planets on a day other than an ACD? In this case, the ACDs are used as fixed points between which we can interpolate, as we did when calculating a natal chart. There are six steps in all to determine the exact location of progressed planets on any date other than an ACD:

Step 1. Determine the two ACDs between which the target date falls, and assign an ephemeris date to each. This is most easily done by subtracting the year of the Birth ACD from the year of each of the two ACDs above. The result will represent the number of days to count ahead from the birthdate to locate the corresponding ephemeris date. Remember, the birth ACD may fall in the same year or the previous year to the birth date.

Step 2. Calculate the number of days that have elapsed from the earlier ACD to the target date. This is most easily done by using the "Numbered Days in a Year" Table, subtracting the day number of the target date from the day number of the previous ACD.

Step 3. Divide the number of days from Step 2 by 365. The result will be the proportion of the year that has elapsed from earlier ACD to the target date, expressed as a decimal, and will be used as the "constant multiplier" for interpolation.

Step 4. Determine the daily motion of each planet between the ephemeris dates assigned in Step 1.

Step 5. Multiply the daily motion of each planet by the constant multiplier from Step 3.

Step 6. Add the results of Step 5 to the planetary positions on the earlier ephemeris date from Step 1. The result will be the exact progressed positions of all planets on the target date.

Example 4.

Let's demonstrate how this is done with an example. We will use the same birth data used in Example 2 of the previous lesson:

Birth date: April 10, 1997, at 2:15 GMT
ACD = March 7, 1997

As determined in that lesson, this person's ACD falls on March 7, 1997. This means that on every March 7th during this person's life, the progressed planets will correspond to the planets listed at 0 hour in the ephemeris, using a day for a year ratio. But let's say we want to pinpoint the exact positions of the progressed planets on August 10, 2003 - a day other than an ACD.

Target Date = August 10, 2003

Step 1. Determine the two ACDs between which the target date falls, and assign an ephemeris date to each. In this case, the target date of August 10, 2003 falls between the ACDs March 7, 2003 and March 7, 2004. March 7, 2003 is the ACD falling before this person's 6th birthday, because 2003 - 1997 = 6. March 7, 2004 is the ACD falling before this person's 7th birthday, because 2004 - 1997 = 7. Therefore, in day for a year symbolism:

ACD March 7, 2003 (ACD before 6th birthday) = 0 hour April 16, 1997 (6 days after birth)
ACD March 7, 2004 (ACD before 7th birthday) = 0 hour April 17, 1997 (7 days after birth)

Step 2. Calculate the number of days that have elapsed from the earlier ACD to the target date. The target date is August 10, 2003. The Table of Numbered Days is used below to determine how many days have elapsed between March 7, 2003 and August 10, 2003:

(Target Date) August 10   Day # 222
(Earlier ACD) March 7   - Day # 66

= 156

Notice that the earlier ACD is subtracted from the target date, not the other way around. In certain cases this may require using the numbered day from the second year's table for the target date in order to subtract.

When calculating the number of elapsed days,
Always subtract the earlier ACD from the target date.

Step 3. Divide the number of days from Step 2 by 365.

$$\frac{156}{365} = .427$$

156 days out of a possible 365 have elapsed from the earlier ACD to the target date. This proportion represents .427 of a year. This becomes the constant multiplier.

Finally, Steps 4-6 are carried out in much the same way as if we were calculating planetary positions for a natal chart. We can even use the same calculation form used in natal calculation:

Step 4. Determine the daily motion of each planet between the ephemeris dates assigned in Step 1. This is accomplished on lines 1-3 on the form, below.

Step 5. Multiply the daily motion of each planet by the constant multiplier from Step 3. This is done on line 4 of the form, below.

Step 6. Add the results of Step 5 to the planetary positions on the earlier ephemeris date from Step 1. The result on line 5 below represents the exact progressed positions of the planets on the target date of August 10, 2003.

	☉	☽	☿	♀	♂	♃
1. Position at 0 hr on Later Ephemeris Date (April 17, 1997)	26°♈62' ~~27°♈02'~~	21°♌68' ~~22°♌08'~~	9°♉27'℞	30°♈44' ~~0°♉44'~~	17°♍29'℞	17°♒38'
2. Position at 0 hr on Earlier Ephemeris Date (April 16, 1997)	26°♈03'	10°♌17'	9°♉36'℞	29°♈30'	17°♍38'℞	17°♒29'
3. Line 1 - Line 2 = Total Daily Travel	59'	11°51' = 711'	9'℞	1°14' = 74'	9'℞	9'
4. Line 3 X CM (.427) = Travel to Target Date	25'	304' = 5°04'	4'℞	32'	4'℞	4'
5. Add lines 2 + 4 = Progressed Position on Target Date	26°♈28'	15°♌21'	9°♉32'℞	29°♈62' = 0°♉02'	17°♍34'℞	17°♒33'

	♄	♅	♆	♇	☊	
1. Position at 0 hr on Later Ephemeris Date (April 17, 1997)	12°♈23'	8°♒23'	29°♑54'	5°♐11'℞	28°♍29'	
2. Position at 0 hr on Earlier Ephemeris Date (April 16, 1997)	12°♈15'	8°♒22'	29°♑53'	5°♐12'℞	28°♍27'	
3. Line 1 - Line 2 = Total Daily Travel	8'	1'	1'	1'℞	2'	
4. Line 3 X CM (.427) = Travel to Target Date	3'	0'	0'	0'℞	1'	
5. Add lines 2 + 4 = Progressed Position on Target Date	12°♈18'	8°♒22'	29°♑53'	5°♐12'℞	28°♍28'	

Example 5.

Let's review the whole process again, including the calculation of the ACD. In this example, we will locate the progressed Moon on February 5, 1998 for a person born November 5, 1952, 6:30 GMT. Before proceeding, the ACD must be determined:

6.5 (GMT of birth as decimal) ÷ 24 = .271
365 days x .271 = 99 days
Day #309 (birthday) - 99 = Day #210, or July 29, 1952.

This person's ACD is July 29, 1952. Now we can proceed with Steps 1 through 3 to determine the constant multiplier needed to progress the Moon to the target date of February 5, 1998:

Step 1. Determine the two ACDs between which the target date falls, and assign an ephemeris date to each.

ACD July 29, 1997	=	0 hour Dec. 20, 1952
(ACD before 45th birthday: 1997-1952 = 45)		(45 days after birthdate)

ACD July 29, 1998	=	0 hour Dec. 21, 1952
(ACD before 46th birthday: 1998-1952 = 46)		(46 days after birthdate)

Step 2. Calculate the number of days that have elapsed from the earlier ACD to the target date.

(Target Date) February 5   Day # 401
(Earlier ACD) July 29   - Day # 210
                            = 191

Step 3. Divide the number of days from Step 2 by 365.

$$\frac{191}{365} = .523$$

Step 4. Determine the daily motion of each planet between the ephemeris dates assigned in Step 1.

Moon at 0 hour Dec. 21, 1952 =   21° ♒ 44'
Moon at 0 hour Dec. 20, 1952 = - 7° ♒ 15'
                                 14°   29', or 869'

Step 5. Multiply the daily motion of each planet by the constant multiplier from Step 3.

869' x .523 = 454', or 7° 34'

Step 6. Add the results of Step 5 to the planetary positions on the earlier ephemeris date from Step 1.

Moon at 0 hour Dec. 20, 1952 =   7° ♒ 15'
                             +   7°   34'
                             = 14° ♒ 49'

On February 5, 1998, this person's Moon had progressed to 14° ♒ 49'.

Lesson 22 Exercises

Determine the location of the progressed planets in the exercises below. The first two exercises require you to progress planets to an ACD, which you must also determine. Exercises 3 & 4 require interpolation. Answers can be found in the Answer Key located in the Appendix.

1. Locate the progressed Sun & Moon on the ACD before the 53rd birthday for a person born July 4, 1950 at 14:23 GMT.

2. Locate the progressed Sun & Moon on the ACD before the 29th birthday for a person born February 8, 1964 (a leap year), at 8:50 GMT.

3. Locate the progressed ☉,☽,☿,♀,♂, and ♃ on the target date May 5, 1995 for a person born November 20, 1972, at 5:19 GMT. A calculation form is provided below for your use.

	☉	☽	☿	♀	♂	♃
1. Position at 0 hr on Later Ephemeris Date						
2. Position at 0 hr on Earlier Ephemeris Date						
3. Line 1 - Line 2 = Total Daily Travel						
4. Line 3 X CM _____ = Travel to Target Date						
5. Add lines 2 + 4 = Progressed Position on Target Date						

4. Locate the progressed ☉ and ☽ on the target date September 5, 1989 for a person born April 3, 1948 at 19:50 GMT, without the aid of forms.

Lesson 23: Progressing Chart Angles & House Cusps

The previous two lessons discussed how to progress planets to any given date. Now we complete the process of progressing a chart by explaining how to progress chart angles and intermediate house cusps. As you will see, this process is very similar to that used in calculating natal house cusps.

The Progressed Midheaven

Determining the location of the progressed Midheaven is the first step in erecting a progressed chart as all remaining house cusps are derived from the progressed MC. Just as various systems exist for calculating natal house cusps, various methods have been devised by astrologers over the centuries for progressing the Midheaven as well. The four most common methods are defined below, which all produce a progressed Midheaven within a degree or so of each other.

Solar Arc: This is the most common method used for progressing the Midheaven and is the method used in this book. The **solar arc**, which is the difference between the progressed Sun and the natal Sun, is simply added to the natal Midheaven. The result is the progressed MC.

Naibod: Named for the medieval astrologer Valentine Naibod, this method uses the average daily motion of the Sun (0° 59' 08") per year of life to progress the MC.

Mean Sidereal Time: This method recalculates the LST of birth based on one's birth GMT for each day after birth, then uses this new LST to calculate a corresponding progressed chart.

Mean Quotidian: Latin for "recurring daily", the Quotidian method uses the same standard as is applied to progressed planets by progressing the MC each year according to its own daily motion. Because the MC moves approximately 361° during the course of a day, this produces a progressed MC that changes about 1° *per day* rather than per year, and results in the progressed MC making a full circuit, plus one degree, around the chart each year.

Locating the Progressed MC using the Solar Arc Method

Progressing the MC using the solar arc method is a very straightforward process and requires only two simple steps:

Step 1. Determine the Solar Arc by calculating the difference between the progressed Sun and the natal Sun. In order to accomplish this step, you must have a copy of the person's complete natal chart and have already calculated the exact position of the progressed Sun (as covered in lesson 22).

Step 2. Add the Solar Arc to the natal Midheaven. The result is the progressed Midheaven.

Progressed Sun - Natal Sun = Solar Arc

Natal Midheaven + Solar Arc = Progressed Midheaven

Example 1.

Let's demonstrate how to progress the MC using the solar arc method. This example will use the same data used in Example 4 of the previous lesson.

Birth Data:
April 10, 1997
2:15 GMT
London, England
51°N 30', 0°W 10'

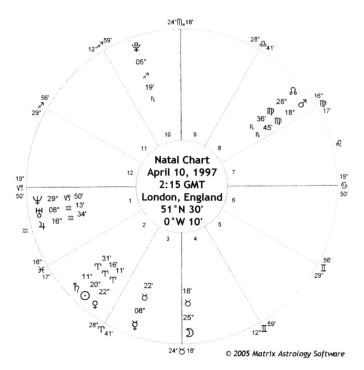

Natal Chart
April 10, 1997
2:15 GMT
London, England
51°N 30'
0°W 10'

© 2005 Matrix Astrology Software

In that example, we progressed the planets to August 10, 2003, and determined that this person's Sun had progressed to 26°♈ 28'. Manned with this information and referring to this person's natal chart shown to the right to locate the position of the natal Sun, subtract the birth Sun from the progressed Sun to find the Solar Arc:

Progressed Sun	26°♈ 28'
- Birth Sun	- 20°♈ 16'
= Solar Arc	= 6° 12'

Notice that this person's age on the target progression date is 6 years and 4 months. Similarly, the solar arc is just a little over 6 degrees, because the average daily motion of the Sun is just under a degree (59' 08"). Translated into day-for-a-year symbolism, this equates to a solar arc equaling just under a degree per year of life. This is a good rule of thumb to keep in mind to double-check your solar arc result: The solar arc should be equal to or a little less than the person's age, allowing a slightly greater variance for more mature ages.

Once the solar arc has been determined, simply add it to the natal Midheaven to determine the progressed Midheaven:

Natal Midheaven	24°♏ 18'
+ Solar Arc	+ 6° 12'
= Progressed Midheaven	30°♏ 30', or 0°♐ 30'.

This person's progressed Midheaven on August 10, 2003 was 0°♐ 30'.

234

Example 2.

Let's calculate the solar arc and progressed MC for a 68 year old person with a natal Sun position of 8° ♌ 39', a progressed Sun position of 14° ♎ 37', and a natal MC of 10° ♊ 32'. When dealing with higher ages and multiple sign changes it is often easier to calculate the solar arc using absolute longitude:

	193° 97'	
Progressed Sun	~~194° 37'~~	(14° ♎ 37' in absolute longitude)
- Birth Sun	- 128° 39'	(8° ♌ 39' in absolute longitude)
= Solar Arc	= 65° 58'	

Notice that this person's solar arc is about 2 degrees less than their age. This is because the Sun's average daily motion is slightly less than a degree, which adds up and can result in differences of several degrees when dealing with older individuals. Now, the solar arc is added to the natal Midheaven to find the position of the progressed Midheaven:

Natal MC	70° 32'	(10° ♊ 32' in absolute longitude)
+ Solar Arc	+ 65° 58'	
= Progressed MC	135° 90', or 16° ♌ 30'	

Example 3.

Using absolute longitude to calculate solar arcs becomes more crucial when dealing with progressions from later signs to earlier signs. Let's calculate the solar arc for another 68 year old person with a natal Sun of 9° ♓ 50', a progressed Sun of 16° ♉ 50', and a natal MC of 28° ♑ 40'.

	406° 50'	add 360° if necessary to subtract
Progressed Sun	~~46° 50'~~	(16° ♉ 50' in absolute longitude)
- Birth Sun	- 339° 50'	(9° ♓ 50' in absolute longitude)
= Solar Arc	67° 00'	

Notice that this person's solar arc is a full degree less than the person in Example 2, even though their ages are the same. This is due to the fact that the Sun's daily motion varies slightly depending on the time of year of birth. Now let's use this solar arc to determine the progressed MC:

Natal MC	298° 40'	(28° ♑ 40' in absolute longitude)
+ Solar Arc	+ 67° 00'	
	365° 40'	
	- 360° 00'	subtract 360° if necessary
= Progressed MC	5° 40', or 5° ♈ 40'	

Progressing the Remaining House Cusps

As you can see, locating the progressed Midheaven is quite simple, but progressing the remaining house cusps requires a bit more math. Just as latitude plays a large part in determining the ascendant and intermediate house cusps in natal chart calculation, latitude must be taken into consideration when progressing these cusps as well. This requires three different interpolation procedures very similar to those used to calculate natal house cusps:

Step 1. First, calculate each house cusp using the closest higher latitude, but instead of interpolating between <u>sidereal times</u> to calculate each cusp as was done in natal calculation, interpolate between listed <u>Midheaven positions</u>.

Step 2. Next, repeat this process using values given for the closest lower latitude, again interpolating between listed Midheaven positions.

Step 3. Finally, interpolate between the results from Steps 1 and 2 using the exact latitude of birth.

Let's demonstrate this procedure with an example.

Example 4.

For this example the same natal chart and target progression date from Example 1 will be used. In order to locate the remaining progressed house cusps, the following information is needed:

Progressed Midheaven: 0° ♐ 30'
Latitude of Birth: 51°N 30'

The target MC of 0° ♐ 30' falls between these two listed MC positions: 00° ♐ 11' and 01° ♐ 08'.

The target Latitude of 51° N 30' falls between these two listed Latitudes: 51° and 52°.

Therefore, we will be working with these two rows of data to calculate the progressed house cusps in this example.

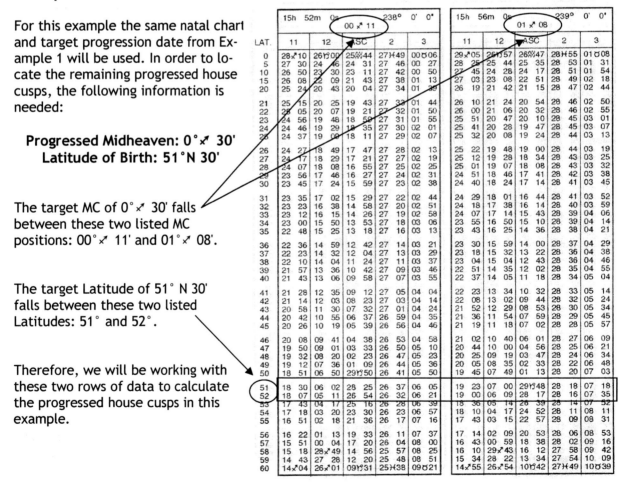

236

In order to interpolate between listed Midheavens, a constant multiplier must be determined which is equal to the portion of the whole (that is, the number of degrees and minutes of arc from earlier to later listed MCs) represented by the target MC. We will call this constant multiplier "MC-CM" to differentiate it from previous constant multipliers used in chart calculation:

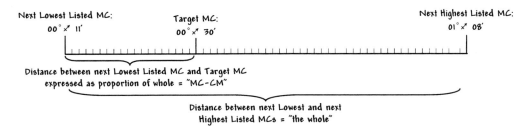

To find this constant multiplier, first determine the number of degrees/minutes' difference between the next lowest listed MC and the target MC:

$$\begin{array}{ll} & ↗\ 00°\ 30' \quad \textit{Target MC} \\ - & ↗\ 00°\ 11' \quad \textit{Next lowest listed MC} \\ \hline & 19' \quad \textit{Difference} \end{array}$$

Then determine how many degrees/minutes represent "the whole". This is done by subtracting the next lowest listed MC from the next highest listed MC:

$$\begin{array}{ll} & ↗\ 01°\ 08' \quad \textit{Next highest listed MC} \\ - & ↗\ 00°\ 11' \quad \textit{Next lowest listed MC} \\ \hline & 57' \quad \textit{Difference} \end{array}$$

Finally, divide the first result by the second, to determine its proportion of the whole expressed in decimal format:

$$\frac{19'}{57'} = .33$$

The MC-CM for this example is .33.

We have provided a Chart Progression Form in the Appendix of this book which contains a handy calculation box for the MC-CM, reproduced here. You may wish to use this form while learning the math of progressions but remember that, like natal calculations, you will not be allowed to take any preprinted forms with you into a certification exam setting. Eventually you will need to commit all of these calculations to memory. Try to gain a firm understanding of the reasoning behind each calculation step in order to make memorization easier.

Midheaven CM (MC-CM)
(Constant Multiplier for Part D: House Cusps,
Lines 4 & 9: MC Interpolation)

Progressed MC	↗ 00° 30'
- Next lowest MC from Table	- ↗ 00° 11'
	= 19 ' (a)
Next highest MC from Table	↗ 01° 08'
- Next lowest MC from Table	- ↗ 00° 11'
	= 57 ' (b)
19' (a) ÷ 57' (b) = MC-CM	.33

Now that the "MC-CM" is determined we can begin calculating the house cusps. Let's start with the Ascendant. First, calculate the progressed Ascendant using the higher latitude of 52°. Refer to *The Book of Tables* excerpt on page 236 to follow along.

	27° 77'
ASC given for later MC, at 52°:	♑ ~~28° 17'~~
ASC given for earlier MC, at 52°:	- ♑ 26° 54'
Difference:	1° 23', or 83'
Multiply difference by MC-CM:	83' x .33 = 27'
Add result to earlier ASC:	♑ 26° 54'
	+ 27'
The result is the progressed ASC at 52°:	♑ 26° 81', or ♑ 27° 21'

Then repeat the process using the lower latitude of 51°:

ASC given for later MC, at 51°:	♑ 29° 48'
ASC given for earlier MC, at 51°:	- ♑ 28° 25'
Difference:	1° 23', or 83'
Multiply difference by MC-CM:	83' x .33 = 27'
Add result to earlier ASC:	♑ 28° 25'
	+ 27'
The result is the progressed ASC at 51°:	♑ 28° 52'

Finally, interpolate between these two values for Latitude. This final step is exactly the same as in natal cusp calculation, and uses the same constant multiplier "CM-3":

ASC at higher Latitude (52°):	♑ 27° 21'	
ASC at lower Latitude (51°):	♑ 28° 52'	
Difference:	- 1° 31'	
	or - 91'	
Multiply difference by CM-3:	- 91' x .5 = - 46'	
Add result to lower Latitude:	♑ 28° 52'	
	+ - 46'	
The result is the final progressed Ascendant:	♑ 28° 06'	

CM-3

(Constant Multiplier for Part D: House Cusps, Line 14: Latitude Interpolation)

Latitude of Birth	51 ° 30 '
- Next lowest Latitude from Table	51 ° 00 '
=	° 30 '
Convert result to decimal CM-3 =	.50

Exception: If Birth Latitude is less than 20°, divide result by 5 ÷ 5 = CM-3 _____

On the following page, the Chart Progression Form has been used to calculate the remaining cusps.

House Cusp Calculation for Higher Latitude

Latitude ___52___ °	11th	12th	ASC	2nd	3rd
1. House Cusps at Higher MC (1°♐ 08')	18°♐ 60' ~~19°♐ 00'~~	5°♑ 69' ~~6°♑ 09'~~	27°♑ 77' ~~28°♑ 17'~~	27°♓ 76' ~~28°♓ 16'~~	7°♉ 35'
2. House Cusps at Lower MC (0°♐ 11')	18°♐ 07'	5°♑ 11'	26°♑ 54'	26°♓ 32'	6°♉ 21'
3. Line 1 - Line 2 =	53'	58'	1° 23' = 83'	1° 44' = 104'	1° 14' = 74'
4. Line 3 X MC-CM (.33) =	17'	19'	27'	34'	24'
5. Add lines 2 + 4 =	18°♐ 24'	5°♑ 30'	26°♑ 81' = 27°♑ 21'	26°♓ 66' = 27°♓ 06'	6°♉ 45'

House Cusp Calculation for Lower Latitude

Latitude ___51___ °	11th	12th	ASC	2nd	3rd
6. House Cusps at Higher MC (1°♐ 08')	18°♐ 83' ~~19°♐ 23'~~	6°♑ 60' ~~7°♑ 00'~~	29°♑ 48'	27°♓ 78' ~~28°♓ 18'~~	7°♉ 18'
7. House Cusps at Lower MC (0°♐ 11')	18°♐ 30'	6°♑ 02'	28°♑ 25'	26°♓ 37'	6°♉ 05'
8. Line 6 - Line 7 =	53'	58'	1° 23' = 83'	1° 41' = 101'	1° 13' = 73'
9. Line 8 X MC-CM (.33) =	17'	19'	27'	33'	24'
10. Add lines 7 + 9 =	18°♐ 47'	6°♑ 21'	28°♑ 52'	26°♓ 70' = 27°♓ 10'	6°♉ 29'

Latitude Interpolation

	11th	12th	ASC	2nd	3rd
11. House Cusps at Higher Latitude (from line 5)	18°♐ 24'	5°♑ 30'	27°♑ 21'	27°♓ 06'	6°♉ 45'
12. House Cusps at Lower Latitude (from line 10)	18°♐ 47'	6°♑ 21'	28°♑ 52'	27°♓ 10'	6°♉ 29'
13. Line 11 - Line 12 =	- 23'	- 51'	- 1° 31' = - 91'	- 4'	16'
14. Line 13 X CM-3 (.5) =	- 12'	- 26'	- 46'	- 2'	8'
15. Add lines 12 + 14 = Progressed House Cusps	18°♐ 35'	5°♑ 55'	28°♑ 06'	27°♓ 08'	6°♉ 37'

Lesson 23 Exercises

Using the following natal chart, progress the Midheaven and Ascendant to the ACD before the 40th birthday. Relevant sections of the Chart Progression Form have been reproduced on the following two pages for your use. Answers can be found in the Answer Key located in the Appendix.

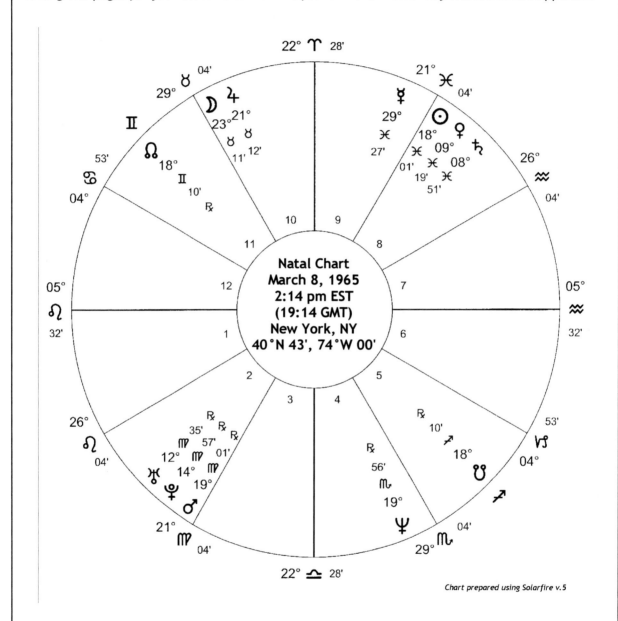

Chart prepared using Solarfire v.5

Part A: ACD

ACD Calculation:

1. CM-1 (Convert GMT of Birth to decimal: _____ ÷ 24 = CM-1) _____

2. 365 days x CM-1 *(line 1)* = ACD Interval   X 365 = _____

3a. GMT Birthdate Day Number *(from Table of Numbered Days)*   _____

  b. - ACD Interval *(from line 2)*   - _____

  c. = ACD Day Number   = _____

  d. = Birth ACD *(line 3c date equivalent from Table of Numbered Days)*   Birth ACD = _____ Year _____

ACD Equivalent Ephemeris Date:

4. Year of ACD prior to Target Date _____ - Year of Birth ACD *(line 3d)* _____ = Elapsed Years(Days) _____

5. GMT Birthdate Day No.*(line 3a)* _____ + Elapsed Years(Days) *(line 4)* _____ = Equivalent Ephemeris Day No. _____

   = Equivalent Ephemeris Date to earlier ACD _____

Solar Arc

Progressed Sun   _____

- Birth Sun   - _____

= Solar Arc   = _____

Progressed MC

Birth MC   _____

+ Solar Arc   + _____

= Progressed MC   = _____

Midheaven CM (MC-CM)
(Constant Multiplier for Part D: House Cusps,
Lines 4 & 9: MC Interpolation)

Progressed MC   _____

- Next lowest MC from Table   - _____

       = _____ ' (a)

Next highest MC from Table   _____

- Next lowest MC from Table   - _____

       = _____ ' (b)

_____ (a) ÷ _____ (b) = **MC-CM** _____

Latitude CM (CM-3)
(Constant Multiplier for Part D: House Cusps,
Line 14: Latitude Interpolation)

Latitude of Birth (or other prog. location) _____° _____'

- Next lowest Latitude from Table   - _____° <u>00</u> '

       = _____° _____'

Convert result to decimal   CM-3 = _____

Exception: If Birth Latitude is
less than 20°, divide result by 5   ÷ 5 = CM-3 _____

House Cusp Calculation for Higher Latitude	
Latitude _____°	ASC
1. House Cusps at Higher MC _____	
2. House Cusps at Lower MC _____	
3. Line 1 - Line 2 =	
4. Line 3 X MC-CM _____ =	
5. Add lines 2 + 4 =	

House Cusp Calculation for Lower Latitude	
Latitude _____°	ASC
6. House Cusps at Higher MC _____	
7. House Cusps at Lower MC _____	
8. Line 6 - Line 7 =	
9. Line 8 X MC-CM _____ =	
10. Add lines 7 + 9 =	

Latitude Interpolation	
	ASC
11. House Cusps at Higher Latitude (from line 5)	
12. House Cusps at Lower Latitude (from line 10)	
13. Line 11 - Line 12 =	
14. Line 13 X CM-3 _____ =	
15. Add lines 12 + 14 = **Progressed House Cusps**	

Lesson 24: Timing Progressed Events:
Aspects, Sign & House Ingresses

This lesson will cover how to calculate the exact date when a progressed planet or point will change sign or house, or when an applying aspect will become exact by progression. Interpolation between ACD positions will be used to time these progressed events.

Three Major Progressed Events

When evaluating progressions, the three most important events to look for are:

- Progressed planet or angle changing sign
- Progressed planet or angle changing house
- Aspects perfecting between progressed planets, natal planets and/or angles

Often, a life event will be triggered by a transiting aspect around the time one of the above is taking place. Therefore, it is important to be able to precisely time these progressed events.

Progressed Orbs

You will recall from Lesson 21 that the Sun, Mercury, and Venus all progress at an average of 1° per year, while the Moon progresses about 13° per year. Mars progresses only about 30 minutes a year, and the outer planets progress much more slowly. As a result, most astrologers will only consider progressed aspects which are within 1° orb for the Sun and planets. A larger orb is given to the progressed Moon.

How to Precisely Time Progressed Events

The invaluable process of interpolation between ACDs is used to precisely time progressed events. The use of ACDs allows us to pinpoint planetary positions once a year without any calculations at all. These two known ACD positions can then be used as interpolation "bookends" between which a third unknown value—the date of the event—can be found.

Step 1. Locate the two ephemeris dates between which the event occurs and determine the two ACDs corresponding to these dates.

Step 2. Calculate a Constant Multiplier, using (a) the distance the planet or point must travel from the earlier ACD to create the event, divided by (b) the total distance the planet or point traveled between the two ACDs.

Step 3. Multiply 365 days by this Constant Multiplier to determine the number of days that will elapse from the earlier ACD to the event date. Then add this number of days to the earlier ACD to pinpoint the exact date of the event.

The Bi-Wheel Chart

A **bi-wheel** is a chart with two rings allowing for the insertion and comparison of two sets of astrological data. Usually, the inner wheel contains a natal chart, while the outer wheel may contain **transits** (the planets as they were actually positioned in the sky on a particular day at a given time), progressions, or the natal chart of a second native. The chart on the inner wheel determines the chart angles and house cusps. Then a second set of planets and chart points is entered around the natal chart in the outer wheel.

The following bi-wheel will be used for the next four examples. The inner wheel contains the natal chart and all house cusps are those of the natal chart. The second wheel contains the planets and points progressed to January 27, 1997, the ACD before this person's 35th birthday.

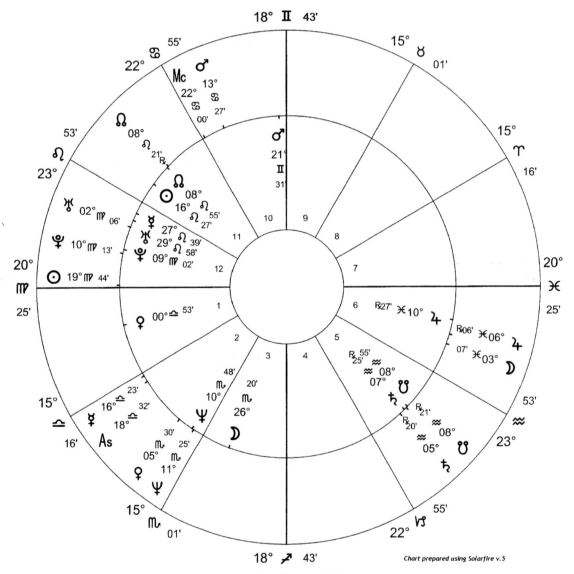

Inner Wheel: Natal Chart
August 9, 1962 8:45 am EDT (12:45 GMT) Boston, MA
ACD = January 27, 1962

Chart prepared using Solarfire v.5

Outer Wheel: Progressions on January 27, 1997
(ACD before 35th birthday)

244

Example 1.

Notice in the chart to the left that the progressed Sun is just about to cross the natal Ascendant and enter the 1st house. Let's pinpoint the exact date when this event will occur.

Step 1. Locate the two ephemeris dates between which the event occurs and determine the two ACDs corresponding to these dates.

Start by checking the ephemeris and locating the two dates between which the Sun will reach 20° ℗ 25', the degree and minute of the natal Ascendant. Starting with the birthdate <u>in the birth year</u>, scan forward one day at a time until locating this 24-hour window. Notice in *The ACS Ephemeris* listing below that this event occurs sometime between 0 hour September 13 and 0 hour September 14, 1962:

LONGITUDE   SEPTEMBER 1962

Day	Sid.Time	☉	0 hr ☽	Noon ☽	True ☊	☿	♀	♂	♃	♄	♅	♆	♇
1 Sa	22 38 42	8℗ 4 57	28℗30 44	4♎26 1	8♌42.7	3♎ 7.2	24♎12.8	6♋ 3.3	7♓39.7	5♒55.9	1℗22.0	11♏ 8.0	9℗48.1
2 Su	22 42 39	9 3 2	10♎21 3	16 16 9	8R37.4	4 24.4	25 11.6	6 41.0	7R31.7	5R52.6	1 25.7	11 9.3	9 50.1
3 M	22 46 36	10 1 9	22 11 38	28 7 52	8 31.9	5 40.0	26 10.0	7 18.5	7 23.8	5 49.3	1 29.5	11 10.5	9 52.2
4 Tu	22 50 32	10 59 17	4♏ 5 13	10♏ 4 6	8 26.9	6 53.7	27 8.1	7 55.9	7 15.9	5 46.0	1 33.2	11 11.8	9 54.3
5 W	22 54 29	11 57 27	16 4 58	22 8 18	8 22.9	8 5.7	28 5.7	8 33.1	7 8.0	5 42.9	1 36.9	11 13.2	9 56.4
6 Th	22 58 25	12 55 38	28 14 37	4♐24 25	8 20.2	9 15.7	29 2.8	9 10.3	7 0.1	5 39.8	1 40.6	11 14.5	9 58.4
7 F	23 2 22	13 53 51	10♐38 14	16 56 38	8D19.1	10 23.7	29 59.6	9 47.3	6 52.3	5 36.8	1 44.3	11 15.9	10 0.5
8 Sa	23 6 18	14 52 6	23 20 7	29 49 13	8 19.4	11 29.6	0♏55.8	10 24.3	6 44.5	5 33.8	1 48.0	11 17.3	10 2.6
9 Su	23 10 15	15 50 22	6♑24 21	13♑ 5 56	8 20.6	12 33.3	1 51.6	11 1.1	6 36.8	5 30.9	1 51.7	11 18.7	10 4.7
10 M	23 14 11	16 48 39	19 54 16	26 49 34	8 22.1	13 34.6	2 46.9	11 37.8	6 29.1	5 28.2	1 55.4	11 20.2	10 6.7
11 Tu	23 18 8	17 46 58	3♒51 50	11♒ 1 1	8R23.0	14 33.3	3 41.7	12 14.4	6 21.5	5 25.5	1 59.0	11 21.7	10 8.8
12 W	23 22 5	18 45 18	18 16 46	25 38 38	8 22.7	15 29.4	4 36.0	12 50.8	6 13.9	5 22.8	2 2.7	11 23.2	10 10.9
13 Th	23 26 1	19 43 41	3♓ 5 53	10♓37 39	8 20.7	16 22.7	5 29.7	13 27.2	6 6.4	5 20.3	2 6.3	11 24.7	10 12.9
14 F	23 29 58	20 42 4	18 12 49	25 50 11	8 16.7	17 12.9	6 22.8	14 3.4	5 59.0	5 17.8	2 9.9	11 26.3	10 15.0
15 Sa	23 33 54	21 40 30	3♈28 26	11♈ 6 10	8 11.1	17 59.8	7 15.3	14 39.5	5 51.6	5 15.4	2 13.5	11 27.8	10 17.0
16 Su	23 37 51	22 38 58	18 42 4	26 14 51	8 4.6	18 43.1	8 7.2	15 15.4	5 44.3	5 13.1	2 17.1	11 29.4	10 19.1
17 M	23 41 47	23 37 27	3♉43 23	11♉ 6 43	7 58.0	19 22.7	8 58.5	15 51.3	5 37.1	5 10.9	2 20.7	11 31.1	10 21.1
18 Tu	23 45 44	24 35 59	18 24 4	25 34 55	7 52.2	19 58.2	9 49.1	16 27.0	5 30.0	5 8.8	2 24.2	11 32.7	10 23.2

Now let's assign equivalent ACDs to these dates. On the facing page the outer wheel shows the progressed Sun at 19° ℗ 44' on the ACD before this person's 35th birthday January 27, 1997. Notice in *The ACS Ephemeris* that this is the position of the Sun on September 13, 1962. Therefore, the following day, September 14, 1962 will be the equivalent of the following ACD, or January 27, 199<u>8</u>.

If this information had not been provided, these dates could have been determined by simply counting days between the birth date and each of the designated dates above, or by using the Table of Numbered Days as follows:

September 13, 1962 (earlier position of Sun)   Day #256
- Birthdate August 9, 1962   -   221
                                        =   35

Once the number of days between these two dates has been determined, add the equivalent number of years to the birth ACD to find the equivalent ACD to the earlier date. The later date would then correspond to the ACD of the following year:

Birth ACD: January 27, 1962
                           + 35
= Equivalent ACD   January 27, 1997

Actual (ephemeris) position on September 13, 1962 = Progressed position on January 27, 1997
Actual (ephemeris) position on September 14, 1962 = Progressed position on January 27, 1998

Example 1 (continued)

Step 2. Calculate a Constant Multiplier, using (a) the distance the planet or point must travel from the earlier ACD to create the event, divided by (b) the total distance the planet or point traveled between the two ACDs.

Determine how far the Sun needs to travel between these two markers to cross the Ascendant, and what portion of the whole this represents. Start by finding the difference between the Sun's position at the earlier 0 hour and 20° ♍ 25', when it will cross the Ascendant:

Sun's position at "event" (p.☉ ☌ n.ASC):	20° ♍ 25'	
Sun's position 0 hour September 13, 1962	- 19° ♍ 44'	
= travel to event	41' **(a)**	

Then determine the total distance the Sun traveled during this 24-hour period:

Sun's position 0 hour September 14, 1962	20° ♍ 42'	
Sun's position 0 hour September 13, 1962	- 19° ♍ 44'	
= total travel	58' **(b)**	

Last, divide **(a)** by **(b)** to find the portion of the total travel this represents. This should be carried out to three decimal places to ensure accuracy:

$$\frac{41}{58} = .707$$

Step 3. Multiply 365 days by this Constant Multiplier to determine the number of days that will elapse from the earlier ACD to the event date. Then add this number of days to the earlier ACD to pinpoint the exact date of the event.

Multiply 365 days by .707, the constant multiplier found in Step 2 above, to find the number of days between the earlier ACD and the date the Sun hits the degree and minute of the Ascendant:

365 days x .707 (constant multiplier found in Step 2 above) = 258 days

Finally, add this number of days to the earlier ACD (equivalent of September 13, 1962) to arrive at the exact date the Sun reaches the Ascendant:

January 27, 1997 = Day # 27 (ACD before event)
+ 258 days   + 258

= Day of Event   = Day #285 = October 12, 1997

The progressed Sun will reach 20° ♍ 25' and cross the natal Ascendant on October 12, 1997.

Example 2.

Let's go through the whole process more briefly this time. You will notice in the example bi-wheel that the progressed Moon at 3° ♓ 07' is about to form a conjunction with the natal Jupiter at 10° ♓ 27'. Let's determine the precise date when this event will occur.

Step 1. Referring to *The ACS Ephemeris* September 1962 listing reprinted earlier in this lesson, find the following 0 hour positions for the Moon:

Moon's position 0 hour September 14, 1962   18° ♓ 13'
Moon's position 0 hour September 13, 1962   3° ♓ 06'

In Example 1 we have established that:

Actual position on September 13, 1962 = Progressed position on January 27, 1997
Actual position on September 14, 1962 = Progressed position on January 27, 1998

Step 2. Now determine the distance the Moon must progress to form the conjunction with Jupiter, then divide it by the Moon's total travel during the equivalent ephemeris 24-hour period in order to establish a constant multiplier:

	17° ♓ 73'
Moon's position 0 hour September 14, 1962	~~18° ♓ 13'~~
Moon's position at "event" (p.☽ ♂ n.♃)	- 10° ♓ 27'
= travel to event	7° 46', or 466'
Moon's position 0 hour September 14, 1962	18° ♓ 13'
Moon's position 0 hour September 13, 1962	- 3° ♓ 06'
= total travel	= 15° 07', or 907'

$$\frac{466}{907} = .514$$

Step 3. Now convert this proportion into the equivalent number of days of a year, and add the result to the earlier ACD to arrive at the exact date of the event:

365 days x .514 = 188 days

January 27, 1997 = Day # 27 (ACD before event)
+ 188 days   + 188

= Day of Event   = Day #215 = August 3, 1997

The progressed Moon will exactly conjoin the natal Jupiter at 10° ♓ 27' on August 3, 1997.

Example 3.

In this example, we will determine on what date the progressed Moon moved into the sign Pisces.

Step 1. Because the Moon had already moved into Pisces by January 27, 1997 (the equivalent of September 13, 1962 in actual time), interpolation between this and the previous ACD is necessary to arrive at the exact date of this event.

$$\text{Moon 0 hour Sept. 12, 1962 (18}°\approx\text{17')} = \text{ACD January 27, 1996}$$
$$\text{Moon 0 hour Sept. 13, 1962 (3}°\times\text{06')} = \text{ACD January 27, 1997}$$

Step 2. Having established the ACD "bookends" for this interpolation, determine the constant multiplier. Start by finding the Moon's travel from the earlier "bookend" (ACD) to the moment of the event:

	29° ≈ 60'
Moon at event (☽ = 0°✕):	0°✕00'
Moon 0 hour Sept. 12, 1962:	- 18° ≈ 17'
= travel to event	11° 43', or 703' **(a)**

Then determine the total travel between the two ACD "bookend" dates:

	32° ≈ 66'
Moon's position 0 hour September 13, 1962	3°✕06'
Moon's position 0 hour September 12, 1962	- 18° ≈ 17'
= total travel	= 14° 49', or 889' **(b)**

Last, divide **(a)** by **(b)** to arrive at the constant multiplier:

$$\frac{703}{889} = .791$$

Step 3. Finally, convert the proportion .791 into the equivalent number of days of a year, and add the result to the earlier ACD to arrive at the exact date of the event:

$$365 \text{ days x .791} = 289 \text{ days}$$

January 27, 1996	=	Day # 27 (ACD before event)
+ 289 days		+ 289
= Day of Event	=	Day #316 = November 12, 1996

The progressed Moon will reach 0° 00' Pisces on November 12, 1996.

Example 4.

In this example let's pinpoint a date farther out into the future to determine when progressed Venus will form a conjunction to natal Neptune at 10°♏48'.

Step 1. Refer back to *The ACS Ephemeris* September 1962 listings shown earlier in this lesson to locate the following ACD "bookend" dates for progressed Venus, between which 10°♏48' falls:

Venus September 19, 1962 = 10°♏39'   September 19, 1962 = ACD January 27, 2003
Venus September 20, 1962 = 11°♏28'   September 20, 1962 = ACD January 27, 2004

As in the previous examples, we arrived at the ACD equivalent dates by finding the number of days between the birthdate and the dates on which Venus arrived at each of these positions, then adding the same number of years as days to the birth ACD.

Step 2.

Next, determine how far Venus needs to progress between these two ACD markers to reach natal Neptune at 10°♏48', and what portion of the daily travel between 0 hour September 19th and 0 hour September 20th this represents. Start by finding the difference between Venus's position at the earlier 0 hour to 10°♏48', when it will conjunct Neptune:

Venus at event (p. ♀ ☌ n.♆):   10°♏48'
Venus at 0 hour Sept. 19, 1926:   - 10°♏39'

= travel to event   09'

Then the total travel between the two 0-hour dates:

                                             10°♏88'
Venus at 0 hour Sept. 20, 1926:   11°♏28'
Venus at 0 hour Sept. 19, 1926:   - 10°♏39'

= total travel   49'

Then the proportion:

$$\frac{9}{49} = .184$$

Step 3. Now apply this proportion to the number of days in a year to arrive at the number of days that will need to elapse between the earlier ACD and the date of the "event", when Venus will reach 10°♏48' and conjunct natal Neptune:

365 days x .184 = 67 days

(earlier ACD) January 27, 2003 = Day # 27
            + 67 days   + 67

        = Day of Event   = Day # 94 = April 4, 2003

Progressed Venus will exactly conjoin the natal Neptune at 10°♏48' on April 4, 2003.

Lesson 24 Exercises

Determine the exact dates of the following progressed events, using the natal chart below. Answers can be found in the Answer Key in the Appendix.

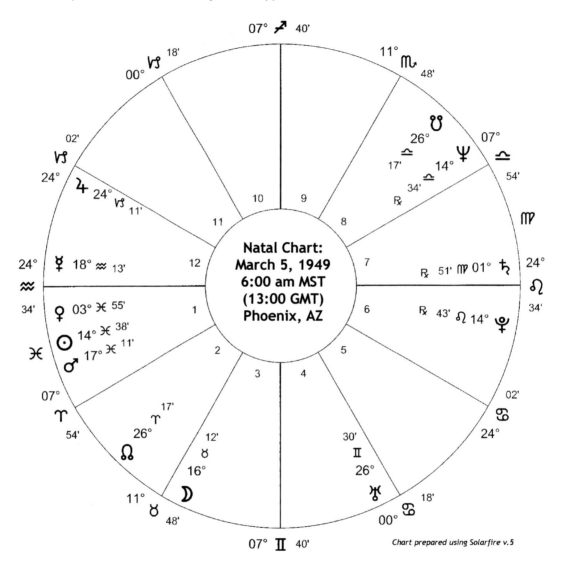

07° ♐ 40'

11° ♏ 48'

00° ♑ 18'

02' ♑ 24°

♃ 24° ♑ 11'

26° ☊ ♎ 17' ♎ 34' ℞

07° ♎ 54' ♍

14° ♆ ♎

51' ♍ 01' ♄ ℞ 24° ♌ 34'

24° ♒ ♀ 18° ♒ 13'

34' ♀ 03° ♓ 55'

43' ♌ 14° ♇ ℞

14° ♓ 38' ☉

07° ♈ 54' ♈ 17° ♓ 11' ♂

02' ♋ 24°

♈ 17' 26° ♈

☊ ♊ 26° 30'

♊ 12' ♉ 16°

18' ♋

00° ♋ ♅

11° ♉ 48' ☽

Natal Chart:
March 5, 1949
6:00 am MST
(13:00 GMT)
Phoenix, AZ

10 9 8 7 6 5 4 3 2 1 12 11

07° ♊ 40'

Chart prepared using Solarfire v.5

1. Calculate this native's ACD:

2. Determine the exact date when progressed Mercury will cross the natal Ascendant.

3. Determine the exact date when progressed Moon will first oppose the natal Sun.

Lesson 25: Section Exam

Two calculation exams are provided here so that you may test yourself. Forms are provided on the following 3 pages for your use in the first exam. The second exam does not include any forms to simulate an actual certification exam. Answers can be found in the Answer Key in the Appendix.

Exam 1

Using the following natal chart, determine the ACD and progress all planets and house cusps to May 1, 2004. Then enter the progressed planets, Ascendant, and Midheaven in the outer wheel below.

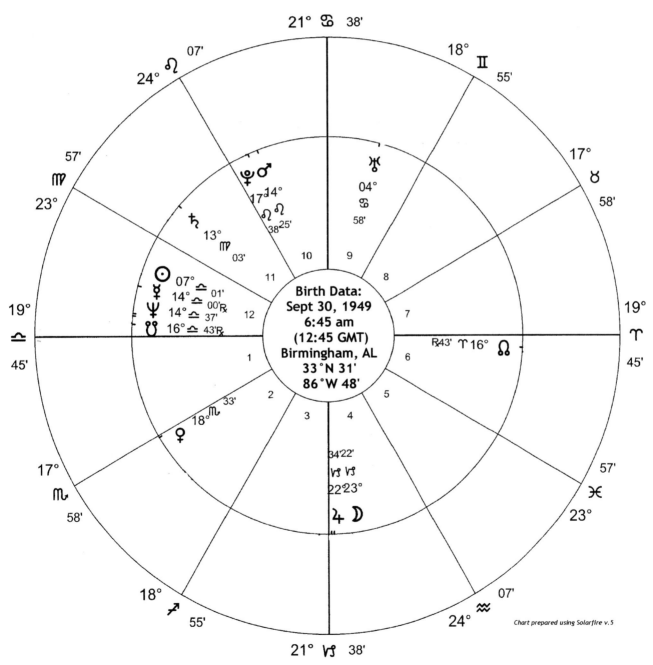

Chart prepared using Solarfire v.5

Part A: ACD

ACD Calculation:

1. CM-1 (Convert GMT of Birth to decimal: _____ ÷ 24 = CM-1) _____

2. 365 days x CM-1 *(line 1)* = ACD Interval   X 365 = _____

3a. GMT Birthdate Day Number *(from Table of Numbered Days)*   _____

   b. - ACD Interval *(from line 2)*   - _____
   _____

   c. = ACD Day Number   = _____

   d. = Birth ACD *(line 3c date equivalent from Table of Numbered Days)*   **Birth ACD = _____ Year _____**

ACD Equivalent Ephemeris Date:

4. Year of ACD prior to Target Date _____ - Year of Birth ACD *(line 3d)* _____ = Elapsed Years(Days) _____

5. GMT Birthdate Day No. *(line 3a)* _____ + Elapsed Years(Days) *(line 4)* _____ = Equivalent Ephemeris Day No. _____

   = Equivalent Ephemeris Date to earlier ACD _____

6. **Equivalent Ephemeris Date to later ACD** *(final date from line 5 plus 1 day)*_____

Part B: Progressed Planetary CM (PP-CM)

7. Target Date Day Number *(from Table of Numbered Days)*   _____

8. - ACD Day Number *(from Table of Numbered Days)*   - _____
   _____

9. = Days elapsed from ACD to Target   = _____

10. Line 9 ÷ 365 = PPCM   PPCM = _____

Solar Arc

Progressed Sun *(Part C, line 5)* _____

- Birth Sun   - _____
_____

= Solar Arc   = _____

Progressed MC

Birth MC   _____

+ Solar Arc   + _____
_____

= Progressed MC   = _____

Part C: Progressed Planetary Positions

	☉	☽	☿	♀	♂	♃
1. Position at 0 hr on later ephemeris date *(Part A, line 6)* _____						
2. Position at 0 hr on earlier ephemeris date *(Part A, line 5)* _____						
3. Line 1 - Line 2 = Total Daily Travel						
4. Line 3 X PPCM _____ = Travel to Target Date						
5. Add lines 2 + 4 = Progressed Position on Target Date						

	♄	♅	♆	♇	☊	
6. Position at 0 hr on later ephemeris date *(Part A, line 6)* _____						
7. Position at 0 hr on earlier ephemeris date *(Part A, line 5)* _____						
8. Line 6 - Line 7 = Total Daily Travel						
9. Line 8 X PPCM _____ = Travel to Target Date						
10. Add lines 7 + 9 = Progressed Position on Target Date						

Midheaven CM (MC-CM)
(Constant Multiplier for Part D: House Cusps, Lines 4 & 9: MC Interpolation)

Progressed MC   _____

- Next lowest MC from Table   - _____

                       =   _____ ' *(a)*

Next highest MC from Table   _____

- Next lowest MC from Table   - _____

                       =   _____ ' *(b)*

_____ *(a)* ÷ _____ *(b)* = **MC-CM** _____

Latitude CM (CM-3)
(Constant Multiplier for Part D: House Cusps, Line 14: Latitude Interpolation)

Latitude of Birth (or other prog. location) ____° ____'

- Next lowest Latitude from Table   - ____° _00_ '

                    =   ____° ____'

Convert result to decimal   **CM-3** = _____

Exception: If Birth Latitude is less than 20°, divide result by 5   ÷ 5 = CM-3 _____

Part D: Progressed House Cusp Calculation

House Cusp Calculation for Higher Latitude					
Latitude _____ °	11th	12th	ASC	2nd	3rd
1. House Cusps at Higher MC _____					
2. House Cusps at Lower MC _____					
3. Line 1 - Line 2 =					
4. Line 3 X MC-CM _____ =					
5. Add lines 2 + 4 =					

House Cusp Calculation for Lower Latitude					
Latitude _____ °	11th	12th	ASC	2nd	3rd
6. House Cusps at Higher MC _____					
7. House Cusps at Lower MC _____					
8. Line 6 - Line 7 =					
9. Line 8 X MC-CM _____ =					
10. Add lines 7 + 9 =					

Latitude Interpolation					
	11th	12th	ASC	2nd	3rd
11. House Cusps at Higher Latitude (from line 5)					
12. House Cusps at Lower Latitude (from line 10)					
13. Line 11 - Line 12 =					
14. Line 13 X CM-3 _____ =					
15. Add lines 12 + 14 = **Progressed House Cusps**					

Exam 2

Using the following natal chart, determine the ACD and progress all planets, Ascendant and Midheaven to the 43rd birthday without the use of forms. Then enter the progressed planets, Ascendant, and Midheaven in the outer wheel below. Three blank pages have been provided for your work.

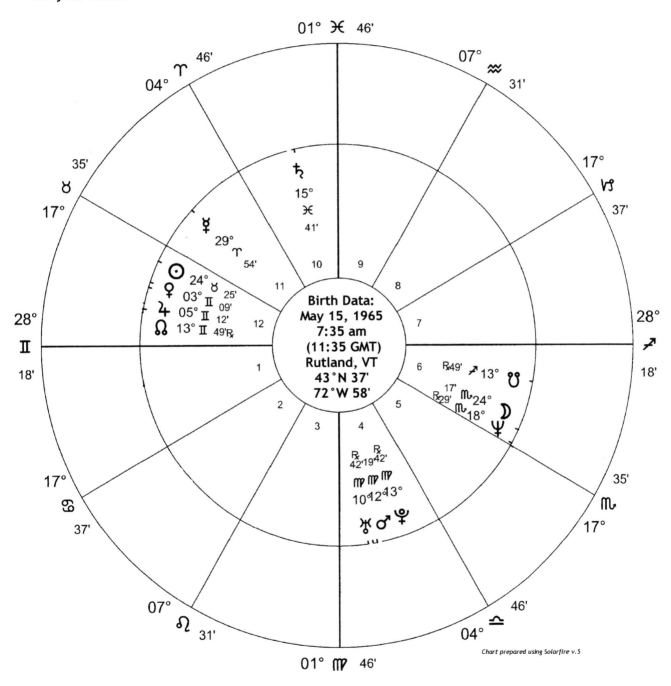

01° ♓ 46'

07° ♒ 31'

04° ♈ 46'

17° ♑ 37'

35' ♉
17°

17° ♑ 37' ... (inner)

♄ 15° ♓ 41'

☿ 29° ♈ 54'

☉ 24° ♉
♀ 03° ♊ 25'
♃ 05° ♊ 09' 12'
☊ 13° ♊ 49' ℞

Birth Data:
May 15, 1965
7:35 am
(11:35 GMT)
Rutland, VT
43°N 37'
72°W 58'

28°
♊
18°

28°
♐
18°

℞ 49' ♐ 13° ☋

℞ 17' ♏ 24'
℞ 29' ♏ 18'
♏ ♆

℞ 42' 19' ℞ 42'
♍ ♍ ♍
10° 12° 13°
♅ ♂ ♇

17° ♋ 37'

35' ♏ 17°

07° ♌ 31'

46' ♎ 04°

01° ♍ 46'

Chart prepared using Solarfire v.5

257

Section 8:

Additional Predictive Techniques

Lesson 26: Solar Arc Directions

Solar Arc Directions are another variation on the "day for a year" principle. Based on the Sun's daily motion, solar arc directions apply the same rate of progression to every planet and point in the horoscope. This lesson explains the simple process of progressing planets and chart angles through time via solar arc direction.

Rotating the Chart through Time

Solar Arc Directions are based entirely on the Sun's motion, and advance the chart as a whole for each year of life according to the Sun's movement each day after birth. Solar Arc Directions differ from other methods of chart progression in that they preserve the patterns and aspects in a natal chart by moving the chart as a fixed unit through time. Natal aspects and aspect patterns are maintained in exactly the same configurations as they were at birth. If two planets are in square aspect natally, they will always remain in square with the same orb via solar arc.

Take a look at the bi-wheel example below. The inner wheel contains a natal chart, and the outer wheel contains the solar arc directed chart for the ACD prior to this person's 40th birthday. Notice that all aspects and configurations remain intact in the solar arc directed chart. It is as if the entire chart were simply rotated counter-clockwise, one degree for each degree of the Sun's movement by progression. Notice the 10th house Venus/Sun conjunction in the natal chart. These two planets have remained in conjunction with the same orb by solar arc, but have now simply "rotated" into the sign of Leo in the 12th house.

Solar arcs are often roughly estimated by adding 1° per year of age to any natal planet or point, but this does not produce accurate results. The Sun's daily movement varies from 57' to 1° 01' during the course of a year, traveling faster in the winter than in the summer. Thus, a person born in June will have a shorter solar arc than someone born in January. In this example, the natal chart was solar arc directed to the ACD before the 40th birthday, when this person was roughly 39½ years old. However, because the birth occurred in June, the solar arc was only 37½ degrees - 2° less than his age. If an estimate of 1° per year had been used instead of the actual solar arc, any predictions made for this person would have been off by two years.

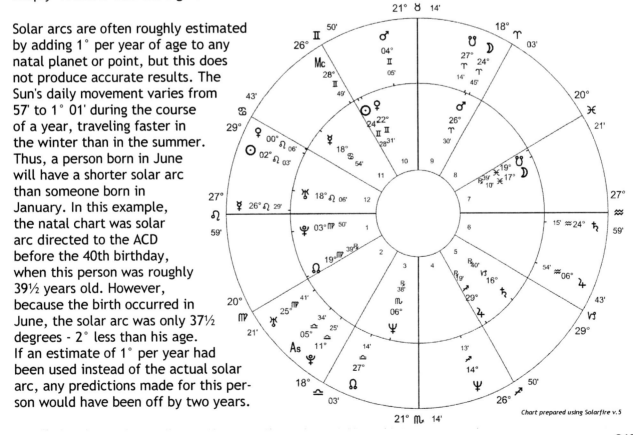

Chart prepared using Solarfire v.5

Calculating Solar Arc Directions

If you have mastered secondary progressions, solar arc directions will seem simple to calculate:

Step 1. Determine the Solar Arc by calculating the difference between the progressed Sun and the natal Sun. In order to accomplish this step, you must have a copy of the person's complete natal chart and have already calculated the exact position of the progressed Sun (covered in lesson 22).

Step 2. Add the Solar Arc to every natal planet and chart angle. That's all there is to it!

Before we tackle progressing a full chart by solar arc, let's review some math skills by calculating a few solar arcs. The easiest way to accomplish this is to convert the natal and progressed Sun positions into absolute longitude first, as demonstrated below. Then the natal position of the Sun is subtracted from the progressed Sun to arrive at the solar arc:

Example 1.

Natal Sun position is 24° ♑ 35',
progressed Sun position is 14° ♓ 53'.

$$24° ♑ 35' = 294.58°$$
$$14° ♓ 53' = 344.88°$$

p. ☉:	344.88°
n. ☉:	- 294.58°
= solar arc	= 50.30° = 50° 18'

Example 2.

Natal Sun position is 10° ♊ 12',
progressed Sun position is 5° ♋ 59'.

$$10° ♊ 12' = 70.20°$$
$$5° ♋ 59' = 95.98°$$

p. ☉:	95.98°
n. ☉:	- 70.20°
= solar arc	= 25.78° = 25° 47'

Example 3.

Natal Sun position is 5° ♓ 18',
progressed Sun position is 14° ♉ 49'.

$$5° ♓ 18' = 335.30°$$
$$14° ♉ 49' = 44.82°$$

	404.82° *(add 360°)*
p. ☉:	~~44.82°~~
n. ☉:	- 335.30°
= solar arc	= 69.52° = 69° 31'

Example 4.

Natal Sun position is 18° ♒ 30',
progressed Sun position is 3° ♈ 26'.

$$18° ♒ 30' = 318.50°$$
$$3° ♈ 26' = 3.43°$$

	363.43° *(add 360°)*
p. ☉:	~~3.43°~~
n. ☉:	- 318.50°
= solar arc	= 44.93° = 44° 56'

Notice in these last two examples that the Sun had progressed from the "end" of the zodiac into an early sign. Remember that 360° can be added if needed to subtract without affecting the accuracy of the answer.

Example 5.

This example demonstrates the entire procedure of progressing a chart by solar arc direction. Below is the natal chart of a person born January 10, 1955, 8:00 am EST, in New York, NY. The ACD June 27, 1954 has been provided. (Refer to Lesson 21 if you need to review how to calculate an ACD.) Now let's progress this chart by solar arc to the ACD before this person's 50th birthday.

Step 1. Determine the Solar Arc by calculating the difference between the progressed Sun and the natal Sun.

The first step is to determine the position of the progressed Sun on the target date, which is the equivalent of 50 days after the date of birth by progression, or March 1, 1955. (Again, refer to Lesson 21 if you need to review how this date was calculated.) Referring to a midnight ephemeris, you will find that on March 1, 1955 the Sun was at 9° ♓ 38'. In the natal chart below the natal Sun is located at 19° ♑ 31'. Now let's calculate the solar arc:

$$
\begin{aligned}
\text{p. } \odot: \quad & 339.63° \quad (9° ♓ 38' \text{ expressed in absolute longitude}) \\
\text{n. } \odot: \quad & \underline{-\ 289.52°} \quad (19° ♑ 31' \text{ expressed in absolute longitude}) \\
= \text{solar arc} = \ & 50.11° = 50° \ 07'
\end{aligned}
$$

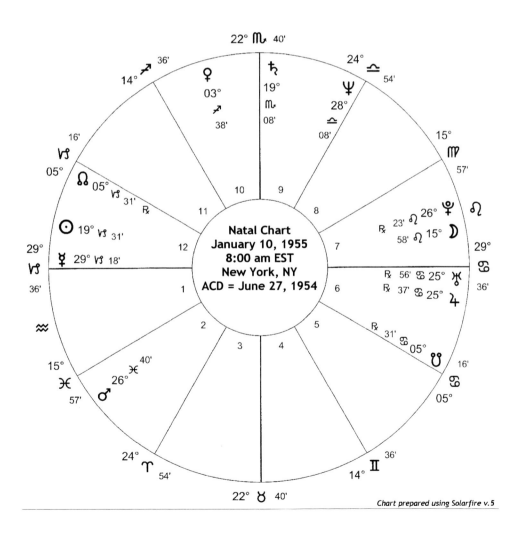

Chart prepared using Solarfire v.5

265

Example 5 (continued)

Step 2. Add the Solar Arc to every natal planet and chart angle.

Now simply add 50° 07', or 50.11° in absolute longitude, to every remaining planet and angle in the natal chart. Notice that all zodiacal positions are first converted to absolute longitude in order to make addition easier:

Natal ☽	135.97° (15° ♌ 58')		Natal ☿	299.30° (29° ♑ 18')	
+ Solar Arc	+ 50.11°		+ Solar Arc	+ 50.11°	
= Progressed ☽	= 186.08° = 6° ♎ 05'		= Progressed ☿	= 349.41° = 19° ♓ 25'	

Natal ♀	243.63° (3° ♐ 38')		Natal ♂	356.67° (26° ♓ 40')	
+ Solar Arc	+ 50.11°		+ Solar Arc	+ 50.11°	
= Progressed ♀	= 293.74° = 23° ♑ 44'			= 406.78°	
			- 360°	- 360.00°	
			= Progressed ♂	= 46.78° = 16° ♉ 47'	

Natal ♃	115.62° (25° ♋ 37')		Natal ♄	229.13° (19° ♏ 08')	
+ Solar Arc	+ 50.11°		+ Solar Arc	+ 50.11°	
= Progressed ♃	= 165.73° = 15° ♍ 44'		= Progressed ♄	= 279.24° = 9° ♑ 14'	

Natal ♅	115.93° (25° ♋ 56')		Natal ♆	208.13° (28° ♎ 08')	
+ Solar Arc	+ 50.11°		+ Solar Arc	+ 50.11°	
= Progressed ♅	= 166.04° = 16° ♍ 02'		= Progressed ♆	= 258.24° = 18° ♐ 14'	

Natal ♇	146.38° (26° ♌ 23')		Natal ☊	275.52° (5° ♑ 31')	
+ Solar Arc	+ 50.11°		+ Solar Arc	+ 50.11°	
= Progressed ♇	= 196.49° = 16° ♎ 29'		= Progressed ☊	= 325.63° = 25° ♒ 38'	

Natal ASC	299.60° (29° ♑ 36')		Natal MC	232.67° (22° ♏ 40')	
+ Solar Arc	+ 50.11°		+ Solar Arc	+ 50.11°	
= Progressed ASC	= 349.71° = 19° ♓ 43'		= Progressed MC	= 282.78° = 12° ♑ 47'	

All planets and angles are directed <u>forward</u>
regardless of whether or not they are retrograde in the natal chart

The solar arc directed planetary positions and angles have been inserted around the natal chart in a bi-wheel, shown below.

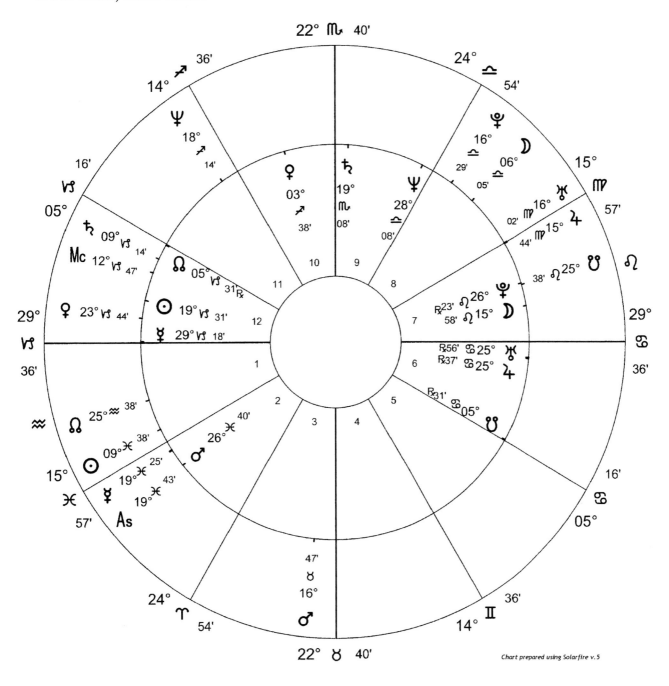

Chart prepared using Solarfire v.5

(Note: You may find that hand-calculated solar arc directed planets differ from computer-generated solar arc directed planets by 1 or 2 minutes of arc. This is due to the fact that computers calculate zodiacal positions to several decimal places.)

Lesson 26 Exercises

Progress the following chart by solar arc direction to the ACD before this person's 38th birthday, then enter the solar arc directed planets and angles in the outer wheel below. The ACD is given below. Two blank pages have been provided following this page for your calculations. Answers can be found in the Answer Key in the Appendix.

Birthdate: April 12, 1948, 5:45 am PDT (12:45 GMT)
San Francisco, CA
Adjusted Calculation Date = October 1, 1947

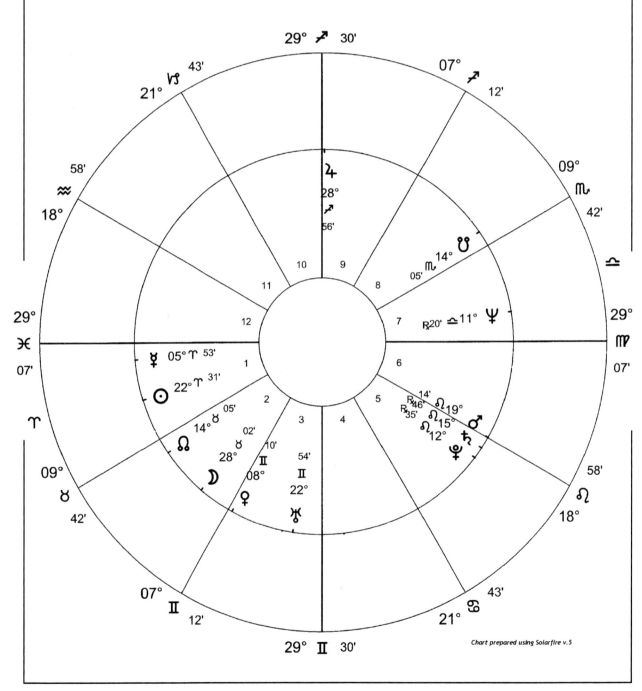

Lesson 27: Solar Returns

A **Solar Return** is a chart based on the time the Sun returns to its exact natal position each year, and is used to gain an overview of the year ahead. In this lesson, we demonstrate how to locate a precise natal position for the Sun, and how to use this position to calculate a Solar Return.

Solar Returns

Every year around the time of one's birthday, the transiting Sun on its annual trip around the zodiac passes through the same zodiacal degree, minute and second that it occupied at the moment of birth. In a **Solar Return** chart, the exact moment this "solar return" occurs is used to erect a new chart representing the new year ahead. This Solar Return chart can then be used to predict the events, opportunities, and challenges one is likely to encounter during the coming year.

Calculating a Solar Return is very much like calculating a new natal chart, but uses the date and time when the Sun returns to the exact position it held at the moment of birth. In order to determine the precise time this event occurs, the position of the natal Sun must be known to the nearest second of arc. Thus, before proceeding with Solar Return calculation, we must begin by going back to the natal chart and recalculating the Sun's position in greater detail.

Accuracy is Everything!

It is crucial that the position of the natal Sun be accurately calculated to the nearest second of arc, because this position will determine the correct time to use for calculating the Solar Return. As explained in previous lessons, for each minute of time the Ascendant advances by 15 minutes of zodiacal longitude, which is why an exact time of birth is essential for an accurate natal chart. Because the Sun moves an average of 59 minutes per day, or 1 minute of arc for each 24 minutes of time, each minute the Sun's position is changing by approximately 2 seconds of zodiacal longitude. In other words, a difference of just 2 *seconds* in the Sun's natal position will change the Ascendant in the Solar Return chart by *15 minutes* of zodiacal arc. This means that in order to calculate a correct Solar Return, the exact minute when the Sun returns to its natal position must be pinpointed, and in order to do this its natal position must be calculated to the nearest second.

Solar Return Location

The location used for a Solar Return is not unanimously agreed upon by astrologers. A Solar Return chart can be calculated using one's actual location at the time of the Solar Return, which can be quite a distance from home if one happens to be traveling at the time. Some astrologers prefer to use the current place of residence regardless of where the person happens to be on the particular day of their Solar Return, while others prefer to always use the birth location. Normally, in an exam setting, you will be told which location to use when calculating the Solar Return. If you are not given this information, you should state clearly on your exam which location you have chosen to use.

Calculating the Solar Return

Three steps are needed to calculate a Solar Return:

Step 1. Determine the exact position of the natal Sun to the nearest second of arc.

Step 2. Determine the exact date and GMT during the target year when the transiting Sun returns to the exact natal position. This is done by:

> a) determining the Sun's motion from 0 hour on the day of its return to its natal position
>
> b) determining the Sun's full daily motion on the day of its return
>
> c) dividing "a" by "b" to determine the portion of the day that elapsed from 0 hour to it's return
>
> d) applying this portion to 24 hours, to determine the exact GMT of the solar return.

Step 3. Calculate a natal chart, using the date and GMT found in Step 2, and the location of choice.

Example 1.

Let's calculate a Solar Return for someone's 30th birthday. This example will use the same birth data and natal chart used in Lesson 13, shown on page 125.

April 9, 1968, 12:13 pm CST (18:13 GMT)
Des Moines, Iowa

Step 1. Determine the exact position of the natal Sun to the nearest second of arc.
In Lesson 13, we determined that this person's natal Sun was located at 19°♈ 57', but now the position of the natal Sun must be recalculated to the nearest second, using a GMT of birth of 18:13 and a CM-1 of .759 as calculated in that lesson. Referring back to an ephemeris for the Sun's position on the birth date and day after, we find the exact position of the Sun as follows:

1. Position at 0 hr on day after birth date **(4/10/68)**	19°♈ 70' 73" ~~20°♈ 11' 13"~~
2. Position at 0 hr on Birth date **(4/9/68)**	19°♈ 12' 20"
3. Line 1 - Line 2 = Total Daily Travel	58' 53" Or 58.883'
4. Line 3 X CM-1 **(.759)** =Travel to birth time	44.692' Or 44' 42"
5. Add lines 2 + 4 = Position at Birth	19°♈ 56' 62" = 19°♈ 57' 02"

Seconds are converted into a decimal of a minute to simplify the calculation process

After the "formula" is applied, the decimal is converted back into seconds

Step 2. Determine the exact date and GMT during the target year when the transiting Sun returns to the exact natal position. Now that the Sun's position has been calculated, we can move ahead to the target year and determine the exact date and time the Sun returns to 19° ♈ 57' 02". Because we are calculating a return for this person's 30th birthday, the target will be around April 9, 1998 (1968 + 30 = 1998). Look in *The ACS Ephemeris* for April 1998 and notice that the Sun reached this position sometime between 0 hour April 10 and 0 hour April 11, 1998:

APRIL 1998   LONGITUDE

Day	Sid.Time	☉	0 hr ☽	Noon ☽	True ☊	☿	♀	♂	♃	♄	♅	♆	♇
1 W	12 36 36	11♈ 3 56	5Ⅱ 1 16	12Ⅱ 7 6	10♏ 9.1	20♈28.2	24♒37.8	20♈56.5	13♓11.1	21♈46.2	11♒52.1	1♒51.5	7♐56.5
2 Th	12 40 33	12 3 10	19 5 55	25 57 41	10R 6.9	19R57.4	25 38.7	21 41.9	13 24.7	21 53.7	11 54.3	1 52.5	7R 55.8
3 F	12 44 29	13 2 21	2♋42 30	9♋20 36	10D 4.1	19 21.6	26 39.9	22 27.3	13 38.3	22 1.3	11 56.4	1 53.6	7 55.1
4 Sa	12 48 26	14 1 30	15 52 19	22 18 6	10 3.6	18 41.7	27 41.4	23 12.6	13 51.7	22 8.8	11 58.5	1 54.6	7 54.3
5 Su	12 52 23	15 0 37	28 38 27	4♌53 52	10 4.4	17 58.5	28 43.3	23 57.8	14 5.2	22 16.4	12 0.5	1 55.5	7 53.5
6 M	12 56 19	15 59 41	11♌ 4 54	17 12 8	10 5.9	17 12.9	29 45.4	24 43.0	14 18.5	22 23.9	12 2.5	1 56.5	7 52.7
7 Tu	13 0 16	16 58 43	23 16 6	29 17 19	10 7.6	16 25.8	0♓47.8	25 28.2	14 31.9	22 31.5	12 4.4	1 57.4	7 51.9
8 W	13 4 12	17 57 43	5♍16 17	11♍13 30	10R 8.6	15 38.2	1 50.4	26 13.3	14 45.1	22 39.1	12 6.4	1 58.3	7 51.0
9 Th	13 8 9	18 56 40	17 9 24	23 4 22	10 8.5	14 51.1	2 53.4	26 58.3	14 58.3	22 46.7	12 8.2	1 59.1	7 50.1
10 F	13 12 5	19 55 36	28 58 46	4♎52 58	10 6.6	14 5.2	3 56.6	27 43.3	15 11.5	22 54.3	12 10.0	1 59.9	7 49.2
11 Sa	13 16 2	20 54 29	10♎47 13	16 41 50	10 2.8	13 21.3	5 0.0	28 28.2	15 24.6	23 1.9	12 11.8	2 0.7	7 48.2

In this case the Sun is returning to its natal position on the day after this person's 30th birthday, not on the birthday itself. Often, the Solar Return will occur on the day before or after one's birthday. This is because there are actually 365 1/4 days in a year; the extra 1/4 day accounts for the difference.

Now let's pinpoint the exact time during April 10, 1998 when the Sun returned to 19° ♈ 57' 02" :

First, determine the Sun's motion from 0 hour on April 10th to its natal position:

	19° ♈ 56' 62"
Sun's Natal Position	~~19° ♈ 57' 02"~~
- Position at 0 hr on April 10, 1998	19° ♈ 55' 36"
= Daily Travel	1' 26"
	Or 1.433'

Second, determine the Sun's total daily motion on April 10, 1998:

	19° ♈ 113' 89"
Position at 0 hr on April 11, 1998	~~20° ♈ 54' 29"~~
- Position at 0 hr on April 10, 1998	19° ♈ 55' 36"
= Daily Travel	58' 53"
	Or 58.883'

Then divide these two results to determine the portion of the day that elapsed from 0 hour to the Sun's return:

Sun's travel from 0 hr to natal position $\frac{1.433}{58.883}$ *divided by Sun's total daily travel* = .0243 *portion of day elapsed from 0 hour to Sun's Return*

Now this proportion can be used to determine the exact GMT of the Solar Return. This is done by multiplying the proportion by the total number of minutes in a day. The result, converted into hours and minutes if necessary, will be the GMT of the Solar Return:

.0243 X 1440 (total number of minutes in a day) = 35 minutes

Remember that there are 1440 minutes in a day, because 24 hours x 60 minutes = 1440. In this example, the result is less than a full hour. Therefore, the GMT to use when calculating this Solar Return will be 00:35. This means that the Sun returned to its natal position of 19°♈ 57' 02" at 00:35 GMT on April 10, 1998. If this result had been greater than 60 minutes, we would have converted it into hours:minutes and taken that as the GMT.

Step 3. Calculate a natal chart, using the date and GMT found in Step 2, and the location of choice. Below is the Solar Return chart erected for April 10, 1998, 00:35 GMT, Des Moines, Iowa.

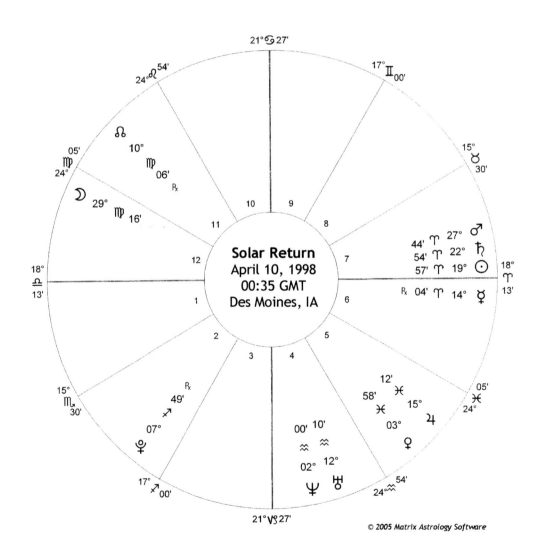

© 2005 Matrix Astrology Software

274

Lesson 27 Exercises

Calculate the chart data to be used in erecting the following Solar Return. Answers can be found in the Answer Key in the Appendix.

1. Using the following natal chart, calculate the date and GMT to be used to erect a Solar Return corresponding to this person's 48th birthday.

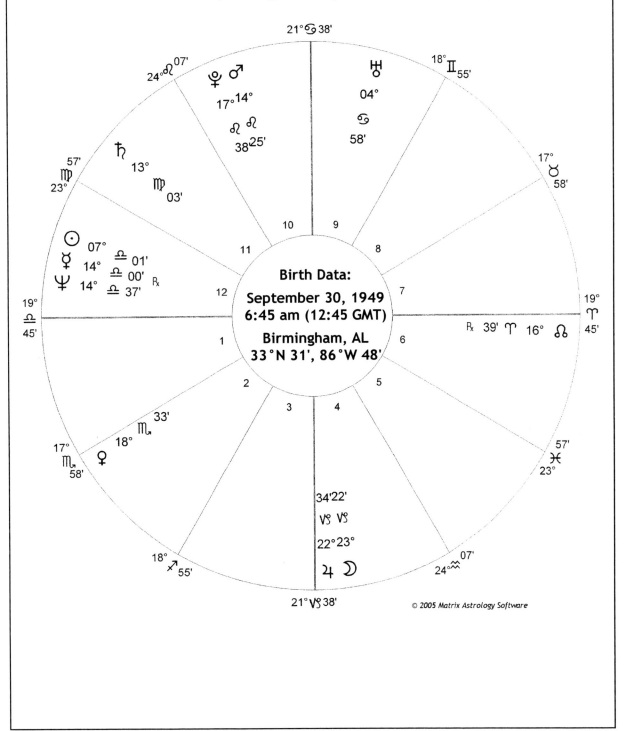

Birth Data:
September 30, 1949
6:45 am (12:45 GMT)
Birmingham, AL
33°N 31', 86°W 48'

© 2005 Matrix Astrology Software

Lesson 28 : Lunar Returns

Lunar Returns are charts cast for the exact moment the Moon makes a monthly return to its natal position, and provide information for the month during which they are in effect. At present we are not aware of any certification exams that require calculating a Lunar Return. However, we chose to include this lesson for those interested in learning Lunar Return calculation.

Lunar Returns

While the transiting Sun returns to its natal position once every year, the faster transiting Moon returns to its natal position once a month. A chart calculated for the exact moment when the Moon makes its return in any particular month is called a **Lunar Return**. A Lunar Return can be used to gain insight into the month for which it is cast, and will reveal the general emotional tone and day-to-day events of the month. Each Lunar Return will only be in effect for 28-29 days, until the transiting Moon again returns to its natal position and establishes a new Lunar Return.

Recall that the Moon moves 12-14° per day. In other words, the Moon is moving 1 minute of zodiacal arc for each 1.7 to 2 minutes of time. You will remember that for each minute of time, the angles of a chart move about 15 minutes of arc. Therefore, in order to calculate the angles of a Lunar Return to within 1 minute of arc, the natal position of the Moon to within 2-3 seconds of zodiacal longitude is required.

Remember that the Moon does not move at a uniform speed throughout the day; This is why most ephemerides give two daily listings for the Moon - one at Noon and one at 0-hour. In order to calculate an exact position for the natal Moon, interpolation is necessary between these **semi-diurnal**, or half-daily positions. Keep in mind that even within these 12-hour windows the speed of the Moon is still fluctuating somewhat. Although semi-diurnal interpolation makes it possible to do fairly precise manual calculations, we cannot hope to achieve the degree of exactitude possible with a computer. Therefore, manually calculated results may differ from a computer-generated Lunar Return by several minutes of arc on the angles.

Semi-Diurnal Interpolation

Semi-diurnal interpolation involves interpolating between two positions 12 hours apart to locate the exact birth position of the Moon. This means either interpolating between 0 hour and Noon, if the GMT of birth is less than 12:00, or interpolating between Noon and 0 hour of the following day, if the GMT of birth is more than 12:00. Because we are dealing with the portion of a 12-hour period represented by the GMT of birth, the constant multiplier used will be different than that used for the rest of the planets which is based on a portion of a full 24-hour day. Finding this new semi-diurnal constant multiplier and how to use it is demonstrated in the following example.

Semi-diurnal (or "half-day") positions for the Moon are used to pinpoint it's exact natal position, necessary for an accurate lunar return

APRIL 1968 **LONGITUDE**

Day	Sid.Time	☉	0 hr ☽	Noon ☽	True ☊	☿	♀	♂
1 M	12 37 39	11♈19 48	14♉54 6	20♉48 51	18♈40.6	20♓ 1.3	20♓15.5	2♉57.3
2 Tu	12 41 36	12 19 0	26 43 7	2♊37 20	18 41.4	21 36.7	21 29.4	3 41.3
3 W	12 45 32	13 18 10	8♊31 57	14 27 27	18 42.0	23 13.6	22 43.3	4 25.4
4 Th	12 49 29	14 17 17	20 24 22	26 23 14	18 42.5	24 51.9	23 57.2	5 9.3
5 F	12 53 25	15 16 22	2♋24 36	8♋29 3	18 42.8	26 31.7	25 11.2	5 53.2
6 Sa	12 57 22	16 15 25	14 37 7	20 49 23	18R42.9	28 12.9	26 25.1	6 37.1
7 Su	13 1 19	17 14 26	27 6 23	3♌28 37	18 42.9	29 55.6	27 39.0	7 20.9
8 M	13 5 15	18 13 24	9♌56 32	16 30 31	18D42.8	1♈39.8	28 52.9	8 4.7
9 Tu	13 9 12	19 12 20	23 10 52	29 57 47	18 42.8	3 25.4	0♈ 6.7	8 48.4
10 W	13 13 8	20 11 13	6♍51 21	13♍51 29	18 43.0	5 12.5	1 20.6	9 32.1
11 Th	13 17 5	21 10 5	20 58 0	28 10 30	18 43.1	7 1.1	2 34.5	10 15.7
12 F	13 21 1	22 8 54	5♎28 27	12♎51 9	18R43.3	8 51.3	3 48.4	10 59.3
13 Sa	13 24 58	23 7 41	20 17 46	27 47 20	18 43.4	10 42.9	5 2.2	11 42.8

Calculating Lunar Returns

Step 1. Determine the exact position of the natal Moon to the nearest second of arc by interpolating between semi-diurnal positions of the Moon. This is done by:

  a) determining a new Constant Multiplier based on the proportion of the half-day that elapsed from 0-hour to the time of birth for births with a GMT of less than 12:00, or from Noon to the time of birth for births with a GMT greater than 12:00.

  b) applying this Constant Multiplier to the Moon's semi-diurnal motion (0-hour to Noon for births with a GMT of less than 12:00, or Noon to 0 hour on the following day for births with a GMT greater than 12:00) to arrive at a precise natal position.

Step 2. Determine the exact date and GMT during the target month when the transiting Moon returns to the exact natal position. This is done by:

  a) determining the Moon's motion from its next earlier listed position in the ephemeris, which may be a Noon or 0-hour listing, to its natal position

  b) determining the Moon's full semi-diurnal motion during the 12-hour period of its return. If the lunar return occurred before Noon, this entails determining the Moon's movement from 0-hour to Noon. If it occurred after Noon, this entails determining the Moon's movement from Noon to 0-hour on the following day.

  c) dividing "a" by "b" to determine the portion of the half-day that elapsed to it's return

  d) applying this portion to 12 hours to find the exact GMT of the Lunar Return.

Step 3. Calculate a natal chart, using the date and GMT found in Step 2, and the location of choice.

Example 1.

Let's work through an example by calculating the Lunar Return in effect at the time of this person's 30th birthday (the natal chart is shown on page 125):

April 9, 1968, 12:13 pm CST (18:13 GMT)
Des Moines, Iowa

Because this person's GMT of birth is greater than 12:00, we will be interpolating between the Moon's positions at Noon (12:00) on the birthday and 0 hour (0:00) on the day after birth. The following positions were taken from the ephemeris for April 1968 (refer to *The ACS Ephemeris* excerpt on the previous page).

☽ Position 12:00 April 9, 1968	♌ 29° 57' 47"
☽ Position at birth 18:13 April 9, 1968	?
☽ Position 0:00 April 10, 1968	♍ 6° 51' 21"

Step 1. Determine the exact position of the natal Moon to the nearest second of arc by interpolating between semi-diurnal positions of the Moon. This is done by:

a) determining a new Constant Multiplier based on the proportion of the half-day that elapsed from 0-hour to the time of birth for births with a GMT of less than 12:00, or from Noon to the time of birth for births with a GMT greater than 12:00.

In this case, the GMT of birth (18:13) is greater than 12:00. Start by subtracting 12:00 from the GMT of birth to find out how many hours and minutes after Noon the birth occurred:

18:13
- 12:00

6:13, or 6.217 hours

Now divide this by 12, the total number of hours in the semi-diurnal or half-day period we are dealing with, to find what proportion of this period 6.217 hours represents. This should be taken to 4 decimal places for accuracy.

6.217 ÷ 12 = .5180

.5180 is the constant multiplier, because it represents the portion of the half-day that elapsed from Noon to the GMT of birth. We can now proceed to Step 1, part b.

Step 1 b) Apply this Constant Multiplier to the Moon's semi-diurnal motion (0-hour to Noon for births with a GMT of less than 12:00, or Noon to 0 hour on the following day for births with a GMT greater than 12:00) to arrive at a precise natal position.

Lines 1-3 below determine the Moon's full semi-diurnal motion from Noon April 9th to 0 hour April 10th. Then on line 4 the constant multiplier is applied to determine the Moon's movement from Noon to the time of birth. Finally, this movement is added to the Moon's Noon position on line 2 to arrive at the exact position of the Moon at the time of birth:

1. Later listed semi-diurnal position to birth GMT **(0-hour 4/10/68)**	♌ 35° 110' 81" ~~♍ 6° 51' 21"~~
2. Earlier listed semi-diurnal position to birth GMT **(Noon 4/9/68)**	♌ 29° 57' 47"
3. Line 1 - Line 2 = Total Semi-diurnal Travel	6° 53' 34" Or 413.567'
4. Line 3 X CM (.5180) =Travel to birth time	214.228' Or 3° 34' 14"
5. Add lines 2 + 4 = Position at Birth	♌ 32° 91' 61" = ♍ 3° 32' 01"

Seconds are converted into a decimal of a minute to simplify the calculation process

After the "formula" is applied, the decimal is converted back into seconds

Step 2. Determine the exact date and GMT during the target month when the transiting Moon returns to the exact natal position.

In this example, we are looking for the moment the Moon returned to its natal position of 3° ♍ 32' 01" on or before this person's 30th birthday, which is April 9, 1998. Look in *The ACS Ephemeris* for April 1998 and notice that this occurred sometime between Noon on April 7th and 0 hour on April 8th. In this example the Moon happens to be returning on a date that is close to the birthday, but keep in mind that the Moon's return can occur up to 28 days before the actual birthday.

The Moon's natal position of 3° ♍ 32' 01" falls between these two listed positions. Therefore, the lunar return occurred some time between Noon on April 7 and 0 hour on April 8, 1998.

APRIL 1998   LONGITUDE

Day	Sid.Time	☉	0 hr ☽	Noon ☽	True ☊	☿	♀	♂	♃	♄	♅	♆	♇
1 W	12 36 36	11 ♈ 3 56	5 ♊ 1 16	12 ♊ 7 6	10 ♍ 9.1	20 ♈ 28.2	24 ♒ 37.8	20 ♈ 56.5	13 ♓ 11.1	21 ♈ 46.2	11 ♒ 52.1	1 ♒ 51.5	7 ♐ 56.5
2 Th	12 40 33	12 3 10	19 5 55	25 57 41	10R 5.9	19R 57.4	25 38.7	21 41.9	13 24.7	21 53.7	11 54.3	1 52.5	7R 55.8
3 F	12 44 29	13 2 21	2 ♋ 42 30	9 ♋ 20 36	10D 4.1	19 21.6	26 39.9	22 27.3	13 38.3	22 1.3	11 56.4	1 53.6	7 55.1
4 Sa	12 48 26	14 1 30	15 ♋ 2 19	22 18 6	10 3.6	18 41.7	27 41.4	23 12.6	13 51.7	22 8.8	11 58.5	1 54.6	7 54.3
5 Su	12 52 23	15 0 37	28 38 27	4 ♌ 43 52	10 4.4	17 58.5	28 43.3	23 57.8	14 5.2	22 16.4	12 0.5	1 55.5	7 53.5
6 M	12 56 19	15 59 41	11 ♌ 4 54	17 ♍ 2 8	10 5.9	17 12.9	29 45.4	24 43.0	14 18.5	22 23.9	12 2.5	1 56.5	7 52.7
7 Tu	13 0 16	16 58 43	23 ♌ 7	29 17 19	10 7.6	16 25.8	0 ♓ 47.8	25 28.2	14 31.9	22 31.5	12 4.4	1 57.4	7 51.9
8 W	13 4 12	17 57 43	5 ♍ 16 17	11 ♍ 13 30	10R 8.6	15 38.2	1 50.4	26 13.3	14 45.1	22 39.1	12 6.4	1 58.3	7 51.0
9 Th	13 8 9	18 56 40	17 9 24	23 4 22	10 8.5	14 51.1	2 53.4	26 58.3	14 58.3	22 46.7	12 8.2	1 59.1	7 50.1
10 F	13 12 5	19 55 36	28 58 46	4 ♎ 52 58	10 6.6	14 5.2	3 56.6	27 43.3	15 11.5	22 54.3	12 10.0	1 59.9	7 49.2
11 Sa	13 16 2	20 54 29	10 ♎ 47 13	16 41 50	10 2.8	13 21.3	5 0.0	28 28.2	15 24.6	23 1.9	12 11.8	2 0.7	7 48.2

Step 2 a) Determine the Moon's motion from its next earlier listed position in the ephemeris, which may be a Noon or 0-hour listing, to its natal position.

The next earliest listed position for the Moon is at Noon on April 7, 1998. Therefore the Moon's motion from Noon to its birth position must be calculated:

Moon's Natal Position	♌ 33° 31' 61" ~~♍ 3° 32' 01"~~
− Position at Noon on April 7, 1998	♌ 29° 17' 19"
= Travel to Birth Position	4° 14' 42" Or 254.7'

Step 2 b) Determine the Moon's full semi-diurnal motion during the 12-hour period of its return.

Next, calculate the full semi-diurnal motion from Noon April 7 to 0 hour April 8, 1998:

Position at 0 hour on April 8, 1998 *(later semi-diurnal position)*	♌ 34° 75' 77" ~~♍ 5° 16' 17"~~
− Position at Noon on April 7, 1998 *(earlier semi-diurnal position)*	♌ 29° 17' 19"
= Total Semi-diurnal Travel	5° 58' 58" Or 358.967'

Step 2 c) Divide "a" by "b" to determine the portion of the half-day that elapsed to it's Return.

The distances the Moon traveled from Noon to its return, and from Noon to 0 hour the following day have been calculated. This information is now converted into a fraction which will indicate the portion of the 12 hour period between Noon and 0 hour that had elapsed to the exact time of the Moon's return:

Moon's travel from Noon to natal position $\dfrac{254.7}{358.967}$ = .7095 *portion of half-day elapsed*
divided by Moon's total semi-diurnal travel   *from Noon to Moon's Return*

Step 2 d) Apply this portion to 12 hours to find the exact GMT of the Lunar Return.

Finally, use this proportion to arrive at the exact GMT of the Moon's return by applying it to the total number of minutes between Noon and 0 hour:

.7095 x 720 (total number of minutes in 12 hours) = 511 minutes, or 8:31

The Moon returned to its natal position of 3°♍ 32' 01" on April 7, 1998, 8 hours and 31 minutes after Noon, which is 20:31 GMT. This then becomes the GMT date and time to use for calculating the Lunar Return chart.

Step 3. Calculate a natal chart, using the date and GMT found in Step 2, and the location of choice. In this case, a chart for April 7, 1998, 20:31 GMT, Des Moines, IA would be calculated.

Remember that the Moon's rate of speed can fluctuate over the course of a day. Computers are able to take this into account when calculating charts, but we cannot when calculating charts manually. Because of this, the Moon in a computer-generated natal chart may differ from a manually-calculated chart by 1-3 minutes. With semi-diurnal interpolation this discrepancy is reduced to a matter of seconds, but even several seconds will create a difference of several minutes in the angles of a Lunar Return. Therefore, if you are checking your results against a computer, do not be discouraged if your Lunar Return does not match precisely.

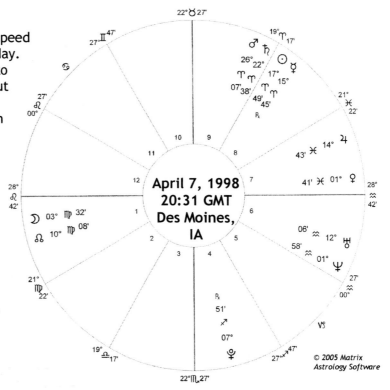

© 2005 Matrix
Astrology Software

Lesson 28 Exercises

Calculate the chart data to be used in erecting following Lunar Return. Answers can be found in the Answer Key in the Appendix.

1. Using the following natal chart, calculate the date and GMT to be used to erect the Lunar Return in effect at the time of this person's 48th birthday.

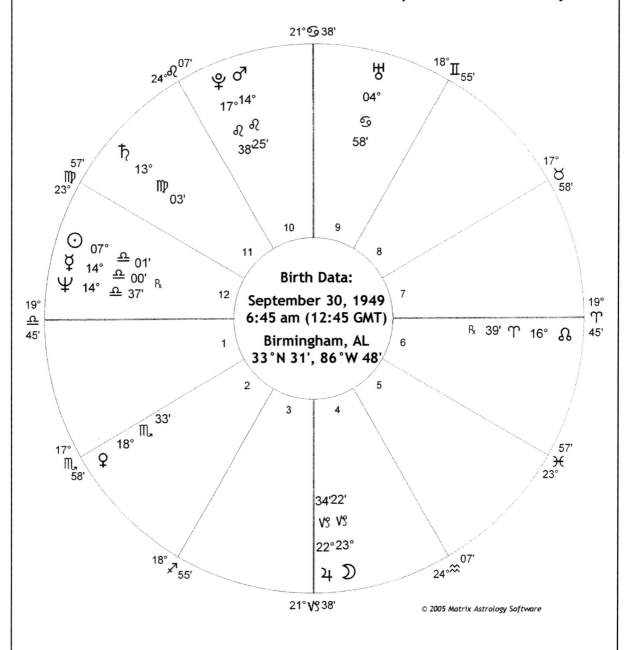

© 2005 Matrix Astrology Software

Section 9:

Composite Charts
& Other Charting Techniques

Lesson 29: Composite & Relationship Charts

Lesson 30: Relocation Charts & Other Charting Techniques

Lesson 29 : Composite & Relationship Charts

Composite and **Relationship Charts** are erected to provide insight into the nature of a relationship and the manner in which the separate energies of the individuals involved will combine. In this lesson calculating a composite chart using two different methods will be demonstrated. An explanation of Davison Relationship Chart calculation will also be included.

Chart Combination Methods

Composite charts and relationship charts are mathematically-derived charts based on the combination of two or more "actual" charts, and are used to describe the manner in which two or more individuals or entities will behave when together. There are three different methods commonly used to combine individual charts for this purpose:

Midpoint Composite Chart: A Midpoint Composite Chart is based solely on the midpoints between all planets and house cusps in the two charts involved. The midpoint between the two Suns becomes the composite Sun, the midpoint between the two Ascendants becomes the composite Ascendant, and so on for all planets and house cusps.

Derivative Composite Chart: Like the Midpoint Composite Chart, the Derivative Composite takes the midpoints between the planets to determine the position of the composite planets, but the composite house cusps are calculated differently. In this method, the midpoint between the two Midheavens is used as the composite Midheaven, then this new Midheaven is used to erect the remaining house cusps according to the latitude of the location of the relationship.

Davison Relationship Chart: The Davison Relationship Chart, named after astrologer Ronald Davison, differs dramatically from the two methods above. Rather than calculating separate midpoints for each chart factor, the Davison Relationship Chart erects a new full chart using the midpoint in time and space between the two birth times and birth locations.

Let us take a closer look at the calculations involved in each of these methods. The two natal charts below will be used to demonstrate composite chart calculations in the next few examples.

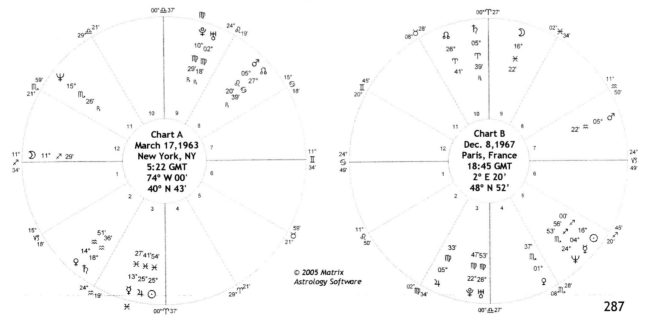

Chart A
March 17,1963
New York, NY
5:22 GMT
74° W 00'
40° N 43'

Chart B
Dec. 8,1967
Paris, France
18:45 GMT
2° E 20'
48° N 52'

© 2005 Matrix
Astrology Software

Determining Composite Chart Planetary Positions

The positions of the planets in both the Midpoint Composite and the Derivative Composite charts are calculated by finding the midpoint of the two natal planets in each chart. The midpoint of the Sun in one chart and the Sun in the second chart is calculated to determine the Sun in the composite chart, the midpoint of the Moon in one chart and the Moon in the other chart is calculated to determine the composite Moon, and so on, as demonstrated in the following example.

Example 1.

Let's calculate the midpoint between the two Suns in the natal charts on the previous page.

Chart A's Sun:	355.9	(25° ♓ 54' in absolute longitude)
Chart B's Sun:	+ 256.0	(16° ♐ 00' in absolute longitude)
	611.9 ÷ 2 = 305.95, or 5 °♒ 57'	

The midpoint Sun position is: 5 °♒ 57'.

Calculating the remaining planets in a Midpoint or Derivative Composite Chart is done in the same manner and is quite straightforward, however there is one situation to be aware of. Depending on the natal charts involved, midpoint calculations can produce positions for Mercury or Venus that oppose the Sun, which is impossible in reality since Mercury cannot be more than 28° and Venus cannot be more than 48° from the Sun. In this case, some astrologers prefer to use the opposite midpoint in order to produce a chart with Mercury or Venus more naturally placed.

Determining Midpoint Composite Chart House Cusps

A Midpoint Composite Chart is erected by finding the midpoints of the house cusps in the two charts. The midpoint of the two Midheavens becomes the composite Midheaven, the midpoint of the two 11th house cusps becomes the 11th house cusp in the composite, and so on.

Example 2.

In this example let's calculate the midpoint between Midheavens in the two natal charts on the previous page.

Chart A's MC:	180.62	(00° ♎ 37' in absolute longitude)
Chart B's MC:	+ 0. 45	(00° ♈ 27' in absolute longitude)
	181.07 ÷ 2 = 90.535 or 0 ° ♋ 32' (farther midpoint)	

The midpoint Midheaven position is 0 ° ♑ 32' (nearer midpoint).

In this case the calculation produced the farther midpoint instead of the nearer midpoint. You will recall from Lesson 16 on Midpoints that it is possible for calculations to produce the farther midpoint instead of the nearer midpoint. As with all midpoints, the nearer midpoint is the stronger midpoint and is the one to be used. Remember to check all results against a chart wheel to confirm that the answer is actually the nearer midpoint. If not, simply swap the sign of the result for its opposite.

Example 3.

Let's calculate the midpoint between Chart A's Ascendant at 11° ♐ 34' and Chart B's Ascendant at 24° ♋ 49'.

Chart A's ASC:	251.57
Chart B's ASC:	+ 114.82
	366.39 ÷ 2 = 183.2 or 3 ° ♎ 12' (farther midpoint)

The closest midpoint is 3 ° ♈ 12', which becomes the Ascendant of the Midpoint Composite chart.

After calculating the midpoints of all house cusps, it is helpful to scan the chart to make certain that all house cusps follow in zodiacal order. This will ensure that no errors have been made due to using farther midpoints instead of nearer midpoints.

The final chart is shown below, calculated by finding the midpoints of all houses cusps and planets of the natal charts of the two individuals on the first page of this Lesson.

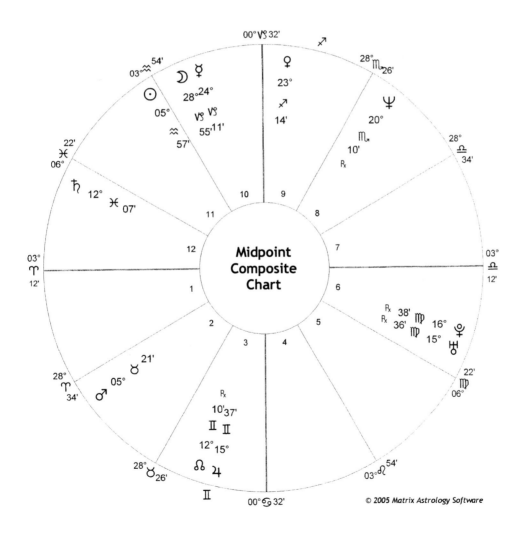

© 2005 Matrix Astrology Software

Determining Derivative Composite Chart House Cusps

Derivative composite chart house cusps are based on the latitude of the location where the relationship exists, requiring more extensive calculations than the midpoint composite chart. First, a composite Midheaven is determined based on the midpoint between the two natal Midheavens. Then, all remaining house cusps are determined by erecting a new chart using the midpoint MC and the latitude where the couple resides. This is very similar to the procedure used to erect a progressed chart in Lesson 23.

There are four steps to determine Derived House Cusps:

Step 1. Find the midpoint between the two natal Midheavens. This becomes the Midheaven of the Derivative Composite chart.

Step 2. Using a Table of Houses, calculate each house cusp using the closest higher latitude to the latitude of the relationship, but instead of interpolating between <u>sidereal times</u> to calculate each cusp as was done in natal calculation, interpolate between listed <u>Midheaven positions</u>.

Step 3. Repeat this process using values given for the closest lower latitude, again interpolating between listed Midheaven positions.

Step 4. Finally, interpolate between these two sets of results using the exact latitude for the relationship.

The Derived House Cusp composite chart shown below has been erected from the natal charts of the couple on the first page of this lesson, using a relationship location of New York, New York. Notice that the Midheaven in this chart is the same as the Midheaven in the Midpoint Composite chart shown on the previous page, however all remaining house cusps differ. Notice also that the zodiacal positions of the planets are the same for both the Midpoint Composite and the Derivative House Cusp Composite charts, however the placement of planets within houses has changed due to the difference in house cusps.

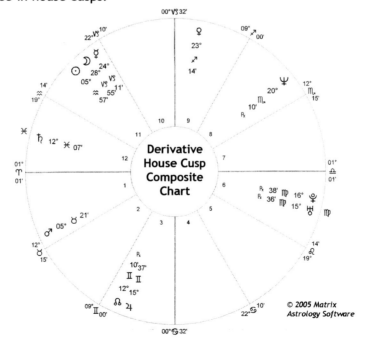

Davison Relationship Charts

Davison Relationship Charts, also called simply "relationship charts", are another tool used to evaluate the combination of two natal charts. In a relationship chart the midpoints between the time and place of birth of the two natal charts are used as the birth information and a chart is erected from this data as if it were a natal chart. Some astrologers prefer this method because the resulting chart represents an actual astronomical event occurring at an actual time and place, unlike the previous two methods which are mathematically derived and do not reflect a real moment in time.

The "place of birth" for the relationship chart is determined by finding the midpoint in longitude and latitude of the two birth locations. For example, the midpoint between birth latitudes for the example couple is calculated below. This procedure is then repeated to find the longitude midpoint:

$$
\begin{array}{lr}
\text{Chart A Latitude} & 40.72° \\
+ \text{Chart B Latitude} & + \ 48.87° \\
\hline
= 89.59 \div 2 = 44.795°, \text{ or } 44°\text{N } 48'
\end{array}
$$

Calculating the midpoint between birth times is more involved due to the occurrence of leap years but is made easier with the use of **Julian Dates**. The Julian dating system assigns each date a number without using months or years. *The ACS Ephemeris* gives the Julian Day number for the first of each month in the "Astro Data" box at the bottom of each page. The day number for any other day within the month can then be deduced by adding the relevant number of days. This date together with the GMT of birth expressed as a decimal of a day is then used to calculate the midpoint in time between the two births, as follows:

Person A: 23086.2236 (Julian date for March 17, 1963 + 5:22 GMT as decimal)
Person B: + 24813.7813 (Julian date for December 8, 1967 + 18:45 GMT)

= 47900.0049

÷ 2 = 23950.0025

Or July 28, 1965, 00:03:36 GMT

The relationship chart for the example couple is shown to the right. Notice that the midpoint location is given by coordinates only as it often falls in highly improbable places. In this case the midpoint between New York and Paris falls somewhere in the middle of the Atlantic Ocean.

At this time we are not aware of any certification exams which require manual calculation of relationship charts.

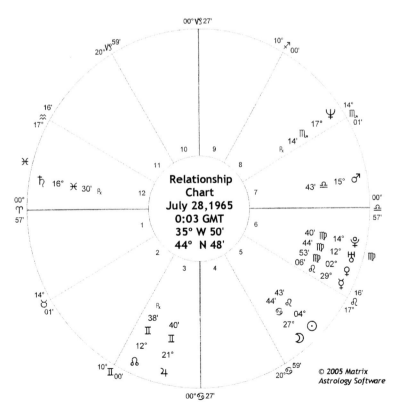

Lesson 29 Exercises

Using the two charts below, erect a Midpoint Composite Chart using the midpoints of all planets and house cusps. Fill in the chart on the following page. Answers can be found in the Answer Key in the Appendix.

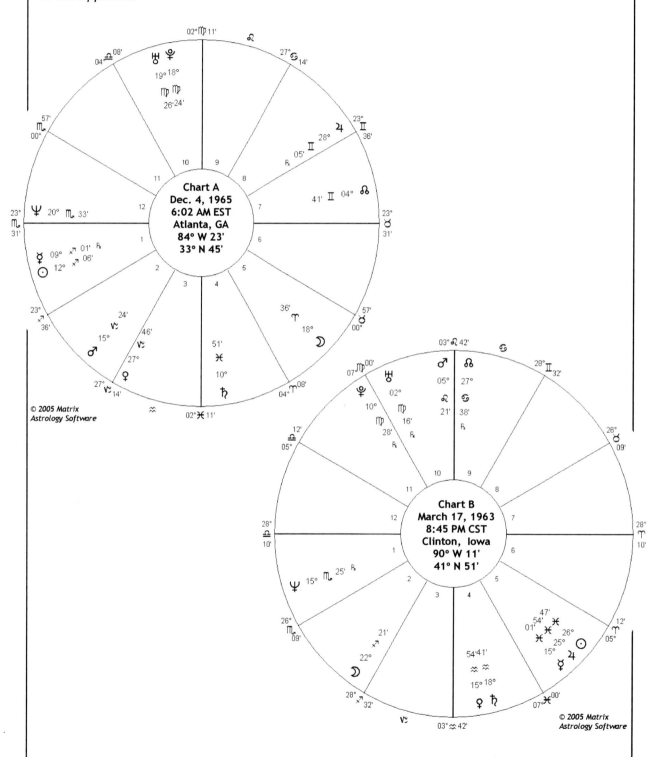

© 2005 Matrix
Astrology Software

© 2005 Matrix
Astrology Software

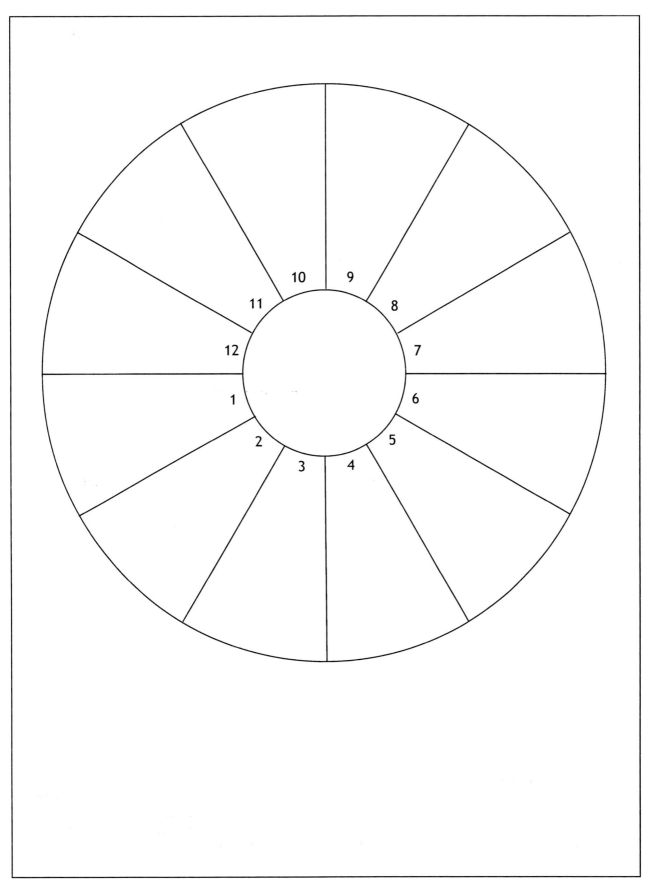

Lesson 30 : Relocation Charts &
Other Charting Techniques

There are many charting techniques that astrologers use to look more deeply into various aspects of a native's life, time major events, or examine global issues. In this final lesson the mathematical basis for erecting the most common of these charting techniques such as Relocation, Electional, Horary, Mundane, and Aries Ingress charts will be explained. These charts are calculated using the same mathematical processes used to erect natal charts, it is simply a matter of understanding what "birth information" to use to construct the chart in question. There are no exercises included for this lesson.

Relocation Charts

Relocation Charts re-calculate a birth chart for a new location and are used to analyze how a person's life situation will change due to the change in location. The same date of birth and GMT are used, but the latitude and longitude of the new location are substituted for the birthplace coordinates. This will produce a change in house cusps, but all planetary positions within the zodiac will remain the same as in the natal chart. When erecting a relocation chart, be sure to use the GMT of birth, and not the local time of birth.

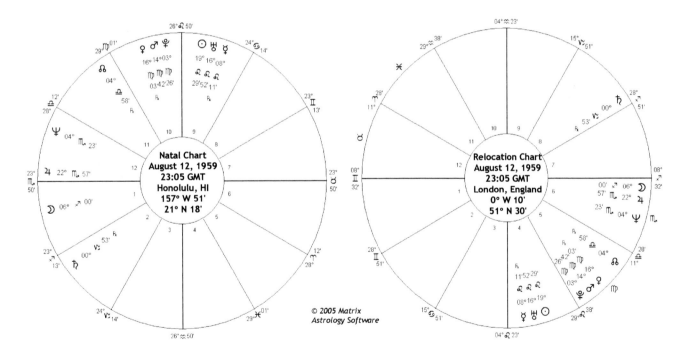

© 2005 Matrix
Astrology Software

In the examples above notice that the only change in birth information required for the Relocation Chart is the location. All of the other birth information remains the same. Also notice that the zodiacal positions of all planets have remained the same, only the house placements differ because the house cusps have changed with the new location.

Event Charts

Event Charts are charts cast for the moment an event occurs, such as the pronouncement of marriage, the signing of a contract, or the start of a business. Just as natal charts contain information on the life involved, event charts can provide information on the "life" of a marriage, business, or other undertaking. The location of the actual event is used to erect the chart.

Electional Charts

Electional Charts are used to select the best time to begin a new undertaking or enter into an agreement. In effect, electional charts choose the resultant event chart in advance in order to take advantage of the best astrological energies available. Electional astrology is a branch of mundane astrology (see below), and has been used in the past to initiate all sorts of events including military invasions, the signing of treaties, and the marriage of royals.

Mundane Charts

Mundane astrology is one of the major branches of traditional astrology and deals with the astrology of world or political events. The most common chart types used by mundane astrology are charts cast for the "birth" or establishment of a nation or entity, ingress and lunation charts (described below), and charts cast for the moment of major planetary conjunctions or aspect patterns. These charts are used to evaluate nations and their leaders, wars and other political conflicts, as well as weather and agricultural conditions and natural disasters.

Ingress Charts

Ingress charts are charts cast for the moment the transiting Sun or other planet enters a new sign. The most common of these charts is the Aries Ingress Chart, cast for the moment the Sun enters the sign Aries each Spring. Aries Ingress Charts are used to evaluate the social, political, and/or physical climate of the year ahead. The Sun's ingress into the other cardinal signs (Cancer, Libra, and Capricorn), signaling the start of each season, is also commonly used for additional insight into each subsequent 3-month period. Generally a nation's capital is used as the "birth location" for ingress charts. Other planetary ingresses into signs are also used in weather prediction and other mundane topics.

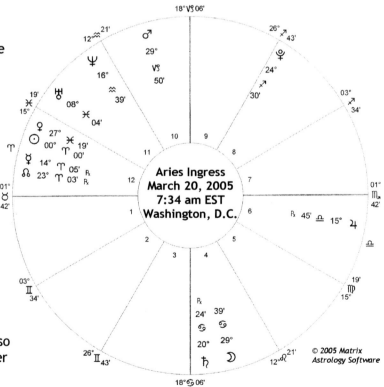

Aries Ingress
March 20, 2005
7:34 am EST
Washington, D.C.

© 2005 Matrix
Astrology Software

Lunation Charts

Lunation Charts are charts cast for the moment a New or Full Moon occurs. An example of a lunation chart is shown below. Like ingress charts, lunation charts generally use a nation's capital for the location if the chart is used for political insight. Lunation charts are also commonly used in weather prediction, in which case the location of the area being investigated for weather conditions is used.

Horary Charts

Horary astrology is another major branch of traditional astrology in which charts are cast for the moment and place a question is asked and the resultant chart is analyzed to obtain an answer. Horary astrology is based on the premise that the planetary positions at the time a question is asked reflect the "birth" of the question and so contain its answer. Each horary chart is only applicable to the question for which it was drawn.

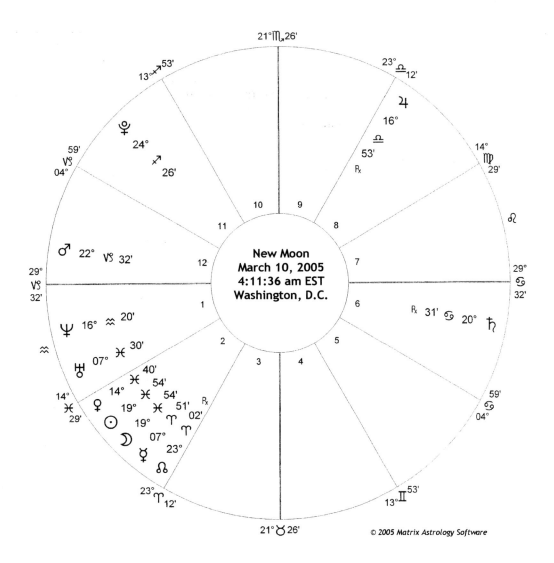

© 2005 Matrix Astrology Software

Section 10:

Appendix

Name_____ Birth Date _____ Birth Time _____ am/pm

Birth Place _____ GMT of Birth _____

10 9
11   8
12   7
1   6
2   5
3   4

☽
☉   ☉
☿   ☿
♀   ♀
♂   ♂
♃   ♃
♄   ♄
♅   ♅
♆   ♆
♇   ♇
☊   ☊
Asc   Asc
Mc   Mc

Chart Calculated By:

_____

Date:_____

©2005 Fowks & Sellon

Chart Calculation Form

Chart Calculation for:

Name_____ Birth Date _____ Birth Time _____ am / pm

Birth Place _____ Lat _____ Long _____

Longitude/Time Equivalent *(from Atlas, or calculate manually in Step 9)* _____

Part A: GMT of Birth

1. Given Time of Birth ____:____ am / pm

2. + PM Adjustment *(+12:00 if pm)* + ____:____

3. +/-Time Zone

    a. Standard Time Zone *(+W, -E)* ____:____

    b. DST Adjustment *(- 1:00 if DST)* - ____:____
    (Include only if not already factored into (a) above)

    c. = Time Zone Adjustment *(Enter on Line 3, right)* = ____:____ ⟶ +W,-E ____:____

                                  Subtotal = ____:____

4. +/- 24 hours if date change required +/- ____:____

5. = GMT of Birth   Date _____   Time = ____:____

Part B: LST of Birth

6. Sidereal Time at 0 hr on birth date *(from ephemeris; use birth date from Step 5)* ____:____:____

7. + GMT of birth *(from Step 5)* ____:____: 00

8. + Solar/Sidereal Time Correction on GMT *(from Table or calculate below:)* ____:____

    (GMT *(as decimal)*_____ hrs x 9.86 secs = _____)   Subtotal = ____:____:____

9. +/- Longitude/Time Equivalent *(from Atlas or calculate below; -W, +E)* +/- ____:____:____

    (Longitude *(as decimal)* _____ x 4 min = _____)   Subtotal = ____:____:____

10. +/- 24:00:00 if required +/- ____:____:____

11. = LST of Birth   LST = ____:____:____

- -

12. Southern Latitude Adjustment *(+/- 12:00:00 if Southern Latitude)* +/- ____:____:____

13. "LST + 12" *(use in place of LST for Southern Latitude births)*   LST+12 = ____:____:____

CM-1
(Constant Multiplier for Part C: Planetary Position)

Convert GMT of Birth *(from line 5)* to decimal: _____ ÷ 24 = **CM-1** _____

© 2004 Fowks & Sellon

Part C: Planetary Position

	☉	☽	☿	♀	♂	♃
1. Position at 0 hr on day After birth date _____						
2. Position at 0 hr on Birth date _____						
3. Line 1 - Line 2 = Total Daily Travel						
4. Line 3 X CM-1 _____ = Travel to birth time						
5. Add lines 2 + 4 = Position at Birth						

	♄	♅	♆	♇	☊	
6. Position at 0 hr on day After birth date _____						
7. Position at 0 hr on Birth date _____						
8. Line 6 - Line 7 = Total Daily Travel						
9. Line 8 X CM-1 _____ = Travel to birth time						
10. Add lines 7 + 9 = Position at Birth						

CM-2
(Constant Multiplier for Part D: House Cusps, Lines 4 & 9: LST Interpolation)

LST of Birth   ___:___:___

- Next lowest Sid Time from Table   - ___:___:___

           = ___:___

Convert result to decimal   _____

        ÷ 4 = CM-2 _____

CM-3
(Constant Multiplier for Part D: House Cusps, Line 14: Latitude Interpolation)

Latitude of Birth   ____° ____ '

- Next lowest Latitude from Table   - ____° 00 '

           = ____° ____ '

Convert result to decimal   CM-3 = _____

Exception: If Birth Latitude is less than 20°, divide result by 5   ÷ 5 = CM-3 _____

Part D: House Cusp Calculation

House Cusp Calculation for Higher Latitude

Latitude _____°	MC	11th	12th	ASC	2nd	3rd
1. House Cusps at Later Sid Time						
2. House Cusps at Earlier Sid Time						
3. Line 1 - Line 2 =						
4. Line 3 X CM-2 _____ =						
5. Add lines 2 + 4 =						

House Cusp Calculation for Lower Latitude

Latitude _____°		11th	12th	ASC	2nd	3rd
6. House Cusps at Later Sid Time						
7. House Cusps at Earlier Sid Time						
8. Line 6 - Line 7 =						
9. Line 3 X CM-2 _____ =						
10. Add lines 7 + 9 =						

Latitude Interpolation

		11th	12th	ASC	2nd	3rd
11. House Cusps at Higher Latitude (from line 5)						
12. House Cusps at Lower Latitude (from line 10)						
13. Line 11 - Line 12 =						
14. Line 13 X CM-3 _____ =						
15. Add lines 12 + 14 = **House Cusps at Birth**						

Part E: Aspects

	☽	☉	☿	♀	♂	♃	♄	♅	♆	♇	☊	ASC	MC
☽													
☉													
☿													
♀													
♂													
♃													
♄													
♅													
♆													
♇													
☊													
ASC													
MC													

Major Aspects			Minor Aspects		
Aspect	**Orb**	**Range**	**Aspect**	**Orb**	**Range**
☌			⚼		
✶			∠		
□			⚏		
△			⚻		
☍					

304

Part F: Declinations

(N = +, S = -)	☽	☉	☿	♀	♂	♃	♄
1. Declination 0 hr day after birth date _____							
2. Declination 0 hr on Birth date _____							
3. Line 1 - Line 2 = Total Daily Change in Declination							
4. Line 3 X CM-1 _____ = Declination change to Birth GMT							
5. Add lines 2 + 4 = Declination at Birth (N = +, S = -)							

♅ _____   ♆ _____   ♇ _____   ☊ _____

Ascendant Declination Calculation		Midheaven Declination Calculation		Declinations Listed in Ascending order
Zodiacal Position _____ Convert minutes to decimal = CM _____ *(use for Step 4 below)*	**Asc**	Zodiacal Position _____ Convert minutes to decimal = CM _____ *(use for Step 4 below)*	**MC**	
1. **Declination** of next highest listed zodiacal degree		1. **Declination** of next highest listed zodiacal degree		
1. **Declination** of next lowest listed zodiacal degree		1. **Declination** of next lowest listed zodiacal degree		
3. Line 1 - Line 2 = Change in Declination		3. Line 1 - Line 2 = Change in Declination		
4. Line 3 x CM _____		4. Line 3 x CM _____		
Add lines 2+4 = ASC Declination at Birth (N = +, S = -)		Add lines 2+4 = MC Declination at Birth (N = +, S = -)		

Parallel and Contraparallel Aspects

Part G: Vertex Calculation

Vertex Calculation for:

Name:_____

Birth Latitude: _____ Birth IC: _____

Co-Latitude:

  90°:   90.00°

  Birth Latitude (as decimal):   -_____

  = Co-Latitude: = _____

Vertex Interpolation At Higher Latitude

Co-Latitude _____°	ASC
1. ASC at Higher MC _____	
2. ASC at Lower MC _____	
3. Line 1 - Line 2 =	
4. Line 3 X CM-V _____ =	
5. Add lines 2 + 4 =	

CM-V
(Constant Multiplier for Vertex Interpolation)

A. IC of Birth   _____

  - Next lowest MC from Table   -_____

  = Difference   _____

B. Higher listed MC   _____

  - Lower listed MC   -_____

  = Interval between MCs   _____

(A)_____ ÷ (B)_____ = **CM-V:** _____
Divide the difference from part A by interval from B.

Vertex Interpolation At Lower Latitude

Co-Latitude _____°	ASC
6. ASC at Higher MC _____	
7. ASC at Lower MC _____	
8. Line 6 - Line 7 =	
9. Line 8 X CM-V _____ =	
10. Add lines 7 + 9 =	

CM-3
(Constant Multiplier for Latitude Interpolation)

Co-Latitude of Birth   _____

- Next lowest Latitude from Table   _____

                      =   _____

Convert result to decimal   = **CM-3** _____

*Exception: If Co-Latitude is
less than 20°, divide result by 5* ÷ 5 = CM-3 _____

Vertex Latitude Interpolation

11. Asc at Higher Latitude (from line 5)	
12. Asc. at Lower Latitude (from line 10)	
13. Line 11 - Line 12 =	
14. Line 13 X CM-3 _____ =	
15. Add lines 12 + 14 = **Vertex at Birth**	

Chart Progression Form

Chart Progression for:

Name _____ GMT of Birth: Date _____ Time _____

Progessed to: *(Target Date)* _____

Birth Location _____ Lat _____ Long _____

Part A: ACD

ACD Calculation:

1. CM-1 (Convert GMT of Birth to decimal: _____ ÷ 24 = CM-1) _____

2. 365 days x CM-1 *(line 1)* = ACD Interval   X 365 = _____

3a. GMT Birthdate Day Number *(from Table of Numbered Days)*   _____

 b. - ACD Interval *(from line 2)*   - _____
    _____

 c. = ACD Day Number   = _____

 d. = Birth ACD *(line 3c date equivalent from Table of Numbered Days)*   Birth ACD = _____ Year _____

ACD Equivalent Ephemeris Date:

4. Year of ACD prior to Target Date _____ - Year of Birth ACD *(line 3d)* _____ = Elapsed Years(Days) _____

5. GMT Birthdate Day No. *(line 3a)* _____ + Elapsed Years(Days) *(line 4)* _____ = Equivalent Ephemeris Day No. _____

   = Equivalent Ephemeris Date to earlier ACD _____

6. **Equivalent Ephemeris Date to later ACD** *(final date from line 5 plus 1 day)* _____

Part B: Progressed Planetary CM (PP-CM)

7. Target Date Day Number *(from Table of Numbered Days)*   _____

8. - ACD Day Number *(from Table of Numbered Days)*   - _____
   _____

9. = Days elapsed from ACD to Target   = _____

10. Line 9 ÷ 365 = PPCM   PPCM = _____

Solar Arc

Progressed Sun *(Part C, line 5)* _____

- Birth Sun   - _____

= Solar Arc   = _____

Progressed MC

Birth MC   _____

+ Solar Arc   + _____
                        _____

= Progressed MC   = _____

© 2004 Fowks & Sellon

Part C: Progressed Planetary Positions

	☉	☽	☿	♀	♂	♃
1. Position at 0 hr on later ephemeris date *(Part A, line 6)* _____						
2. Position at 0 hr on earlier ephemeris date *(Part A, line 5)* _____						
3. Line 1 - Line 2 = Total Daily Travel						
4. Line 3 X PPCM _____ = Travel to Target Date						
5. Add lines 2 + 4 = Progressed Position on Target Date						

	♄	♅	♆	♇	☊	
6. Position at 0 hr on later ephemeris date *(Part A, line 6)* _____						
7. Position at 0 hr on earlier ephemeris date *(Part A, line 5)* _____						
8. Line 6 - Line 7 = Total Daily Travel						
9. Line 8 X PPCM _____ = Travel to Target Date						
10. Add lines 7 + 9 = Progressed Position on Target Date						

Midheaven CM (MC-CM)
(Constant Multiplier for Part D: House Cusps, Lines 4 & 9: MC Interpolation)

Progressed MC _____

- Next lowest MC from Table   - _____

= _____ ' *(a)*

Next highest MC from Table _____

- Next lowest MC from Table   - _____

= _____ ' *(b)*

_____ *(a)* ÷ _____ *(b)* = **MC-CM** _____

Latitude CM (CM-3)
(Constant Multiplier for Part D: House Cusps, Line 14: Latitude Interpolation)

Latitude of Birth (or other prog. location) ____° ____'

- Next lowest Latitude from Table   - ____° __00__'

= ____° ____'

Convert result to decimal   **CM-3 =** _____

Exception: If Birth Latitude is less than 20°, divide result by 5 ÷ 5 = CM-3 _____

Part D: Progressed House Cusp Calculation

House Cusp Calculation for Higher Latitude

Latitude _____°	11th	12th	ASC	2nd	3rd
1. House Cusps at Higher MC _____					
2. House Cusps at Lower MC _____					
3. Line 1 - Line 2 =					
4. Line 3 X MC-CM _____ =					
5. Add lines 2 + 4 =					

House Cusp Calculation for Lower Latitude

Latitude _____°	11th	12th	ASC	2nd	3rd
6. House Cusps at Higher MC _____					
7. House Cusps at Lower MC _____					
8. Line 6 - Line 7 =					
9. Line 8 X MC-CM _____ =					
10. Add lines 7 + 9 =					

Latitude Interpolation

	11th	12th	ASC	2nd	3rd
11. House Cusps at Higher Latitude (from line 5)					
12. House Cusps at Lower Latitude (from line 10)					
13. Line 11 - Line 12 =					
14. Line 13 X CM-3 _____ =					
15. Add lines 12 + 14 = **Progressed House Cusps**					

TABLE OF ABSOLUTE LONGITUDE
Signs of the Zodiac

		♈	♉	♊	♋	♌	♍	♎	♏	♐	♑	♒	♓	
0		0	30	60	90	120	150	180	210	240	270	300	330	**0**
1		1	31	61	91	121	151	181	211	241	271	301	331	**1**
2		2	32	62	92	122	152	182	212	242	272	302	332	**2**
3		3	33	63	93	123	153	183	213	243	273	303	333	**3**
4		4	34	64	94	124	154	184	214	244	274	304	334	**4**
5		5	35	65	95	125	155	185	215	245	275	305	335	**5**
6		6	36	66	96	126	156	186	216	246	276	306	336	**6**
7		7	37	67	97	127	157	187	217	247	277	307	337	**7**
8		8	38	68	98	128	158	188	218	248	278	308	338	**8**
9		9	39	69	99	129	159	189	219	249	279	309	339	**9**
10		10	40	70	100	130	160	190	220	250	280	310	340	**10**
11		11	41	71	101	131	161	191	221	251	281	311	341	**11**
12		12	42	72	102	132	162	192	222	252	282	312	342	**12**
13		13	43	73	103	133	163	193	223	253	283	313	343	**13**
14		14	44	74	104	134	164	194	224	254	284	314	344	**14**
15		15	45	75	105	135	165	195	225	255	285	315	345	**15**
16		16	46	76	106	136	166	196	226	256	286	316	346	**16**
17		17	47	77	107	137	167	197	227	257	287	317	347	**17**
18		18	48	78	108	138	168	198	228	258	288	318	348	**18**
19		19	49	79	109	139	169	199	229	259	289	319	349	**19**
20		20	50	80	110	140	170	200	230	260	290	320	350	**20**
21		21	51	81	111	141	171	201	231	261	291	321	351	**21**
22		22	52	82	112	142	172	202	232	262	292	322	352	**22**
23		23	53	83	113	143	173	203	233	263	293	323	353	**23**
24		24	54	84	114	144	174	204	234	264	294	324	354	**24**
25		25	55	85	115	145	175	205	235	265	295	325	355	**25**
26		26	56	86	116	146	176	206	236	266	296	326	356	**26**
27		27	57	87	117	147	177	207	237	267	297	327	357	**27**
28		28	58	88	118	148	178	208	238	268	298	328	358	**28**
29		29	59	89	119	149	179	209	239	269	299	329	359	**29**
		♈	♉	♊	♋	♌	♍	♎	♏	♐	♑	♒	♓	

Degree of each Sign (left and right margins)

SIGNS OF THE ZODIAC NUMBERED

♈	♉	♊	♋	♌	♍	♎	♏	♐	♑	♒	♓
1	2	3	4	5	6	7	8	9	10	11	12

CONVERSION TABLES

MINUTES PER DEGREE	
1°	60'
2°	120'
3°	180'
4°	240'
5°	300'
6°	360'
7°	420'
8°	480'
9°	540'
10°	600'
11°	660'
12°	720'
13°	780'
14°	840'
15°	900'
16°	960'
17°	1020'
18°	1080'
19°	1140
20°	1200'
21°	1260'
22°	1320'
23°	1380'
24°	1440'
25°	1500'
26°	1560'
27°	1620'
28°	1680'
29°	1740'
30°	1800'

MINUTES AS DECIMAL OF A DEGREE OR HOUR			
1'	.017	31'	.517
2'	.033	32'	.533
3'	.05	33'	.55
4'	.067	34'	.567
5'	.083	35'	.583
6'	.1	36'	.6
7'	.117	37'	.617
8'	.133	38'	.633
9'	.15	39'	.65
10'	.167	40'	.667
11'	.183	41'	.683
12'	.2	42'	.7
13'	.217	43'	.717
14'	.233	44'	.733
15'	.25	45'	.75
16'	.267	46'	.767
17'	.283	47'	.783
18'	.3	48'	.8
19'	.317	49'	.817
20'	.333	50'	.833
21'	.35	51'	.85
22'	.367	52'	.867
23'	.383	53'	.883
24'	.4	54'	.9
25'	.417	55'	.917
26'	.433	56'	.933
27'	.45	57'	.95
28'	.467	58'	.967
29'	.483	59'	.983
30'	.5	60'	1.0

TABLE OF DECLINATION OF DEGREES ON THE ECLIPTIC (+N, -S)

Signs of the Zodiac

	♈	♉	♊	♋	♌	♍	♎	♏	♐	♑	♒	♓	
0	0°00'	+11°29'	+20°10'	+23°28'	+20°10'	+11°29'	0°00'	-11°29'	-20°10'	-23°28'	-20°10'	-11°29'	**0**
1	+0°24'	+11°50'	+20°23'	+23°28'	+19°57'	+11°08'	-0°24'	-11°50'	-20°23'	-23°28'	-19°57'	-11°08'	**1**
2	+0°48'	+12°11'	+20°35'	+23°27'	+19°44'	+10°46'	-0°48'	-12°11'	-20°35'	-23°27'	-19°44'	-10°46'	**2**
3	+1°12'	+12°32'	+20°47'	+23°26'	+19°31'	+10°25'	-1°12'	-12°32'	-20°47'	-23°26'	-19°31'	-10°25'	**3**
4	+1°36'	+12°52'	+20°58'	+23°24'	+19°17'	+10°03'	-1°36'	-12°52'	-20°58'	-23°24'	-19°17'	-10°03'	**4**
5	+2°00'	+13°12'	+21°09'	+23°22'	+19°02'	+9°41'	-2°00'	-13°12'	-21°09'	-23°22'	-19°02'	-9°41'	**5**
6	+2°23'	+13°32'	+21°20'	+23°20'	+18°48'	+9°19'	-2°23'	-13°32'	-21°20'	-23°20'	-18°48'	-9°19'	**6**
7	+2°47'	+13°52'	+21°30'	+23°17'	+18°33'	+8°57'	-2°47'	-13°52'	-21°30'	-23°17'	-18°33'	-8°57'	**7**
8	+3°11'	+14°11'	+21°40'	+23°13'	+18°17'	+8°35'	-3°11'	-14°11'	-21°40'	-23°13'	-18°17'	-8°35'	**8**
9	+3°34'	+14°31'	+21°49'	+23°10'	+18°02'	+8°12'	-3°34'	-14°31'	-21°49'	-23°10'	-18°02'	-8°12'	**9**
10	+3°58'	+14°50'	+21°58'	+23°05'	+17°46'	+7°50'	-3°58'	-14°50'	-21°58'	-23°05'	-17°46'	-7°50'	**10**
11	+4°21'	+15°09'	+22°07'	+23°01'	+17°29'	+7°27'	-4°21'	-15°09'	-22°07'	-23°01'	-17°29'	-7°27'	**11**
12	+4°45'	+15°27'	+22°15'	+22°56'	+17°13'	+7°05'	-4°45'	-15°27'	-22°15'	-22°56'	-17°13'	-7°05'	**12**
13	+5°08'	+15°45'	+22°23'	+22°50'	+16°56'	+6°41'	-5°08'	-15°45'	-22°23'	-22°50'	-16°56'	-6°41'	**13**
14	+5°32'	+16°03'	+22°30'	+22°44'	+16°39'	+6°18'	-5°32'	-16°03'	-22°30'	-22°44'	-16°39'	-6°18'	**14**
15	+5°55'	+16°21'	+22°37'	+22°37'	+16°21'	+5°55'	-5°55'	-16°21'	-22°37'	-22°37'	-16°21'	-5°55'	**15**
16	+6°18'	+16°39'	+22°44'	+22°30'	+16°03'	+5°32'	-6°18'	-16°39'	-22°44'	-22°30'	-16°03'	-5°32'	**16**
17	+6°41'	+16°56'	+22°50'	+22°23'	+15°45'	+5°08'	-6°41'	-16°56'	-22°50'	-22°23'	-15°45'	-5°08'	**17**
18	+7°05'	+17°13'	+22°56'	+22°15'	+15°27'	+4°45'	-7°05'	-17°13'	-22°56'	-22°15'	-15°27'	-4°45'	**18**
19	+7°27'	+17°29'	+23°01'	+22°07'	+15°09'	+4°21'	-7°27'	-17°29'	-23°01'	-22°07'	-15°09'	-4°21'	**19**
20	+7°50'	+17°46'	+23°05'	+21°58'	+14°50'	+3°58'	-7°50'	-17°46'	-23°05'	-21°58'	-14°50'	-3°58'	**20**
21	+8°12'	+18°02'	+23°10'	+21°49'	+14°31'	+3°34'	-8°12'	-18°02'	-23°10'	-21°49'	-14°31'	-3°34'	**21**
22	+8°35'	+18°17'	+23°13'	+21°40'	+14°11'	+3°11'	-8°35'	-18°17'	-23°13'	-21°40'	-14°11'	-3°11'	**22**
23	+8°57'	+18°33'	+23°17'	+21°30'	+13°52'	+2°47'	-8°57'	-18°33'	-23°17'	-21°30'	-13°52'	-2°47'	**23**
24	+9°19'	+18°48'	+23°20'	+21°20'	+13°32'	+2°23'	-9°19'	-18°48'	-23°20'	-21°20'	-13°32'	-2°23'	**24**
25	+9°41'	+19°02'	+23°22'	+21°09'	+13°12'	+2°00'	-9°41'	-19°02'	-23°22'	-21°09'	-13°12'	-2°00'	**25**
26	+10°03'	+19°17'	+23°24'	+20°58'	+12°52'	+1°36'	-10°03'	-19°17'	-23°24'	-20°58'	-12°52'	-1°36'	**26**
27	+10°25'	+19°31'	+23°26'	+20°47'	+12°32'	+1°12'	-10°25'	-19°31'	-23°26'	-20°47'	-12°32'	-1°12'	**27**
28	+10°46'	+19°44'	+23°27'	+20°35'	+12°11'	+0°48'	-10°46'	-19°44'	-23°27'	-20°35'	-12°11'	-0°48'	**28**
29	+11°08'	+19°57'	+23°28'	+20°23'	+11°50'	+0°24'	-11°08'	-19°57'	-23°28'	-20°23'	-11°50'	-0°24'	**29**
	♈	♉	♊	♋	♌	♍	♎	♏	♐	♑	♒	♓	

Degree of each Sign (left and right margins)

TABLE OF NUMBERED DAYS

Days of the Month

Months of the Year

Day	Jan	Feb	Mar	Apr	May	Jun	Jul	Aug	Sep	Oct	Nov	Dec
1	1	32	60	91	121	152	182	213	244	274	305	335
2	2	33	61	92	122	153	183	214	245	275	306	336
3	3	34	62	93	123	154	184	215	246	276	307	337
4	4	35	63	94	124	155	185	216	247	277	308	338
5	5	36	64	95	125	156	186	217	248	278	309	339
6	6	37	65	96	126	157	187	218	249	279	310	340
7	7	38	66	97	127	158	188	219	250	280	311	341
8	8	39	67	98	128	159	189	220	251	281	312	342
9	9	40	68	99	129	160	190	221	252	282	313	343
10	10	41	69	100	130	161	191	222	253	283	314	344
11	11	42	70	101	131	162	192	223	254	284	315	345
12	12	43	71	102	132	163	193	224	255	285	316	346
13	13	44	72	103	133	164	194	225	256	286	317	347
14	14	45	73	104	134	165	195	226	257	287	318	348
15	15	46	74	105	135	166	196	227	258	288	319	349
16	16	47	75	106	136	167	197	228	259	289	320	350
17	17	48	76	107	137	168	198	229	260	290	321	351
18	18	49	77	108	138	169	199	230	261	291	322	352
19	19	50	78	109	139	170	200	231	262	292	323	353
20	20	51	79	110	140	171	201	232	263	293	324	354
21	21	52	80	111	141	172	202	233	264	294	325	355
22	22	53	81	112	142	173	203	234	265	295	326	356
23	23	54	82	113	143	174	204	235	266	296	327	357
24	24	55	83	114	144	175	205	236	267	297	328	358
25	25	56	84	115	145	176	206	237	268	298	329	359
26	26	57	85	116	146	177	207	238	269	299	330	360
27	27	58	86	117	147	178	208	239	270	300	331	361
28	28	59	87	118	148	179	209	240	271	301	332	362
29	29		88	119	149	180	210	241	272	302	333	363
30	30		89	120	150	181	211	242	273	303	334	364
31	31		90		151		212	243		304		365

Months of the Year

Day	Jan	Feb	Mar	Apr	May	Jun	Jul	Aug	Sep	Oct	Nov	Dec
1	366	397	425	456	486	517	547	578	609	639	670	700
2	367	398	426	457	487	518	548	579	610	640	671	701
3	368	399	427	458	488	519	549	580	611	641	672	702
4	369	400	428	459	489	520	550	581	612	642	673	703
5	370	401	429	460	490	521	551	582	613	643	674	704
6	371	402	430	461	491	522	552	583	614	644	675	705
7	372	403	431	462	492	523	553	584	615	645	676	706
8	373	404	432	463	493	524	554	585	616	646	677	707
9	374	405	433	464	494	525	555	586	617	647	678	708
10	375	406	434	465	495	526	556	587	618	648	679	709
11	376	407	435	466	496	527	557	588	619	649	680	710
12	377	408	436	467	497	528	558	589	620	650	681	711
13	378	409	437	468	498	529	559	590	621	651	682	712
14	379	410	438	469	499	530	560	591	622	652	683	713
15	380	411	439	470	500	531	561	592	623	653	684	714
16	381	412	440	471	501	532	562	593	624	654	685	715
17	382	413	441	472	502	533	563	594	625	655	686	716
18	383	414	442	473	503	534	564	595	626	656	687	717
19	384	415	443	474	504	535	565	596	627	657	688	718
20	385	416	444	475	505	536	566	597	628	658	689	719
21	386	417	445	476	506	537	567	598	629	659	690	720
22	387	418	446	477	507	538	568	599	630	660	691	721
23	388	419	447	478	508	539	569	600	631	661	692	722
24	389	420	448	479	509	540	570	601	632	662	693	723
25	390	421	449	480	510	541	571	602	633	663	694	724
26	391	422	450	481	511	542	572	603	634	664	695	725
27	392	423	451	482	512	543	573	604	635	665	696	726
28	393	424	452	483	513	544	574	605	636	666	697	727
29	394		453	484	514	545	575	606	637	667	698	728
30	395		454	485	515	546	576	607	638	668	699	729
31	396		455		516		577	608		669		730

Days of the Month

Lunar Phase Dial

To assemble, photocopy this page onto card stock, then cut out both dials. Place the Lunar Phase Dial on top of the plain dial and attach them together with a paper fastener through the center.

To use, point the arrow on the inner dial to the sign and degree of the Sun (or other slower moving planet) on the outer dial. Then locate the position of the Moon (or faster moving planet) on the outer dial and note into which phase segment it falls.

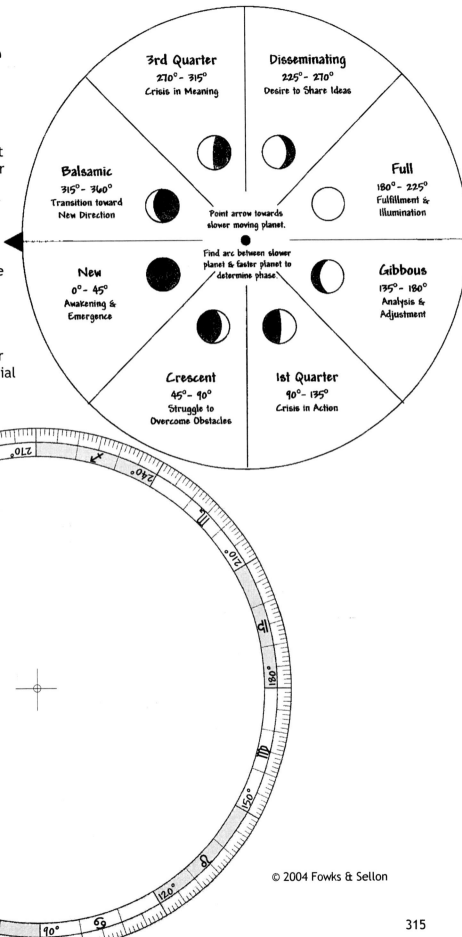

3rd Quarter
270° - 315°
Crisis in Meaning

Disseminating
225° - 270°
Desire to Share Ideas

Balsamic
315° - 360°
Transition toward
New Direction

Full
180° - 225°
Fulfillment &
Illumination

Point arrow towards
slower moving planet.

Find arc between slower
planet & faster planet to
determine phase.

New
0° - 45°
Awakening &
Emergence

Gibbous
135° - 180°
Analysis &
Adjustment

Crescent
45° - 90°
Struggle to
Overcome Obstacles

1st Quarter
90° - 135°
Crisis in Action

© 2004 Fowks & Sellon

315

Answer Key

Lesson 1: Math Basics I - Answer Key

1.

```
      10:16:05 (Jan 3, 1985)
  +    3:02:20
  =   13:18:25 (Jan 3, 1985)
```

2.

```
      15:33:12 (Aug 8, 2002)
  +    4:45:08
  =   19:78:20
  -       60:00 (-60 min, +1 hr)
  +     1:00:00
  =   20:18:20 (Aug 8, 2002)
```

3.

```
      20:16:52 (May 5, 1973)
  +     7:38:15
  =    27:54:67
  -          60 (-60 sec, + 1 min)
  +        1:00
  =    27:55:07
  -    24:00:00 (-24 hrs, +1 day)
  =     3:55:07 May 6, 1973
```

4.

```
      17:42:55 (June 10, 1953)
  +     9:30:00
  +     0:02:46
  =    26:74:101
  -           60 (-60 sec, + 1 min)
  +         1:00
  =    26:75:41
  -        60:00 (-60 min, +1 hr)
  +      1:00:00
  =    27:15:41
  -    24:00:00 (-24 hrs, +1 day)
  =     3:15:41 June 11, 1953
```

5.

```
       3:08:40 (Feb 21, 1994)
  +     2:45:10
  +     0:03:18
  =     5:56:68
  -          60 (-60 sec, +1 min)
  +        1:00
  =     5:57:08 (Feb 21, 1994)
```

6.

```
      12:33:21 (Nov 8, 1975)
  +     5:00:00
  +     0:01:12
  =    17:34:33 (Nov 8, 1975)
```

7.

```
       51 70 (-1 min, +60 sec)
      13:52:10 (Feb 10, 1997)
  -     6:43:52
  =     7:08:18 (Feb 10, 1997)
```

8.

```
       8 68      (-1 hr, +60 min)
       9:08:45 (Jun 20, 1962)
  -     4:36:15
  =     4:32:30 (Jun 20, 1962)
```

9.

```
      29       (-1 day, +24 hrs)
       5 92     (-1 hr, +60 min)
       6:32:56 (Apr 13, 2003)
  -   12:45:15
  =   17:47:41 Apr 12, 2003
```

10.

```
           ♏ (8) 22° 49'
  +            14° 22'
  =        (8) 36° 71'
  -                60' (-60 min, +1 degree)
  +             1°
  =        (8) 37° 11'
  -               30°  (-30 degrees, +1 sign)
  +           (1)
  =        ♐ (9) 07° 11'
```

Lesson 1: Math Basics I - Answer Key (continued)

11.

$$
\begin{array}{rlll}
 & \text{II} \ (3) & 14° & 53' \\
+ & & 28° & 18' \\
= & \text{II} \ (3) & 42° & 71' \\
- & & & 60' \quad \text{(-60 min, +1 degree)} \\
+ & & 1° & \\
= & \text{II} \ (3) & 43° & 11' \\
- & & 30° & \quad \text{(-30 degrees, +1 sign)} \\
+ & (1) & & \\
= & \text{♋} \ (4) & 13° & 11' \\
\end{array}
$$

12.

$$
\begin{array}{rlll}
 & \text{♈} \ (1) & 9° & 30' \\
+ & & 26° & 48' \\
= & (1) & 35° & 78' \\
- & & & 60' \quad \text{(-60 min, +1 degree)} \\
+ & & 1° & \\
= & (1) & 36° & 18' \\
- & & 30° & \quad \text{(-30 degrees, + 1 sign)} \\
+ & (1) & & \\
= & \text{♉} \ (2) & 6° & 18' \\
\end{array}
$$

13.

$$
\begin{array}{rll}
 & (4) \ 37° \quad {}' & \text{-1 sign, +30 degrees} \\
 & \text{♐} \ 86' & \text{-1 degree, +60 minutes} \\
\text{♌} & (5) \ \cancel{8°} \ \cancel{26'} & \\
- \ \text{♋} & (4) \ 23° \ 52' & \\
= & 14° \ 34' & \\
\end{array}
$$

14.

$$
\begin{array}{rll}
 & (13) & \text{+12 signs} \\
 & \text{♏} \ 26° \ 69' & \text{-1 degree, +60 minutes} \\
 & \text{♈} \ (1) \ \cancel{27°} \ \cancel{09'} & \\
- \ \text{♓} & (12) \ 19° \ 23' & \\
= & (1) \ 7° \ 46' & = 30° \ (1 \ \text{sign}) + 7° + 46' \\
= & 37° \ 46' & \\
\end{array}
$$

15.

$$
\begin{array}{rll}
 & \text{♒} \ (11) \ 18° \ 42' & \\
- & \text{♎} \ (7) \ 7° \ 30' & \\
= & (4) \ 11° \ 12' & = 120° \ (4 \ \text{signs}) + 11° + 12' \\
= & 131° \ 12' & \\
\end{array}
$$

16.

$$
\begin{array}{rll}
 & 295° \ 68' & \text{-1 deg, +60 min} \\
26° \ \text{♑} \ 08' & \cancel{296°} \ \cancel{08'} & \\
- \ 10° \ \text{♎} \ 29' & - \ 190° \ 29' & \\
= & = 105° \ 39' & \\
\end{array}
$$

17.

$$
\begin{array}{rll}
 & 439° & \text{+360 degrees} \\
19° \ \text{II} \ 47' & \cancel{79°} \ 47' & \\
- \ 21° \ \text{♍} \ 12' & - \ 171° \ 12' & \\
= & = 268° \ 35' & \\
\end{array}
$$

18.

$$
\begin{array}{rll}
 & 243° \ 79' & \text{-1 deg, +60 min} \\
4° \ \text{♐} \ 19' & \cancel{244°} \ \cancel{19'} & \\
- \ 22° \ \text{♉} \ 37' & - \ 52° \ 37' & \\
= & = 191° \ 42' & \\
\end{array}
$$

Lesson 2: Math Basics II - Answer Key

1. 12:48 = **12.8 hrs**

12:48 = 12 + $\frac{48}{60}$ hours = 12.8 hours

(48 minutes ÷ 60 = .8 of an hour)

2. 3:52:15 = **3.87 hrs**

3:52:15 = 3 hrs + $52\frac{15}{60}$ min = 3 hrs 52.25 min

= 3 $\frac{52.25}{60}$ hours = 3.87 hours

(52.25 minutes ÷ 60 = .87 of an hour)

3. 18:08:30 = **18.14 hrs**

18:08:30 = 18 hrs + 8 $\frac{30}{60}$ = 18 hrs 8.5 mins

= 18 $\frac{8.5}{60}$ hours = 18.14 hours

4. 12.63 hours = **12:37:48**

Record whole hours	12:__:__
.63 x 60 = 37.8	
Record whole minutes	12:37:__
.8 x 60 = 48	
Record seconds	12:37:48

5. 4.14 hours = **4:08:24**

Record whole hours	4:__:__
.14 x 60 = 8.4	
Record whole minutes	4:08:__
.4 x 60 = 24	
Record seconds	4:08:24

6. .69 days = **16:33:36**

.69 x 24 hours = 16.56	
Record whole hours	16:__:__
.56 x 60 = 33.6	
Record whole minutes	16:33:__
.6 x 60 = 36	
Record seconds	16:33:36

7. 45° W 36' = **45.6° W**

45° 36' = 45 $\frac{36}{60}$ degrees = 45.6° W

8. 23° 58' = **23.97°**

23° 58' = 23 $\frac{58}{60}$ degrees = 23.97°

9. 18.682° = **18° 40' 55"**

Record whole degrees	18° __' __"
.682 x 60 = 40.92	
Record whole minutes	18° 40' __"
.92 x 60 = 55	
Record seconds	18° 40' 55"

10. 3° 52' = **232 minutes**

180' (3 x 60 minutes) + 52' = 232'

11. 12° 13' = **733 minutes**

720' (12 x 60 minutes) + 13' = 733'

12. 758' = **12° 38'**

758' ÷ 60 = 12.633°	
Record whole degrees	12° __'
.633 x 60 = 37.98, rounded to 38'	12° 38'

Lesson 3: Time & GMT - Answer Key

1. 3:14 am, Dec. 10. 1944 **San Elizario, TX** MWT +6:00 (Mountain Standard Time Zone, War Time in effect)	**2.** 7:30 pm, June 14, 1968 **Bowling Green, IN** EST +5:00 (Eastern Standard Time Zone, No Daylight Savings Time in effect)
3. 4:40 pm, April 18, 1938 **Brooklyn, Kings Co, NY** EST +5:00 (Eastern Standard Time Zone, No Daylight Savings Time in effect)	**4.** 11:30 pm, Sept. 25, 1948 **Chattanooga, TN** CDT +5:00 (Central Standard Time Zone, Daylight Savings Time in effect)
5. 5:18 am, June 15, 1978 **Eugene, Oregon** PDT +7:00 (Pacific Standard Time Zone, Daylight Savings Time in effect.)	**6.** 3:45 pm, February 8, 1946 **Honolulu, Hawaii** HST + 10:30 (Hawaii Standard Time Zone, No Daylight Savings Time in effect)
7. 9:35 pm, August 5, 1915 **Tokyo, Japan** -9:00	**8.** 9:30 pm, Sept. 30, 1970 **Dingo, Australia** - 10:00
9. 7:00 am, May 10, 1942 **London, England** - 2:00	**10.** 1:15 pm, July 10, 1983 **Istanbul, Turkey** - 3:00

Lesson 3: Time & GMT - Answer Key (continued)

11. 7:35 pm, September 10, 1985, Boise, Idaho

1. Given Time of Birth   7 : 35 am (pm)
2. + PM Adjustment *(+12:00 if pm)*   + 12 : 00
3. +/-Time Zone   **MDT**
     a. Standard Time Zone *(+W, -E)*   7 :00
     b. DST Adjustment *(- 1:00 if DST)*   - 1 :00
     (Include only if not already factored into (a) above)
     c. = Time Zone Adjustment *(Enter on Line 3, right)*   = 6 :00 ⟶ (+W,)E 6 : 00

           Subtotal = 25 : 35

4. +/- 24 hours if date change required   +(-) 24 : 00   *Notice date change!*

5. = GMT of Birth   Date Sept 11, 1985   Time = 1 : 35

12. 3:15 am, March 20, 1945, Brooklyn, Kings Co, New York

1. Given Time of Birth   3 : 15 (am)/pm
2. + PM Adjustment *(+12:00 if pm)*   + ___:___
3. +/-Time Zone   **EWT**
     a. Standard Time Zone *(+W, -E)*   5 :00
     b. DST Adjustment *(- 1:00 if DST)*   - 1 :00
     (Include only if not already factored into (a) above)
     c. = Time Zone Adjustment *(Enter on Line 3, right)*   = 4 :00 ⟶ (+W,)E 4 :00   *Notice War Time Adjustment!*

           Subtotal = 7 : 15

4. +/- 24 hours if date change required   +/- ___:___

5. = GMT of Birth   Date Mar 20, 1945   Time = 7 : 15

13. 12:40 pm, December 5, 1943, London, England

1. Given Time of Birth   12 : 40 am /(pm)
2. + PM Adjustment *(+12:00 if pm)*   + ___:___
3. +/-Time Zone
     a. Standard Time Zone *(+W (-E))*   1 :00
     b. DST Adjustment *(- 1:00 if DST)*   - ___:___
     (Include only if not already factored into (a) above)
     c. = Time Zone Adjustment *(Enter on Line 3, right)*   = 1 :00 ⟶ +W,(-E) 1 :00   *Notice PM Adjustment is not necessary for times between 12:00-12:59pm*

           Subtotal = 11 : 40

4. +/- 24 hours if date change required   +/- ___:___

5. = GMT of Birth   Date Dec. 5, 1943   Time = 11 : 40

Lesson 3: Time & GMT - Answer Key (continued)

14. 3:30 am, April 12, 1986, Leningrad, Russia

1. Given Time of Birth   3 : 30 (am) pm
2. + PM Adjustment *(+12:00 if pm)*   + ___:___
3. +/-Time Zone
     a. Standard Time Zone *(+W, -E)*   4 :00
     b. DST Adjustment *(- 1:00 if DST)*   - ___:___
     (Include only if not already factored into (a) above)
     c. = Time Zone Adjustment *(Enter on Line 3, right)* = 4 :00   →   +W (-E) 4 :00

                                      Subtotal = - : 30

4. +/- 24 hours if date change required   (+)- 24 :00   *Notice date change!*

5. = GMT of Birth   Date Apr. 11, 1986   Time = 23 : 30

15. 8:30 pm, August 5, 1972, Honolulu, Hawaii

1. Given Time of Birth   8 : 30 am / (pm)
2. + PM Adjustment *(+12:00 if pm)*   + 12 : 00
3. +/-Time Zone   **AHST**
     a. Standard Time Zone *(+W, -E)*   10:00
     b. DST Adjustment *(- 1:00 if DST)*   - ___:___
     (Include only if not already factored into (a) above)
     c. = Time Zone Adjustment *(Enter on Line 3, right)* = 10 :00   →   (+W) E 10 :00

                                        Subtotal = 30 : 30

4. +/- 24 hours if date change required   +(-) 24 :00   *Notice date change!*

5. = GMT of Birth   Date Aug. 6, 1972   Time = 6 : 30

16. 11:45 am, February 11, 1957, Melbourne, Australia

1. Given Time of Birth   11 : 45 (am) pm
2. + PM Adjustment *(+12:00 if pm)*   + ___:___
3. +/-Time Zone
     a. Standard Time Zone *(+W, -E)*   10:00
     b. DST Adjustment *(- 1:00 if DST)*   - ___:___
     (Include only if not already factored into (a) above)
     c. = Time Zone Adjustment *(Enter on Line 3, right)* = 10 :00   →   +W (-E) 10 :00

                                        Subtotal = 1 : 45

4. +/- 24 hours if date change required   +/- ___:___

5. = GMT of Birth   Date Feb. 11, 1957   Time = 1 : 45

17.   4:12 pm, March 19, 1959, Santa Fe, New Mexico

1. Given Time of Birth   __4__ : __12__ am (pm)

2. + PM Adjustment *(+12:00 if pm)*   + __12__ : __00__

3. +/-Time Zone   **MST**
   a. Standard Time Zone *(+W, -E)*   __7__ :00
   b. DST Adjustment *(- 1:00 if DST)*   - ___:___
      (Include only if not already factored into (a) above)   ——————
   c. = Time Zone Adjustment *(Enter on Line 3, right)* = __7__ :00   ——→ (+W,)E __7__ : __00__

                                                               Subtotal = __23__ : __12__

4. +/- 24 hours if date change required   +/- ___:___
                                                                    ——————

5. = GMT of Birth	Date Mar. 19, 1959	Time = __23__ : __12__

Lesson 4: Latitude & Longitude - Answer Key

1. Charlotte, North Carolina
80° W 51'

80° W 51' = 80.85°
80.85 x 4 minutes = 323.40 minutes
323 ÷ 60 = 5.38 hours
Record whole hours   5:__:__
.38 x 60 = 22.8 minutes
Record whole minutes 5:23:__
.4 x 60 = 24 seconds
Record seconds   5:23:24
Longitude/Time Equivalent = - 5:23:24

2. Laramie, Wyoming
105° W 35'

105° W 35' = 105.58°
105.58 x 4 minutes = 422.32 minutes
422 ÷ 60 = 7.03 hours
Record whole hours   7:__:__
.03 x 60 = 1.8 minutes
Record whole minutes 7:02:__
.32 x 60 = 19 seconds
Record seconds   7:02:19
Longitude/Time Equivalent = - 7:02:19

3. Miami, Florida
80° W 12'

80° W 12' = 80.2°
80.2 x 4 minutes = 320.80 minutes
320 ÷ 60 = 5.33 hours
Record whole hours   5:__:__
.33 x 60 = 19.8 minutes
Record whole minutes 5:20:__
.80 x 60 = 48 seconds
Record seconds   5:20:48
Longitude/Time Equivalent = - 5:20:48

4. Rome, Italy
12° E 29'

12° E 29' = 12.48°
12.48 x 4 minutes = 49.92 minutes

Record whole hours   0:__:__
Record whole minutes 0:49:__
.92 x 60 = 55 seconds
Record seconds   0:49:55
Longitude/Time Equivalent = + 0:49:55

5. Hornby, New Zealand
172° E 32'

172° E 32' = 172.53°
172.53 x 4 minutes = 690.12 minutes
690 ÷ 60 = 11.5 hours
Record whole hours   11:__:__
.5 x 60 = 30 minutes
Record whole minutes 11:30:__
.12 x 60 = 7 seconds
Record seconds   11:30:07
Longitude/Time Equivalent = +11:30:07

6. Beijing, China
116° E 25'

116° E 25' = 116.42°
116.42 x 4 minutes = 465.68 minutes
465 ÷ 60 = 7.75 hours
Record whole hours   7:__:__
.75 x 60 = 45 minutes
Record whole minutes 7:45:__
.68 x 60 = 40.8 seconds
Record seconds   7:45:41
Longitude/Time Equivalent = + 7:45:41

Lesson 5: Sidereal Time - Answer Key

(Note that in all Lesson 5 exercises we have calculated the Longitude/Time equivalent manually. Your LST may differ by 2-3 seconds if you used the longtitude/time equivalent listed in the Atlas instead. A difference of 2-3 seconds is acceptable and will not affect the accuracy of the final chart, but if your difference is greater than this you need to check your calculations for errors.)

1. 6:29 GMT, February 16, 1985, Atlanta, Georgia (84° W 23')

Sidereal Time at 0 hr on birth date   9 : 43 : 43

+ GMT of birth   6 : 29 : 00

+ Solar/Sidereal Time Correction on GMT *(from Table or calculate below:)*   01 : 04

(GMT *(as decimal)* __6.48__ hrs x 9.86 secs = __64 secs__)   Subtotal =   15 : 73 : 47

+/- Longitude/Time Equivalent *(from Atlas or calculate below; -W, +E)*   +⊙ 5 : 37 : 31

(Longitude *(as decimal)* __84.38__ x 4 min = __337.52__)   Subtotal =   10 : 36 : 16

+/- 24:00:00 if required   +/- ___ : ___ : ___

= LST of Birth   LST =   10 : 36 : 16

2. 14:05 GMT, August 30, 1965, Athens, Greece (23° E 43')

Sidereal Time at 0 hr on birth date   22 : 31 : 54

+ GMT of birth   14 : 05 : 00

+ Solar/Sidereal Time Correction on GMT *(from Table or calculate below:)*   02 : 19

(GMT *(as decimal)* __14.08__ hrs x 9.86 secs = __139 secs__)   Subtotal =   36 : 38 : 73

+/- Longitude/Time Equivalent *(from Atlas or calculate below; -W, +E)*   ⊕/- 1 : 34 : 52

(Longitude *(as decimal)* __23.72__ x 4 min = __94.88__)   Subtotal =   37 : 72 : 125

                 Or 38   14   05

+/- 24:00:00 if required   +/- 24 : 00 : 00

= LST of Birth   LST =   14 : 14 : 05

Lesson 5: Sidereal Time - Answer Key (continued)

3. 8:45 GMT, March 4, 1942, Newark, New Jersey (74° W 10')

Sidereal Time at 0 hr on birth date	10 : 44 : 30
+ GMT of birth	8 : 45 : 00
+ Solar/Sidereal Time Correction on GMT *(from Table or calculate below:)*	01 : 26
(GMT *(as decimal)* **8.75** hrs x 9.86 secs = **86 secs**) Subtotal =	18 : 90 : 56
+/- Longitude/Time Equivalent *(from Atlas or calculate below; -W, +E)*	+⊖ 4 : 56 : 41
(Longitude *(as decimal)* **74.17** x 4 min = **296.68**) Subtotal =	14 : 34 : 15
+/- 24:00:00 if required +/-	___ : ___ : ___
= LST of Birth LST =	14 : 34 : 15

4. 1:52 GMT, July 10, 1979, Vienna, Austria (16° E 20')

Sidereal Time at 0 hr on birth date	19 : 09 : 18
+ GMT of birth	1 : 52 : 00
+ Solar/Sidereal Time Correction on GMT *(from Table or calculate below:)*	00 : 18
(GMT *(as decimal)* **1.87** hrs x 9.86 secs = **18 secs**) Subtotal =	20 : 61 : 36
+/- Longitude/Time Equivalent *(from Atlas or calculate below; -W, +E)*	⊕ - 1 : 05 : 19
(Longitude *(as decimal)* **16.33** x 4 min = **65.32**) Subtotal =	21 : 66 : 55
	Or 22 06 55
+/- 24:00:00 if required +/-	___ : ___ : ___
= LST of Birth LST =	22 : 06 : 55

Lesson 6: Section Review - Answer Key

1.

July 11, 1975
8:45pm
Des Moines, Iowa
Latitude: 41° N 36', Longitude: 93° W 37'

Part A: GMT of Birth

1. Given Time of Birth   __8__ :__45__ am / (pm)

2. + PM Adjustment *(+12:00 if pm)*   + __12__ :__00__

3. +/-Time Zone

     a. Standard Time Zone *(+W, -E)*   __6__ :__00__

     b. DST Adjustment *(- 1:00 if DST)*   - __1__ :__00__
     (Include only if not already factored into (a) above)

     c. = Time Zone Adjustment *(Enter on Line 3, right)* = __5__ :__00__ ⟶ (+W,)E __5__ : __00__

                               Subtotal = __25__ : __45__

4. +/- 24 hours if date change required   + (-) __24__ : __00__

5. = GMT of Birth   Date __July 12, 1975__   Time = __1__ : __45__

Part B: LST of Birth

6. Sidereal Time at 0 hr on birth date *(from ephemeris; use birth date from Step 5)*   __19__ : __17__ : __05__

7. + GMT of birth *(from Step 5)*   __1__ : __45__ : __00__

8. + Solar/Sidereal Time Correction on GMT *(from Table or calculate below:)*   __:17__

     (GMT *(as decimal)* __1.75__ hrs x 9.86 secs = __17__)   Subtotal = __20__ : __62__ : __22__

9. +/- Longitude/Time Equivalent *(from Atlas or calculate below; -W, +E)*   + (-) __6__ : __14__ : __29__

     (Longitude *(as decimal)* __93.62__ x 4 min = __374.48__)   Subtotal = __14__ : __47__ : __53__

10. +/- 24:00:00 if required   +/- __:__:__

11. = LST of Birth   LST = __14__ : __47__ : __53__

2.

December 8, 1987
5:52 am
Tokyo, Japan
Latitude: 35° N 42', Longitude: 139° E 46'

Part A: GMT of Birth

1. Given Time of Birth   _5_ :_52_ (am)/ pm

2. + PM Adjustment *(+12:00 if pm)*   + ____:____

3. +/-Time Zone

     a. Standard Time Zone *(+W, -E)*   _9_ : _00_

     b. DST Adjustment *(- 1:00 if DST)*   - ____:____
     (Include only if not already factored into (a) above)

     c. = Time Zone Adjustment *(Enter on Line 3, right)*   = _9_ : _00_ ⟶ +W (-E) _9_ : _00_

                                            Subtotal = _-3 : 08_

4. +/- 24 hours if date change required   (+)- _24 : 00_

5. = GMT of Birth   Date _Dec 7, 1987_   Time = _20 : 52_

Part B: LST of Birth

6. Sidereal Time at 0 hr on birth date *(from ephemeris; use birth date from Step 5)*   _5_ : _00_ : _56_

7. + GMT of birth *(from Step 5)*   _20_ : _52_ : _00_

8. + Solar/Sidereal Time Correction on GMT *(from Table or calculate below:)*   _3_ : _26_

   (GMT *(as decimal)* _20.87_ hrs x 9.86 secs = _206_)   Subtotal = _25_ : _55_ : _82_

9. +/- Longitude/Time Equivalent *(from Atlas or calculate below; -W, +E)*   (+)- _9_ : _19_ : _05_

   (Longitude *(as decimal)* _139.77_ x 4 min = _559.08_)   Subtotal = _34_ : _74_ : _87_
                                                   Or 35   15   27

10. +/- 24:00:00 if required   +(-) _24_ : _00_ : _00_

11. = LST of Birth   LST = _11_ : _15_ : _27_

3.

August 25, 1962
6:58 pm
Portland, Maine
Latitude: 43° N 40', Longitude: 70° W 15'

Part A: GMT of Birth

1. Given Time of Birth   6 :58   am / (pm)

2. + PM Adjustment *(+12:00 if pm)*   + 12 :00

3. +/-Time Zone

    a. Standard Time Zone *(+W, -E)*   5 : 00

    b. DST Adjustment *(- 1:00 if DST)*   - 1 : 00
    (Include only if not already factored into (a) above)

    c. = Time Zone Adjustment *(Enter on Line 3, right)* = 4 : 00 ⟶ (+W,)E 4 : 00

                                            Subtotal = 22 : 58

4. +/- 24 hours if date change required   +/- ___ : ___

5. = GMT of Birth   Date Aug 25, 1962   Time = 22 : 58

Part B: LST of Birth

6. Sidereal Time at 0 hr on birth date *(from ephemeris; use birth date from Step 5)*   22 : 11 : 07

7. + GMT of birth *(from Step 5)*   22 : 58 : 00

8. + Solar/Sidereal Time Correction on GMT *(from Table or calculate below:)*   3 : 46

    (GMT *(as decimal)* 22.97 hrs x 9.86 secs = 226)   Subtotal = 44 : 72 : 53

9. +/- Longitude/Time Equivalent *(from Atlas or calculate below; -W, +E)*   + (-) 4 : 41 : 00

    (Longitude *(as decimal)* 70.25 x 4 min = 281)   Subtotal = 40 : 31 : 53

10. +/- 24:00:00 if required   + (-) 24 : 00 : 00

11. = LST of Birth   LST = 16 : 31 : 53

Lesson 7: Daily Motion - Answer Key

1. May 10th, 1987

	☉	☽	☿	♀	♂	♃
1. Position at 0 hr on day After birth date **(5/11/87)**	18° ♉ 108' ~~19° ♉ 48'~~	16° ♎ 48'	23° ♉ 65' ~~24° ♉ 05'~~	21° ♈ 68' ~~22° ♈ 08'~~	22° ♊ 83' ~~23° ♊ 23'~~	16° ♈ 24'
2. Position at 0 hr on Birth date **(5/10/87)**	18° ♉ 50'	3° ♎ 32'	21° ♉ 55'	20° ♈ 56'	22° ♊ 44'	16° ♈ 10'
3. Line 1 - Line 2 = Total Daily Travel	58'	13° 16' = 796'	2° 10' = 130'	1° 12' = 72'	39'	14'

	♄	♅	♆	♇	☊
6. Position at 0 hr on day After birth date **(5/11/87)**	19° ♐ 53' Rx	26° ♐ 05' Rx	7° ♑ 45' Rx	8° ♏ 16' Rx	11° ♈ 03' Rx
7. Position at 0 hr on Birth date **(5/10/87)**	19° ♐ 56' Rx	26° ♐ 07' Rx	7° ♑ 46' Rx	8° ♏ 17' Rx	11° ♈ 03' Rx
8. Line 6 - Line 7 = Total Daily Travel	-3' Rx	- 2' Rx	-1' Rx	-1' Rx	0'

2. April 15, 1985

	☉	☽	☿	♀	♂	♃
1. Position at 0 hr on day After birth date **(4/16/85)**	25° ♈ 57'	39° ♒ 53' ~~9° ♓ 53'~~	6° ♈ 47' Rx	7° ♈ 38' Rx	22° ♉ 44'	13° ♒ 16'
2. Position at 0 hr on Birth date **(4/15/85)**	24° ♈ 58'	27° ♒ 42'	6° ♈ 56' Rx	7° ♈ 60' Rx ~~8° ♈ 00' Rx~~	22° ♉ 02'	13° ♒ 08'
3. Line 1 - Line 2 = Total Daily Travel	59'	12° 11' = 731'	-9' Rx	-22' Rx	42'	8'

	♄	♅	♆	♇	☊
6. Position at 0 hr on day After birth date **(4/16/85)**	26° ♏ 54' Rx	17° ♐ 44' Rx	3° ♑ 35' Rx	3° ♏ 35' Rx	18° ♉ 22' Rx
7. Position at 0 hr on Birth date **(4/15/85)**	26° ♏ 57' Rx	17° ♐ 46' Rx	3° ♑ 35' Rx	3° ♏ 36' Rx	18° ♉ 26' Rx
8. Line 6 - Line 7 = Total Daily Travel	-3' Rx	-2' Rx	0	-1' Rx	-4' Rx

Lesson 8: Finding Planets - Answer Key

1. October 12, 1987, 16:44 GMT

CM-1
(Constant Multiplier for Part C: Planetary Position)

Convert GMT of Birth to decimal: ____16.73____ ÷ 24 = **CM-1** ___.697___

	☉	☽	☿	♀	♂	♃
1.Position at 0 hr on day After birth date **10/13/87**	18°♎ 67' ~~19°♎ 07'~~	29°♊ 44'	11°♏ 85' ~~12°♏ 25'~~	2°♏ 39'	2°♎ 42'	25°♈ 26' Rx
2.Position at 0 hr on Birth date **10/12/87**	18°♎ 08'	17°♊ 25'	11°♏ 58'	1°♏ 25'	2°♎ 03'	25°♈ 34' Rx
3. Line 1 - Line 2 = Total Daily Travel	59'	12° 19' = 739'	27'	1° 14' = 74'	39'	-8' Rx
4. Line 3 X CM-1 __.697__ = Travel to birth time	41'	515' = 8° 35'	19'	52'	27'	-6' Rx
5. Add lines 2 + 4 = Position at Birth	18°♎ 49'	25°♊ 60' = 26°♊ 00'	11°♏ 77' = 12°♏ 17'	1°♏ 77' 2°♏ 17'	2°♎ 30'	25°♈ 28' Rx

	♄	♅	♆	♇	☊	
6.Position at 0 hr on day After birth date **10/13/87**	16°♐ 51'	23°♐ 26'	5°♑ 25'	9°♏ 04'	2°♈ 14' Rx	
7. Position at 0 hr on Birth date **10/12/87**	16°♐ 46'	23°♐ 24'	5°♑ 24'	9°♏ 02'	2°♈ 16' Rx	
8. Line 6 - Line 7 = Total Daily Travel	5'	2'	1'	2'	-2' Rx	
9. Line 8 X CM-1 _.697__ = Travel to birth time	3'	1'	1'	1'	-1' Rx	
10. Add lines 7 + 9 = Position at Birth	16°♐ 49'	23°♐ 25'	5°♑ 25'	9°♏ 03'	2°♈ 15' Rx	

Lesson 9: Chiron & Asteroids - Answer Key

1. Determine Chiron's position on February 11, 1963, 13:39 GMT.

Step 1. CM-1 = 13.65 ÷ 24 = .569

Step 2. 10 days + .569 (CM-1) = 10.569

Step 3. 10.569 ÷ 28 (days) = .377

Step 4. Chiron's position 0-hour March 1, 1963: 10° ♓ 26'

Chiron's position 0-hour Feb 1, 1963: <u>8° ♓ 41'</u>

= Monthly Motion   1° 45', or 105'

Step 5. 105' x .377 = 39.59, rounded to 40'

Step 6. Chiron's position 0-hour Feb 1, 1963:   8° ♓ 41'

\+   40'

= **Chiron's position at birth**   = 9° ♓ 21'

---

2. Determine the position of the asteroid Ceres for the same birth date.

Step 1. CM-1 = 13.65 ÷ 24 = .569

Step 2. Next earliest listing is Feb 7, 1963.

Feb 11-Feb 7 = 4 days

4 days + .569 (CM-1) = 4.569

Step 3. 4.569 ÷ 10 (days) = .457

Step 4. Ceres' position 0-hour Feb 17, 1963: 14° ♍ 11' R_x

Ceres' position 0-hour Feb 7, 1963: 15° ♍ 59' R_x

= 10-day Motion   -1° 48' R_x, or 108' R_x

Step 5. 108' R_x x .457 = 49.35 R_x, rounded to 49' R_x

Step 6. Ceres' position 0-hour Feb 7, 1963: 15° ♍ 59' R_x

\-   49' R_x

= **Ceres' position at birth**   = 15° ♍ 10' R_x

Lesson 10: House Cusps I - Answer Key

1. 8:51:42 LST

CM-2

LST of Birth	8 : 51 : 42
- Next lowest Sid Time from Table	- 8 : 48 : 00
=	3 : 42
Convert result to decimal	3.7
÷ 4 = CM-2	.93

1. MC at Later LST **(8:52:00)**	10° ♌ 33'
2. MC at Earlier LST **(8:48:00)**	9° ♌ 34'
3. Line 1 - Line 2 =	59'
4. Line 3 X CM-2 __.93__ =	55'
5. Add lines 2 + 4 =	9° ♌ 89' = 10° ♌ 29'

MC = 10° ♌ 29'

IC = 10° ♒ 29'

2. 14:10:45 LST

CM-2

LST of Birth	14 : 10 : 45
- Next lowest Sid Time from Table	- 14 : 08 : 00
=	2 : 45
Convert result to decimal	2 .75
÷ 4 = CM-2	.69

1. MC at Later LST **(14:12:00)**	5° ♏ 18'
2. MC at Earlier LST **(14:08:00)**	4° ♏ 16'
3. Line 1 - Line 2 =	1° 02', or 62'
4. Line 3 X CM-2 __.69__ =	43'
5. Add lines 2 + 4 =	4° ♏ 59'

MC = 4° ♏ 59'

IC = 4° ♉ 59'

17:24:49 LST
Houston, Texas 29° N 46'

CM-2
(Constant Multiplier for LST Interpolation)

LST of Birth	17: 24: 49
- Next lowest Sid Time from Table	- 17 :24 :00
=	00: 49
Convert result to decimal	.82
÷ 4 = CM-2	.21

CM-3
(Constant Multiplier for Latitude Interpolation)

Latitude of Birth	29° 46 '
- Next lowest Latitude from Table	- 29° 00 '
=	° 46 '
Convert result to decimal = CM-3 =	.77

Exception: If Birth Latitude is less than 20°, divide result by 5   ÷ 5 = CM-3 _____

1st Cusp	17° ♓ 19'		7th Cusp	17° ♍ 19'
2nd Cusp	27° ♈ 13'		8th Cusp	27° ♎ 13'
3rd Cusp	27° ♉ 25'		9th Cusp	27° ♏ 25'
4th Cusp	21° ♊ 56'		10th Cusp	21° ♐ 56'
5th Cusp	15° ♋ 20'		11th Cusp	15° ♑ 20'
6th Cusp	11° ♌ 56'		12th Cusp	11° ♒ 56'

House Cusp Calculation for Higher Latitude

Latitude __30°__	MC	11th	12th	ASC	2nd	3rd
1. House Cusps at Later Sid Time (17:28:00)	21° ♐ 99' ~~22° ♐ 39'~~	15° ♑ 62' ~~16° ♑ 02'~~	12° ♒ 46'	17° ♓ 85' ~~18° ♓ 25'~~	28° ♈ 15'	28° ♉ 15'
2. House Cusps at Earlier Sid Time (17:24:00)	21° ♐ 44'	15° ♑ 05'	11° ♒ 38'	16° ♓ 59'	27° ♈ 00'	27° ♉ 14'
3. Line 1 - Line 2 =	55'	57'	1° 08' = 68'	1° 26' = 86'	1° 15' = 75'	1° 01' = 61'
4. Line 3 X CM-2 __ .21 __ =	12'	12'	14'	18'	16'	13'
5. Add lines 2 + 4 =	21° ♐ 56'	15° ♑ 17'	11° ♒ 52'	16° ♓ 77' =17° ♓ 17'	27° ♈ 16'	27° ♉ 27'

House Cusp Calculation for Lower Latitude

Latitude __29°__		11th	12th	ASC	2nd	3rd
6. House Cusps at Later Sid Time (17:28:00)		15° ♑ 73' ~~16° ♑ 13'~~	12° ♒ 64' ~~13° ♒ 04'~~	18° ♓ 34'	27° ♈ 62' ~~28° ♈ 02'~~	28° ♉ 05'
7. House Cusps at Earlier Sid Time (17:24:00)		15° ♑ 16'	11° ♒ 57'	17° ♓ 09'	26° ♈ 48'	27° ♉ 04'
8. Line 6 - Line 7 =		57'	1° 07' = 67'	1° 25' = 85'	1° 14' = 74'	1° 01' = 61'
9. Line 3 X CM-2 _ .21 __ =		12'	14'	18'	16'	13'
10. Add lines 7 + 9 =		15° ♑ 28'	11° ♒ 71' = 12° ♒ 11'	17° ♓ 27'	26° ♈ 64' = 27° ♈ 04'	27° ♉ 17'

Latitude Interpolation

		11th	12th	ASC	2nd	3rd
11. House Cusps at Higher Latitude (from line 5)		15° ♑ 17'	11° ♒ 52'	17° ♓ 17'	27° ♈ 16'	27° ♉ 27'
12. House Cusps at Lower Latitude (from line 10)		15° ♑ 28'	12° ♒ 11'	17° ♓ 27'	27° ♈ 04'	27° ♉ 17'
13. Line 11 - Line 12 =		- 11' Rx	- 19' Rx	- 10' Rx	12'	10'
14. Line 13 X CM-3 _ .77 __ =		- 8' Rx	- 15' Rx	- 8' Rx	9'	8'
15. Add lines 12 + 14 = **House Cusps at Birth**		15° ♑ 20'	11° ♒ 56'	17° ♓ 19'	27° ♈ 13'	27° ♉ 25'

Lesson 12: Southern Latitude Births - Answer Key

1. January 9, 1974
3:25 am
Sydney, Australia 33°S 52' 151°E 13'

Part A: GMT of Birth

1. Given Time of Birth   __3__:25 (am)/ pm

2. + PM Adjustment *(+12:00 if pm)*   + ____:____

3. +/-Time Zone

    a. Standard Time Zone *(+W, -E)*   11 : 00

    b. DST Adjustment *(- 1:00 if DST)*   - ____:____
    (Include only if not already factored into (a) above)

    c. = Time Zone Adjustment *(Enter on Line 3, right)* = 11 : 00 ⟶ +W,(-E) 11 : 00

                                            Subtotal = ____:____

4. +/- 24 hours if date change required   ⟶ (+/)- __24__:00

5. = GMT of Birth   Date __Jan 8, 1974__   Time = __16__:25

Part B: LST of Birth

6. Sidereal Time at 0 hr on birth date *(from ephemeris; use birth date from Step 5)*   7 : 08 : 39

7. + GMT of birth *(from Step 5)*   16 : 25 : 00

8. + Solar/Sidereal Time Correction on GMT *(from Table or calculate below:)*   2 : 42

    (GMT *(as decimal)* __16.42__ hrs x 9.86 secs = __162__)   Subtotal = 23 : 35 :81

9. +/- Longitude/Time Equivalent *(from Atlas or calculate below; -W, +E)*   (+)- 10 :04 :53

    (Longitude *(as decimal)* __151.22__ x 4 min = __604.88__)   Subtotal = 33 : 39 :134
                                                Or 33 41 14

10. +/- 24:00:00 if required   +(-) 24: 00 :00

11. = LST of Birth   LST = 9 : 41 : 14

12. Southern Latitude Adjustment *(+/- 12:00:00 if Southern Latitude)*   (+)- 12: 00 :00

13. "LST + 12" *(use in place of LST for Southern Latitude births)*   LST+12 = 21 : 41 : 14

CM-2
(Constant Multiplier for LST Interpolation)

LST of Birth	21 : 41 : 14
- Next lowest Sid Time from Table	- 21 : 40 : 00
=	1 : 14
Convert result to decimal	1.23
÷ 4 = CM-2	.31

CM-3
(Constant Multiplier for Latitude Interpolation)

Latitude of Birth	33 ° 52 '
- Next lowest Latitude from Table	- 33 ° ___ '
=	___ ° 52 '
Convert result to decimal = CM-3 =	.87

Exception: If Birth Latitude is less than 20°, divide result by 5   ÷ 5 = CM-3 _____

1st Cusp	12° ♐ 46'	7th Cusp	12° ♊ 46'
2nd Cusp	5° ♑ 59'	8th Cusp	5° ♋ 59'
3rd Cusp	28° ♑ 05'	9th Cusp	28° ♋ 05'
4th Cusp	22° ♒ 58'	10th Cusp	22° ♌ 58'
5th Cusp	24° ♓ 20'	11th Cusp	24° ♍ 20'
6th Cusp	3° ♉ 18'	12th Cusp	3° ♏ 18'

House Cusp Calculation for Higher Latitude

Latitude __34°__	MC	11th	12th	ASC	2nd	3rd
1. House Cusps at Later Sid Time (21:44:00)	23°♒ 41'	24°♓ 70' ~~25°♓ 10'~~	3°♉ 71' ~~4°♉ 11'~~	13°♊ 34'	5°♋ 99' ~~6°♋ 39'~~	27°♋ 103' ~~28°♋ 43'~~
2. House Cusps at Earlier Sid Time (21:40:00)	22°♒ 39'	23°♓ 58'	2°♉ 57'	12°♊ 32'	5°♋ 45'	27°♋ 49'
3. Line 1 - Line 2 =	1° 02' = 62'	1° 12' = 72'	1° 14' = 74'	1° 02' = 62'	54'	54'
4. Line 3 X CM-2 __.31__ =	19'	22'	23'	19'	17'	17'
5. Add lines 2 + 4 =	~~22°♒ 58'~~ 22°♌ 58'	23°♓ 80' = 24°♓ 20'	2°♉ 80' = 3°♉ 20'	12°♊ 51'	5°♋ 62' = 6°♋ 02'	27°♋ 66' = 28°♋ 06'

House Cusp Calculation for Lower Latitude

Latitude __33°__		11th	12th	ASC	2nd	3rd
6. House Cusps at Later Sid Time (21:44:00)		24°♓ 71' ~~25°♓ 11'~~	3°♉ 55'	12°♊ 56'	5°♋ 76' ~~6°♋ 16'~~	27°♋ 93' ~~28°♋ 33'~~
7. House Cusps at Earlier Sid Time (21:40:00)		23°♓ 59'	2°♉ 41'	11°♊ 54'	5°♋ 22'	27°♋ 38'
8. Line 6 - Line 7 =		1° 12' = 72'	1° 14' = 74'	1° 02' = 62'	54'	55'
9. Line 3 X CM-2 _ .31 __ =		22'	23'	19'	17'	17'
10. Add lines 7 + 9 =		23°♓ 81' = 24°♓ 21'	2°♉ 64' = 3°♉ 04'	11°♊ 73' = 12°♊ 13'	5°♋ 39'	27°♋ 55'

Latitude Interpolation

		11th	12th	ASC	2nd	3rd
11. House Cusps at Higher Latitude (from line 5)		24°♓ 20'	3°♉ 20'	12°♊ 51'	5°♋ 62' ~~6°♋ 02'~~	27°♋ 66' ~~28°♋ 06'~~
12. House Cusps at Lower Latitude (from line 10)		24°♓ 21'	3°♉ 04'	12°♊ 13'	5°♋ 39'	27°♋ 55'
13. Line 11 - Line 12 =		- 1' ℞	16'	38'	23'	11'
14. Line 13 X CM-3 _ .87 __ =		- 1' ℞	14'	33'	20'	10'
15. Add lines 12 + 14 = **House Cusps at Birth**		~~24°♓ 20'~~ 24°♍ 20'	~~3°♉ 18'~~ 3°♏ 18'	~~12°♊ 46'~~ 12°♐ 46'	~~5°♋ 59'~~ 5°♑ 59'	~~27°♋ 65' = 28°♋ 05'~~ 28°♑ 05'

Lesson 13: Natal Chart Exams - Answer Key

Exam 1. (Completed natal chart is shown on page 342.)

August 15, 1983, 5:52 am
Cairo, Egypt 30°N 03' 31°E 15'

Part A: GMT of Birth

1. Given Time of Birth   <u> 5 </u>:<u> 52 </u> (am)/ pm

2. + PM Adjustment *(+12:00 if pm)*   + <u>   </u>:<u>   </u>

3. +/-Time Zone
   a. Standard Time Zone *(+W, -E)*   <u> 3 </u>:<u> 00 </u>

   b. DST Adjustment *(- 1:00 if DST)*   - <u>   </u>:<u>   </u>
   (Include only if not already factored into (a) above)
   c. = Time Zone Adjustment *(Enter on Line 3, right)* = <u> 3 </u>:<u> 00 </u> ⟶ +W,-Ⓔ <u> 3 </u>:<u> 00 </u>

                                                   Subtotal = <u> 2 </u>:<u> 52 </u>

4. +/- 24 hours if date change required   +/- <u>   </u>:<u>   </u>

5. = GMT of Birth   Date <u> August 15, 1983 </u>   Time = <u> 2 </u>:<u> 52 </u>

Part B: LST of Birth

6. Sidereal Time at 0 hr on birth date *(from ephemeris; use birth date from Step 5)*   <u> 21 </u>:<u> 31 </u>:<u> 20 </u>

7. + GMT of birth *(from Step 5)*   <u> 2 </u>:<u> 52 </u>:<u> 00 </u>

8. + Solar/Sidereal Time Correction on GMT *(from Table or calculate below:)*   <u>   </u>:<u> 28 </u>

   (GMT *(as decimal)* <u> 2.87 </u> hrs x 9.86 secs = <u> 28 </u>)   Subtotal = <u> 23 </u>:<u> 83 </u>:<u> 48 </u>

9. +/- Longitude/Time Equivalent *(from Atlas or calculate below; -W, +E)*   ⊕- <u> 2 </u>:<u> 05 </u>:<u> 00 </u>

   (Longitude *(as decimal)* <u> 31.25 </u> x 4 min = <u> 125.0 </u>)   Subtotal = <u> 25 </u>:<u> 88 </u>:<u> 48 </u>
                                                                       Or 26   28   48
10. +/- 24:00:00 if required   +Ⓒ <u> 24 </u>:<u> 00 </u>:<u> 00 </u>

11. = LST of Birth   LST = <u> 2 </u>:<u> 28 </u>:<u> 48 </u>

12. Southern Latitude Adjustment *(+/- 12:00:00 if Southern Latitude)*   +/- <u>   </u>:<u>   </u>:<u>   </u>

13. "LST + 12" *(use in place of LST for Southern Latitude births)*   LST+12 = <u>   </u>:<u>   </u>:<u>   </u>

CM-1
(Constant Multiplier for Part C: Planetary Position)

Convert GMT of Birth to decimal: <u> 2.87 </u> ÷ 24 = **CM-1** <u> .120 </u>

Lesson 13: Natal Chart Exams - Answer Key (continued)

	☉	☽	☿	♀	♂	♃
1.Position at 0 hr on day After birth date 8/16/83	21° ♌ 95' ~~22° ♌ 35'~~	27° ♏ 67' ~~28° ♏ 07'~~	19° ♍ 41'	6° ♍ 37' ℞	0° ♌ 89' ~~1° ♌ 29'~~	1° ♐ 33'
2.Position at 0 hr on Birth date 8/15/83	21° ♌ 37'	15° ♏ 12'	18° ♍ 33'	6° ♍ 64' ℞ ~~7° ♍ 04' ℞~~	0° ♌ 50'	1° ♐ 30'
3. Line 1 - Line 2 = Total Daily Travel	58'	12° 55' = 775'	1° 08' = 68'	- 27' ℞	39'	3'
4. Line 3 X CM-1 __.120__ = Travel to birth time	7'	93' = 1° 33'	8'	3' ℞	5'	0'
5. Add lines 2 + 4 = Position at Birth	21° ♌ 44'	16° ♏ 45'	18° ♍ 41'	7° ♍ 01' ℞	0° ♌ 55'	1° ♐ 30'

	♄	♅	♆	♇	☊	
6.Position at 0 hr on day After birth date 8/16/83	29° ♎ 22'	5° ♐ 04'	26° ♐ 36' ℞	27° ♎ 09'	23° ♊ 18'	
7. Position at 0 hr on Birth date 8/15/83	29° ♎ 18'	5° ♐ 04'	26° ♐ 37' ℞	27° ♎ 08'	23° ♊ 19'	
8. Line 6 - Line 7 = Total Daily Travel	4'	0'	- 1' ℞	1'	-1' ℞	
9. Line 8 X CM-1 _.120__ = Travel to birth time	0'	0'	0'	0'	0'	
10. Add lines 7 + 9 = Position at Birth	29° ♎ 18'	5° ♐ 04'	26° ♐ 37' ℞	27° ♎ 08'	23° ♊ 19'	

CM-2
(Constant Multiplier for LST Interpolation)

LST of Birth	2 : 28 : 48
- Next lowest Sid Time from Table	- 2 : 28 : 00
	= 00 : 48
Convert result to decimal	.8
÷ 4 = CM-2	.2

CM-3
(Constant Multiplier for Latitude Interpolation)

Latitude of Birth	30 ° 03 '
- Next lowest Latitude from Table	- 30 ° 00 '
	= 00 ° 03 '
Convert result to decimal	= CM-3 = .05
Exception: If Birth Latitude is less than 20°, divide result by 5	÷ 5 = CM-3 _____

House Cusp Calculation for Higher Latitude

Latitude __31°__	MC	11th	12th	ASC	2nd	3rd
1. House Cusps at Later Sid Time **(2:32:00)**	10° ♉ 25'	13° ♊ 69' ~~14° ♊ 09'~~	15° ♋ 73' ~~16° ♋ 13'~~	14° ♌ 94' ~~15° ♌ 34'~~	8° ♍ 99' ~~9° ♍ 39'~~	8° ♎ 01'
2. House Cusps at Earlier Sid Time **(2:28:00)**	9° ♉ 24'	13° ♊ 12'	15° ♋ 20'	14° ♌ 44'	8° ♍ 44'	7° ♎ 01'
3. Line 1 - Line 2 =	1° 01' = 61'	57'	53'	50'	55'	1° = 60'
4. Line 3 X CM-2 __ .2 __ =	12'	11'	11'	10'	11'	12'
5. Add lines 2 + 4 =	9° ♉ 36'	13° ♊ 23'	15° ♋ 31'	14° ♌ 54'	8° ♍ 55'	7° ♎ 13'

House Cusp Calculation for Lower Latitude

Latitude __30°__		11th	12th	ASC	2nd	3rd
6. House Cusps at Later Sid Time **(2:32:00)**		13° ♊ 58'	14° ♋ 113' ~~15° ♋ 53'~~	14° ♌ 74' ~~15° ♌ 14'~~	8° ♍ 92' ~~9° ♍ 32'~~	8° ♎ 02'
7. House Cusps at Earlier Sid Time **(2:28:00)**		13° ♊ 01'	14° ♋ 59'	14° ♌ 23'	8° ♍ 37'	7° ♎ 02'
8. Line 6 - Line 7 =		57'	54'	51'	55'	1° = 60'
9. Line 3 X CM-2 _ .2 __ =		11'	11'	10'	11'	12'
10. Add lines 7 + 9 =		13° ♊ 12'	14° ♋ 70' = 15° ♋ 10'	14° ♌ 33'	8° ♍ 48'	7° ♎ 14'

Latitude Interpolation

		11th	12th	ASC	2nd	3rd
11. House Cusps at Higher Latitude (from line 5)		13° ♊ 23'	15° ♋ 31'	14° ♌ 54'	8° ♍ 55'	7° ♎ 13'
12. House Cusps at Lower Latitude (from line 10)		13° ♊ 12'	15° ♋ 10'	14° ♌ 33'	8° ♍ 48'	7° ♎ 14'
13. Line 11 - Line 12 =		11'	21'	21'	7'	-1' Rx
14. Line 13 X CM-3 _ .05 __ =		1'	1'	1'	0'	0'
15. Add lines 12 + 14 = **House Cusps at Birth**		13° ♊ 13'	15° ♋ 11'	14° ♌ 34'	8° ♍ 48'	7° ♎ 14'

Exam 1 (continued)

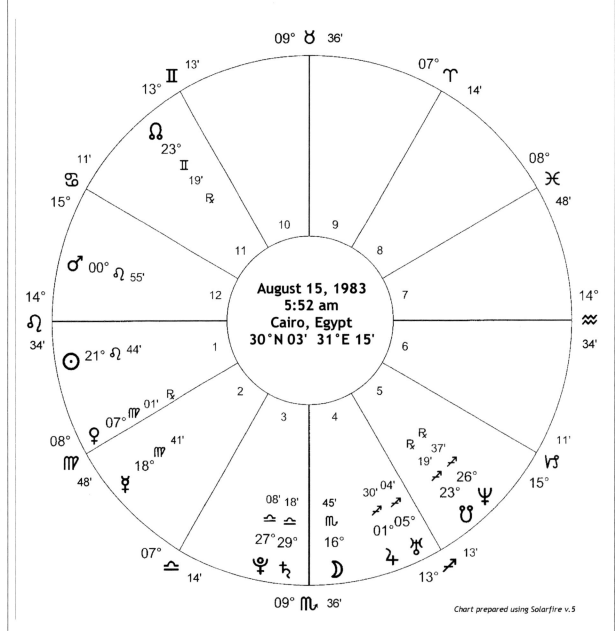

August 15, 1983
5:52 am
Cairo, Egypt
30°N 03' 31°E 15'

Chart prepared using Solarfire v.5

Lesson 13: Natal Chart Exams - Answer Key

Exam 2. (Completed natal chart is shown on page 346.)

April 10, 1995, 10:50 pm
Seattle, WA 47°N 36' 122°W 20'

Part A: GMT of Birth

1. Given Time of Birth   _10_ : _50_ am / (pm)

2. + PM Adjustment *(+12:00 if pm)*   +   _12_ : _00_

3. +/-Time Zone

    a. Standard Time Zone *(+W, -E)*   _8_ : _00_

    b. DST Adjustment *(- 1:00 if DST)*   - _1_ : _00_
    (Include only if not already factored into (a) above)

    c. = Time Zone Adjustment *(Enter on Line 3, right)* = _7_ : _00_ ⟶ (+W)-E _7_ : _00_

                                       Subtotal = _29_: _50_

4. +/- 24 hours if date change required   ⟶ +(-) _24_ : _00_

5. = GMT of Birth   Date _April 11, 1995_   Time = _5_ : _50_

Part B: LST of Birth

6. Sidereal Time at 0 hr on birth date *(from ephemeris; use birth date from Step 5)*   _13_: _14_ : _58_

7. + GMT of birth *(from Step 5)*   _5_ : _50_ : _00_

8. + Solar/Sidereal Time Correction on GMT *(from Table or calculate below:)*   __ : _57_

    (GMT *(as decimal)* _5.83_ hrs x 9.86 secs = _57_)   Subtotal = _18_ : _64_ : _115_

9. +/- Longitude/Time Equivalent *(from Atlas or calculate below; -W, +E)*   +(-) _8_ : _09_ : _19_

    (Longitude *(as decimal)* _122.33_ x 4 min = _489.32_)   Subtotal = _10_ : _55_ : _96_
                                           Or 10   56   36

10. +/- 24:00:00 if required   +/- ___ : ___ : ___

11. = LST of Birth   LST = _10_: _56_ : _36_

- - - - - - - - - -

12. Southern Latitude Adjustment *(+/- 12:00:00 if Southern Latitude)*   +/- ___ : ___ : ___

13. "LST + 12" *(use in place of LST for Southern Latitude births)*   LST+12 = ___ : ___ : ___

CM-1
(Constant Multiplier for Part C: Planetary Position)

Convert GMT of Birth to decimal: _5.83_ ÷ 24 = CM-1 _.243_

Lesson 13: Natal Chart Exams - Answer Key (continued)

	☉	☽	☿	♀	♂	♃
1. Position at 0 hr on day After birth date 4/12/95	20°♈ 98' ~~21°♈ 38'~~	35°♌ 44' ~~5°♍ 44'~~	18°♈ 52'	17°♓ 45'	14°♌ 63' ~~15°♌ 03'~~	15°♐ 13'℞
2. Position at 0 hr on Birth date 4/11/95	20°♈ 39'	22°♌ 33'	16°♈ 49'	16°♓ 32'	14°♌ 51'	15°♐ 15'℞
3. Line 1 - Line 2 = Total Daily Travel	59'	13° 11' = 791'	2° 03' = 123'	1° 13' = 73'	12'	-2' ℞
4. Line 3 X CM-1 __.243__ = Travel to birth time	14'	192' = 3° 12'	30'	18'	3'	0'
5. Add lines 2 + 4 = Position at Birth	20°♈ 53'	25°♌ 45'	16°♈ 79' 17°♈ 19'	16°♓ 50'	14°♌ 54'	15°♐ 15'℞

	♄	♅	♆	♇	☊	
6. Position at 0 hr on day After birth date 4/12/95	19°♓ 24'	0°♒ 15'	25°♑ 29'	0°♐ 12' ℞	5°♏ 39' ℞	
7. Position at 0 hr on Birth date 4/11/95	19°♓ 17'	0°♒ 14'	25°♑ 28'	0°♐ 13' ℞	5°♏ 41' ℞	
8. Line 6 - Line 7 = Total Daily Travel	7'	1'	1'	1' ℞	2' ℞	
9. Line 8 X CM-1 _.243__ = Travel to birth time	2'	0'	0'	0'	0'	
10. Add lines 7 + 9 = Position at Birth	19°♓ 19'	0°♒ 14'	25°♑ 28'	0°♐ 13' ℞	5°♏ 41' ℞	

CM-2
(Constant Multiplier for LST Interpolation)

LST of Birth	10 : 56 : 36
- Next lowest Sid Time from Table	-10 : 56 : 00
=	00 : 36
Convert result to decimal	.6
÷ 4 = CM-2	.15

CM-3
(Constant Multiplier for Latitude Interpolation)

Latitude of Birth	47° 36'
- Next lowest Latitude from Table	- 47° 00'
=	00° 36'
Convert result to decimal = CM-3 =	.6
Exception: If Birth Latitude is less than 20°, divide result by 5 ÷ 5 = CM-3	_____

House Cusp Calculation for Higher Latitude

Latitude __48°__	MC	11th	12th	ASC	2nd	3rd
1. House Cusps at Later Sid Time (11:00:00)	13° ♍ 43'	13° ♎ 63' ~~14° ♎ 03'~~	5° ♏ 108' ~~6° ♏ 48'~~	24° ♏ 53'	25° ♐ 72' ~~26° ♐ 12'~~	5° ♒ 09'
2. House Cusps at Earlier Sid Time (10:56:00)	12° ♍ 39'	13° ♎ 07'	5° ♏ 59'	24° ♏ 09'	25° ♐ 18'	4° ♒ 04'
3. Line 1 - Line 2 =	1° 04' = 64'	56'	49'	44'	54'	1° 05' = 65'
4. Line 3 X CM-2 __ .15 __ =	10'	8'	7'	7'	8'	10'
5. Add lines 2 + 4 =	12° ♍ 49'	13° ♎ 15'	5° ♏ 66' = 6° ♏ 06'	24° ♏ 16'	25° ♐ 26'	4° ♒ 14'

House Cusp Calculation for Lower Latitude

Latitude __47°__		11th	12th	ASC	2nd	3rd
6. House Cusps at Later Sid Time (11:00:00)		13° ♎ 67' ~~14° ♎ 07'~~	6° ♏ 66' ~~7° ♏ 06'~~	24° ♏ 89' ~~25° ♏ 29'~~	25° ♐ 111' ~~26° ♐ 51'~~	5° ♒ 27'
7. House Cusps at Earlier Sid Time (10:56:00)		13° ♎ 11'	6° ♏ 17'	24° ♏ 45'	25° ♐ 57'	4° ♒ 22'
8. Line 6 - Line 7 =		56'	49'	44'	54'	1° 05' = 65'
9. Line 3 X CM-2 _ .15 __ =		8'	7'	7'	8'	10'
10. Add lines 7 + 9 =		13° ♎ 19'	6° ♏ 24'	24° ♏ 52'	25° ♐ 65' = 26° ♐ 05'	4° ♒ 32'

Latitude Interpolation

		11th	12th	ASC	2nd	3rd
11. House Cusps at Higher Latitude (from line 5)		13° ♎ 15'	6° ♏ 06'	24° ♏ 16'	25° ♐ 26'	4° ♒ 14'
12. House Cusps at Lower Latitude (from line 10)		13° ♎ 19'	6° ♏ 24'	24° ♏ 52'	26° ♐ 05'	4° ♒ 32'
13. Line 11 - Line 12 =		- 4'	- 18'	- 36'	- 39'	- 18'
14. Line 13 X CM-3 _ .6 __ =		- 2'	- 11'	- 22'	- 23'	- 11'
15. Add lines 12 + 14 = **House Cusps at Birth**		13° ♎ 17'	6° ♏ 13'	24° ♏ 30'	25° ♐ 42'	4° ♒ 21'

Exam 2 (continued)

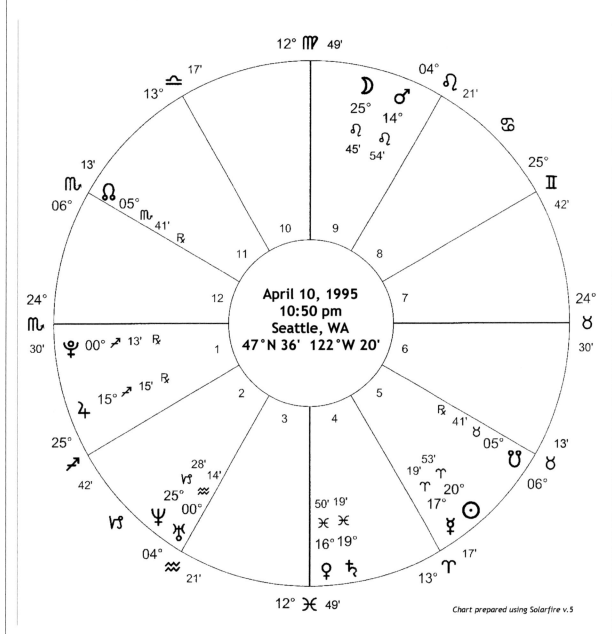

Chart prepared using Solarfire v.5

Lesson 13: Natal Chart Exams - Answer Key (continued)

Exam 3. (Completed natal chart is shown on page 350.)

January 5, 1961, 4:45 am
Perth, Australia 31°S 57' 115°E 51'

Part A: GMT of Birth

1. Given Time of Birth   __4_ :_45_ (am)/ pm

2. + PM Adjustment *(+12:00 if pm)*   + ___:___

3. +/-Time Zone
    a. Standard Time Zone *(+W, -E)*   _8_ :_00_

    b. DST Adjustment *(- 1:00 if DST)*   - ___:___
    (Include only if not already factored into (a) above)

    c. = Time Zone Adjustment *(Enter on Line 3, right)* = _8_ :_00_ ⟶ +(W),-E _8_ :_00_

                                            Subtotal = _-3_ : _15_

4. +/- 24 hours if date change required   (+/)- _24_ : _00_

5. = GMT of Birth   Date _Jan 4, 1961_   Time = _20_ : _45_

Part B: LST of Birth

6. Sidereal Time at 0 hr on birth date *(from ephemeris; use birth date from Step 5)*   _6_ : _53_ : _27_

7. + GMT of birth *(from Step 5)*   _20_ : _45_ : _00_

8. + Solar/Sidereal Time Correction on GMT *(from Table or calculate below:)*   _3_ : _25_

    (GMT *(as decimal)* _20.75_ hrs x 9.86 secs = ___205___)   Subtotal = _26_ :_101_ : _52_

9. +/- Longitude/Time Equivalent *(from Atlas or calculate below; -W, +E)*   (+)- _7_ : _43_ : _24_

    (Longitude *(as decimal)* _115.85_ x 4 min = ___463.4___)   Subtotal = _33_ :_144_ : _76_
                                                    Or 35 25   16

10. +/- 24:00:00 if required   +(-) _24_:_00_ :_00_

11. = LST of Birth   LST = _11_ : _25_ : _16_

12. Southern Latitude Adjustment *(+/- 12:00:00 if Southern Latitude)*   (+)- _12_ : _00_ : _00_

13. "LST + 12" *(use in place of LST for Southern Latitude births)*   LST+12 = _23_ : _25_ : _16_

CM-1
(Constant Multiplier for Part C: Planetary Position)

Convert GMT of Birth to decimal: _20.75_ ÷ 24 = **CM-1** _.865_

Lesson 13 Answer Key (continued)

	☉	☽	☿	♀	♂	♃
1. Position at 0 hr on day After birth date 1/5/61	14° ♑ 25'	16° ♌ 76' ~~17° ♌ 16'~~	13° ♑ 50'	29° ♒ 50'	6° ♋ 35' ℞	14° ♑ 61' ~~15° ♑ 01'~~
2. Position at 0 hr on Birth date 1/4/61	13° ♑ 24'	5° ♌ 28'	12° ♑ 14'	28° ♒ 42'	6° ♋ 58' ℞	14° ♑ 47'
3. Line 1 - Line 2 = Total Daily Travel	1° 01' 61'	11° 48' = 708'	1° 36' = 96'	1° 08' = 68'	-23' ℞	14'
4. Line 3 X CM-1 __.865__ = Travel to birth time	53'	612' = 10° 12'	83' = 1° 23'	59'	-20' ℞	12'
5. Add lines 2 + 4 = Position at Birth	13° ♑ 77 =14° ♑ 17'	15° ♌ 40'	13° ♑ 37'	28° ♒ 101' =29° ♒ 41	6° ♋ 38' ℞	14° ♑ 59'

	♄	♅	♆	♇	☊	
6. Position at 0 hr on day After birth date 1/5/61	19° ♑ 63' ~~20° ♑ 03'~~	25° ♌ 16' ℞	10° ♏ 55'	7° ♍ 58' ℞	7° ♍ 20' ℞	
7. Position at 0 hr on Birth date 1/4/61	19° ♑ 56'	25° ♌ 18' ℞	10° ♏ 54'	7° ♍ 59' ℞	7° ♍ 25' ℞	
8. Line 6 - Line 7 = Total Daily Travel	7'	-2' ℞	1'	- 1' ℞	-5' ℞	
9. Line 8 X CM-1 _.865__ = Travel to birth time	6'	-2' ℞	1'	- 1' ℞	-4' ℞	
10. Add lines 7 + 9 = Position at Birth	19° ♑ 62' 20° ♑ 02'	25° ♌ 16' ℞	10° ♏ 55'	7° ♍ 58' ℞	7° ♍ 21' ℞	

CM-2
(Constant Multiplier for LST Interpolation)

LST of Birth	23 25 16
- Next lowest Sid Time from Table	- 23 : 24 : 00
	= 1 : 16
Convert result to decimal	1.27
÷ 4 = CM-2	.318

CM-3
(Constant Multiplier for Latitude Interpolation)

Latitude of Birth	31° 57'
- Next lowest Latitude from Table	- 31° 00'
	= 00° 57'
Convert result to decimal	= CM-3 = __.95__
Exception: If Birth Latitude is *less than 20°, divide result by 5*	÷ 5 = CM-3 _____

348

House Cusp Calculation for Higher Latitude

Latitude __32°__	MC	11th	12th	ASC	2nd	3rd
1. House Cusps at Later Sid Time **(23:28:00)**	21° ♓ 17'	25° ♈ 61' ~~26° ♈ 01'~~	3° ♊ 12'	6° ♋ 58'	27° ♋ 110' ~~28° ♋ 50'~~	21° ♌ 98' ~~22° ♌ 38'~~
2. House Cusps at Earlier Sid Time **(23:24:00)**	20° ♓ 12'	24° ♈ 52'	2° ♊ 09'	6° ♋ 04'	27° ♋ 57'	21° ♌ 41'
3. Line 1 - Line 2 =	1° 05' = 65'	1° 09' = 69'	1° 03' = 63'	= 54'	53'	57'
4. Line 3 X CM-2 __ .318 __ =	21'	22'	20'	17'	17'	18'
5. Add lines 2 + 4 =	20° ♓ 33' **20° ♍ 33'**	24° ♈ 74' = 25° ♈ 14'	2° ♊ 29'	6° ♋ 21'	27° ♋ 74' = 28° ♋ 14'	=21° ♌ 59'

House Cusp Calculation for Lower Latitude

Latitude __31°__		11th	12th	ASC	2nd	3rd
6. House Cusps at Later Sid Time **(23:28:00)**		25° ♈ 55'	2° ♊ 49'	5° ♋ 85' ~~6° ♋ 25'~~	27° ♋ 91' ~~28° ♋ 31'~~	21° ♌ 91' ~~22° ♌ 31'~~
7. House Cusps at Earlier Sid Time **(23:24:00)**		24° ♈ 46'	1° ♊ 46'	5° ♋ 32'	27° ♋ 39'	21° ♌ 34'
8. Line 6 - Line 7 =		1° 09' = 69'	1° 03' = 63'	53'	52'	57'
9. Line 3 X CM-2 _ .318__ =		22'	20'	17'	17'	18'
10. Add lines 7 + 9 =		= 24° ♈ 68' = 25° ♈ 08'	1° ♊ 66' = 2° ♊ 06'	5° ♋ 49'	27° ♋ 56'	21° ♌ 52'

Latitude Interpolation

		11th	12th	ASC	2nd	3rd
11. House Cusps at Higher Latitude (from line 5)		25° ♈ 14'	2° ♊ 29'	5° ♋ 81' ~~6° ♋ 21'~~	27° ♋ 74' ~~28° ♋ 14'~~	21° ♌ 59'
12. House Cusps at Lower Latitude (from line 10)		25° ♈ 08'	2° ♊ 06'	5° ♋ 49'	27° ♋ 56'	21° ♌ 52'
13. Line 11 - Line 12 =		6'	23'	32'	18'	7'
14. Line 13 X CM-3 _ .95 __ =		6'	22'	30'	17'	7'
15. Add lines 12 + 14 = **House Cusps at Birth**		~~25° ♈ 14'~~ **25° ♎ 14'**	~~2° ♊ 28'~~ **2° ♐ 28'**	5° ♋ 79' =~~6° ♋ 19'~~ **6° ♑ 19'**	27° ♋ 73' =~~28° ♋ 13'~~ **28° ♑ 13'**	~~21° ♌ 59'~~ **21° ♒ 59'**

Exam 3 (continued)

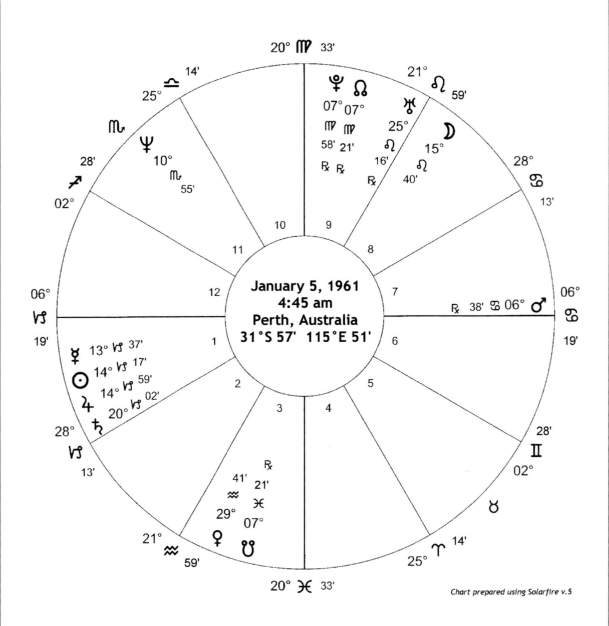

January 5, 1961
4:45 am
Perth, Australia
31°S 57' 115°E 51'

Chart prepared using Solarfire v.5

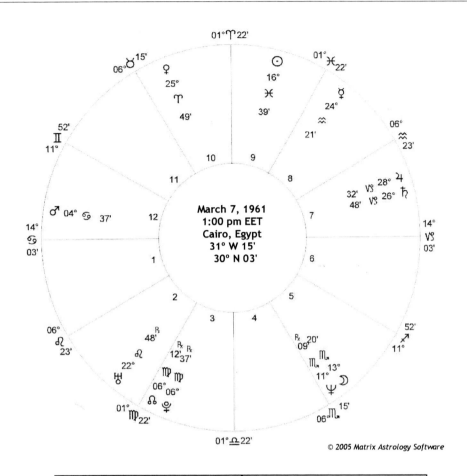

01°♈22'

06°♉15'
♀
25°
♈
49'

☉
16°
♓
39'

01°♓22'
☿
24°
♒
21'

06°
♒
23'

52'
♊
11°

10   9

8

32' ♑ 28° ♃
48' ♑ 26° ♄

14°
♑
03'

♂ 04° ♋ 37'
14°
♋
03'

12

March 7, 1961
1:00 pm EET
Cairo, Egypt
31° W 15'
30° N 03'

11

7

6

52'
♐
11°

06°
♌
23'

48' ℞
♌
22°
♅

℞ ℞
12' 37'
♍ ♍
06° 06'

2

3   4

5

℞ 20'
09° ♏
♏ 13°
11° ☽
☽

01°
♍ 22'
☊
06° ♏
15'
06° ♏

01°♎22'

© 2005 Matrix Astrology Software

Aspect	Orb	Aspect	Orb
Conjunction	8°	Semi-sextile	3°
Opposition	8°	Semi-square	4°
Trine	8°	Sextile	6°
Square	8°	Sesquisquare	2°
Sextile	6°	Quincunx	2°

1. The closest aspect in the chart is: ♀ ☌ ☊   **Separating with and orb of 25'**

2. What was the last aspect made by the Moon? ☽ ☌ ♆   **Separating , 2° 11' orb**

3. What is the next aspect made by the Moon? ☽ △ ASC   **Applying: 43' orb**

Lesson 14: Aspects - Answer Key

	☽ 13°♏20 / 223.33	☉ 16°♓39 / 346.65	☿ 24°♒21 / 324.35	♀ 25°♈49 / 25.82	♂ 4°♋37 / 94.62	♃ 28°♑32 / 298.53	♄ 26°♑48 / 296.80	♅ 22°♌48 / 142.80	♆ 11°♏09 / 221.15	♇ 6°♍37 / 156.62	☊ 6°♍12 / 156.20	ASC 14°♋03 / 104.05	MC 1°♈22 / 1.37
☽ 13°♏20 / 223.33		223.33 =123.32 △	223.33 =101.02	223.33 197.51 -360 =162.49	223.33 =128.71	223.33 =75.2	223.33 =73.47	223.33 =80.53	223.33 =2.18 ☌	223.33 =66.71	223.33 =67.13	223.33 =119.28 △	223.33 =221.96 -360 =138.1
☉ 16°♓39 / 346.65	△		346.65 =22.3	346.65 320.83 -360 =39.17	346.65 252.03 -360 =107.97	346.65 =48.12 ∠	346.65 =49.85	346.65 203.85 =156.15	346.65 =125.5 △	346.65 190.03 -360 =169.97	346.65 190.45 -360 =169.55	346.65 242.6 -360 =117.4 △	346.65 345.28 -360 =14.72
☿ 24°♒21 / 324.35				324.35 298.53 -360 =61.47 ✳	324.35 229.73 -360 =130.27	324.35 =25.82	324.35 =27.55 ⚺	324.35 =181.55 ☍	324.35 =103.2	324.35 =167.73	324.35 =168.15	324.35 =220.3	324.35 322.98 -360 =37.02
♀ 25°♈49 / 25.82			✳		25.82 =68.8	25.82 272.71 -360 =87.29 □	25.82 271.98 -360 =89.02 □	25.82 =116.98 △	25.82 195.33 -360 =164.67	25.82 =130.8	25.82 =130.38	25.82 =78.23	25.82 =24.45
♂ 4°♋37 / 94.62						94.62 203.91 -360 =156.09	94.62 202.18 -360 =157.82	94.62 =48.18 ∠	94.62 =126.53 △	94.62 =62.0 ✳	94.62 =61.58 ✳	94.62 =9.43	94.62 =93.25 □
♃ 28°♑32 / 298.53		∠		□			298.53 =1.73 ☌	298.53 =155.73	298.53 =77.38	298.53 =141.91	298.53 =142.33	298.53 194.48 -360 =165.52	298.53 297.16 -360 =62.84 ✳
♄ 26°♑48 / 296.80			⚺	□	☌			296.80 =154.0	296.80 =75.65	296.80 =140.18	296.80 =140.6	296.80 192.75 -360 =167.25	296.80 295.43 -360 =64.57 ✳
♅ 22°♌48 / 142.80			☍	△	∠				142.80 =78.35	142.80 =13.82	142.80 =13.4	142.80 =38.75	142.80 =141.4
♆ 11°♏09 / 221.15	☌	△		△				△		221.15 =64.53 ✳	221.15 =64.95 ✳	221.15 =117.1 △	221.15 219.78 -360 =140.2
♇ 6°♍37 / 156.62				✳				✳			156.62 =.42 ☌	156.62 =52.57	156.62 =155.2
☊ 6°♍12 / 156.20				✳				✳	☌			156.20 =52.15	156.20 =154.8
ASC 14°♋03 / 104.05	△	△							△				104.05 =102.6
MC 1°♈22 / 1.37					□	✳	✳						

Lesson 15: Declinations - Answer Key

February 2, 1995 at 8:02 GMT, Asc: 21° ♒ 23', MC: 13° ♐ 55'

(N = +, S = -)	☽	☉	☿	♀	♂	♃	♄
1. Declination 0 hr day after birth date **2/03/95**	+0° 21' N	-16° 43' S	-12° 49' S	-20° 42' S	+16°55' N	-21° 17' S	-8° 57' S
2. Declination 0 hr on Birth date **2/02/95**	-4° 07' S	-17° 00' S	-12° 37' S	-20° 37' S	+16°46' N	-21° 15' S	-9° 00' S
3. Line 1 - Line 2 = Total Daily Change in Declination	4° 28' = 268'	17'	-12'	-5'	9'	-2'	3'
4. Line 3 X CM-1 **.335** = Declination change to Birth GMT	90' = 1° 30'	6'	-4'	-2'	3'	-1'	1'
5. Add lines 2 + 4 = Declination at Birth (N = +, S = -)	-2° 37' S	-16° 54' S	-12° 41' S	-20° 39' S	+16°49' N	-21° 16' S	-8° 59' S

♅ -21° 11' S   ♆ -20° 49' S   ♇ -7° 01' S   ☊ -14° 43' S

Ascendant Declination Calculation		Midheaven Declination Calculation		Declinations Listed in Ascending order	
Zodiacal Position **21° ♒ 23'** Convert minutes to decimal = CM **.38** *(use for Step 4 below)*	**Asc**	Zodiacal Position **13° ♐ 55'** Convert minutes to decimal = CM **.92** *(use for Step 4 below)*	**MC**	☽	2° 37' S
1. **Declination** of next highest listed zodiacal degree **22° ♒ 00'**	-14° 11' S	1. **Declination** of next highest listed zodiacal degree **14° ♐ 00'**	-22° 30' S	♇	7° 01' S
				♄	8° 59' S
2. **Declination** of next lowest listed zodiacal degree **21° ♒ 00'**	-14° 31' S	2. **Declination** of next lowest listed zodiacal degree **13° ♐ 00'**	-22° 23' S	☿	12° 41' S
				ASC	14° 23' S
3. Line 1 - Line 2 = Change in Declination	20'	3. Line 1 - Line 2 = Change in Declination	-7'	☊	14° 43' S
				♂	16° 49' N
4. Line 3 x CM **.38**	8'	4. Line 3 x CM **.92**	-6'	☉	16° 54' S
				♀	20° 39' S
Add lines 2+4 = ASC Declination at Birth (N = +, S = -)	-14° 23' S	Add lines 2+4 = MC Declination at Birth (N = +, S = -)	-22° 29' S	♆	20° 49' S
				♅	21° 11' S
				♃	21° 16' S
				MC	22° 29' S

Parallel and Contraparallel Aspects

Asc ‖ ☊   ☉ # ♅ ♂   ♀ ‖ ♆   ♀ ‖ ♅   ♀ ‖ ♃   ♃ ‖ ♆   ♃ ‖ ♅   ♅ ‖ ♆

Lesson 16: Midpoints & Antiscia - Answer Key

1. ♆/♇ Midpoint

♆ 20° ♍ 26' = 170.43
♇ 28° ♋ 27' = + 118.45
288.88 ÷ 2 = 144.44

Closest Midpoint = 24° ♌ 26'

2. ASC/MC Midpoint

ASC 9° ♊ 53' = 69.88
MC 14° ♒ 54' = + 314.90
384.78 ÷ 2 = 192.39
= 12° ♎ 23'

Closest Midpoint = 12° ♈ 23'

(Notice that this calculation resulted in the farther midpoint 12° ♎ 39', not the nearer midpoint 12° ♈ 23'.)

3. ☉/☽ Midpoint

☉ 25° ♒ 22' = 325.37
☽ 25° ♌ 14' = + 145.23
470.60 ÷ 2 = 235.30

Two Strong 25° ♏ 18'
Midpoints = 25° ♉ 18'

(Because the Sun and Moon are in exact opposition by degree, both midpoints will be equally strong.)

4. Antiscion of ♅

♅ 10° ♉ 03' = 40.05

90° + (90° - 40.05) = 139.95

Antiscion = 19° ♌ 57'

5. Antiscion of ☉

☉ 25° ♒ 22' = 325.37

270° + (270° - 325.37) = 214.63

Antiscion = 4° ♏ 38'

6. Antiscion of ASC

ASC 9° ♊ 53' = 69.88

90° + (90° - 69.88) = 110.12

Antiscion = 20° ♋ 07'

Part of Fortune: Male (Diurnal)

Ascendant		10.40	(10°♈24' in absolute longitude)
+ Moon	+	134.32	(14°♌19' in absolute longitude)
- Sun	-	346.22	(16°♓13' in absolute longitude)
	=	-201.50	
	+	360.00	+ or - 360°
= Part of Fortune	=	158.50	= 8°♍30'

Part of Spirit: Male (Diurnal)

Ascendant		10.40	(10°♈24' in absolute longitude)
+ Sun	+	346.22	(16°♓13' in absolute longitude)
- Moon	-	134.32	(14°♌19' in absolute longitude)
= Part of Spirit	=	222.30	= 12°♏18'

Part of Marriage: Male

Ascendant		10.40	(10°♈24' in absolute longitude)
+ Venus	+	303.52	(3°♒31' in absolute longitude)
- Saturn	-	317.57	(17°♒34' in absolute longitude)
	=	- 3.65	
	+	360.00	+ or - 360°
= Part of Marriage	=	356.35	= 26°♓21'

Lesson 17: Arabic Parts - Answer Key (continued)

Part of Fortune: Female (Nocturnal)

Ascendant		114.82	(24°♋ 49' in absolute longitude)
+ Sun	+	256.00	(16°♐ 00' in absolute longitude)
- Moon	-	346.37	(16°♓ 22' in absolute longitude)
= Part of Fortune	=	24.45	= 24°♈ 27'

Part of Spirit: Female (Nocturnal)

Ascendant		114.82	(24°♋ 49' in absolute longitude)
+ Moon	+	346.37	(16°♓ 22' in absolute longitude)
- Sun	-	256.00	(16°♐ 00' in absolute longitude)
= Part of Spirit	=	205.19	= 25°♎ 11'

Part of Marriage: Female

Ascendant		114.82	(24°♋ 49' in absolute longitude)
+ Saturn	+	5.65	(5°♈ 39' in absolute longitude)
- Venus	-	211.62	(1°♏ 37' in absolute longitude)
	=	- 91.15	
	+	360.00	+ or - 360°
= Part of Marriage	=	268.85	= 28°♐ 51'

Lesson 18: Equatorial Ascendant & Vertex - Answer Key

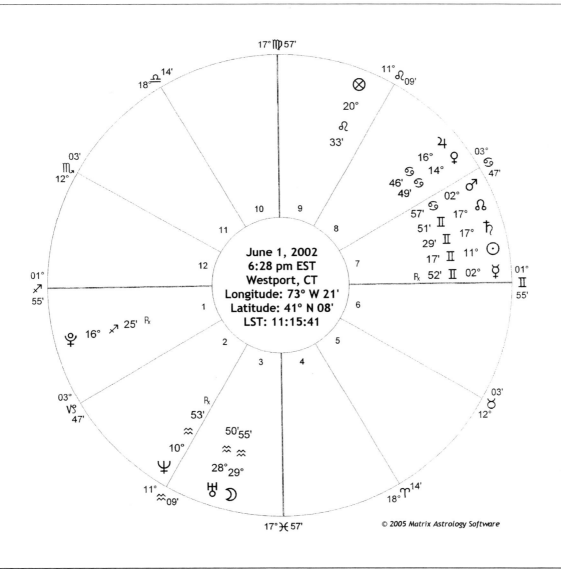

17° ℏ 57'

18° ♎ 14'

11° ♌ 09'

⊗

20°
♌
33'

03°
03' ♍

♏ 03'
12°

16° ♋ ♃
14° ♀
46' ♋
49' ♋
02°
57' ♋ 17' ☊
51' ♊ 17'
29' ♊ 11° ♄
17' ♊
Rx 52' ♊ 02° ☿

01°
♐
55'

June 1, 2002
6:28 pm EST
Westport, CT
Longitude: 73° W 21'
Latitude: 41° N 08'
LST: 11:15:41

01°
♊
55'

16° ♐ 25' Rx
♇

03°
♑
47'

Rx
53'
♒
50' 55'
10° ♒ ♒
28' ♒ 29'
♅ ☽

03°
♉
12°

11°
♒ 09'

17° ♓ 57'

18° ♈ 14'

© 2005 Matrix Astrology Software

Equatorial Ascendant Calculation

CM-2 *(Constant Multiplier for Equatorial Ascendant Interpolation)*		Latitude 0°	Equatorial ASC
		1. Asc at Later Sid Time (11:16:00)	♐ 19° 53'
LST of Birth	11 : 15 : 41	2. Asc at Earlier Sid Time (11:12:00)	♐ 18° 58'
- Next lowest Sid Time from Table	- 11 : 12 : 00	3. Line 1 - Line 2 =	55'
=	3 : 41		
Convert result to decimal	3.68	4. Line 3 X CM-2 = .92	51'
÷ 4 = CM-2	.92	5. Add lines 2 + 4 = **Equatorial Ascendant =**	♐ 18° 109' = ♐ 19° 49'

357

Lesson 18: Equatorial Ascendant & Vertex - Answer Key (continued)

Vertex Calculation for:		Vertex Interpolation At Higher Latitude		

Vertex Calculation for:

Name: **Lesson 19 Answer Key**

Birth Latitude: <u>41° N 08'</u> Birth IC: <u>17° ♓ 57'</u>

Co-Latitude:

90°:		**90.00°**
- Birth Latitude *(as decimal):*	-	<u>41.13</u>
= Co-Latitude:	=	**48.87**
	=	**48 ° N 52'**

Co-Latitude 49°	ASC
1. ASC at Higher MC(18° ♓ 02')	16° ♋ 04'
2. ASC at Lower MC (16° ♓ 57')	15° ♋ 16'
3. Line 1 - Line 2 =	48'
4. Line 3 X CM-V .92 =	44'
5. Add lines 2 + 4 =	16° ♋ 00'

CM-V
(Constant Multiplier for Vertex Interpolation)

A. IC of Birth	17°	♓	57'	
- Next lowest MC from Table	- 16°	♓	57'	
= Difference			1°	
B. Higher listed MC	18°	♓	02'	
- Lower listed MC	- 16°	♓	57'	
= Interval between MCs	1°		05'	
		or	65'	

(A) <u>60</u> ÷ *(B)* <u>65</u> = **CM-V: .92**

Divide the difference from part A by interval from B.

Vertex Interpolation At Lower Latitude

Co-Latitude 48°	ASC
6. ASC at Higher MC (18° ♓ 02')	15° ♋ 12'
7. ASC at Lower MC (16° ♓ 57')	14° ♋ 24'
8. Line 6 - Line 7 =	48'
9. Line 8 X CM-V .92 =	44'
10. Add lines 7 + 9 =	15° ♋ 08'

CM-3
(Constant Multiplier for Latitude Interpolation)

Co-Latitude of Birth	48° N 52'
- Next lowest Latitude from Table	48° 00'
=	52'
Convert result to decimal = CM-3	.87

Exception: If Co-Latitude is less than 20°, divide result by 5   ÷ 5 = CM-3 _____

Vertex Latitude Interpolation

11. Asc at Higher Latitude (from line 5)	16° ♋ 00'
12. Asc. at Lower Latitude (from line 10)	15° ♋ 08'
13. Line 11 - Line 12 =	52'
14. Line 13 X CM-3 .87 =	45'
15. Add lines 12 + 14 = **Vertex at Birth**	15° ♋ 53'

Lesson 19: Lunar Phases - Answer Key

1. Natal Lunar Phase = New Phase

Moon		142.77°
- Sun	-	117.37°
= Natal Lunar Phase	=	25.4

2. Pluto and Mercury are in the Disseminating Phase

Mercury (faster)		143.28°
	+	360.00
subtotal		503.28
- Pluto (slower)	-	259.98°
= Phase	=	243.3

3. Mars and Venus are in the Third Quarter Phase.

Venus (faster)		76.07°
	+	360.00
subtotal		436.07
- Mars (slower)	-	136.30°
= Phase	=	299.77

4. The Prenatal Eclipse was a total lunar eclipse occurring on May 4, 2004 at 20:31 GMT, at 14°♏ 42'.

Lesson 20: Section Exam - Answer Key

	☽ 1°♑01' 271.02	☉ 6°♊51' 66.85	☿ 5°♊14 ℞ 65.23	♀ 9°♋20' 99.33	♂ 29°♊55' 89.92	♃ 15°♋51' 105.85	♄ 16°♊53' 76.88	♅ 28°♒49' 328.82	♆ 10°♒55℞ 310.92	♇ 16°♐32 ℞ 256.53	☊ 17°♊45' 77.75	ASC 16°♌37' 136.62	MC 28°♈28 28.47
☽ 1°♑1' 271.02		271.02 204.17 -360 155.83	271.02 205.79 -360 154.21	271.02 171.69	271.02 181.11 ☍	271.02 165.17	271.02 194.14 -360 165.86	271.02 57.8 ✶	271.02 39.9	271.02 14.49	271.02 193.27 -360 166.73	271.02 134.4 ⚼	271.02 242.55 -360 117.45 △
☉ 6°♊51' 66.85			66.85 1.62 ☌	66.85 32.48 ⚺	66.85 23.07	66.85 39.0	66.85 10.03	66.85 261.97 - 360 98.03	66.85 244.97 - 360 115.93 △	66.85 189.68 - 360 170.32	66.85 10.9	66.85 69.77	66.85 38.38
☿ 5°♊14'℞ 65.23		☌		65.23 34.1	65.23 24.69	65.23 40.62	65.23 11.65	65.23 263.59 -360 96.41 □	65.23 245.69 -360 114.31 △	65.23 191.3 -360 168.7	65.23 12.52	65.23 71.39	65.23 36.76
♀ 9°♋20' 99.33		⚺			99.33 9.41	99.33 6.52 ☌	99.33 22.45	99.33 229.49 -360 130.51	99.33 211.59 -360 148.41 ⚻	99.33 157.2	99.33 21.58	99.33 37.29	99.33 70.86
♂ 29°♊55' 89.92	☍					89.92 15.93	89.92 13.04	89.92 238.9 -360 121.1 △	89.92 221.0 -360 139.0	89.92 166.61	89.92 12.17	89.92 46.7 ∠	89.92 61.45 ✶
♃ 15°♋51' 105.85				☌			105.85 28.97 ⚺	105.85 222.97 -360 137.03	105.85 205.07 -360 154.93	105.85 150.68 ⚻	105.85 28.1 ⚺	105.85 30.77 ⚺	105.85 77.38
♄ 16°♊53' 76.88						⚺		76.88 251.9 -360 108.06	76.88 234.04 -360 125.96 △	76.88 179.65 ☍	76.88 .87 ☌	76.88 59.74 ✶	76.88 48.41 ∠
♅ 28°♒49' 328.82	✶		□		△				328.82 17.9	328.82 72.29	328.82 251.07 -360 108.93	328.82 192.2 -360 167.8	328.82 300.35 -360 59.65 ✶
♆ 10°♒55'℞ 310.92		△	△	⚻			△			310.92 54.39 ✶	310.92 233.17 -360 126.83 △	310.92 174.3 ☍	310.92 282.45 -360 77.55
♇ 16°♐32'℞ 256.53						⚻	☍		✶		256.53 178.78 ☍	256.53 119.91 △	256.53 228.06 -360 131.94
☊ 17°♊45' 77.75						⚺	☌		△	☍		77.75 58.87 ✶	77.75 49.28
ASC 16°♌37' 136.62	⚼				∠	⚺	✶		☍	△	✶		136.62 108.15
MC 28°♈28 28.47	△				✶		∠	✶					

(N = +, S = -)	☽	☉	☿	♀	♂	♃	♄
1. Declination 0 hr day after birth date 5/29/02	24° 63' ~~-25° 03' S~~	+21°33' N	+18°54' N	+24°49' N	+24°25' N	+22°44' N	+21°30' N
2. Declination 0 hr on Birth date 5/28/02	-24°08' S	+21°24' N	+19°16' N	+24°53' N	+24°25' N	+22°45' N	+21°29' N
3. Line 1 - Line 2 = Total Daily Change in Declination	55'	9'	-22'	-4'	0	-1'	1'
4. Line 3 X CM-1 .363 = Declination change to Birth GMT	20'	3'	-8'	-1'	0	0	0
5. Add lines 2 + 4 = Declination at Birth (N = +, S = -)	-24°28' S	+21°27' N	+19°08' N	+24°52' N	+24°25' N	+22°45' N	+21°29' N

♅ -12° 35' S   Ψ -17° 25' S   ♇ -12° 40' S   ☊ +22° 53' N

Ascendant Declination Calculation		Midheaven Declination Calculation		Declinations Listed in Ascending order
Zodiacal Position 16° ♌ 37' Convert minutes to decimal = CM .62 *(use for Step 4 below)*	Asc	Zodiacal Position 28° ♈ 28' Convert minutes to decimal = CM .47 *(use for Step 4 below)*	MC	MC 10° 56' N
1. **Declination** of next highest listed zodiacal degree 17° ♌	+15 ° 45' N	1. **Declination** of next highest listed zodiacal degree 29° ♈	10 ° 68' +11 ° ~~08~~ N	♅ 12° 35' S
				♇ 12° 40' S
2. **Declination** of next lowest listed zodiacal degree 16° ♌	+16 ° 03' N	2. **Declination** of next lowest listed zodiacal degree 28° ♈	+10 ° 46' N	ASC 15° 52' N
				Ψ 17° 25' S
3. Line 1 - Line 2 = Change in Declination	-18'	3. Line 1 - Line 2 = Change in Declination	22'	☿ 19° 08' N
				☉ 21° 27' N
				♄ 21° 29' N
4. Line 3 x CM .62	-11'	4. Line 3 x CM .47	10'	♃ 22° 45' N
				☊ 22° 53' N
				♂ 24° 25' N
Add lines 2+4 = ASC Declination at Birth (N = +, S = -)	+15 ° 52' N	Add lines 2+4 = MC Declination at Birth (N = +, S = -)	+10 ° 56' N	☽ 24° 28' S
				♀ 24° 52' N

Parallel and Contraparallel Aspects

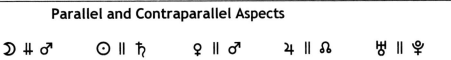

☽ ‖ ♀   ☽ ‖ ♂   ☉ ‖ ♄   ♀ ‖ ♂   ♃ ‖ ☊   ♅ ‖ ♇

3. **What is the closest aspect in this Chart?** ♀ △ Ascendant, 5' orb

4. **Which was the last aspect made by the Moon?** ☽ ☌ ♂ 1° 06' separating orb

5. **What will be the next aspect made by the Moon?** ☽ ☍ ♀

    This aspect has an orb of 8° 19', just out of the given allowable orb of 8° for an opposition. However because the Moon is applying toward the opposition to Venus, the Moon will soon move within the allowable 8° orb.

6. **What aspect is made between Mars and the Ascendant?** ∠ (semi-square)

7. **What is the midpoint between Saturn and Jupiter?** 1° ♋ 22'

    $$
    \begin{aligned}
    ♃ \text{ position} &= 105.85° \text{ (15° ♋ 51' in absolute longitude)} \\
    + ♄ \text{ position} &= + 76.88° \text{ (16° ♊ 53' in absolute longitude)} \\
    &= 182.73° \\
    ÷ 2 = {}& 91.37 = 1° ♋ 22'
    \end{aligned}
    $$

8. **Calculate the antiscion of the Sun:** 23° ♋ 09'

    Sun's position 66.85° (6° ♊ 51' in absolute longitude)
    Antiscion = 90° + (90° − 66.85) = 90° + 23.15 = 113.15 or **23° ♋ 09'**

9. **Calculate the antiscion of the Moon:** 28° ♐ 59'

    Moon's position 271.02° (1° ♑ 01' in absolute longitude)
    Antiscion = 270° + (270° − 271.02) = 270° + -1.02 = 268.98 or **28° ♐ 59'**

10. **Calculate the Natal Lunar Phase:** Full Phase

Moon	271.02°
- Sun	- 66.85°
= Lunar Phase	= 204.17°

11. **Calculate Part of Fortune:** 10° ♓ 47'

    Day Birth Formula:

	Ascendant	136.62
	+ Moon	+ 271.02
	- Sun	- 66.85
	= Part of Fortune	340.79° = **10° ♓ 47'**

12. **Calculate the Equatorial Ascendant** 24° ♋ 32' **& the Vertex:** 7° ♑ 18'

    (Calculations for Equatorial Ascendant and Vertex are shown on the following page.)

CM-2		Latitude 0°	Equatorial ASC
(Constant Multiplier for Equatorial Ascendant Interpolation)		1. Asc at Later Sid Time (1:48:00)	24 ° 63' ♋ 25° 03'
LST of Birth	1 : 45 : 49	2. Asc at Earlier Sid Time (1:44:00)	♋ 24°06'
- Next lowest Sid Time from Table	- 1 : 44 : 00	3. Line 1 - Line 2 =	57'
=	1 : 49	4. Line 3 X CM-2 = .46	26'
Convert result to decimal	1.82	5. Add lines 2 + 4 = Equatorial Ascendant =	= ♋ 24° 32'
÷ 4 = CM-2	.46		

12. Vertex Calculation for:		Vertex Interpolation At Higher Latitude	
		Co-Latitude 37°	ASC
Name: <u>Woman</u>		1. ASC at Higher MC 29 ° ♎ 03'	6° 88' ♑ 7° 28'
Birth Latitude: 53 ° N 33' Birth IC: 28 ° ♎ 28'		2. ASC at Lower MC 28 ° ♎ 00'	♑ 6° 30'
Co-Latitude:		3. Line 1 - Line 2 =	58'
90°: 90.00°		4. Line 3 X CM-V .44 =	26'
Birth Latitude *(as decimal)*: - 53.55		5. Add lines 2 + 4 =	♑ 6° 56'
= Co-Latitude: = 36.45° or 36 ° 27'			

CM-V		Vertex Interpolation At Lower Latitude	
(Constant Multiplier for Vertex Interpolation)		Co-Latitude 36°	ASC
A. IC of Birth	28 ° ♎ 28'	6. ASC at Higher MC 29 ° ♎ 03'	7° 68' ♑ 8° 08'
- Next lowest MC from Table	- 28 ° ♎ 00'	7. ASC at Lower MC 28 ° ♎ 00'	♑ 7° 10'
= Difference	28'	8. Line 6 - Line 7 =	58'
B. Higher listed MC	29 ° ♎ 03'	9. Line 8 X CM-V .44 =	26'
- Lower listed MC	- 28 ° ♎ 00'	10. Add lines 7 + 9 =	♑ 7° 36'
= Interval between MCs	63'		
(A) 28' ÷ *(B)* 63' = CM-V: .44			
Divide the difference from part A by interval from B.			

CM-3		Vertex Latitude Interpolation	
(Constant Multiplier for Latitude Interpolation)		11. Asc at Higher Latitude (from line 5)	♑ 6° 56'
Co-Latitude of Birth	36° 27'	12. Asc. at Lower Latitude (from line 10)	♑ 7° 36'
- Next lowest Latitude from Table	36 ° 00'	13. Line 11 - Line 12 =	-40'
=	27'	14. Line 13 X CM-3 .45 =	-18'
Convert result to decimal = CM-3 .45		15. Add lines 12 + 14 = Vertex at Birth	♑ 7° 18'
Exception: If Co-Latitude is less than 20°, divide result by 5 ÷ 5 = CM-3 _____			

Lesson 21: Introduction to Progressions - Answer Key

1. December 12, 1983, 3:55 GMT

(GMT of Birth as decimal) 3.92 ÷ 24 = (CM-1) .163
365 days x .163 = 59 days
(Birthdate) December 12 = Day #346 - 59 days = Day #287
ACD = October 14, 1983

2. July 16, 1995, 20:33 GMT

(GMT of Birth as decimal) 20.55 ÷ 24 = (CM-1) .856
365 days x .856 = 312 days
(Birthdate) July 16 = Day #562 - 312 days = Day #250
ACD = September 7, 1994

3. November 30, 1996, 13:45 GMT

(GMT of Birth as decimal) 13.75 ÷ 24 = (CM-1) .573
365 days x .573 = 209 days
(Birthdate) November 30 = Day #334 - 209 days = Day #125
ACD = May 5, 1996

Lesson 22: Progressing Planets - Answer Key

1. July 4, 1950 at 14:23 GMT.

(GMT of Birth as decimal) 14.38 ÷ 24 = (CM-1) .599
365 days x .599 = 219 days
(Birthdate) July 4 = Day #550 - 219 days = Day #331
ACD = November 27, 1949

ACD before 53rd birthday = November 27, 2002 (1949 + 53 = 2002)
(Birthdate Day Number) #185 + (Elapsed Years) 53 = Day #238
Equivalent Ephemeris Date = August 26, 1950

Progressed Sun on November 27, 2002 = 2° ♍ 12'
Progressed Moon on November 27, 2002 = 12° ♒ 04'
(Sun and Moon positions taken from Ephemeris listing for August 26, 1950)

2. February 8, 1964 at 8:50 GMT.

(GMT of Birth as decimal) 8.83 ÷ 24 = (CM-1) .368
365 days x .368 = 134 days
(Birthdate) February 8 = Day #404 - 134 days = Day #270
ACD = September 27, 1963

ACD before 29th birthday = September 27, 1992 (1963 + 29 = 1992)
(Birthdate Day Number) #39 + (Elapsed Years) 29 = Day #68
Equivalent Ephemeris Date = March 8, 1964 *(1 is added to all day numbers occurring after February 28th to account for February 29th because 1964 was a leap year)*

Progressed Sun on September 27, 1992 = 17° ♓ 27'
Progressed Moon on September 27, 1992 = 4° ♑ 42'
(Sun and Moon positions taken from Ephemeris listing for March 8, 1964)

Lesson 22: Progressing Planets - Answer Key (continued)

3. November 20, 1972 at 5:19 GMT.

ACD Calculation:
(GMT of Birth as decimal) 5.32 ÷ 24 = (CM-1) .222
365 days x .222 = 81 days
(Birthdate) November 20 = Day #324 - 81 days = Day #243
ACD = August 31, 1972

ACD Equivalent Ephemeris Date:
(Year of ACD prior to Target Date) 1994 - (Year of Birth ACD) 1972 = 22 (Elapsed Years)
(Birthdate Day Number) #324 + (Elapsed Years) 22 = Day #346
Equivalent Ephemeris Date to earlier ACD = December 12, 1972
Equivalent Ephemeris Date to later ACD = December 13, 1972

Progressed Planetary CM (PP-CM):
(Target Date Day Number) #490 - (ACD Day Number) #243 = 247 (Days elapsed ACD to Target)

247 ÷ 365 = **(PP-CM) .677**

	☉	☽	☿	♀	♂	♃
1. Position at 0 hr on Later Ephemeris Date (12/13/72)	21° ♐ 05'	40° ♒ 96' ~~11° ♓ 36'~~	29° ♏ 62' ~~0° ♐ 02'~~	22° ♏ 49'	17° ♏ 63' ~~18° ♏ 03'~~	13° ♑ 28'
2. Position at 0 hr on Earlier Ephemeris Date (12/12/72)	20° ♐ 04'	28° ♒ 39'	29° ♏ 09'	21° ♏ 35'	17° ♏ 23'	13° ♑ 15'
3. Line 1 - Line 2 = Total Daily Travel	1° 01' = 61'	12° 57' = 777'	53'	1° 14' = 74'	40'	13'
4. Line 3 X CM (.677) = Travel to Target Date	41'	526' = 8° 46'	36'	50'	27'	9'
5. Add lines 2 + 4 = Progressed Position on Target Date	20° ♐ 45'	36° ♒ 85' = 7° ♓ 25'	29° ♏ 45'	21° ♏ 85' = 22° ♏ 25'	17° ♏ 50'	13° ♑ 24'

Lesson 22: Progressing Planets - Answer Key (continued)

4. April 3, 1948 at 19:50 GMT.

ACD Calculation:
(GMT of Birth as decimal) 19.83 ÷ 24 = (CM-1) .826
365 days x .826 = 301 days
(Birthdate) April 3 = Day #458 - 301 days = Day #157
ACD = June 6, 1947

ACD Equivalent Ephemeris Date:
(Year of ACD prior to Target Date) 1989 - (Year of Birth ACD) 1947 = 42 (Elapsed Years)
(Birthdate Day Number) #93 + (Elapsed Years) 42 = Day #135
Equivalent Ephemeris Date to earlier ACD = May 15, 1948
Equivalent Ephemeris Date to later ACD = May 16, 1948

Progressed Planetary CM (PP-CM):
(Target Date Day Number) #248 - (ACD Day Number) #157 = *91* (Days elapsed ACD to Target)

91 ÷ 365 = **(PP-CM) .249**

	☉	☽
1. Position at 0 hr on Later Ephemeris Date (5/16/48)	24° ♉ 62' ~~25° ♉ 02'~~	24° ♌ 31'
2. Position at 0 hr on Earlier Ephemeris Date (5/15/48)	24° ♉ 04'	10° ♌ 17'
3. Line 1 - Line 2 = Total Daily Travel	58'	14° 14' = 854'
4. Line 3 X CM (.249) = Travel to Target Date	14'	213' = 3° 33'
5. Add lines 2 + 4 = Progressed Position on Target Date	24° ♉ 18'	13° ♌ 50'

Lesson 23: Progressing Chart Angles - Answer Key

Part A: ACD

ACD Calculation:

1. CM-1 (Convert GMT of Birth to decimal: ___19.23___ ÷ 24 = CM-1) ___.801___

2. 365 days x CM-1 *(line 1)* = ACD Interval   X 365 = ___292___

3a. GMT Birthdate Day Number *(from Table of Numbered Days)* ___432___

  b. - ACD Interval *(from line 2)*   - ___292___

  c. = ACD Day Number   = ___140___

  d. = Birth ACD *(line 3c date equivalent from Table of Numbered Days)*   Birth ACD = ___May 20___ Year ___1964___

ACD Equivalent Ephemeris Date:

4. Year of ACD prior to Target Date ___(n/a)___ - Year of Birth ACD *(line 3d)* ___(n/a)___ = Elapsed Years(Days) ___40___

5. GMT Birthdate Day No. *(line 3a)* ___432___ + Elapsed Years(Days) *(line 4)* ___40___ = Equivalent Ephemeris Day No. ___472___

  = Equivalent Ephemeris Date to earlier ACD ___April 17, 1965___

Solar Arc   +360.00

Progressed Sun	♈ 26° 46' = 26.77
- Birth Sun	- ♓ 18° 01' = 348.02
= Solar Arc	= ___38.75___
	= 38° 45'

Progressed MC

Birth MC	___♈ 22° 28'___
+ Solar Arc	+ ___38° 45'___
= Progressed MC	= ___61° 13'___
	= 1° ♊ 13'

Midheaven CM (MC-CM)
(Constant Multiplier for Part D: House Cusps,
Lines 4 & 9: MC Interpolation)

Progressed MC	♊ 1° 13'
- Next lowest MC from Table	- ♊ 1° 08'
	= ___05'___ ' *(a)*
Next highest MC from Table	♊ 2° 05'
- Next lowest MC from Table	- ♊ 1° 08'
	= ___57'___ ' *(b)*

___5'___ *(a)* ÷ ___57'___ *(b)* = MC-CM ___.088___

Latitude CM (CM-3)
(Constant Multiplier for Part D: House Cusps,
Line 14: Latitude Interpolation)

Latitude of Birth (or other prog. location)	___40°___	___43___ '
- Next lowest Latitude from Table	- ___40°___	___00___ '
	= ___°___	___43___ '
Convert result to decimal	CM-3 =	___.717___

Exception: If Birth Latitude is
less than 20°, divide result by 5   ÷ 5 = CM-3 _____

House Cusp Calculation for Higher Latitude	
Latitude __41__ °	ASC
1. House Cusps at Higher MC ___2° ♊ 05'___	♍ 6° 20'
2. House Cusps at Lower MC ___1° ♊ 08'___	♍ 5° 32'
3. Line 1 - Line 2 =	48'
4. Line 3 X MC-CM ___.088___ =	4'
5. Add lines 2 + 4 =	♍ 5° 36'

House Cusp Calculation for Lower Latitude	
Latitude __40__ °	ASC
6. House Cusps at Higher MC ___2° ♊ 05'___	♍ 6° 06'
7. House Cusps at Lower MC ___1° ♊ 08'___	♍ 5° 19'
8. Line 6 - Line 7 =	47'
9. Line 8 X MC-CM ___.088___ =	4'
10. Add lines 7 + 9 =	♍ 5° 23'

Latitude Interpolation	
	ASC
11. House Cusps at Higher Latitude (from line 5)	♍ 5° 36'
12. House Cusps at Lower Latitude (from line 10)	♍ 5° 23'
13. Line 11 - Line 12 =	13'
14. Line 13 X CM-3 ___.717___ =	9'
15. Add lines 12 + 14 = **Progressed House Cusps**	♍ 5° 32'

Lesson 24: Timing Progressed Events - Answer Key

1. ACD for March 5, 1949, 13:00 GMT

(GMT of Birth as decimal) 13.00 ÷ 24 = .542
365 days x .542 = 198 days
(Birthdate) March 5 = Day #429 - 198 days = Day #231 = August 19
ACD = August 19, 1948

2. Progressed Mercury to 24°♒ 34' (natal Ascendant)

Mercury 0 hour March 11, 1949 = 25°♒ 14'   Equivalent ACD = August 19, 1954
(March 11,1949 is 6 days after birth, therefore equivalent ACD is 6 <u>years</u> after <u>birth ACD</u>)

Mercury 0 hour March 10, 1949 = 23°♒ 53'   Equivalent ACD = August 19, 1953
(March 10,1949 is 5 days after birth, therefore equivalent ACD is 5 <u>years</u> after <u>birth ACD</u>)

☿ target position	♒ 24° 34'
- ☿ 0 hr 3/10/49	- ♒ 23° 53'
= travel to target	41' (a)

☿ 0 hr 3/11/49	♒ 25° 14'
- ☿ 0 hr 3/10/49	- ♒ 23° 53'
= total travel	1° 21', or 81' (b)

$$\frac{41' \ (a)}{81' \ (b)} = .506$$

365 days x .506 = 185 days

August 19, 1953 (earlier ACD) + 185 days = **February 20, 1954**

3. Progressed Moon to 14°♍ 38' (opposing natal Sun)

Moon 0 hour March 15, 1949 = 27°♍ 02'   Equivalent ACD = August 19, 1958
(March 15, 1949 is 10 days after birth, therefore equivalent ACD is 10 years after birth ACD)

Moon 0 hour March 14, 1949 = 11°♍ 46'   Equivalent ACD = August 19, 1957
(March 14, 1949 is 9 days after birth, therefore equivalent ACD is 9 years after birth ACD)

☽ target position	♍ 14° 38'
- ☽ 0 hr 3/14/49	- ♍ 11° 46'
= travel to target	2° 52', or 172' (a)

☽ 0 hr 3/15/49	♍ 27° 02'
- ☽ 0 hr 3/14/49	- ♍ 11° 46'
= total travel	15° 16', or 916' (b)

$$\frac{172' \ (a)}{916' \ (b)} = .188$$

365 days x .188 = 69 days

August 19, 1957 (earlier ACD) + 69 days = **October 27, 1957**

Lesson 25: Progression Calculation Exam One - Answer Key

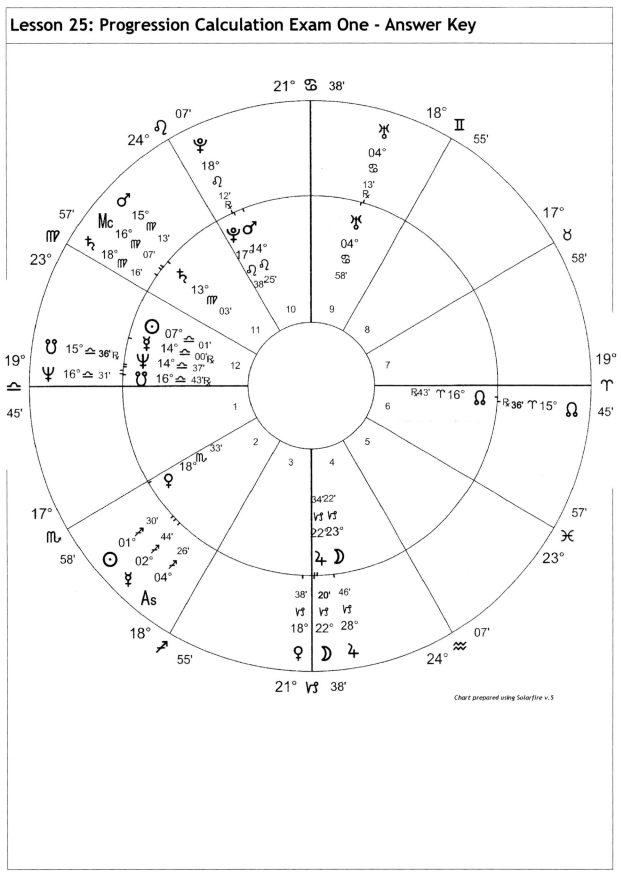

Exam 1. Birth Data: September 30, 1949, 12:45 GMT, Birmingham, AL (Target Date May 1, 2004)

Part A: ACD

ACD Calculation:

1. CM-1 (Convert GMT of Birth to decimal: ___**12.75**___ ÷ 24 = CM-1) ___**.531**___

2. 365 days x CM-1 *(line 1)* = ACD Interval ⠀⠀⠀⠀⠀ X 365 = ___**194**___

3a. GMT Birthdate Day Number *(from Table of Numbered Days)* ___**273**___

⠀b. - ACD Interval *(from line 2)* ⠀⠀⠀⠀⠀⠀⠀⠀⠀⠀ - ___**194**___

⠀c. = ACD Day Number ⠀⠀⠀⠀⠀⠀⠀⠀⠀⠀⠀⠀ = ___**79**___

⠀d. = Birth ACD *(line 3c date equivalent from Table of Numbered Days)* ⠀⠀ Birth ACD = <u>**March 20**</u> ⠀ Year **1949**

ACD Equivalent Ephemeris Date:

4. Year of ACD prior to Target Date **2004** - Year of Birth ACD *(line 3d)* **1949** = Elapsed Years(Days) **55**

5. GMT Birthdate Day No.*(line 3a)* **273** + Elapsed Years(Days) *(line 4)* **55** = Equivalent Ephemeris Day No. **328**

⠀= Equivalent Ephemeris Date to earlier ACD <u>**November 24,**</u> 1949

6. Equivalent Ephemeris Date to later ACD *(final date from line 5 plus 1 day)* <u>**November 25,**</u> 1949

Part B: Progressed Planetary CM (PP-CM)

7. Target Date Day Number *(from Table of Numbered Days)* ⠀⠀⠀ ___**121**___ May 1st

8. - ACD Day Number *(from Table of Numbered Days)* ⠀⠀⠀⠀ - ___**79**___

9. = Days elapsed from ACD to Target ⠀⠀⠀⠀⠀⠀⠀ = ___**42**___

10. Line 9 ÷ 365 = PPCM ⠀⠀⠀⠀⠀⠀⠀⠀ PPCM = ___**.115**___

Solar Arc	
Progressed Sun *(Part C, line 5)*	**241° 30' (♐ 1° 30')**
- Birth Sun	**-187° 01' (♎ 7° 01')**
= Solar Arc	**= 54° 29'**

Progressed MC		
Birth MC		**111° 38' (♋ 21° 38')**
+ Solar Arc	+	**54° 29'**
= Progressed MC	=	**165° 67'**
		Or 166° 07'
		= ♍ 16° 07'

372

Lesson 25: Progression Calculation Exam One - Answer Key (continued)

	☉	☽	☿	♀	♂	♃
1. Position at 0 hr on later ephemeris date *(Part A, line 6)* (11/25/49)	2° ♐ 23'	33° ♑ 72' ~~4° ♒ 12'~~	3° ♐ 68' ~~4° ♐ 08'~~	18° ♑ 90' ~~19° ♑ 30'~~	15° ♍ 40'	28° ♑ 56'
2. Position at 0 hr on earlier ephemeris date *(Part A, line 5)* (11/24/49)	1° ♐ 23'	20° ♑ 47'	2° ♐ 33'	18° ♑ 31'	15° ♍ 09'	28° ♑ 45'
3. Line 1 - Line 2 = Total Daily Travel	1° = 60'	13° 25' = 805'	1° 35' = 95'	59'	31'	11'
4. Line 3 X PPCM (.115) = Travel to Target Date	7'	93' = 1° 33'	11'	7'	4'	1'
5. Add lines 2 + 4 = Progressed Position on Target Date	1° ♐ 30'	21° ♑ 80' = 22° ♑ 20'	2° ♐ 44'	18° ♑ 38'	15° ♍ 13'	28° ♑ 46'

	♄	♅	♆	♇	☊	
6. Position at 0 hr on later ephemeris date *(Part A, line 6)* (11/25/49)	18° ♍ 20'	4° ♋ 11' ℞	16° ♎ 32'	18° ♌ 12' ℞	15° ♈ 32' ℞	
7. Position at 0 hr on earlier ephemeris date *(Part A, line 5)* (11/24/49)	18° ♍ 16'	4° ♋ 13' ℞	16° ♎ 31'	18° ♌ 12' ℞	15° ♈ 37' ℞	
8. Line 6 - Line 7 = Total Daily Travel	4'	- 2' ℞	1'	0'	- 5' ℞	
9. Line 8 X PPCM (.115) = Travel to Target Date	0'	0'	0'	0'	- 1' ℞	
10. Add lines 7 + 9 = Progressed Position on Target Date	18° ♍ 16'	4° ♋ 13' ℞	16° ♎ 31'	18° ♌ 12' ℞	15° ♈ 36' ℞	

Midheaven CM (MC-CM)
(Constant Multiplier for Part D: House Cusps, Lines 4 & 9: MC Interpolation)

Progressed MC		16° ♍ 07'
- Next lowest MC from Table	-	15° ♍ 53'
	=	14' ' *(a)*
Next highest MC from Table		16° ♍ 57'
- Next lowest MC from Table	-	15° ♍ 53'
	=	64' ' *(b)*

14' *(a)* ÷ 64' *(b)* = MC-CM .219

Latitude CM (CM-3)
(Constant Multiplier for Part D: House Cusps, Line 14: Latitude Interpolation)

Latitude of Birth (or other prog. location) 33° 31'

- Next lowest Latitude from Table   - 33° 00'

                                    = ___° 31'

Convert result to decimal   CM-3 = .517

Exception: If Birth Latitude is less than 20°, divide result by 5 ÷ 5 = CM-3 _____

Lesson 25: Progression Calculation Exam One - Answer Key (continued)

House Cusp Calculation for Higher Latitude

Latitude (34°)	11th	12th	ASC	2nd	3rd
1. House Cusps at Higher MC (16°♍ 57')	16°♎ 108' ~~17°♎ 48'~~	12°♏ 68' ~~13°♏ 08'~~	4°♐ 51'	5°♑ 71' ~~6°♑ 11'~~	11°♒ 29'
2. House Cusps at Lower MC (15°♍ 53')	16°♎ 49'	12°♏ 15'	4°♐ 01'	5°♑ 15'	10°♒ 25'
3. Line 1 - Line 2 =	59'	53'	50'	56'	1° 04' = 64'
4. Line 3 X MC-CM (.219) =	13'	12'	11'	12'	14'
5. Add lines 2 + 4 =	16°♎ 62' = 17°♎ 02'	12°♏ 27'	4°♐ 12'	5°♑ 27'	10°♒ 39'

House Cusp Calculation for Lower Latitude

Latitude (33°)	11th	12th	ASC	2nd	3rd
6. House Cusps at Higher MC (16°♍ 57')	16°♎ 112' ~~17°♎ 52'~~	12°♏ 82' ~~13°♏ 22'~~	4°♐ 80' ~~5°♐ 20'~~	5°♑ 96' ~~6°♑ 36'~~	11°♒ 39'
7. House Cusps at Lower MC (15°♍ 53')	16°♎ 53'	12°♏ 29'	4°♐ 30'	5°♑ 39'	10°♒ 35'
8. Line 6 - Line 7 =	59'	53'	50'	57'	1° 04' = 64'
9. Line 8 X MC-CM (.219) =	13'	12'	11'	12'	14'
10. Add lines 7 + 9 =	16°♎ 66' = 17°♎ 06'	12°♏ 41'	4°♐ 41'	5°♑ 51'	10°♒ 49'

Latitude Interpolation

	11th	12th	ASC	2nd	3rd
11. House Cusps at Higher Latitude (from line 5)	17°♎ 02'	12°♏ 27'	4°♐ 12'	5°♑ 27'	10°♒ 39'
12. House Cusps at Lower Latitude (from line 10)	17°♎ 06'	12°♏ 41'	4°♐ 41'	5°♑ 51'	10°♒ 49'
13. Line 11 - Line 12 =	- 04'	- 14'	- 29'	- 24'	- 10'
14. Line 13 X CM-3 (.517) =	- 02'	- 07'	- 15'	- 12'	- 05'
15. Add lines 12 + 14 = **Progressed House Cusps**	17°♎ 04'	12°♏ 34'	4°♐ 26'	5°♑ 39'	10°♒ 44'

374

Lesson 25: Progression Calculation Exam Two - Answer Key

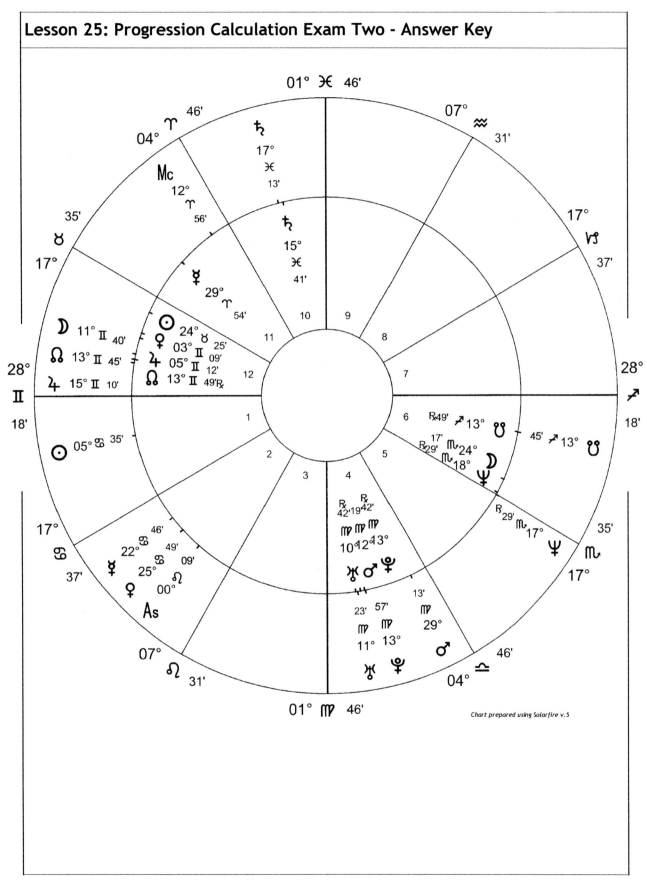

Chart prepared using Solarfire v.5

Lesson 25: Progression Calculation Exam Two - Answer Key

Exam 1. Birth Data: May 15, 1965, 11:35 GMT, Rutland, VT (Target Date May 15, 2008)

Part A: ACD

ACD Calculation:

1. CM-1 (Convert GMT of Birth to decimal: __**11.58**__ ÷ 24 = CM-1) __**.483**__

2. 365 days x CM-1 *(line 1)* = ACD Interval   X 365 = __**176**__

3a. GMT Birthdate Day Number *(from Table of Numbered Days)* __**500**__

   b. - ACD Interval *(from line 2)*   - __**176**__

   c. = ACD Day Number   = __**324**__

   d. = Birth ACD *(line 3c date equivalent from Table of Numbered Days)*   Birth ACD = __Nov. 20__   Year __1964__

ACD Equivalent Ephemeris Date:

4. Year of ACD prior to Target Date __2007__ - Year of Birth ACD *(line 3d)* __1964__ = Elapsed Years(Days) __43__

5. GMT Birthdate Day No.*(line 3a)* __500__ + Elapsed Years(Days) *(line 4)* __43__ = Equivalent Ephemeris Day No. __543__

   = Equivalent Ephemeris Date to earlier ACD __June 27, 1965__

6. **Equivalent Ephemeris Date to later ACD** *(final date from line 5 plus 1 day)* __June 28, 1965__

Part B: Progressed Planetary CM (PP-CM)

7. Target Date Day Number *(from Table of Numbered Days)*   __**500**__ (May 15th)

8. - ACD Day Number *(from Table of Numbered Days)*   - __**324**__

9. = Days elapsed from ACD to Target   = __**176**__

10. Line 9 ÷ 365 = PPCM   PPCM = __**.482**__

Solar Arc

Progressed Sun *(Part C, line 5)* $\cancer$ 5°35' = 95°35'

- Birth Sun   - $\taurus$ 24°25' = 54°25'

= Solar Arc   = __41° 10'__

Progressed MC

Birth MC $\pisces$ 1°46' = 331°46'

+ Solar Arc   + __41° 10'__

= Progressed MC   = __372°56'__
                                     - 360° 00'
                                     = 12°56' = 12$\aries$56'

Lesson 25: Progression Calculation Exam Two - Answer Key (continued)

	☉	☽	☿	♀	♂	♃
1. Position at 0 hr on later ephemeris date *(Part A, line 6)* (6/28/65)	♋ 5°65' ~~♋ 6°05'~~	♊ 18°74' ~~♊ 19°14'~~	♋ 22°102' ~~♋ 23°42'~~	♋ 26°27'	♍ 28° 89' ~~♍ 29°29'~~	♊ 15°17'
2. Position at 0 hr on earlier ephemeris date *(Part A, line 5)* (6/27/65)	♋ 5°08'	♊ 4°37'	♋ 21°53'	♋ 25°14'	♍ 28° 59'	♊ 15°03'
3. Line 1 - Line 2 = Total Daily Travel	57'	14° 37' = 877'	1° 49' = 109'	1° 13' = 73'	30'	14'
4. Line 3 X PPCM (.482) = Travel to Target Date	27'	423' = 7° 03'	53'	35'	14'	7'
5. Add lines 2 + 4 = Progressed Position on Target Date	♋ 5° 35'	♊ 11° 40'	♋ 22° 46'	♋ 25° 49'	♍ 29° 13'	♊ 15° 10'

	♄	♅	♆	♇	☊
6. Position at 0 hr on later ephemeris date *(Part A, line 6)* (6/28/65)	♓17° 13' ℞	♍ 11° 24'	♏17°29' ℞	♍ 13° 58'	♊ 13° 46'
7. Position at 0 hr on earlier ephemeris date *(Part A, line 5)* (6/27/65)	♓17° 13'	♍ 11° 22'	♏17°30' ℞	♍ 13° 57'	♊ 13° 45'
8. Line 6 - Line 7 = Total Daily Travel	0'	2'	-1' ℞	1'	1'
9. Line 8 X PPCM (.482) = Travel to Target Date	0'	1'	0'	0'	0'
10. Add lines 7 + 9 = Progressed Position on Target Date	♓17° 13'	♍ 11° 23'	♏17°29' ℞	♍ 13° 57'	♊ 13° 45'

Midheaven CM (MC-CM)
(Constant Multiplier for Part D: House Cusps, Lines 4 & 9: MC Interpolation)

Progressed MC	12° ♈ 56'
- Next lowest MC from Table	- 11° ♈ 58'
=	58' ' (a)
Next highest MC from Table	12° ♈ 63' ~~13° ♈ 03'~~
- Next lowest MC from Table	- 11° ♈ 58'
=	65' ' (b)

58' (a) ÷ 65' (b) = MC-CM .892

Latitude CM (CM-3)
(Constant Multiplier for Part D: House Cusps, Line 14: Latitude Interpolation)

Latitude of Birth (or other prog. location)	43° 37'
- Next lowest Latitude from Table	- 43° 00'
=	° 37'
Convert result to decimal	CM-3 = .617

Exception: If Birth Latitude is less than 20°, divide result by 5 ÷ 5 = CM-3 _____

House Cusp Calculation for Higher Latitude	
Latitude (44°)	**ASC**
1. House Cusps at Higher MC (13°♈ 03')	♋ 29° 87' ~~♌ 0° 27'~~
2. House Cusps at Lower MC (11°♈ 58')	♋ 29° 40'
3. Line 1 - Line 2 =	47'
4. Line 3 X MC-CM (.892) =	42'
5. Add lines 2 + 4 =	♋ 29° 82'

House Cusp Calculation for Lower Latitude	
Latitude (43°)	**ASC**
6. House Cusps at Higher MC (13°♈ 03')	♋ 29° 52'
7. House Cusps at Lower MC (11°♈ 58')	♋ 29° 05'
8. Line 6 - Line 7 =	47'
9. Line 8 X MC-CM (.892) =	42'
10. Add lines 7 + 9 =	♋ 29° 47'

Latitude Interpolation	
	ASC
11. House Cusps at Higher Latitude (from line 5)	♋ 29° 82'
12. House Cusps at Lower Latitude (from line 10)	♋ 29° 47'
13. Line 11 - Line 12 =	35'
14. Line 13 X CM-3 (.617) =	22'
15. Add lines 12 + 14 = **Progressed House Cusps**	♋ 29° 69' = ♌ 0° 09'

Lesson 26: Solar Arc Directions - Answer Key

(Completed Solar Arc Directed Bi-wheel is shown on the following page.)

ACD before 38th birthday = October 1, 1985 (1947 (year of birth ACD) + 38 = 1985)
(Birthdate Day Number) #102 + (Elapsed Years) 38 = Day #140
Equivalent Ephemeris Date = May 20, 1948 (38 days after birthdate)

Progressed ☉   58° 53' (28° ♉ 53') = Ephemeris position on May 20, 1948
- Natal ☉   - 22° 31' (22° ♈ 31')

= Solar Arc   = 36° 22' = 36.37°

Natal ☽   58.03° (28° ♉ 02')   Natal ☿   5.88° (5° ♈ 53')
+ Solar Arc   + 36.37°   + Solar Arc   + 36.37°

= Progressed ☽   = 94.40° = 4° ♋ 24'   = Progressed ☿   = 42.25° = 12° ♉ 15'

Natal ♀   68.17° (8° ♊ 10')   Natal ♂   139.23° (19° ♌ 14')
+ Solar Arc   + 36.37°   + Solar Arc   + 36.37°

= Progressed ♀   = 104.54° = 14° ♋ 32'   = Progressed ♂   = 175.60° = 25° ♍ 36'

Natal ♃   268.93° (28° ♐ 56')   Natal ♄   135.77° (15° ♌ 46')
+ Solar Arc   + 36.37°   + Solar Arc   + 36.37°

= Progressed ♃   = 305.30° = 5° ♒ 18'   = Progressed ♄   = 172.14° = 22° ♍ 08'

Natal ♅   82.90° (22° ♊ 54')   Natal ♆   191.33° (11° ♎ 20')
+ Solar Arc   + 36.37°   + Solar Arc   + 36.37°

= Progressed ♅   = 119.27° = 29° ♋ 16'   = Progressed ♆   = 227.70° = 17° ♏ 42'

Natal ♇   132.58° (12° ♌ 35')   Natal ☊   44.08° (14° ♉ 05')
+ Solar Arc   + 36.37°   + Solar Arc   + 36.37°

= Progressed ♇   = 168.95° = 18° ♍ 57'   = Progressed ☊   = 80.45° = 20° ♊ 27'

Natal ASC   359.12° (29° ♓ 07')   Natal MC   269.50° (29° ♐ 30')
+ Solar Arc   + 36.37°   + Solar Arc   + 36.37°

                   = 395.49°   = Progressed MC   = 305.87° = 5° ♒ 52'
                   - 360.00°

= Progressed ASC   = 35.49° = 5° ♉ 29'

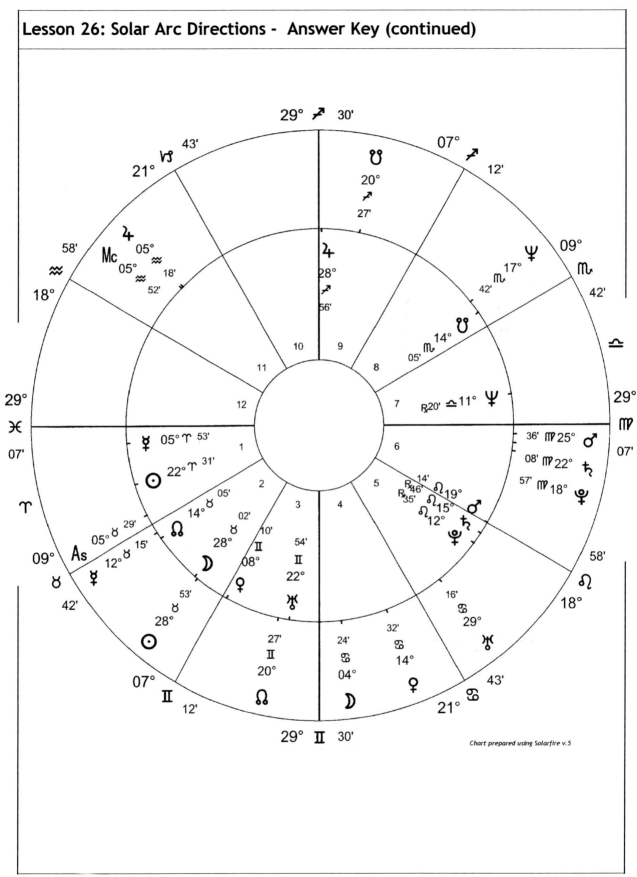

Chart prepared using Solarfire v.5

Lesson 27: Solar Returns - Answer Key

1. Date & GMT of Solar Return nearest to 48th birthday
   = 3:40 GMT, September 30, 1997

1. Position at 0 hr on day after birth date **(10/1/49)**	♎ 6°87' 107" ~~♎ 7°28' 47"~~
2. Position at 0 hr on Birth date **(9/30/49)**	♎ 6°29' 48"
3. Line 1 - Line 2 = Total Daily Travel	58' 59" Or 58.983'
4. Line 3 X CM-1 **(.531)** =Travel to birth time (12.75 (GMT of birth) ÷ 24 = .531)	31.320' or 31' 19"
5. Add lines 2 + 4 = Position at Birth	♎ 6°60' 67" = ♎ 7°01' 07"

Sun's Natal Position   ♎ 6°61' 07"
                              ~~♎ 7°01' 07"~~

- Position at 0 hr on Sept 30, 1997   ♎ 6°52' 07"

= Travel to Natal Position   9' 00"
                           Or   9.0'

Position at 0 hr on Oct 1, 1997   ♎ 6°110' 66"
                              ~~♎ 7°51' 06"~~

- Position at 0 hr on Sept 30, 1997   ♎ 6°52' 07"

= Daily Travel   58' 59"
                 Or 58.983'

Sun's travel from 0 hr to natal position $\frac{9.0}{58.983}$ = .1526 *portion of day elapsed*
divided by Sun's total daily travel   *from 0 hour to Sun's Return*

.1526 X 1440 (total number of minutes in a day) = 219.744 minutes, rounded to 220 = 3:40

Date & GMT of Solar Return nearest to 48th birthday
= 3:40 GMT, September 30, 1997

Lesson 28: Lunar Returns - Answer Key

**1. Date & GMT of Lunar Return in effect at the time of the 48th birthday
  = 16:59 GMT, September 12, 1997**

1. Later listed semi-diurnal position to birth GMT (0 hour 10/1/49)	♑ 28° 80' 79" <s>♑ 29° 21' 19"</s>
2. Earlier listed semi-diurnal position to birth GMT (Noon 9/30/49)	♑ 22° 57' 53"
3. Line 1 - Line 2 = Total Semi-diurnal Travel	6° 23' 26" Or 383.433'
4. Line 3 X CM (.0625) =Travel to birth time (0.75 ÷ 12 = .0625)	23.965' Or 23' 58"
5. Add lines 2 + 4 = Position at Birth	♑ 22° 80' 111" = ♑ 23° 21' 51"

Moon's Natal Position	♑ 22° 81' 51" <s>♑ 23° 21' 51"</s>
- Position at Noon on Sept 12, 1997	♑ 20° 24' 51"
= Travel to Birth Position	2° 57' 00" Or 177.0'

Position at 0 hour on Sept 13, 1997 *(later semi-diurnal position)*	♑ 27° 29' 99" <s>♑ 27° 30' 39"</s>
- Position at Noon on Sept 12, 1997 *(earlier semi-diurnal position)*	♑ 20° 24' 51"
= Total Semi-diurnal Travel	7° 05' 48" Or 425.80'

Moon's travel from Noon to natal position $\frac{177.0}{425.8}$ = .4157 *portion of half-day elapsed*
divided by Moon's total semi-diurnal travel   *from Noon to Moon's Return*

.4157 X 720 (total number of minutes in 12 hours) = 299.30 minutes, rounded to 299
= 4:59 hours after noon on September 12, 1997, or 16:59 GMT

**Date & GMT of Lunar Return in effect at the time of the 48th birthday
= 16:59 GMT, September 12, 1997**

Lesson 29: Composite Charts - Answer Key

(Midpoint calculations are shown on the following page.)

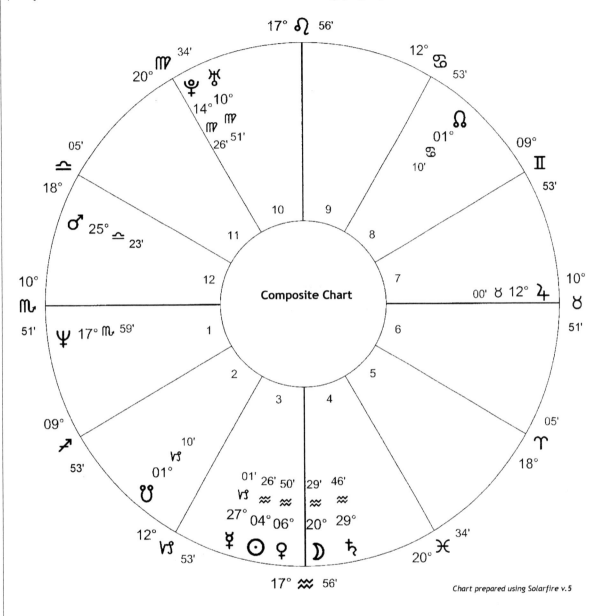

Chart prepared using Solarfire v.5

Lesson 29: Composite Charts - Answer Key

Midpoint Composite House Cusps:

Midheaven:
	Chart A	152.18°	(2° ♍ 11')
+	Chart B	+ 123.70°	(3° ♌ 42')
		275.88° ÷ 2 = 137.94°	

Composite Midpoint MC = **17° ♌ 56'**
Composite Midpoint 4th house cusp = **17° ♒ 56'**

11th Cusp:
	Chart A	184.13°	(4° ♎ 08')
+	Chart B	+ 157.00°	(7° ♍ 00')
		341.13° ÷ 2 = 170.57°	

Composite Midpoint 11th house cusp = **20° ♍ 34'**
Composite Midpoint 5th house cusp = **20° ♓ 34'**

12th Cusp:
	Chart A	210.95°	(0° ♏ 57')
+	Chart B	+ 185.20°	(5° ♎ 12')
		396.15° ÷ 2 = 198.08°	

Composite Midpoint 12th house cusp = **18° ♎ 05'**
Composite Midpoint 6th house cusp = **18° ♈ 05'**

Ascendant:
	Chart A	233.52°	(23° ♏ 31')
+	Chart B	+ 208.17°	(28° ♎ 10')
		441.69° ÷ 2 = 220.85°	

Composite Midpoint ASC = **10° ♏ 51'**
Composite Midpoint DSC = **10° ♉ 51'**

2nd Cusp:
	Chart A	263.60°	(23° ♐ 36')
+	Chart B	+ 236.15°	(26° ♏ 09')
		499.75° ÷ 2 = 249.88°	

Composite Midpoint 2nd house cusp = **9° ♐ 53'**
Composite Midpoint 8th house cusp = **9° ♊ 53'**

3rd Cusp:
	Chart A	297.23°	(27° ♑ 14')
+	Chart B	+ 268.53°	(28° ♐ 32')
		565.76° ÷ 2 = 282.88°	

Composite Midpoint 3rd house cusp = **12° ♑ 53'**
Composite Midpoint 9th house cusp = **12° ♋ 53'**

Midpoint Composite House Planets:

☉	252.10°	(12° ♐ 06') Chart A
+	356.78°	(26° ♓ 47') Chart B
	608.88° ÷ 2 = 304.44°	☉ = **4° ♒ 26'**

☽	18.60°	(18° ♈ 36') Chart A
+	262.35°	(22° ♐ 21') Chart B
	280.95° ÷ 2 = 140.48°	☽ = **20° ♌ 29'**

☿	249.02°	(9° ♐ 01') Chart A
+	345.02°	(15° ♓ 01') Chart B
	594.04° ÷ 2 = 297.02°	☿ = **27° ♑ 01'**

♀	297.77°	(27° ♑ 46') Chart A
+	315.90°	(15° ♒ 54') Chart B
	613.67° ÷ 2 = 306.84°	♀ = **6° ♒ 50'**

♂	285.40°	(15° ♑ 24') Chart A
+	125.35°	(5° ♌ 21') Chart B
	410.75° ÷ 2 = 205.38°	♂ = **25° ♎ 23'**

♃	88.08°	(28° ♊ 05') Chart A
+	355.90°	(25° ♓ 54') Chart B
	443.98° ÷ 2 = 221.99°	= 12° ♏ 00'

Nearer midpoint ♃ = 12° ♉ 00'

♄	340.85°	(10° ♓ 51') Chart A
+	318.68°	(18° ♒ 41') Chart B
	659.53° ÷ 2 = 329.77°	♄ = **29° ♒ 46'**

♅	169.43°	(19° ♍ 26') Chart A
+	152.27°	(2° ♍ 16') Chart B
	321.70° ÷ 2 = 160.85°	♅ = **10° ♍ 51'**

♆	230.55°	(20° ♏ 33') Chart A
+	225.42°	(15° ♏ 25') Chart B
	455.97° ÷ 2 = 227.99°	♆ = **17° ♏ 59'**

♇	168.40°	(18° ♍ 24') Chart A
+	160.47°	(10° ♍ 28') Chart B
	328.87° ÷ 2 = 164.44°	♇ = **14° ♍ 26'**

☊	64.68°	(4° ♊ 41') Chart A
+	117.63°	(27° ♋ 38') Chart B
	182.31° ÷ 2 = 91.16°	☊ = **1° ♋ 10'**

Glossary

Absolute Longitude: Zodiacal longitude expressed in degrees from 0 to 360 without the use of zodiacal signs.

Adjusted Calculation Date (ACD): A date used in "day for a year" progressions representing the equivalent of 0 hour GMT for a particular individual.

Altitude: The elevation of a point above the horizon.

Angles: The four points (**Ascendant, Midheaven, Descendant,** and **Imum Coeli**) forming the horizontal and vertical axes of a birth chart and dividing it into four quadrants of three houses each.

Antiscia: Points equidistant to and on opposite sides of the 0° Cancer/0° Capricorn axis. Singular **Antiscion.**

Anti-Vertex: The point where the prime vertical intersects the Ecliptic in the east directly opposite the Vertex.

Applying Aspect: An aspect in which a faster moving planet is approaching an exact aspect with a slower moving planet or point.

Arabic Parts: Points derived from the distance between two planets or points which is then projected from a third point usually the Ascendant, following the formula Part = A + (B − C). Also referred to as "Lots".

Arc: The angular distance between two points.

Ascendant (ASC): The point of the zodiac where the celestial horizon intersects with the Ecliptic in the east.

Aspect: The angular relationship created by the distance or arc between two planets or points.

Aspectarian: A grid showing the aspects between all planets and sensitive points in a chart.

Azimuth: An object's compass bearing measured in degrees along the horizon from due south.

Bi-Wheel: A chart with two rings allowing for the insertion and comparison of two sets of astrological data.

Celestial Equator: A great circle formed by the Earth's Equator projected into space. The Celestial Equator intersects with the Ecliptic at 0° Aries and 0° Libra.

Celestial Horizon: A great circle parallel to the plane of the visible horizon which passes through the center of the Earth. The Ascendant, Descendant, and the Equatorial Ascendant are all determined by locating the points in the east and west where the celestial horizon intersects with the Ecliptic.

Celestial Meridian: A great circle formed by a meridian of longitude projected into space. The Celestial Meridian passes through due north and due south on the celestial horizon and through the Zenith directly above and the Nadir directly below. The Midheaven and the Imum Coeli are located at the points where the Celestial Meridian intersects with the highest point on the Ecliptic and the lowest point on the Ecliptic respectively.

Ceres: The largest of the four primary asteroids comprising Ceres, Juno, Vesta and Pallas.

Chiron: A comet located between the orbits of Saturn and Uranus.

Co-Latitude: A location's distance north or south as measured from one of the poles instead of the Equator. Co-latitude is easily calculated by subtracting the birth latitude from 90°.

Composite Chart: A chart derived from the midpoints between two or more natal charts

Conjunction (σ): Planets or points sharing the same degree of zodiacal longitude, or within an allowable orb.

Constant Multiplier: An unvarying proportion used in mathematical calculation.

Contraparallel (‖): Two planets or points sharing the same degree of declination but in opposite polarities, with one north and the other south of the Celestial Equator.

Converse directions: A symbolic chart progression technique in which the chart is moved backwards through time instead of forward.

Cosmobiology: An astrological system developed by Reinhold Ebertin (1901-1988) using midpoints and eliminating the use of houses.

Cusp: The boundary establishing the start of each of the twelve astrological houses.

Daily Motion: The apparent distance a planet travels in 24 hours measured along the Ecliptic.

Daily Retardation: The later rising of the Moon each night by approximately 50 minutes due to the Moon's eastward orbital motion around the Earth.

Davison Relationship Chart: See **Relationship Chart.**

Day for a Year: A symbolic method of progression in which each day is equated to a year of life.

Daylight Savings Time (DST or DT): A method used to extend the evening daylight hours for convenience sake by moving clocks one hour ahead of standard time.

Declination: A planet or point's distance north or south of the Celestial Equator.

Derivative Composite Chart: A composite chart in which the house cusps are calculated based on the latitude of the location where the relationship exists.

Descendant (DSC): The point of the zodiac directly opposite the Ascendant, where the celestial horizon intersects with the Ecliptic in the west.

Direct Motion: The apparent forward motion of a planet.

Diurnal: Of or pertaining to the day.

Diurnal Motion: The daily rotation of the Earth on its axis creating the apparent daily motion of celestial bodies from east to west.

Ecliptic: A great circle formed by the orbit of the Earth projected onto the celestial sphere; commonly referred to as "the apparent path of the Sun".

Ecliptic System: A coordinate system using the Ecliptic as the fundamental horizontal plane.

Electional Astrology: A branch of astrology dealing with the selection of the most astrologically advantageous time to begin new undertakings.

Elements: The classification of zodiacal signs into Fire, Earth, Air and Water.

Ephemeris: Tables of planetary positions and other astrological data. Plural **ephemerides.**

Equator: A great circle around the middle of the Earth that is equidistant from both poles which is designated as 0° latitude.

Equatorial Ascendant: The point formed by the intersection of the celestial horizon, Celestial Equator, and the Ecliptic in the east. It is the rising degree of the Ascendant if the location of birth were on the Equator.

Equatorial System: A coordinate system using the Celestial Equator as the fundamental horizontal plane.

Equinoctial Points: The two points where the Ecliptic intersects with the Celestial Equator, designated 0° Aries and 0° Libra.

Event Chart: A chart cast for the moment an event occurs.

GMT of Birth: Time of birth expressed in Greenwich Mean Time.

Grand Cross: See **Grand Square.**

Grand Square: Four planets or points 90° apart, usually in the same modality.

Grand Trine: Three planets or points 120° apart, usually in the same element.

Great Circles: Imaginary planes passing through the center of the Earth and projected out into the celestial sphere.

Greenwich Mean Time (GMT): Local Mean Time for Greenwich, England at 0° longitude.

Harmonics: The study of aspects formed by various divisions of the circle.

Horary Astrology: A branch of astrology in which charts are cast for the moment questions are asked and then analyzed to obtain answers.

Horizon System: A coordinate system using the celestial horizon as the fundamental horizontal plane.

House Divisional System: A system for dividing an astrological chart into 12 houses based on various astronomical or astrological criteria.

Imum Coeli (IC): Meaning "bottom of the sky" in Latin, the point of the zodiac opposite to the Midheaven and formed by the anti-culminating intersection of the Ecliptic and the Celestial Meridian.

Inferior planets: The inner planets Mercury and Venus whose orbits are closer to the Sun than the Earth's.

Ingress: The movement of a planet into a new sign.

Ingress Chart: A chart cast for the moment a planet enters a new sign.

386

Inner Planets: Mercury and Venus, also referred to as **inferior planets.**

Interception: When an entire sign of the zodiac becomes contained within a single house without "owning" the cusp of that house, it is said be **intercepted.**

International Date Line: An imaginary line irregularly following the 180° meridian designating the separation of two consecutive calendar days.

Interpolation: The process of calculating an exact value between two known values based on its proportion of the whole.

Julian Date: A day number assigned consecutively to each date, doing away with the need for month and year designations.

Latitude: The angular distance north or south of the Equator, designated as 0° latitude.

Local Mean Time (LMT): True local time based on the actual position of the Sun.

Local Sidereal Time (LST): Local time based on the position of the 0° Aries point.

Longitude: The angular distance east or west of the Prime Meridian, designated as 0° longitude.

Longitude-Time Equivalent: The difference in time between a location's local mean time and Greenwich Mean Time, determined by converting the location's longitude into time. Also called "Time equivalent to Greenwich".

Lots: See Arabic Parts.

LST of Birth: Time of birth expressed in local sidereal time, used to calculate house cusps.

Lunar Eclipse: The full or partial obscuring of the Moon's reflected light due to the blocking of sunlight by the Earth and occurring when the Earth is directly between the Sun and Moon. Lunar Eclipses are usually notated with a blackened opposition symbol.

Lunar Phase: The angular relationship between the Sun and the Moon revealed by how much of the Moon's surface is illuminated, classified into one of eight possible phases: New, Crescent, First Quarter, Gibbous, Full, Disseminating, Last Quarter, and Balsamic.

Lunar Return: A chart calculated for the exact moment in any particular month when the transiting Moon returns to the exact position it occupied at the time of birth.

Lunation: The period of time between one New Moon and the next New Moon, also called a **synodic month.**

Mean Quotidian: Latin for "recurring daily", a method which progresses the Midheaven of a chart over the course of a year according to its actual daily motion.

Medium Coeli (MC): See Midheaven

Major Aspects or Ptolemaic Aspects: Conjunction (☌), opposition (☍), Trine (△), Square (□), Sextile (✶)

Minor Aspects: Any aspects other than the major Ptolemaic aspects. The most common minor aspects are the Semisextile (⌄), Semisquare (∠), Sesqusquare (⊡), and Quincunx (⊼).

Meridian: A great circle of longitude passing through the North and South Poles and forming one of the vertical (or "long") lines of measurement. Longitude measures the distance east or west of the Prime Meridian.

Midheaven: Also called the **Medium Coeli (MC)** meaning "middle of the sky" in Latin, the most elevated degree of the zodiac formed by the culminating intersection of the Ecliptic and the Celestial Meridian.

Midpoint: The center point between two points

Midpoint Composite Chart: A derived chart based on the midpoints of planets and house cusps of two or more natal charts.

Modality: The classification of zodiacal signs into Cardinal, Fixed, and Mutable.

Mundane Astrology: A branch of astrology dealing with world and political events.

Mystic Rectangle: Four planets or points forming two sextiles, two trines and two oppositions.

Nadir: The point on the celestial sphere directly opposite the Zenith and formed by the lower intersection of the Celestial Meridian and the Prime Vertical.

Naibod: Named for the medieval astrologer Valentine Naibod, a method of progressing the Midheaven each year of life based on the average daily motion of the Sun (0° 59' 08").

Natal Lunar Phase: The angular relationship between the Sun and the Moon at the time of birth, calculated by subtracting the Sun's zodiacal longitude from the Moon's.

Nocturnal: Of or pertaining to the night.

Nodes of the Moon: The points on the zodiac where the plane of the Moon's orbit intersects with the Ecliptic.

Nonile: An aspect formed by the division of the circle by 9.

North Celestial Pole: The Earth's North Pole projected out into space.

Obliquity of the Ecliptic: The 23½° angle between the Ecliptic and the Celestial Equator.

Octile: An aspect formed by the division of the circle by 8.

Opposition (☍): An aspect formed by two points 180° or six signs apart.

Orb: The distance between points qualifying the existence of an aspect.

Outer Planets: The planets located outside the Earth's orbit, and called **superior planets**. These include Mars, Jupiter, Saturn, Uranus, Neptune and Pluto.

Pallas: One of the four major asteroids along with Ceres, Juno and Vesta.

Parallel: Two planets or points sharing the same degree and polarity of declination.

Parallels: Lines of latitude parallel to the Equator and forming the horizontal lines of measurement. Latitude measures a location's distance north or south of the Equator.

Partile Aspect: An aspect which is exact to the degree.

Part of Fortune (⊗): An Arabic Part, *Pars Fortuna* in Latin. Formula for Day Births: Ascendant + Moon - Sun = Part of Fortune. Formula for Night Births: Ascendant + Sun - Moon = Part of Fortune

Part of Marriage: An Arabic Part. Formula for Males (Day or Night: Ascendant + Venus - Saturn = Part of Marriage. Formula for Females (Day or Night): Ascendant + Saturn - Venus = Part of Marriage

Part of Spirit: An Arabic Part, *Pars Spiritus* in Latin. Formula for Day Births: Ascendant + Sun - Moon = Part of Spirit. Formula for Night Births: Ascendant + Moon - Sun = Part of Spirit

Perfection: The process of an aspect becoming exact by degree.

Personal Year: In progressions the "personal year" refers to the year measured from birthday to birthday.

Placidus: A commonly used system of house division created by Placidus De Titus, a 17ᵗʰ century Italian monk.

Planetary Cycle: The time it takes each planet to progress through the zodiac.

Polarity: The classification of zodiacal signs into pairs of opposites.

Prenatal Eclipse: The last Solar or Lunar Eclipse to occur before birth.

Primary Directions: A progression system in which one year of life is equivalent to the time it takes for 1° to pass over the Midheaven, or approximately 4 minutes of time, measured in right ascension along theCcelestial Equator.

Prime Meridian: The meridian passing through Greenwich, England and designated as 0° longitude.

Prime Vertical: A great circle passing through the east and west points on the celestial horizon, directly overhead through the Zenith and down through the Nadir. The Prime Vertical and the Celestial Meridian intersect at right angles at the Zenith and Nadir.

Progressed Lunar Phase: The angular relationship between the progressed Sun and progressed Moon classified into one of eight phases. See **Lunar Phase.**

Progressions: Predictive techniques based on the symbolic movement of planets and points in a birth chart.

Ptolemaic Aspects: See Major Aspects

Quadrant: One fourth of the astrological chart as divided horizontally by the Ascendant-Descendant axis and vertically by the Midheaven/Imum Coeli axis.

Quincunx (⚻): An aspect formed by two points 150° or five signs apart.

Quintile: An aspect formed by the division of the circle by 5.

Relationship Chart: A chart erected using the midpoints in time and place of birth of two natal charts.

Relocation Chart: A natal chart recalculated using the coordinates of a new location and used to analyze the manner in which a native will be affected by relocating to a new area.

Retrograde Motion: The apparent backwards motion of a planet, designated with the glyph (℞).

Right Ascension: A celestial object's distance east of 0° Aries measured along the celestial equator.

Secondary Progressions: A symbolic method of advancing the birthchart one day for each year of life.

Sect: The classification of charts into day births in which the Sun is located above the Ascendant-Descendant axis, or night births in which the Sun is located below the Ascendant-Descendant axis.

Semi-diurnal: Half-daily.

Semioctile: An aspect formed by the division of the circle by 16.

Semisextile (⚺): An aspect formed by two points 30° or one sign apart.

Semisquare (∠): An aspect formed by two points 45° apart.

Sensitive Points: Points in a chart that can produce effects when stimulated via aspect, transit, or progression.

Separating Aspect: An aspect which has already become exact and in which the faster moving planet is receding from the allowable orb.

Septile: An aspect formed by the division of the circle by 7.

Sesquiquadrate: See **sesquisquare.**

Sesquisquare (⚼): An aspect formed by two points 135° apart.

Sexagesimal: Based on the number 60.

Sextile (✶): An aspect formed by two points 60° or two signs apart.

Sidereal: Relative to the stars.

Sidereal Time: Time based on the stars. The zodiac makes one full rotation every 24 sidereal hours.

Signs of Long Ascension: Signs that take longer to rise over the Ascendant due to the obliquity of the Ecliptic. In the Northern Hemisphere these are Cancer through Sagittarius; In the Southern Hemisphere these are Capricorn through Gemini.

Signs of Short Ascension: Signs that rise more quickly over the Ascendant due to the obliquity of the Ecliptic. These are Capricorn through Gemini in the Northern Hemisphere and Cancer through Sagittarius in the Southern Hemisphere.

Solar Arc: The difference in degrees and minutes between the Sun's natal position and its progressed position, used in progressions and solar arc directions.

Solar Arc Directions: A symbolic method of advancing a birth chart through time in which the Sun's daily motion each day after birth is applied to all planets and points for each year of life.

Solar Eclipse: The full or partial obscuring of the Sun by the Moon, occurring when the Moon is directly between the Earth and the Sun. Solar Eclipses are usually notated with a blackened conjunction symbol.

Solar Return: A chart erected for the exact moment the transiting Sun returns to its natal position in any year.

Solar Sidereal Time Correction: The adjustment factor needed to convert solar time into sidereal time.

Solar Time: Time based on the Sun.

Solstice Points: The points 0° Cancer or 0° Capricorn at which the Sun reaches its greatest northern or southern declination.

South Celestial Pole: The Earth's South Pole projected out into space.

Square (□): An aspect formed by two points 90° or 3 signs apart.

Standard Time: Time based on the mean solar time of a designated meridian and applied to an entire time zone.

Standard Time Meridian: The meridian of longitude upon which a standard time zone is based.

Standard Time Zone: A zone in which all localities keep their clocks based on the mean solar time of the same designated standard time meridian.

Stellium: A cluster of three or more planets located in the same sign or house.

Superior Planets: Planets located outside the Earth's orbit: Mars, Jupiter, Saturn, Uranus, Neptune and Pluto.

Synastry: Astrological techniques used to assess relationships by comparing two or more charts.

Table of Houses: A set of tables giving exact zodiacal degrees for each angle and house cusps at various sidereal times and latitudes, used in chart erection.

Tertiary Directions: A symbolic method of progressing a chart correlating each day after birth to a lunar month of life.

Transit: The actual position of the planets in the sky at any particular time.

Trine (△): An aspect formed by two points 120° or four signs apart.

T-Square: Two planets or points in opposition and both forming a square to a third point.

Universal Time (UT): Greenwich Mean Time (GMT) expressed in 24-hour format.

Uranian Astrology: An astrological system founded by Alfred Witte (1878-1941) employing the use of midpoints to form "planetary pictures" and eight additional hypothetical planets.

Vertex: The point where the prime vertical intersects the Ecliptic in the west.

Void of Course: The designation given to the Moon between its last Ptolemaic aspect in a sign and its ingress into the next sign.

Waning: Growing smaller. The Moon is waning from Full Moon to New Moon.

War Time (WT) and **Double War Time:** Methods used to extend daylight hours by advancing clocks one or two hours ahead of actual standard time.

Waxing: Growing larger. The Moon is waxing from New Moon to Full Moon.

Yod: Two planets or points sextile one another with each forming a quincunx to a third planet or point.

Zenith: The point on the celestial sphere directly overhead, formed by the culminating intersection of the Celestial Meridian and Prime Vertical.

Zodiacal Latitude A planet or point's distance north or south of the Ecliptic.

Zero Hour, "0 Hour": Listed in ephemeredes as the moment a day begins.

Zodiacal Longitude: A planet or point's distance east of 0° Aries measured along the Ecliptic.

Resources

Astronomy

Cornelius, Geoffrey & Paul Devereux, *The Secret Language of the Stars and Planets*, 1996 Chronicle Books, San Francisco, CA

Rey, H.A., *The Stars: A New Way to See Them*, 1980 Houghton Mifflin Co., Boston, MA

Wyatt, Stanley P., *Principles of Astronomy*, 2nd edition, 1971 Allyn and Bacon, Inc., Boston, MA

Zeilik, Michael, *Astronomy: The Evolving Universe*, Second Edition, 1971 Harper & Row, New York, NY

Astrology—General

George, Demetra & Douglas Bloch, *Asteroid Goddesses: The Mythology, Psychology, and Astrology of the Re-emerging Feminine*, 2003 Ibis Press, Berwick, ME

Hand, Robert, *Horoscope Symbols*, 1981 Whitford Press, West Chester, PA

Hickey, Isabel M., *The Classic Work on Spiritual Astrology*, 1992 CRCS Publications, Sebastol, CA

National Council for Geocosmic Research, *Essentials of Intermediate Astrology*, 1995 NCGR, Inc.

Naylor, P.I.H., *Astrology: A Fascinating History*, 1970 Wilshire Book Co., North Hollywood, CA

Sasportas, Howard, *The Twelve Houses: An Introduction to the Houses in Astrological Interpretation*, 1985 Aquarian Press, San Francisco, CA

Wickenburg, Joanne, *Your Hidden Powers: Intercepted Signs and Retrograde Planets*, 1992 American Federation of Astrologers, Inc., Tempe, AZ

Astrology—Encyclopedic References

Brau, Jean-Louis, & Helen Weaver & Allan Edmands, *Larousse Encyclopedia of Astrology*, 1982 Plume Printing, New York, NY

DeVore, Nicholas, *Encyclopedia of Astrology*, 2002 Astrology Classics Publishing, New York, NY

Holden, James Herschel, *A History of Horoscopic Astrology: From the Babylonian Period to the Modern Age*, 1996 American Federation of Astrologers, Inc., Tempe, AZ

Leo, Alan, *The Complete Dictionary of Astrology*, 1989 Destiny Books, Rochester, VT

Lewis, James R., *The Astrology Encyclopedia*, 1994 Visible Ink Press, Detroit, MI

Chart Calculation

Doane, Doris Chase, *How to Prepare and Pass an Astrologer's Certificate Exam*, 1973 American Federation of Astrologers, Inc., Tempe, AZ

Filbey, John, *Natal Charting*, 1981 The Cromwell Press, Melksham, Wiltshire, England

March, Marion D. & Joan McEvers, *The Only Way to... Learn Astrology Volume II, Math & Interpretation Techniques*, 1993 ACS Publications, San Diego, CA

Sehested, Ove H., *The Basis of Astrology Volume 1: Chart Erection*, American Federation of Astrologers, Inc., Tempe, AZ

Scofield, Bruce, *Astrological Chart Calculations: An Outline of Conventions and Methodology*, 2002 One Reed Publications, Amherst, MA

Aspects and Other Points & Measurements

Hand, Robert, *Night & Day: Planetary Sect in Astrology*, 1995 ARHAT, Reston, VA

Henson, Donna, *Vertex: The Third Angle*, 2003 American Federation of Astrologers, Inc., Tempe, AZ

Rudhyar, Dane, *The Lunation Cycle*, 1976 Aurora Press, Santa Fe, NM

Tierney, Bil, *Dynamics of Aspect Analysis: New Perceptions in Astrology*, 1983 CRCS Publications, Sebastopol, CA

Tyl, Noel, editor, *Astrology's Special Measurements: How to Expand the Meaning of the Horoscope*, 1994 Llewellyn Publications, St. Paul, MN

Zoller, Robert, *The Arabic Parts in Astrology: A Lost Key to Prediction*, 1980 Inner Traditions International, Rochester, VT

Secondary Progressions & Other Predictive Techniques

Davison, R. C., *The Technique of Prediction*, 1974 L. N. Fowler & Co., London, England

Devine, Carole DeMott, *Solar Arc Directions: How to Read Life's Roadmap*, 2000 L.A.B. Professional Publishing, Woodbridge, VA

Hammerslough, Bruce F., *Forecasting Backward and Forward: Modern Techniques of Timing and Rectification*, 1994 Llewellyn Publications, St. Paul, MN

Hand, Robert, *Planets in Transit: Life Cycles for Living*, 1976 Whitford Press, West Chester, PA

Hastings, Nancy Anne, *Secondary Progressions: Time to Remember*, 1984 Samuel Weiser, Inc., York Beach, ME

March, Marion D. & Joan McEvers, *The Only Way to... Learn About Tomorrow Volume IV*, 1994 ACS Publications, San Diego, CA

Shaw, Christine, *Predictive Astrology: A Practical Guide*, 2001 Llewellyn Publications, St. Paul, MN

Composite & Relationship Charts

Davison, Ronald, *Synastry: Understanding Human Relations Through Astrology*, 1983 Aurora Press, Santa Fe, NM

Hand, Robert, *Planets in Composite: Analyzing Human Relationships*, 1975 Whitford Press, West Chester, PA

Townley, John, *Composite Charts: The Astrology of Relationship*, 2000 Llewellyn Publications, St. Paul, MN

Electional Astrology

Scofield, Bruce, *The Timing of Events: Electional Astrology*, 1985 Astrolabe, Orleans, MA

Horary Astrology

Lehman, Dr. J. Lee, Ph.D., *The Martial Art of Horary Astrology*, 2002 Whitford Press, Atglen, PA

Mundane Astrology

Baigent, Michael & Nicholas Campion & Charles Harvey, *Mundane Astrology: An Introduction to the Astrology of Nations and Groups*, 1992 Aquarian Press, London, UK

Campion, Nicholas, *The Book of World Horoscopes*, 2004 Wessex Astrologer Inc., Bournemouth, UK

Uranian Astrology & Cosmobiology

Brummund, Ruth & Udo Rudolph, *Handbook of Techniques for The Hamburg School*, 1992 Penelope Publications, Plantation, FL

Ebertin, Reinhold, *The Combination of Stellar Influences*, 1994 American Federation of Astrologers, Tempe, AZ

Simms, Maria Kay, *Dial Detective: Investigation with the 90° Dial*, 2001 Cosmic Muse Publications, Kensington, NH

Index

Absolute longitude, **13-14**,20,145,146,149,168, 176,177,178,197,199,235,264,265,266
    adding and subtracting, 13
    converting to decimal, 20
    converting without a table, 14
    degree equivalents of signs, 14
    Table of Absolute Longitude, 310
ACD, see Adjusted Calculation Date
ACS American Atlas, The, **27-28**, 29,30,31
ACS Ephemeris, The, 48,**65**,**66**,75,83,200,212,222, 245,273,277,280,291
    locating Chiron in, 83
    locating eclipses in, 200
    locating ingress & other data in, 66
    locating planetary positions in, 65
    locating sidereal time in, 48
    semi-diurnal positions for Moon in, 277
ACS International Atlas, The, **28**,32
Adjusted calculation date (ACD), 211,**214-215**, 246,247,248,249,265
    ACD Interval, **214-219**,223
    ACD Year, 219,223
    Birth ACD, 223,245
    calculating, **216-219**
    progressing planets to, **221-223**
    reason for, 215
    using to locate progressed Moon, 223
    using to locate progressed planets,**221-228**
Air signs, 142,144
Altitude, 156
Angles, chart, 92
Answer Keys, 317-384
Antiscia, antiscion, 167, **170-172**
    calculating, 171
Anti-vertex, 183,**184**,187
Arabic Parts, **175-179**
Arc, 65,141,**145**,146,151
    calculating between two points, 145
    shorter, 145,146
Aries Ingress charts, 295,**296**
ASC, see Ascendant
Ascendant, **92**,93,103,183,184,187
    declination of,162
    interpolation of, 103
Aspect Calculation Form, 149,**304**
Aspect patterns, 144
Aspectarian, **141**,148,162
    notating applying and separating, 148
Aspects, **141-151**
    applying and separating, 141,**147-148**,151
    as angles, 141
    calculating using form, 149
    glyphs, 143
    identifying closest, 151
    identifying in *The ACS Ephemeris,* 66
    major, 141
    minor, 143

    partile, 147
    Ptolemaic, 141
Asteroid Goddesses, 85,87
Asteroids, 83-86
Azimuth, 156
Balsamic Phase, 195,196,198
Birth ACD, 245
Birth year, 221
Bi-wheel chart, 244,263 267
Bonatti, Guido, 177,178
Borrowing, 9
Cardinal signs, 142,144,147,296
Celestial Equator, 47,155,156,160,**183**,186,211
Celestial horizon, 92,**183**,184,186,187
Celestial meridian, 183,**184**
Celestial sphere, 183
Central Standard Time (CST), 30
Chart angles, 92
    progressing, 233-239
Chart Calculation Form & Blank Wheel, 300-303
Chart calculation, southern latitudes, 110-113
Chart combination methods, 287
Chart Progression Form, 237,238,239,**307-309**
Chart wheel, filling in, 124
Charts, hand calculated vs. computer generated, 77,267,281
Chiron, 83-86
    listed in *The ACS Ephemeris,* 66
CM-1, **73-80**,84,85,86,94,**102**,120,158,216
CM-2, **94-97**,101,**102**,103,104,185
CM-3, **100-104**,123,187,238
CM-V, 187,**189**
Co-Latitude, 187,**188**,190
    calculating, **188**
    of birth, 187
Common errors:
    filling in chart wheel, 125
    GMT of birth, 119
    house cusps, 123
    LST of birth, 120
    natal chart calculation, 119-125
    planetary positions, 121
Composite Charts, **287-290**
    calculating derivative house cusps, 290
    calculating midpoint house cusps, 288-289
    determining planetary positions, 288
Computer generated charts vs. hand calculated, 77,267,281
Conjunction, **141**,143,144,146,156
Constant multipler, 73-80,84,86,94,95,96,**100-103**, 157,158,160,161,184,185,187
    for semi-diurnal interpolation, 277-279
    monthly, 84
    understanding, **102**
    vertex interpolation, 189
Contraparallel, 155
    determining,162

397

About the Authors

Lauran Fowks, PMAFA

Lauran is a member of the second graduating class of Kepler College, earning a B.A. in Astrological Studies. She is currently pursuing her masters degree while serving as teaching assistant for astrological calculation in Kepler's undergraduate program using the methods presented in *Simply Math*. Lauran's previous work included accounting, graphic design, office procedure and forms design, and working as national trainer in bookkeeping and office procedure for an international service company. After her three children were born, Lauran switched tracks to quilting and other fiber arts. She has lectured and taught classes in quilting and cloth doll design, and her work has won numerous national and international awards. Lauran is a professional astrologer in Westchester County, New York. Her website can be found at www.astroreflections.com.

Lynn Gordon Sellon, PMAFA, C.A. NCGR

Lynn has incorporated astrology into her life since childhood. She holds degrees in Sociology and Education with a minor concentration in art. In *Simply Math*, she combines her commitment to teaching astrology with her past experience writing corporate procedure manuals and conducting nationwide computer training courses. She was a contributing author to Llewellyn's *2006 Moon Signs Book*. The painting on the cover was inspired by Lynn's passion for astrology and love of art. Her work as an artist has gained national recognition and is included in many private collections as well as having been featured on the *Today Show*. Lynn lives with her husband and three children in Fairfield County, Connecticut where she maintains a professional astrological practice. Her website is located at www.celestialguidance.com.